The Human Side of Prayer

THE HUMAN SIDE
OF PRAYER

The Psychology of Praying

L.B. BROWN

with chapters by
Anna Wierzbicka
David Turner
Charles Creegan

Religious Education Press

Birmingham, Alabama

Library of Congress Cataloging-in-Publication Data

Brown, Laurence Binet, 1927-
    The human side of prayer: the psychology of praying / L.B. Brown;
    with chapters by Anna Wierzbicka, David Turner, Charles Creegan.
    Includes bibliographical references (p. 284-308) and index.
    ISBN 0-89135-092-6
    1. Prayer—Psychology.   2. Prayer—Christianity. I. Title
  BV225.B76   1994   93-31018
  291.4'3'019—dc20   CIP

Religious Education Press, Inc.
5316 Meadow Brook Road
Birmingham, Alabama 35242
10 9 8 7 6 5 4 3 2

Religious Education Press publishes books exclusively in religious education
and in areas closely related to religious education. It is committed to enhanc-
ing and professionalizing religious education through the publication of
serious, significant, and scholarly works.

PUBLISHER TO THE PROFESSION

Contents

Chapter One
Prayer in religion and psychology   1

Chapter Two
What is prayer? In search of a definition   25
    Anna Wierzbicka

Chapter Three
Early approaches to the psychology of prayer   47

Chapter Four
Reaching in and reaching out: Prayer in
anthropological perspective   67
    David Turner

Chapter Five
Theological guidance about prayer   83

Chapter Six
The real me is the me at private prayer:
a philosophical perspective   97
    Charles Creegan

Chapter Seven
Traditional analogies to prayer   111

Chapter Eight
Anti- and other prayers   133

Chapter Nine
Attitudes to prayer   144

Chapter Ten
Prayer, meditation and control   164

Chapter Eleven
Development and the meaning of prayer   189

Chapter Twelve
Further explanations   208

Chapter Thirteen
Conclusion   240

Chapter Fourteen
Postscript   252

Appendix I
Annotated Bibliography on the psychology of prayer   257
    Emma Shackle and L.B. Brown

Appendix II
Great prayers of the Bible collected by
    David T. Patterson (1927)   282

References   284

Index of Names   309

Index of Subjects   321

Chapter One

Prayer in Religion and Psychology

"Nothing is apt to mask the face of God so much as religion"
— Martin Buber

This book, like Leuba's (1925) account of mysticism, "has been long in the making" (p. x). He noted that mysticism (and I would add prayer) "has suffered as much at the hands of its admirers as its materialist enemies" (p. ix), and that his study "represents an effort to remove (mystical religion) as part of inner life from the domain of the occult . . . to incorporate it in that body of facts of which psychology takes cognizance" (ibid.). My analysis concentrates on prayer, and only indirectly on religious experience. Like Leuba's approach, it uses the comparative and "the inductive method of the descriptive sciences" (p. xii). In a preface to his second edition (1928) he said, "It is neither a book of edification nor a defense of any particular religious belief" (p. xii). Similar disclaimers apply to the arguments and the material discussed here.

Since this is not a book of advice about religion, it makes no specific recommendations about how to pray. Nor does it try to justify or dismiss prayer. Any decision about whether or not to pray must be made by each of us for ourselves. That we can adopt a posture or attitude of prayer, for example by kneeling or folding our hands or being in the prayerful context of a church, without actually praying, emphasizes the intangibility of the subject of this book.

Any account of prayer must recognize at least two separate perspectives on it. There is first an observer's stance on what others might be doing when they appear to pray. This might involve wondering why and how they could be praying, or admiring their 'evident' devotion. An observer may have little knowledge or understanding of the traditions within which prayers are offered, and that could have prescribed them. Those who themselves pray are likely to have a different view, with sympathy, knowledge, and an understanding of what is involved. It is likely, however, that few 'really' understand

1

what is taken-for-granted by those who pray within another religious tradition. While Moslems seem to be active in their prayers, Buddhists appear withdrawn or perfunctory, and it can be hard for Westerners to understand the prejudices, whether for or against those practices.

It is the participants' (or performers') stance on their own prayers that provides the most valid data for any studies of prayer, whether they are to be understood within religious, social-science or psychological contexts. Each of these approaches contains its own assumptions about the meaning of what happens when someone prays, the effects prayer might have on their thought, feelings or emotions, actions, targets, and the contexts for any prayer. None of these offers a neutral perspective, since whether we are praying or watching others at prayer, something of our attitudes and background goes into whatever conclusions or interpretations we make. While no one wants someone else to 'explain' why they are praying (or doing anything), the aim of this book is to understand what might be involved in such prayer.

This broad perspective recognizes many contexts for prayer, and different 'reasons' for praying, and innumerable expectations of what prayers might be able to achieve. Examining the prayers themselves conveys little about those features, especially when the prayer is offered in public, or as part of a formal liturgy or religious service. To expect that every prayer contains a message to, or from God is rather pious, without reference to the intentions of those who offer or are involved with them. Ted Simes' play, 'Herbert III', for example, refers to the strategies that were used in the middle of the night by Marguerite to avoid sex with her husband. They included repeated prayers to 'Sweet Jesus' for the safety of their nineteen-year- old son, Herbert III, and her thanks that he was 'straight'. *Punch* had a joke in 1964, in which a clergyman complained that if his people devoted as much time to the Lord as they did to football, "perhaps we'd win the European cup." This book is, however, about prayer from religious and psychological points of view.

Prayer by itself says little about the attitudes or beliefs of those who pray, although those praying may also need the courage to act or endure, especially if they think that petitionary prayers are its prototypic form. If that were so, we would have to prepare a psychology of complaints,[1] developing a stance about the rectitude of what can be prayed for. But even children agree that it is improper to pray for what they think is wrong (Brown and Thouless, 1964). Perhaps it is more important to recognize that prayers can express reverence, Godly fear, or a sense of the sacred, which some people replace with an expectation about God's authoritarian control, which might make prayer a means for them to share that power or achieve other goals.

But it is hard to look at a text, however it has been recorded, and detect all that it might convey, even for those who produced it. Knowing the context it

---

1. This was in a sense where this study began, when in the later 1960s I began a study of the ways in which complaints to the Ombudsman in New Zealand, Sir Guy Powles, were expressed, after I had worked on petitionary prayer with the late Dr. Thouless.

was designed for, and in which it is being interpreted can help that, although literary critics, theologians, psychologists and other specialists each have their own ways to evaluate their preferred texts and other data. It is therefore easy to parody and criticize prayers, by taking them away from their context, as Monty Python did for "Prayers in time of war," by casting them in pacifist terms. Even a prayer expressing distress in the face of misfortune need not be taken seriously, and we can tell from the context and the intonation in which it is uttered whether someone who says, 'Oh God', is swearing, cursing, or praying and is therefore to be understood in religious terms.

Any examination of a psychology of prayer must recognize these problems, although they are not specific to prayer. We might compare them, for example, to the differences between listening to music, performing it, composing it, adopting the role of a music theorist concerned with the psychological and imaginative processes that might define the quality of the work, or a critic.

Prayer within religion

But what is prayer? Dictionaries stress that it is a devout or earnest supplication, a "solemn request or thanksgiving to God or object of worship" (in the *Concise Oxford*). Its roots are in the Latin *precarius*, which also gives us 'precarious' as "dependent on chance, uncertain." But prayer not only entails what is obtained by treaty, or is perilous, since a precarious tenure is "held during the pleasure of another," and what is past being prayed for is hopeless.

Christian traditions have distinguished between active, passive, and silent prayer, between objective and subjective prayer, spontaneous or ejaculatory prayers, and between participation in the daily offices or in annual cycles of prayer. This shows their variety, and the structuring role that personal or liturgical prayers can occupy. Other religious traditions might be expected to show a similar diversity.

Although many people expect to be able to tell when someone is at prayer, it is hard to know if they are in fact praying (whatever that implies) rather than sitting and thinking, 'being quiet,' meditating, or just 'sitting.' It is not only psychologists who know that any mental state is hard to understand, and that additional information is needed to test or validate conclusions, especially about states of consciousness.

Continuing conflicts among psychologists center on the best ways to access mental states, and how to use such knowledge. While there was little doubt during the nineteenth century that introspection offered valid psychological data, the dominant place that Behaviorism came to occupy, especially in the 1930s, polarized psychologists' opinions and practice. The relevance of what people said when asked to tell what they were thinking about was then questioned. Because it could not be independently verified it was replaced by 'behavioral' data. But the use of carefully designed questionnaires to measure attitudes, beliefs, and values (cf Robinson, Shaver, and Wrightsman, 1991) has persisted (Starbuck's 1897 study of conversion being the first in this line).

The conflicts over data became an important reason for the relative neglect by psychologists of religion of the nature of prayer, apart from the principled or phenomenological arguments about its psychological character and basis, and the studies of its correlates and (poor) material efficacy (cf Wulff, 1991). The annotated bibliography here, on pages 259 to 281, shows that prayer has not been disregarded and is recognized as a crucial component of the "religious variable," which until recently was one of psychology's "taboo topics" (Farberow, 1963). Direct questions about the frequency of prayer as a measure of religiousness, the development of children's concepts of prayer and its relation to meditation, gave prayer some 'psychological respectability' (Spilka, Hood, and Gorsuch, 1985, p. 165-166) and showed the therapeutic potential of religion (Comstock and Partridge, 1972).

Religiousness has been commonly examined by questions like, "What religious group do you belong to? Do you go to church? Do you pray?" (Francis and Brown, 1991). It has, however, been accepted as a single variable or a set of separate dimensions (cf Dittes, 1969) that include belief, experience, and practice, as well as a knowledge of the doctrines, spiritual techniques, and rituals that are received, and then carried by the great variety of religious traditions and groups, and the consequences of accepting or following those traditions. Other distinctions that have been identified include the extrinsic or intrinsic 'motivations,' and the reasons, or forms of religiousness that are accepted by individuals.

Although it seems that the practice of religion in general, and of prayer in particular, might have recently declined, it is hard to establish confidently that that is so, beyond looking at data from social surveys, which have only a fifty year history, or by referring to historical studies of Church growth or decline (cf Currie, Gilbert, and Horsley, 1977). One trend that can be docu-

---

Table 1

Percentages in the British Isles agreeing with specific questions about their religion.from Fogarty, Ryan, and Lee (1984) *Irish Values and Attitudes.*

	Eire	Northern Ireland	Britain	All Europe
Prays and meditates	81	73	50	58
Draws comfort and strength from religion	79	70	46	49
Goes to church weekly or more often	82	52	14	25
Has great confidence in the church	52	44	19	21

mented in Australia with reference to the Census statistics shows an increasing proportion who claim to have no religion (so described) from 8.3 percent in 1976 to 12.7 percent in 1986 (Castles, 1990).

The survey data from the European Values Study in Table 1 shows little uniformity in religious practice from one part of the British Isles to another, although such demographic material must be interpreted cautiously. While Church going and public prayer may have decreased in Europe and Australia, ordinary conversations and casual observations suggest that neither private or public prayer has disappeared, although it might never be talked about in some contexts. That prayer in public schools and other places remains a hot political issue in the USA indicates its potency, although secular substitutes for prayer could include self-directed meditation, relaxation exercises, as well as the search for physical fitness that is now advocated for its health-related advantages, and not for religious reasons that might include respecting one's body. But we know little about what sustains the practice of prayer, or what makes it religiously valid, beyond its habitual practice and the extent to which it is a prescribed and practiced part of any religion.

Psychologists of religion seem to have assumed that prayer is a rather simple activity, and that to be involved with it we must bring our personal, social, and religious background, as well as attitudes and sanctions that recognize particular practices. Beliefs and expectations about prayer and what it might achieve are, however, unlikely to be homogeneous, and they are expected to involve hidden psychological processes that, if they were identified, might explain the 'reasons' or need for prayer among those for whom it is more than a habit or an accepted part of their life, unless it is a 'natural' and religious process implanted by God. However it may be explained, most people know about prayer, and have well-developed attitudes that accept or reject all, or only some aspects, of what it might involve.

The practice of prayer is expected to be as variable across traditions as among individuals, whether because of their training or their temperament. The claims that are made on it, and its validity, propriety, and sanctions are, however, more likely to reflect attitudes than an explicit knowledge of the theological and liturgical implications of prayer. Yet it seems more likely to be prescribed, than to flow like a creative or imaginative force. Whether or not the readers of this book will agree with the validity of prayer and how that might be established depends on the religious or spiritual implications they find in the material that is available. I do not expect you to accept every part of my psychological analyses of prayer, which follow the conventions of social science and not of religion, and that often point to questions that have not yet been resolved, or even explored.

An early argument held that prayer evolved or derives from an inarticulate cry or sigh of relief (Marrett, 1903). While those sighs and cries can be obscured, or embellished and interpreted, any theory about the origins of prayer confuses the practice of those who have been initiated into a particular religious tradition with the assumption that we all look for assistance in our weakness. Other needs or primitive meanings of prayer that have been identified include those implied by Heiler's (1932) account of the phenomenology of prayer, which he describes "as the calm collectedness of a devout individual soul, and as the ceremonial liturgy of a great congregation; as an original creation of a religious genius, and as an imitation on the part of a simple, average religious person; as the spontaneous expression of upspringing religious experiences, and as the mechanical recitation of an incomprehensible formula; as bliss and ecstasy of heart, and as painful fulfillment of the law; as the involuntary discharge of an overwhelming emotion, and as the voluntary concentration on a religious object; as loud shouting and crying, and as still, silent absorption; as artistic poetry, and as stammering speech; as the flight of the spirit to the supreme Light, and as a cry out of the deep distress of the heart; as joyous thanksgiving and ecstatic praise, and as humble supplication for forgiveness and compassion; as a childlike entreaty for life, health, and happiness, and as an earnest desire for power in the moral struggle of existence; as a simple petition for daily bread, and as an all-consuming yearning for God Himself; as a selfish wish, and as an unselfish solicitude for a brother; as wild cursing and vengeful thirst, and as heroic intercession for personal enemies and persecutors; as a stormy clamor and demand, and as joyful renunciation and holy serenity; as a desire to change God's will and make it chime with our petty wishes, and as a self-forgetting vision of an surrender to the Highest Good; as the timid entreaty of the sinner before a stern judge; and as the trustful talk of a child with a kind father; as swelling phrases of politeness and flattery before an unapproachable King, and as a free outpouring in the presence of a friend who cares; as the humble petition of a servant to a powerful master, and as the ecstatic converse of the bride with the heavenly Bridegroom (p. 353)." It seems inherently unlikely that a single explanation could capture such a range of forms or attitudes. But each of those contrasts captures recognized human emotions.

Non-Christian traditions are likely to emphasize other features or forms of prayer that might be hard to recognize without a detailed knowledge of their traditionally prescribed practices. It could, therefore, be impossible to develop a psychology of prayer that can be applied to all religious traditions, as Wierzbicka's essay here shows. Since each religion must be located within a culture, valid psychological analyses of it ought to be recognizable by those within, or sympathetic to it. A deliberate reductionism should be avoided on those grounds alone, and I expect each reader to take issue with at least some parts of my argument.

My own religious background within Methodist and Anglican (or Episcopal) traditions in New Zealand, and then in England, Australia, and elsewhere, has shaped my understanding of prayer and my fascination with the variety of religious forms, traditions, experiences, and disclosures, especially as they impact on the nature, and the roles of prayer.

To expect prayer to be primarily petitional excludes its many other forms and disregards the expressive and adaptive or instrumental uses of religion in general, and of prayer in particular. Over-simplification seems, however, to have been a common strategy among psychologists (and others) in their search for an explanation of prayer and the attitudes that might support it. Petitionary prayer is, however, both controversial and prototypic, since some believe it involves talking to ourselves in an attempt to adjust to reality. A central problem could therefore be to understand how those who pray make sense of their prayers. Whatever that involves, beyond some form of religious commitment, it seems that a positive religious stance should distinguish those who pray, even if others think that could be like whistling in the dark. The expectations about prayer therefore range from literal or concrete to abstract constructions of it, and then to claims on the validity of any insights or support from it, even if that is expected to be delusional. But it could be as hard to support prayer as it is to falsify the validity of any claims about its benefits, except on *a priori* grounds. Whatever effects are anticipated or realized, the 'successes' of prayer must be evaluated subjectively, and we may never be told of the failures, since positive instances draw more attention. Spiritual prayers are less tangible, but probably conform to the social and religious norms defined by the tradition within which they are offered. The faith in prayer itself, however, presents a strong case for developing a psychological account that goes beyond aligning it with other repeated actions, like buying lottery tickets or making risky decisions. We will see that many analogies and explanations of prayer have been proposed. Jung's (1958) analysis, for example, relied heavily on the concept of archetype as a link with myth and tradition which is not, as he said in his *Answer to Job* (p. 409), "fiction: it consists of facts that are continually repeated and can be observed over and over again."

Highly prescriptive solutions hardly seem appropriate to the realities of religion, with its enormous differences in individuals' reactions and practice, and the credibility of their claims on whatever orthodoxies are recognized. They can range from an intensely personal commitment to respecting traditional and institutional formulations because they are embedded in our culture. When Jung was asked if he believed in God, he said that he believed the psyche to be real, although its critics believed only in physical facts (Jung, 1958, pp. 463-4). This focuses the psychology of religion on persons and their beliefs, since "all religious assertions are physical impossibilities" (ibid.), although it disregards the traditional origins of religious doctrines and the beliefs and practices they support.

'Religious psychologies' are, however, built on religious assumptions, while the psychology of religion approaches religious phenomena, and the related beliefs, experiences, and practices, through psychology itself, perhaps with some reference to commonsense interpretations (Kelley, 1992). While it may be naively thought that this involves 'unconscious' processes, even they confront consciousness so that "a balance between the opposites must be found" (Jung, 1958, p. 468).

If someone is seized by the validity of their prayer, they find it unnecessary to argue about its logic, while those "no longer impressed by the revelation of holiness (or with the transcendental power of) prayer" (Jung, 1958, p. 153) must fall back on rationalized or derived religious insights (following W. H. Clark, 1958), which contrast with analyses of the immediacy, and the 'flow' or excitement that sustains creative and dangerous activities, whether in mountaineering, ritual events, games, sports, or artistic experiences (cf Csikszentmihalyi and Csikszentmihalyi, 1988, p. 31).

Religious archetypes

Another place to begin an account of prayer and what it can achieve is with Homer. This locates prayer archaically and puts a distance between current understanding of the workings of God or the gods and what is accepted as one of their root models in Western culture.

In *The Greeks and the Irrational*, E.R. Dodds (1951) points out that in Homer's psychology acceptable explanations of events, especially those producing misfortune, were not concerned with personal intentions, but with the act itself. The causes were ascribed to the intervention of external agencies, whether an 'indeterminate daemon,' 'god' or 'gods' "may inspire courage at a crisis or take away a man's understanding" (p. 11). Dodds identifies such attributions as forms of speech or rhetoric because the supernatural agencies were accepted. He does, however, stress the importance of our techniques of listening when we look back at what we have done and say, "I didn't really mean to do that." With another step one distances oneself by saying, "It wasn't really I who did it" (pp. 13-14). Transposing responsibility from an interior to an external world not only eliminates vagueness by pointing to concrete causal events but, as in the Socratic paradox that virtue is knowledge and no one does wrong on purpose, it excludes from the self what is unsystematized by defining its alien origins.

Dodds stresses that projecting shame to an external power is consistent with the absence of guilt from classical Greek culture, although its later recognition "transformed divine temptation" (*ate*) into a punishment, and then to a doctrine of man's helpless dependence on an arbitrary power (p. 30). Similar doctrines imply the futility of human purpose or suggest that too much success incurs supernatural danger (as when we touch wood) because the gods are jealous. Doctrines like these transformed the gods into agents of justice (p. 31).

In general terms, Dodds concludes that "religion grows out of man's relationship to his total environment, morals out of his relation to his fellow men" (p. 31). The first component of this process involves a sense of 'cosmic justice' that is projected yet disconfirmed by the simple observation that the wicked flourish (p. 33). Dodds argues that to sustain it, beliefs were needed to extend an open time-span beyond the normal limit set by death. Looking beyond that, one could say that the successful sinner would be punished through his descendants or that he would pay his debt in another life.

Early psychologists stressed the origins of our study, rather than the origins of religion (cf Bowker, 1973), while others found solace in current theories or in findings that depended on the "Questionnaire, scaling, factor analysis, and case study procedures" that Dittes (1969) stressed were "part of the search for ways to study religion" (p. 602). In fact, a major problem has been to gain acceptance for the fact that religion could be investigated, and that the "laws of the mind" were not directly revealed and could not be deduced from a phenomenology of 'primitive' religions (Tylor, 1873).

But a continuing problem in any psychological study of religion involves similar strictures against its systematic investigation, in part because of the fear that psychologists are reductionists, or voyeurs invading a domain of privileged relationships. But 'God' might have sanctioned biological adaptation, reinforcement, cognitive problem solving, and social or cultural dynamics since images, models and archetypes of God are inherent in our society. They are, however, unlikely to be built into the psyche as natural cognitions, although they could help to personify or tame the environment in terms of love and reverence, rather than hate and fear. Similarly, a fragmented self might gain a coherent identity when linked to something more than a finite 'social ego.' Alternatively, religion could entail an 'incarnation' in which God supports the self through inward and outward processes that might call on mana, or taboo as well as demonism. These matrices of feeling are carried by many traditions and conveyed through those in particular social roles.

Jung recognized that 'faith' is not commensurable with the rationalist assumptions that criticize faithfulness as an "irrational psychic phenomenon" (1958, p. 153). This, like Freud's claims about religion, involves an interpretation, although in a letter to Freud (on 26 June 1910), Jung emphasized the paradoxical ambiguity of natural events involving life and death, where joyfulness is counterbalanced by fear, or in a culture where pessimism is countered by a "mystery of immortality gained by the total suppression of instinct (through identification with [Christ as] the dead man)" (Freud, 1974, p. 337).

So God exists as a physical entity for some, as nonphysical for others, while God is nonexistent for yet others. Each of these groups may have equally strong convictions. Whether they depend in any sense on psychological factors that are beyond our religious beliefs themselves could itself be a matter of belief. There is little mystery about this, since we recognize the variety of ways in which people can be religious or will repudiate specific constructions and interpretations of religious meaning. So Jung held that "all religions are physical impossibilities" (op. cit.), although others accept religious assertions as literally rather than metaphorically true.

Dodds (1951, p. 2), when considering the nature of religious experience in ancient Greece, stressed the variety of types of religious experience there, many of which are no longer interpreted as 'religious,' citing the "divine, temptation or infatuation (*ate*) which led Agamemnon to compensate himself for the loss of his own mistress by robbing Achilles of his" (pp. 2-3). The religious question there involves an attribution of responsibility, in this case to Zeus who had put infatuation into the understanding—"So what could I do? Deity will always have its way" (p. 3). Nevertheless, Agamemnon accepted the responsibility himself. "Since I was blinded by infatuation and Zeus took away my understanding, I am willing to make my peace and give abundant compensation" (ibid.). Even if that 'simply' involved a "manner of speaking" it is a construction of experience in the dialogue between attitudes, and in the ascriptions to whatever is judged rational or irrational about religious and other experiences.

If it is expected that a place must be found in these analyses for 'unconscious' processes as well as for whatever can be accessed through consciousness, the balance between those opposites may be found with reference to religious symbols which are grounded in the archetypes of wholeness (following Jung, 1958, p. 468), in a sense of the holy (Otto, 1917), or in other categories, such as belief, practice, or experience.

A long tradition of interpretation holds that religions are irrational or that those involved with them are emotionally unstable, regardless of interpretations of the physical or other effects that duplicate 'natural' processes or depend on narratives that make it "vivid to the imagination of the hearers" (Dodds, 1951, p. 14). Dodds argues that to transpose an event from the interior or imagined world to what is outside eliminates its vagueness and its metaphorical or mental qualities. This habit of objectifying or 'projecting' drives and wishes, so that they are 'not-self,' could have opened a door to religious ideas that confuse the boundaries between what is internal and external, thereby sanctioning our beliefs or experience as 'real,' so that we can control our desires in the same way as we control external events or processes. This move is ill-defined, except with reference to a set of doctrinal or ideological principles that may be religious or psychological.

Although Herodotus distinguished supernatural or divine madness from that due to natural causes or disease (Dodds, 1951, p. 65) this contrast has been lost to us. So the effects or the 'location' of the divine is not well articulated psychologically, except in terms of beliefs about it as either subjective or objective. Some of the uses of prayer discussed by Dodds show that there was a modern ring to the ancients' reactions to the supernatural as an 'irrational' domain lying beyond (or behind) 'objective' reality. Perhaps it is hard to live only with the immediacy of the present. As Dodds put it, many sick men accepted the decision of Asclepius that "he does not care for me or want to save me." But true believers were no doubt infinitely patient, waiting "for the significant vision" (p. 113). So people still return again and again to Lourdes, and many who suffer must be content with an indirect revelation of the support that can be found there. Dodds recognized the role of priests, fellow-patients, and any others who might hear their story. Furthermore, "a healing shrine can maintain its reputation on a very low percentage of success, provided a few of them are sensational" (Dodds, 1951, p. 115). A crucial criticism of medical remedies involves their failures, "whereas in dreams, as Aristotle said, the element of judgment is absent" (ibid.).

We should not forget that different standards of criticism are applied to different performances, or to the claims that can be made on them. And we should not confuse the claims on religion with those on the objective world within which it is cast, and to which it need not refer directly. Furthermore, Dodds held that "when Hesiod tells us how the muses spoke to him on

Helicon this is not allegory or poetic ornament, but an attempt to express a real experience in literary terms" (p. 117). Our unwillingness to resolve such questions lies at the heart of the "ambiguity of religion," as does the extent to which remote or mountainous places seem to facilitate numinous experiences, although they do not occur only there. Whether some physiological process might be involved in those experiences or in dreams has been a matter of principled dispute that will not be settled easily, although religious interpretations are still set against scientific constructions of such events. While we might recognize that others (usually thought of as naive traditionalists) accept that psychic excursions in sleep or trance sharpen the mind-body contrast, the phenomena of shamanism provide a model for deliberately forcing the mind, through abstinence or spiritual exercises, to enter a spiritual dimension that might generate ideas about the survival of death, reincarnation, and other-world journeys. Vivid claims on the imagination might enhance one's power (Zaleski, 1987). Those feelings or beliefs have roots in cultural myths and in the experiences of others, and there are few sound reasons for only accepting our own construals of religious beliefs or experiences and disregarding others' traditions or understandings.

If we accept the old anthropological dichotomy between guilt- and shame-oriented cultures, both of them promoted a horror of the body and revulsion at the life of the senses (Dodds, 1951, p. 152) that we associate with Puritanism. The moral sense of that perspective is aligned with Christian doctrines about original sin and denying physical emotions, since 'true' life is lived beyond the body, which is a polluting prison. Such interpretations depended initially on the authority of ancient texts, practices, and doctrines that shaped experience and thought about the problems that religions still present to us. Our problem, as it was for Dodds (1951) in relation to the ancient Greeks, is to come to terms with "the power, the wonder and the peril of the Irrational" (p. 254), in a period which appears to lack an "awareness of mystery and of an ability to penetrate to the deeper, less conscious levels of human experience" (p. 1). Psychological theories and tools are still applied unevenly to our understanding of mystery and prayer, perhaps because the only signs we recognize there are ambiguous. When George Meredith said that "who rises from prayer a better man, his prayer is answered" (*Oxford Dictionary of Quotations*, p. 337, 36), he evaded the disreputable implications of prayer as unreal, or as a technique for individual salvation or personal revelation (cf Dodds, 1951, p. 248).

Martin (1985) identified the archetypal Paradise as pastoral, "with trees, animals, and few people, but no books and certainly no machines" (p. 21). Prayer is often understood at that level. As a medium of communication it is oral, and therefore direct (cf Ong, 1982). Scripture, on the other hand, is a reminder of our alienation from God, as are confessions of sin and petitions for deliverance.

Martin therefore stressed that "The New Testament dramatically conceived, is the enactment of the conflict between the sacred and its licensed interpreters and intermediaries, precipitated by the entrance of an outsider proclaiming a means of direct access to God that circumvents constitutional channels. Scribes (along with Pharisees and tax-collectors) are seen as the *betes noires* of the faithful . . . . (since) 'If any man among you seemeth to be wise in this world, let him become a fool, that he may be wise' (1 Corinthians 3,18)" (p. 23). The holy person is a fool, since knowledge precludes belief.

Martin's (1985) analysis of *The knowledge of ignorance* in the period up to the Renaissance concludes that ignorance was idealized then. Perhaps that is a reason why the Churches seem not to have welcomed psychological enquiries, and why prayers that might try to change, and not accommodate us to our existing fortunes or misfortunes, have been thought futile. Since psychological theories involve commentaries on, rather than prescriptions about the goals of development through self-realizations and individuation, the short answer to questions about what is needed if we are to "believe in prayer" and what validates it, is *faith*. Gambling, on the other hand involves action while prayer depends on the language in which needs or wishes can be expressed. Even if prayer also involves social control, because of the ways it is taught we can avoid such control through covert wishes and intentions, with paradoxical ease.

Psychological accounts of prayer do not need to be committed to a particular theory (unlike Ulanov and Ulanov, 1985) in their search for whatever can clarify or help us understand what it involves, beyond an appeal to the religious sanctions that tell us to pray unceasingly. Other conventional interpretations suggest that prayer has always been available for attempts to control our unpredictable and potentially hostile environment, and that it involves suggestion. In that case we merely pray for ourselves. But what else do we pray for? Are tragic happenings, conflicts, and insoluble problems the staple of petitionary prayer, or thinly disguised appeals for our own security? If they are, how might we increase their efficacy? Can we ever change the natural world, or only ourselves, through prayer? Does our understanding of prayer develop as we grow up? Are prayers necessarily expressions of immature and dependent wishes? Does our increasing scientific knowledge limit the relevance and content of our prayers? Do prayers symbolically model our needs or experience?

Positive answers to questions like these are easily criticized for the egocentricity of whatever expectations prayers seem to carry, unless they express a hopeful relationship with God or with a transcendent order. The language in which many prayers are couched is of little help in trying to understand whatever deep meanings they carry, because it is formal. The inevitable tension that surrounds the critical or skeptical attitudes of anyone who refuses to pray upsets those who can pray easily or regularly. But we do not know exactly what *they* are 'doing,' since it is as hard to give concurrent accounts of our prayers as of scientific work, or when writing or dreaming. The accounts of those activities are necessarily retrospective and secondary, and it is the role of a coach, producer, or spiritual director to shape the performance of an athlete, actor, or religious person. Critics (or psychologists) aim to examine and recast such performances in more abstract ways. This psychology of prayer is therefore to be understood as a critical examination of what prayers and praying might mean. To broaden its range, essays on the semantics, anthropology, and philosophy of prayer have been included.

What is prayer?

Phillips' (1965) philosophical study of the concept of prayer identified the first crucial problem as, "What then is prayer?" He gives the classical answer, "If no one asks me I know; if I wish to explain it to one that asketh, I know not . . . (since the) meaning of 'prayer' is in the activity of praying" (p. 3). The other accounts that have been given, including those in psychological terms, cannot be expected to be commensurate, although they ought to be supported by data or ordinary talk about its nature and practice, and they can be expected to be diverse. Furthermore, the reasons for praying are unlikely to be uniform and will not easily support simple generalizations. If psychologists of religion appeal to 'deeply' analytic interpretations that by-pass rational processes, they tend to neglect the contexts within which prayer is practiced, which are themselves defined by religious traditions. Such psychological explanations may seem artificial, which could be a reason why the Churches have given less support to the psychology than to the sociology of religion, which stresses its social and contextual nature.

Common sense holds that prayer involves talking to God. Should no one be 'there' to talk to, prayers are assumed to be empty, unless other uses or analogues for them can be identified. Agnostics and atheists may not pray, but they probably 'talk' to themselves and to others who are not present when planning interactions with them. Prayer itself might similarly mediate what someone intends to do, strengthening the importance of planned, goal-directed, and deliberate 'actions' within a social context. Those who take 'behavior' as *the* dependent variable in psychology neglect our inner and our social lives, while action-oriented accounts reflect commonsense social knowledge about what is appropriate or expected of us. There must therefore be some interplay between common sense and scientific psychologies because "the common culture affects scientists' thought and activities, as (do) the reverse processes, by which the products of science modify the common culture" (Kelley, 1992). Kelley also notes that "It is impossible for us to avoid the effects of commonsense psychology, but easy for us (as psychologists) to be unaware of them." This is especially so with any attempt to produce a psychology of prayer that does not recognize the religious and everyday demands that prayers carry.

Phillips (1965, p. 37) argues that asking whether someone is praying or not and whether they might be talking to God involves religious and moral questions about the criteria of prayer that hold in particular religious communities. Against that, a philosophical question asks "what it means to affirm or deny that a man is talking to God" (ibid.), while psychological questions center on the attitudes, knowledge, beliefs, experience, and social or religious processes that support prayer, allowing it to be judged a meaningful (or meaningless) activity. Such meanings are carried by religious language in contrasted expressions like, "Lord, hear our prayer, and let our cry come unto Thee" and "Speak, Lord, for thy servant heareth" (Phillips, 1965, p. 52). We do, of course have to learn about those meanings and the uses of such prayers.

When Kierkegaard noted that "prayer does not change God, but it changes the one who offers it" (in Phillips, 1965, p. 56), he identified a reflexive attitude which does not, however, imply that prayer is just like talking to yourself. The simplest objections to prayer reject the spatial implication that God must, like the planets, be external (Phillips, p. 57), and the anthropomorphic explanations that God is like us. There are many other meanings or conceptions of God, and of prayer or worship, in the rhetorical manoeuvres that produce coherence or help us escape from an (unbearable) sense of being. But as Simone Weil asserted, "It is not my business to think about myself. My business is to think about God. It is for God to think about me" (Phillips, 1965, p. 78). Does that imply an abdication of self-control similar to that when a legal case shapes the evidence about a person's character, in ways they might not recognize?

To understand prayer we therefore must develop a "feeling for the game" (Phillips, 1965, p. 83) that those who pray are engaged in, which recognizes the sense they make of religion. This can, however, be as hard to do plausibly if one would dismiss prayer, as it is for those who expect to be able to support it. Arguments about the existence of God or what the world is like could depend on prepared positions that are similar to someone giving themselves "up to what they call the explanation of the text, at the expense of a beautiful poem" (Phillips, p. 103). Whatever it is that religious (and political) attitudes involve, whether it is arrogance, control, collaboration, dependence, or compassion, it is not clear where one's questioning stops and devotion begins. To accept that the language of prayer is performative replaces the notion that intentions are latent in any demand or appeal for help or material success, by reference to its symbolic or sacramental effects on individuals or a community. While covert and unrecognized needs (or 'reasons') might drive people to pray, they are not easily identified, except in principle. Yet most people have some knowledge of prayer, even if they find it uncongenial, and distinguish prayers that are religious from those that are formal or even imprecatory. We might know some people for whom prayer seems 'natural,' and others for whom it is a burden. And we know that private, corporate, and ready-made prayers are not the same, since formal prayers follow the conventions of politeness, moving from adoration in the initial address to petition, if that is what they are about, and that Christians accept the Lord's Prayer as their prototype when expressing dependence, affirmation, longing or seeking, dedication, obedience, and so on. That the prayers of Jesus were short and concise and that he prayed for his enemies with confidence contrasts against preachers' claims and the arguments of theologians. The confessions of mystics, whose metaphors express an inner life, seem too easy to interpret or deconstruct, if in surreal terms.

While prayer is expected to involve seeking after God, it typically entails solemn and humble requests, modeled perhaps on the appeals to other hold-ers of power, which are themselves like prayers. In that sense, prayer *is* peti-tionary, although it is likely to involve more than that as the central phe-nomenon of religion, supporting personal experience and a committed religiousness. The 'best' experience of prayer is held to be primary and pre-propositional, although most prayers share a language which tames and brings the 'word' of religion into a social domain. It is through this lan-guage that we learn to recognize the character of others' experiences, with reli-gious sanctions confirming our interpretations. These experiences can expose the otherness and immediacy of the sacred, or our awareness of the mys-tery of life. Those for whom talking about prayer is as natural as talk about sport or the television have no problems with its reality or validity. When they pray, there is nothing to be 'explained' about the words or the attitudes they carry.

Heiler (1932) began his book on *Prayer, a Study in the History and Psychology of Religion* with a litany of the authorities who had agreed that "there can be no doubt at all that prayer is the heart and center of all religion." This view contrasts with the more usual psychological analyses of the cen-tral role of dogma and doctrines, institutions and rites, ethical ideals, and social control in religion. While prayer is at the heart of life when *labore est orare*, sacraments, purifications, offerings, processions, and asceticism can (indirectly) express an inner experience of what Heiler identified as "awe, trust, surrender, yearning, and enthusiasm" (ibid.), through their "outward and visible signs."

But we know that a conventional scientific rationalism can encompass and exhaust the sense of a transcendent reality with an incorrigible doubt and uncertainty about its validity, and a pessimistic preoccupation with the evils or pettiness of the world that obscures any sense of mystery. This mystery can also be hidden by the reliance of religious people on institutionally con-trolled doctrines, scriptures or liturgies, and other 'guaranteed' paths to enlightenment. Since any claims on them can be manipulated, it is hard to decide who is genuine or conscientious pray-*er*, especially when the newer paths to 'enlightenment' extend from chemical and other ecstasies to the physical exhilaration of jazzercize or dietary control, which are seldom com-pared with prayer by their practitioners who also reject the view that they are not good for one's health.

A utilitarian view avoids such doubts, trusting in a commonsense view of human nature that bothers neither about the lightness or darkness of being. Some awareness of mystery is, however, a prerequisite for the (authentic) reli-gious faith that Luther identified with "prayer and nothing but prayer." These issues were a continuing concern for the early psychologists of religion, who avoided the bleaker features of their contemporary religion by a pre-occupation with its 'primitive' forms in Christian and other traditions.

Prayer then became the most elementary form of the religious life (to mangle one of Emile Durkheim's preoccupations). Karl Girgensohn (1923), a German psychologist of religion who died in 1930, similarly stressed that to know how much religion a person has, one must know how and what is prayed about. But since, almost by definition, it is hard for any outsider to understand that, because of the privacy of religion, most of us must be content with fleeting insights and distorted information about the prayer-lives of the saints and mystics. While we expect prayers to have a 'meaning,' we also accept that a few play games in their prayers, and in what is intended by them.

Saints and mystics

Our basic psychological data about prayer depend on the results of social surveys that ask about religious practice, belief and experience. The Australian Values Study (McCallum, 1987), for example, shows that in 1983 more females (40 percent) than males (26 percent) said they "pray regularly," that 39 percent of females and 28 percent of males hold orthodox Christian beliefs, 31 percent of females and 12 percent of males regularly attend church, and that 12 percent of women and 9 percent of men are engaged in voluntary work for a church or other religious organization. Since our sense of God, or of religion can be concealed from strangers or the profane, we may never know how much acquiescence to socially desirable pressures or self presentation are buried in those answers and what insight they might give into common prayer. These survey results about prayer and religious experience are remarkably consistent across different studies in English-speaking societies, so David Hay's analysis of religious experience in Britain found that "41 percent of the women reported experiences of a presence or power, compared with 31 percent of the men" (1982, p. 119), with these proportions positively related to age, education and social class.

Despite the invasive, perhaps voyeuristic efforts of survey researchers (as well as journalists and many others) to discover the truth of our sexual preferences, financial dealings, honesty *and* our religion, some rely more heavily on the judgements of experts than on survey data. When high profile individuals decide to blow their cover and expose what might have been suspected about their piety or lack of it, their autobiographical assertions can be made to appear ambiguous because of some political agenda.

So McFarland (1990), writing of Dorothea von Montau, described in Gunter Grass's *The Flounder*, notes that "The acceptance of suffering as a form of *imitatio Christi* is common in saints' lives, and it is a didactic requirement that Dorothea should suffer progressively more as she approaches sanctity. Dorothea's sufferings were partly inflicted by her husband and her fellow-citizens, both lay and clerical, as the response of the 'world' to the life of grace to which she was called" (p. 83). McFarland goes on to describe "a specific mode of late medieval discourse which was striving to expand the means of expressing spiritual experience (and hence of psychological states and inwardness in general) beyond those hitherto available in vernacular writing. One of the principal strategies for doing this is to contrast the sensory perceptions of the flesh with those of the spirit, and to use vivid bodily movement and gesture as a means of indicating emotional responses to both the sight of food and to the sound of angels singing" (p. 88).

Despite that, William James relied on spiritual writings in his *Varieties of Religious Experience* (1902), and when he addressed the validity of their authors' credibility he said, "In the natural sciences and industrial arts it never occurs to anyone to try to refute opinions by showing their author's neurotic constitution. Opinions here are invariably tested by logic and by experiment. It should be no otherwise with religious opinions. Their value can only be ascertained by spiritual judgements directly passed upon them, as judgements based on our own immediate feeling primarily; and secondarily on what we ascertain of their experiential relations to our moral needs and to the rest of what we hold as true" (1985, p. 23). The coherence of these accounts has been an important criterion of their validity, although psychological (or scientific) meanings are inevitably intertwined with their use for or against particular theological, pastoral, or psychological interpretations and conclusions. Yet William James rejected the relevance of Saint Teresa's nervous system (or mental state) to her theology, which he judged in terms of its immediate 'luminousness,' philosophical reasonableness, and moral helpfulness as the "only available criteria" (ibid.). He found their psychological origins in immediate intuition, pontifical authority or supernatural revelation, or in a "higher spirit," or as "automatic utterances" (p. 24) (a medical preoccupation at that time), and stressed that "medical materialists" turned "the tables on their predecessors by using their criteria or origins in a destructive instead of an accreditive way" (ibid.). Sacks (1986a and b) shows that those preoccupations have continued, although the credibility of isolated cases is reduced if we expect to be able to test them against a consensus about the reliability and validity of the *evidence* that might refute theories or specific hypotheses that are derived from them.

Those who work out their religion in public make a display that is not present in a flight to solitude in their own room or in nature's open spaces. 'Experts,' and the saints or mystics who speak of a life of prayer to their disciples when they teach them how to pray, seldom hold their intimate conversations with God in public. Their written prayers (for example in Appleton's [1985] *Oxford Book of Prayer*) are, however, part of our liturgical inheritance and obscure the spontaneous cries that might convey the deep needs, yearning, or adoration that, or so we are told, are seldom verbalized.

The followers of any guide or prophet must therefore accept *traces* of their lives, and so William James stressed the importance of the fruits of religion over any roots that could be identified, which are necessarily obscure. The traces of prayer are indirect, although we are assured that when confronted with an ultimate need one makes loud cries to God, and that such involuntary utterances of distress or joy imprint themselves on those who happen to hear. So a rich man of Assisi, who had invited Francis to spend the night at his house to overhear him at his prayer, heard Francis repeat throughout the night "My God and my All." The ardor of that prayer was such that the rich man immediately became a disciple. Confessional and mystical writings therefore extend beyond prayer to accounts of the visions and insights that support their claims and advice. Despite those literary strategies, conceits, and pastoral guidance, the Lord's Prayer has been a continuing stimulus for religious devotion.

Yet the reactions to religious forms and liturgies have been neglected by psychologists, although Welford's (1948) studies of the preferred language for Bible reading, prayer, and public worship support the view that prayers in the 'new' liturgies give traditionalists the sense that they have been 'manufactured,' while familiarity with the 'old' language has made those traditional forms appear venerable. No liturgical form is naive or innocent, and the attitudes to them could be like reactions to works of art or music (Brown and Moore, 1990) that can be enlivened by a knowledge of the authors' intentions. Since others' prayers can be an important stimulus for one's own meditation or contemplation, they have a place in any psychology of prayer that recognizes an inner life and its examination. Although an empirically based psychology of religion began to develop around the turn of this century, it is only in the last thirty years that a Catholic psychology has been based on detached observation (cf Godin, 1985, Vergote, 1988) and not on the wisdom of spiritual direction. So Heiler (1932) described St Teresa as "the woman psychologist among the saints" (p. xxvi). In that sense, psychologies of prayer began within theology and philosophies of religion, to advance the practical and moral claims that might interpret or direct religious experiences. There is continuing debate about the extent to which any account of those experiences can stand as data, even for a psychohistory like Erikson's (1958) *Young Man Luther*, or an examination of Augustine's *Confessions* (in the *Journal for the Scientific Study of Religion* in 1986 and Capps and Dittes, 1990). Commentators can too easily write themselves over such documents.

Testimonies to the validity of prayer, in the prayers themselves, and in the language in which they are conveyed, as well as in the rituals and gestures (especially with the hands) that accompany them, are expected to be more disclosive in private than in public. In both contexts, however, psychological effects are expected on those who pray. Even if they are reflexive, as with St Francis, others can be moved or influenced by them. It is not clear, however, whether the prototypic prayer is found in a spontaneous 'cry' for help, in the well-constructed words of a liturgy, in hymns of praise, or among those who have withdrawn from the world. Any cry can respond to a threat, show trust in life itself, be directed to another person, a transcendent being, or to the order of the universe and its creative powers.

The dominant nineteenth-century theories of religion advanced by Schopenhauer and Feuerbach were echoed by Freud who held that faith in God arose primarily as the projection of a wish or fantasy. This aligns with the classical view that fear itself created the gods, and while Marx held that the gods were created by those in power, to bluff and subdue the rest, some held that those conceptions were forms of a 'natural' cognition or explanation, and others held that they implicate our needs or social relationships. In each case they assume a constructed order beyond the flux of immediate experience. That an ability to form abstract conceptions is accepted as an essential feature of adult thinking could be a more fundamental process here than the feelings of weakness, dependence, or hope that have been expected to support religious responses. None of these assumptions is easily tested, and their plausibility rests on accepting some set of principled psychological doctrines.

Those who have looked for consistent differences in personality or other characteristics among those who are or are not religious have not found consistent support for defined traits beyond religiousness itself and perhaps in gender (Gaston and Brown, 1992). The variety of religious experiences are not plausibly reduced simply to brain dysfunctions, misattributions, or even social influence. Nor can they be discarded, as they are by the skeptical commentators who do not recognize the validity of imaginative constructions and an emotional life. The phenomenology of religion, which Heiler (1932, p. 83) set between trust and distrust, dependence and independence, continues to invite attention, not least because of the conviction or confidence that religious traditions draw.

There are other difficulties in assuming that all contemporary religions depend on primitive psychological processes, especially if they are unfamiliar. Each has its own traditional coherence and base, so that even if someone does not understand the Mass, or the enthusiasm of Pentecostalism, the evidence suggests that we tend to take over (or reject) the 'faith' of the community in which we grew up (Hunsberger and Brown, 1984) and that specific religious forms are integral to the communities that support them (cf Swanson, 1960). While prayer may be rejected because it is too concrete (or abstract), directed to inappropriate targets or expectations, uncommitted (or too personal), not spontaneous, too sacrificial, mindless, and so on, those reactions are themselves likely to depend on how the world in which one lives is represented in experience and understanding. The range of religious emotions includes reverence and admiration, self-confidence or humility, frustration, or hope. Although we may not agree about how those emotions should be handled or the states or events that are likely to drive us to prayer, they could involve reactions to the explicit or implicit relationships that express subjection and kinship or independence. A paramount relationship in prayer is between an inferior and a superior, unless it is assumed that God must always be "on our side."

Other analyses

Some of the attitudes involved in prayer, and in its targets, have been criticized by philosophers and moralists as too concrete, not expressing appropriate values, searching for 'happiness' rather than 'divine favor,' or for material rather than spiritual benefits. But Socrates held that we should pray for whatever *is* good, since the gods know best what is good. The Stoics could therefore surrender unreservedly to the hand of Fate: and while a wise man prays but does not ask, Rousseau prayed simply for "what Thou wilt." Others might pray only in solemn contemplation, or in adoration and praise, despite immense differences from time to time in the intensity of their emotional rapture or abandonment. Not to pray for what we might achieve for ourselves stresses our independence, but could make our prayers circular, since according to Voltaire, we address the God we have made in our own image.

While some might have given up prayer because of the immutability of natural laws, scientific explanations can escape such confidence with "thought experiments" that could be analogous to prayers, although Whitehead held that a religious awareness discerns the permanent side of the universe, exemplified in particular instances. That prayers co-exist with scientific analyses emphasizes the extent to which our understanding of the environment is coherently structured in ways that eliminate neither science or religion, unless they reflect the arrogant egocentricity of religious people. But Penrose (1990, p. 422) notes that "the data are not yet good enough to point clearly to one or other of the proposed cosmological models (nor to determine whether or not the presence of a tiny cosmological constant might have a significant overall effect)." In this sense there can be no "simple prayers."

Reasons for maintaining prayer include respect for an established religious tradition, ignorance of how the world actually works, and faith in or wagering on God's existence. Some retain prayer as a customary practice, or interpret it as a form of contemplation directed to God without any petitionary expectations, or as an imaginative enterprise about what *might* be. Others insist that God's work is incomplete without their recognition or support. Such explanatory strategies attempt to make a compromise between religious demands, thoughts about the validity of prayer, whether in subjective or objective terms, and the worlds of nature and experience. It is the attempts to expose those problems that help to make prayer psychologically interesting, since anyone acquainted with prayer will have developed some attitudes to its validity. Those attitudes might recognize prayer as an expedient that 'mature' people no longer need, as a crutch that the strong can throw away or that without prayer, God and 'man' are kept apart, as Sabatier asserted. Whatever psychological attitudes and beliefs will support, or can be assigned to prayer, it must be grounded in a tradition, in experience, and in some awareness of what it achieves, except when prayer is simply a naive or primitive appeal for help.

Marrett's (1903) anthropological analysis that derived from Frazer's *Golden Bough* aligned incantation with invocation, and spells with prayer, by asking whether "the spell helps to generate the prayer." He concluded, however, that "the spell belongs to magic, and the prayer to religion," and that "certain beliefs, of a kind natural to the infancy of thought, (are) to be accepted at face value in a spirit of naive faith, whilst being in fact illusory." This view presupposed a credulity that questioned what can be taken at "face value" and the relationships between "common sense, religion and science, with reciprocal relationships between the experiences we encounter and revelations of a sacred dimension." Pailin (1990, p. 87f) identified that in terms of an ecstasy beyond the normal, an aesthetically satisfying sense of unity or wholeness, a novel perspective that is self-authenticating, a moral sensibility, a creative, releasing joy, or an encounter with God that has been represented as Buber's 'Thou,' Marcel's 'Presence or Being,' Schleiermacher's 'feeling of absolute dependence,' Otto's 'holy,' or as the contemplative's 'dark night of the soul.'

In line with that, a recent examination of Hinduism by Southeimer (1989, p. 197ff) identifies its components as:

1. the work and teachings of the Brahmans,
2. asceticism and renunciation,
3. tribal religion (at an institutional level),
4. folk religion through an "immediate presence and access to a god or a goddess in the form of a *murti*" or as a living person treated as one, so that the god exists 'here and now,' is earthbound, and does not live in some puranic *svarga* (or religious text), and
5. bhakti as "a fruit of effort and a gift of god" for "the devotee whose essential link with the deity consists precisely" in that reward.

These categories are different from those in any Christian perspective, which Glock and Stark (1965), as sociologists, identified as belief, practice (especially through participation in religious rites and rituals), experience, knowledge, and the consequences or everyday effects of religion. Ninian Smart (1969), from the perspective of religious studies, identified the components of religion as doctrinal, mythological, ethical, ritual, and experiential, adding a social dimension, since "Religions are not just systems of belief: they are also organizations or parts of organizations. They have a communal and social significance" (p. 20). These dimensions adopt an outsider's perspective on religion, in the sense that they do not explicitly refer to the views or experience of insiders to particular religions.

King's (1986) anthropological formulation was in terms of

1. a social tradition or culture that supports and interprets a cosmology with deities, and saints or spirits;
2. sacred knowledge passed on to those who are approved to receive it;
3. the techniques by which spiritual power is found and used in prayer, sacraments, blessings, or ritual;
4. believers, or adherents who align the meaning of their life with some set of religious practices, ideas, or doctrines, and so carry a religion;
5. fellowship and communication with other believers, and with the transcendental world.

An alignment of these features with psychological approaches is outlined in the following table.

While prayer straddles each of these levels, it may be primarily traditional and a spiritual technique or process. But when Clayton and Gladden (1969) linked the ritual, experiential, ideological, intellectual, and consequential dimensions they found a single dimension in which religious belief

Table 2		
Religions involve . . .	Psychology studies . . .	Psychologists identify . . .
a. a tradition	1. knowledge	
b. sacred knowledge	2. belief	cognition
c. spiritual technique	3. experience	affect
and rituals	4. behavior	action
d. adherents or	5. social contexts	content
members		
e. within-group	6. secular consequences	
fellowship		

was central so that the other aspects were referred to it.

Yet it is the institutional, social, and textual structures that carry religions across generations and locations, defining or distinguishing them from whatever is not 'religious.' The diversity of personal commitments that insiders to a religion recognize within their own tradition contrast against their awareness of the institutional processes in other traditions, and so Jung's "*Answer to Job*" holds that "the (Christian) doctrine of the Trinity originally corresponded with a patriarchal order of society." He went on to say that "we cannot tell whether social conditions produced the idea or, conversely, the idea revolutionized the existing social order" (p. 151), so that the concept of the Trinity "moulds the anthropomorphic conceptions of father and son, of the life of different persons into an archetypal and luminous figure, the 'Most Holy Three-in-One,' giving a psychic presence outside consciousness, in religion as a societal rather than an individual process" (p. 151). Other tensions in religion include the opportunistic pressures on some people to show their 'religiousness,' regardless of whether religion has been found 'helpful,' with the common conclusion that "Without question the mentally disturbed are frequently attracted to religion" (Wulff, 1991, p. 307), or that religion can be a danger to mental (and perhaps physical) health because of its illusions. To have been indoctrinated into a religious tradition carries its own impact, and it may be hard to avoid a sense of dependence implicit in the doctrine that, for example, we have been made to serve God, and can find no rest without Him. Prayer might reinforce that process in religious terms, or through its role in coping or in some generalized beliefs about the nature of the world and of one's place and duties within it, despite the difficulties in establishing the direct consequences of whatever outcomes are expected from one's prayers.

As a confusing psychological interpretation, the analysis of prayer by Christopher Bryant (in Wakefield's [1983] *Dictionary of Christian Spirituality*) defines it as "entering into communion with God," and places it "partly in a region beyond the competence of psychology to speak about," while granting that as a "human experience" it is "a valid subject for psychological scrutiny" (p. 317). Bryant aligns Jung's archetypes with God's unconditional authority which presents individuals with "a divine or numinous quality" aroused by symbols that trigger activity, so that in prayer individuals "look through or away from the symbol to the Unknown to which it points." From this point of view, prayers themselves awaken and express fundamental religious attitudes in adoration, confession, thanksgiving, petition and intercession, and in our awareness of a need for, but our estrangement from God. Bryant also believes that these beliefs are supported in "modern psychological medicine," and in our involvement with the crimes of humanity. Nevertheless, he holds that naive or child-like and primitive feelings in petitions are "apt to shock the sophisticated," and that healing forces are at work in the repetition of prayers. He says that "a confident petition which opens the personality to its depths causes either distress signals or impulses of healing and encouragement to be sent out below the level of consciousness" (p. 318).

Despite the prescriptive piety of that entry on prayer, Wakefield's *Dictionary* recognizes 'pietism' and freedom from the guilt of sin as part of our nature. It also refers to the personal response of faith, fasting and abstinence, the receptive nature of feminine spirituality (although there is no entry for "masculine spirituality"), the spiritual power of holy places and pilgrimages, and the reformers' sense of immediacy in an 'inner light.' Modern concepts of 'human nature' or 'person' carry the thread that links prayer with a need to change and with the 'new' therapies, including self-help and meditation.

If, on the other hand, we imagine penitents having to make regular private confessions, the Protestant Reformers took that into public worship, and a post-Vatican II emphasis is now given to the corporate nature of sin and reconciliation while philosophers stress the assertive, rebellious, or self-sufficient nature of 'man' in shaping their destiny. Nevertheless, Christians maintain that penitence is "an indispensable precondition for the communion with God for which man is destined" (Harries, 1984, p. 295). Harries also noted that psychoanalysis has both confused and enriched Christian teaching on penitence by questioning simplistic views about it and stressing the role of counselors in helping to deepen our self-understanding. Behind those practices lie the mysteries of transcendence that align God with awe, the numinous, holy dread, or the "fear that is cast out by love." The spirituality of a contemplative life, the emphasis Christianity gives to the person and the life of Christ, and the social (or pastoral) implications of withdrawal from, or engagement with the world, are at the edges of prayer, which should be handled cautiously by any psychologist.

Common sense
Our point of departure must, however, be found in the practice of prayer, how it is understood, and the claims on what it can 'do.' There are many answers to those questions, depending on the contexts in which they are explored and the prejudices brought to their understanding. That the valid-

ity of any religion is accepted by some and rejected by others, and that religion is expected to carry revealed truths or hoped for illusions emphasizes its ambiguity so that it can be taken for granted as part of our culture, rejected as a cultural relic, or offered as a way to transform lives.

Current meanings of prayer are to be found in the ways it is talked about, and a casual examination of two Penguin books of quotations as repositories of our everyday statements shows that prayer has been judged most appropriate for the aged (since "beads and prayer-books are the toys of age"), and that "words without thoughts never go to heaven." While "long prayers are a pretence," "silent prayers are immediate." To begin a journey on a Sunday enjoys the benefit of the Church's prayers for "all who travel by land or water." But every prayer is for a miracle—"that twice two be not four"—although he "who rises from prayer a better man, his prayer is answered." While a "single grateful thought raised to heaven is the most perfect prayer," the commonest prayer holds that "if I was sure I were to die tonight I would repent at once." That many prayers "don't get through," or are returned with "rejected scrawled across 'em," acknowledges that a prayerful frame of mind is not always reinforced. Although prayer may be "the Church's banquet" and that "more things are wrought by prayer than this world dreams of," others are said to pray "with no very lively hope of success." As the paragon of Christian prayer, Jesus drew attention to the fact that, "My house should be called the house of prayer, but ye have made it a den of thieves."

Those epigrams can be set against explicitly Christian perspectives, including that of La Novalis, the poet of romanticism, who held that praying is to religion what thinking is to philosophy. While the Bible contains prayers that would communicate with God, they are not necessarily directed to, or showing confidence in a divine being, and it is hard to tie down the prayers that are expressed in a word, like the "Jesus prayer," or in wordless sighs of adoration with a glance or gesture towards a sacred object or to the heavens. Boundaries between the sacred and secular are fuzzy, which gives prayer a peculiar attraction for any psychological analysis of what makes it 'effective.' That many common courtesies and blessings or curses derive from simple prayers suggests their power. The next chapter, therefore, examines the semantics of prayer, since prayer, its practice and psychology, depends on language.

Chapter Two

What Is Prayer? In Search of a Definition

ANNA WIERZBICKA

"A careful . . . study of just the terminology that designates acts of human-spiritual communication has yet to be done among even the widespread and best known religious traditions" (Gill, 1987, p. 489).

Introduction

Is prayer a universal human phenomenon? Not everyone prays, of course, but would it be true to say that in all human societies, in all cultures, prayer is, as far as we know, a part of life?

Claims of the kind have often been made. For example, Dubois-Dumee (1989, p. 12) states: "In all places, since the beginning of time, people have prayed; not always, it is true, as I pray—but I can't judge their fervor on those grounds." Similarly, D'Arcy (1918, p. 171) writes: "Face to face with vast and mysterious forces, beset by dangers, urged on by unceasing needs, man turns instinctively for help to powers other and greater than himself. Prayer is wide as the world and older than history." Finally, Brandon (1970, p. 507): "Prayer is a universal religious phenomenon."

On the other hand, Stanner (1976, p. 29) denies the existence of prayer in the life of Australian Aborigines. He summarizes the essence of Aboriginal religion as follows:

"The Aborigines acknowledged that men's lives were under a power or force beyond themselves; . . . they venerated the places where such power or force was believed to concentrate; . . . they imposed a self-discipline to maintain a received tradition relating to the provenance and care of such power; and . . . part of the discipline was to maintain what might be called a 'religious economy.' The elements of belief and action were in a sense an

25

'address' to the givers of life. There was no element of direct petition, so that to speak of 'prayer' would be to go too far, just as it would be to speak of 'worship.' But I agree that we are dealing with lives of religious devotion."

Even these four quotes, however, make it quite clear that any assertions about the universality of prayer (or otherwise) hinge on the definition of this concept; and that without such a definition, the question of the universality of prayer cannot even be raised. In fact, without a working definition of prayer, any rational inquiry into this aspect of human life is severely hampered, to say the least—especially so if one wants to reach beyond the confines of one's own culture and one's own religious tradition.[1]

A survey of definitions

One type of definition of prayer is illustrated by the following formula: "[Prayer is] the attitude of heart that under the inspiration of the Holy Spirit opens itself to the Mystery of the Blessed Trinity" (Boniface Baroffio, quoted in Buono, 1990, p. 6). Obviously, on this kind of definition there couldn't be any question of any universality, or even near-universality, of prayer. On the other hand, it would also be easy to formulate a definition of prayer which would allow us to assert that prayer *is* a part of any culture (including, for example, Australian Aboriginal culture). Clearly, what is needed is not an arbitrary definition of one kind or another but one which would be inherently valid—or at least more valid than the competitors. We need, then, criteria for constructing a valid definition. We also need some principles which would guide us through the maze of existing definitions of prayer, and to help us to sieve the grain from the chaff.

Numerous definitions of prayer have of course already been proposed— by theologians, philosophers, anthropologists, religious writers, and so on. A number of such definitions will be discussed in the course of this chapter. In accordance with Wittgenstein's precept that meaning should be approached within the "stream of life," I will start with some definitions offered by people who have themselves prayed a great deal, and whose discussions of prayer are born of their own experience. As a starting point, then let us consider a selection of definitions gathered from various sources by Dubois-Dumee (1989, p. 9):

Prayer is . . .
1. The raising up of the soul to God (John Damascene, eighth century)
2. Simply, union with God (Curé d'Ars)
3. A conversation with a friend; and that includes knowing how to shut up and listen (St Ignatius of Loyola)
4. A conversation with God (Gregory of Nyssa, fourth century)

---

1. I would like to thank colleagues who have discussed the concept of 'prayer' with me, and who offered many valuable comments. In particular, thanks are due to Tim Curnow, Tony Diller, Jean Harkins, and Ulrike Mosel. Tim Curnow has also read the first draft of this chapter and made helpful criticisms and suggestions.

5. The key to Holy Writ (Isaac the Syrian, seventh century)

6. A heart-to-heart talk, in which the soul flows into God and God flows into the soul, in order to transform it into himself (Elizabeth of the Trinity)

7. Awakening to God's presence within (James Borst)

8. Full attentiveness (Simone Weil)

9. A one-word description of a life-time's journey into God (Delia Smith)

10. Prayer isn't a matter of a lot of thinking; it's a lot of loving (St Teresa of Avila)

11. Prayer is a way of life . . . an attitude to living and breathing . . . an awareness of God in all our experiences, good and bad (Frank Topping)

12. It is a matter of opening yourself to God, just as you open yourself to fire, or to the sun or to the light (Louis Evely)

13. Your prayer is God's word of longing and love in you, God's breathing of the Spirit in you, to make you want the union he wants (Maria Boulding)

Of these thirteen 'definitions' number 5 can be dismissed as a statement *about* prayer rather than an attempt to define this concept. Several others (for example, 1, 7, 9 and 12) are not definitions but metaphors: concepts such as 'raising,' 'awakening,' 'journey' or 'opening,' are used here in a metaphorical, not in a literal sense; in reality, needless to say, there is no 'journey,' or 'awakening,' and nothing is being 'raised up' or 'opened.' In fact, metaphorical definitions of prayer are particularly common and are used extremely widely. To mention two of the most popular ones: "Prayer is the raising of the mind and heart to God, to adore, thank, ask pardon, and seek graces" (St Augustine's definition, used widely in Catholic catechisms; cf O'Donnell, 1977, p. 14); and "Prayer is an ascent of the mind to God" (St Thomas Aquinas' definition, in 'de Oratione,' *Summa theologiae* 2 ii qu. lxxxiii). Some of the metaphors used in the literature on prayer are very bold indeed, as when believers are exhorted to "become prayer" (cf e.g. Dubois-Dumee 1989) or when it is said that, for example, "Our prayer is Jesus Christ" (Hynes, 1989, p. 6). Metaphors of this, or any other kind, can be enlightening, but they cannot offer the kind of conceptual understanding which a definition of the literal sense of a word must aim at.

When we leave aside the metaphorical elements of the proposed definitions, and when we add what is clearly intended though not mentioned explicitly, the following concepts emerge as particularly worthy of further scrutiny: 'God,' 'soul,' 'talk,' 'conversation,' 'listening,' 'attention,' 'thinking,' 'loving,' and 'union.' Reading through various books and articles on prayer, we encounter all these words very frequently—plus a few other ones, such as 'relationship,' 'communion,' 'encounter,' communication' or 'intercourse':

"We have established a working definition of prayer as conscious relationship [with God]." (Barry, 1987, p. 14)

"Prayer is the search for God, encounter with God, and going beyond this encounter in communion." (Metropolitan Anthony of Sourozh, 1987, p. 3)

"Real prayer is a personal relationship with God." (Hynes, 1989, p. 33)

"Prayer [is] loving conversation with God." (St John Chrysostom, quoted in Buono, 1990, p. 4)

"Prayer is a living intercourse [*Verkehr*] of the believer [lit. "the pious person"] with God conceived as personal and as currently experienced, an intercourse which reflects the forms of human social relations." (Heiler, 1918, p. 491; my translation)

Definitions linking prayer with God could be quoted ad infinitum; but there are also others, which consciously omit any reference to God, referring instead to "higher powers," "supernatural powers," or to "divine or spiritual entities," as in the following examples:

"Prayer is not necessarily petition, the asking for benefits. Any intercourse of a human soul with higher powers may rightly be termed prayer." (D'Arcy, 1918, p. 171; characteristically D'Arcy adds, however: "Prayer is, in general, the communion of the human soul with God.")

"In its simplest and most primitive form prayer is the expression of a desire, cast in the form of a request, to influence some force or power conceived as supernatural. Apart from the modern usage of the term, which connotes spiritual communication, it is usually understood to imply reverent entreaty." (Fallaize, 1918, p. 154)

"Prayer, understood as the human communication with divine and spiritual entities, has been present in most of the religions in human history." (Gill, 1987, p. 489)

Definitions of prayer which seek to exclude references to God are often rather ambivalent and sometimes appear to contradict themselves in this respect. For example, Phillips (1981, p. 30) writes: "When a believer prays, he talks to God . . . Not all prayers can be described as talking to God, but they are nevertheless claimed to be meetings with the supernatural or encounters with the divine." Macquarrie (1972, p. 25) describes prayer simply as thinking ("Prayer is thinking"). He elaborates (p. 30): "Prayer is a fundamental style of thinking, passionate and compassionate, responsible and thankful, that is deeply rooted in our humanity and that manifests itself not only among believers but also among serious-minded people who do not profess any religious faith." Having said this, Macquarrie (ibid.) expresses his hope that "if we follow out the instinct to pray that is in all of us, it will finally bring us to faith in God," but apparently he doesn't want to include any explicit mention of God, or even of anything supernatural, in his definitions of prayer and praying. (Thus he says [ibid.]: "To pray is to think in such a way that we dwell with reality," but he hastens to add "and faith's name for reality is God.")

Like the definitions involving the notion of God (or even more so), the definitions which omit any mention of God are usually heavily metaphorical. For example, the *New Catholic Encyclopaedia* (Arbesmann, 1967 p. 667) offers the following:

"In its primal and elemental form it may be defined as an act of cult by which man enters into communion with a higher, superhuman, supersensuous being, somehow conceived as personal and experienced as real and present, upon whose power he feels himself dependent."

Apart from the word *cult*, which carries with it various assumptions whose nature has not been explored, this definition relies crucially on three metaphors: 'higher,' 'superhuman,' and 'enter into communion.' It is by no means clear, however, exactly what these metaphors are meant to imply; for example, is 'higher' meant to imply 'good'? Or 'powerful'? Or both 'good' and 'powerful'? The same questions apply to 'superhuman.' The "entering into communion" could be understood as implying communication (in the sense of 'saying things to' and being understood), as implying a realization of mutual good feelings, or in some other way. Suggestive and intuitively satisfying as formulae of this kind may be, they simply fail to make clear exactly what is being claimed to be conceptually relevant.

Faced with so many different definitions of prayer how do we choose between them? And if we are not entirely satisfied with any of them, how do we construct one which would be in some sense 'better' or more illuminating?

I believe a more illuminating definition (or 'explication') can be arrived at if we distinguish different writers' theories of prayer from the folk theory embodied in the English word *prayer* (and in its equivalents in those languages which do have words corresponding exactly to the English word *prayer*). Phillips (1981, p. 1) opens his book on *The Concept of Prayer* with a quote from Wittgenstein's *Philosophical Investigations* (1953, pp. 123-4): "Philosophy may in no way interfere with the actual use of language; it can in the end only describe it." In my view, this quote gives us the clue to how we should proceed: we should first of all explore the concept embodied in the English word *prayer*, as it is actually used; having done this, we should try to establish whether this concept is universal (encoded in all human languages); and if we find that it isn't, then enquire whether the phenomenon describable in English as *prayer* is attested in all other societies, including those which do not have a corresponding word (nor, by implication, a corresponding concept).

Heiler (1920, p. 488; my translation) writes:

"When we consider all these contrasts [between different types of prayer] and when we survey all the main types of prayer, the question imposes itself: what do they all have in common, what is the basis of all these phenomena, what is the *essence* of prayer? The answer to this question is not easy."

But in fact, what is most problematic is not the answer but the question itself. We cannot simply survey "all the main types of prayer" and then extract their common denominator, because first we would have to know what to include in our survey; and to do this we would have to know what we mean by prayer. Thus, we cannot really ask Heiler's question unless we already know the answer. But if we take the English word *prayer* as our starting point then we can establish the range of 'prayers' in a nonarbitrary way, and then we can indeed ask what they have in common. This is what I will try to do in this chapter.[2]

Gill (1987, p. 493) writes:

"In the general study of prayer, the term *prayer* has been used loosely to designate a variety of human acts, principally speech acts associated with the practice of religion, especially those that are communications with a divine or spiritual entity. There can be no precise definition given the word when used in this way, for it serves as but a general focusing device for more precise comparative and historical study. The term gains definitional precision when seen as any of dozens of terms used in specific religious traditions as articulated in practice or in doctrine."

In a sense he is quite right, because the use of the word *prayer* in the literature on the subject has indeed been extremely fluid. But it is not true that there can be no precise definition of this term: in ordinary English, the word *prayer* does have a definite meaning, and it is this 'ordinary' meaning which can provide the "focusing device" for more precise comparative and historical study. But to be able to use this word as an effective "focusing device" we do need a precise and non-arbitrary definition. I believe that such a definition can be found (as it can be found for any other speech act or speech genre word; cf Wierzbicka 1987 and 1991).

What does it mean to 'define' anything (e.g. *prayer*)?

To define *prayer* we need to elucidate the concept of 'prayer,' but we also need to elucidate the concept of 'defining.' Since this chapter is meant to be on prayer, and not on defining, the latter problem can be discussed here only in an extremely sketchy way. (For further discussion see, e.g. Wierzbicka, 1985, 1987, 1992, and forthcoming; see also Apresjan, 1974.) The most important points (as I see it) are the following ones:

1. A definition aims at capturing the 'semantic invariant' of a word, that is, the stable set of components which are compatible with the entire range of this word's use. (Hypothetical components of meaning which are compatible with some but not all of the word's uses are not part of its semantic invariant.)

2. In some cases it can be established that a word has two (or more) different (though possibly related) meanings. In a case like this, each meaning will be linked with its own semantic invariant. It is not, then, the shared core of the two meanings which represents the semantic invariant but the full set of components associated with a given meaning. For example, the French verb *prier* has two meanings; when it is used transitively it means 'to ask for,' and when it is used intransitively it means 'to pray.' Etymologically, the second meaning is no doubt derived from the first one, but synchronically, they are quite distinct.

---

2. In this chapter, no distinction will be made between the verb *to pray* and the noun *prayer*. It should be pointed out, however, that the noun *prayer* has two meanings: roughly *prayer*[1] designates a certain activity (the activity of praying), whereas *prayer*[2] designates a certain text (which is intended to be used in praying). Only the former meaning (*prayer*[1]) is considered here.

3. The literal meaning must be distinguished from marked usages, involving metaphor, irony, humor, and so on. Marked usages of this kind have to be accounted for in terms of a general theory of metaphor, irony, humor, and similar devices, and not in terms of the postulated invariant of a particular word.

4. The definition of a word should be stated in terms of words that are semantically simpler than the word which is being defined, and, ideally, in terms of 'semantic primitives,' that is, words which are so simple that they are regarded as indefinables. (Without such a condition, all definitions would be potentially circular.)

5. The definition of a word should be stated in terms of 'lexical universals,' that is, words which have their semantic equivalents in all (or nearly all) languages of the world. For example, if 'prayer' were to be defined in terms of words such as *worship, cult, humility*, or *reverence*, this would mean that the definition would have an Anglo, or European, bias (since concepts of this kind are themselves cultural artifacts of European languages, cf Wierzbicka, in press). Furthermore, a definition of this kind could not be readily compared with those of religious speech acts and speech genres from other religious traditions. But if all religious speech acts and speech genres are defined in terms of lexical universals then their definitions can be easily compared, and the similarities and differences between them can be clearly identified.

6. The list of the (hypothetical) lexical universals emerging from the work of the last two decades includes the following thirty-odd elements: I, you, someone; this, all, two, the same; know, say, think, feel, want, do, happen; good, bad, big, small; no, if, can, because, like, very; where, when, after, under; part of, kind of.

7. An adequate definition (that is, one which captures the invariant and thus accounts for the range of a word's use) cannot be expected to take the form of one simple phrase or one simple sentence. Rather, it must be expected to take the form of a set of sentential components, with their own (iconic) 'grammar,' reflected in the visual form of the explicatory formula.

8. The definition (or, as I would call it, explication) of a complex concept such as 'prayer' may take the form of a conceptual 'prototype' rather than any rigid set of 'denotational conditions.' The notion of prototype is not incompatible with that of a semantic invariant: the latter implies a set of necessary and sufficient features (which have to be stated in the explication), whereas the former allows us to seek these features in the subjective conceptualization of a given situation rather than in the 'objective' situation itself.

What is prayer? A preliminary discussion

Religious literature on prayer often insists that prayer is not inherently linked with speech. For example, Dubois-Dumee (1989, p. 6) writes:

"*Prayer* . . . is a state of being . . . And, moreover, it is a way of life . . . What is asked of us, therefore, is not so much that we 'say prayers' as that we 'live in prayer,' constantly in the presence of God, so that we become one huge longing for God, so that we 'become prayer.'"

In ordinary language, however, *to pray* is clearly an 'active' verb, not a 'stative' one; and it does crucially involve the concept of 'speaking,' or, more precisely, of 'saying (something).' This can be shown by a variety of linguistic tests which needn't be discussed here. Suffice it to say that in ordinary English, the two sentences:

A. He was in a state of grace.

B. He was in a state of prayer.

have an entirely difference status, A being a 'normal' English sentence, and B, a creative and intentional violation of the normal usage. In normal usage, praying is something that one does, not something that one can 'be,' 'become,' or 'live in.'

As for 'saying,' we should distinguish, first of all, the two senses of this word: the basic 'saying' which can be done in one's head, or in writing, as well as *viva voce*, and the vocal 'saying.' The English word *pray* can be applied to both 'mental' and 'vocal' acts, but in both kinds 'saying something' is crucially involved. A person thinking about God cannot be described in English as *praying*, no matter what the content of their thoughts. On the other hand, a person who is silently repeating in his or her head the invocation "Jesus!" (as in the shortest version of the so-called "Jesus prayer"; cf Lindbeck, 1981, p. 71) may well be so described—provided that certain conditions are fulfilled which are metaphorically referred to as the "raising of one's mind and heart to God."

The idea that "listening to God" or "paying attention to God" is equally, or more, important than "saying something" is an important part of the Christian conception of prayer, but it cannot be regarded as part of the meaning of the English word *pray*: where nothing is 'said' at all (not even silently) then, from the point of view of the English language, there is no praying. For example, when Brother Roger of Taizé says that "Silence is the whole of prayer; God speaks to us, breathing silently; he touches us in that aloneness that no other human can fill" (Dubois-Dumee, 1989, p. 55), his words have to be seen as a metaphor, and as a creative violation of the ordinary sense of the English word.

Assuming, then, that praying necessarily involves some words at least, some 'saying,' does it have to be saying something *to God*? Here, the answer must be in the negative—if only because one can say in English that somebody was praying to a saint; and although a statement of this kind does refer, in some oblique way, to God, it does not imply that the praying person is saying something to God. Rather, he or she is saying something to a saint, while at the same time, metaphorically speaking, 'raising his mind and heart to God.' Restricting our attention, at this stage, to Christian prayer, we could suggest (at a first approximation) that praying presupposes either 'saying something to God' or 'saying something to someone who is with God' (a saint or an angel) combined with a desire to 'say something to God' (as if one were praying, indirectly, to God, even when one is praying directly to 'someone who is with God'). Schematically, this could be represented as follows:

(a) person X wants to say something to God
(b) because of this, X says something (to someone)

Component (a) would reflect, to some extent, St Augustine's idea of 'raising one's mind and heart to God,' whereas component (b) would reflect the need for some sort of words.[3] Jointly, components (a) and (b) invite the inference that the 'saying of something' is addressed to God, but they allow also the possibility of a mediated address (as when one says something to a saint because of one's desire to say something to God).

But should the word *God* (with a capital G), be incorporated in our definition of *prayer*? Leaving aside, for the time being, the question of speech addressed at 'divine' or 'supernatural' 'powers,' we must first consider the question of the applicability of *prayer* to polytheistic societies, such as ancient Greece. Could one say, for example (without stretching or violating everyday usage) that Homer's heroes *prayed* to Zeus, Apollo, or Athene? And is it possible to use the word *pray* with reference to Aristotle invoking the gods in favor of his adopted son Nicanor, and making the vow that if his wish is granted, he would erect statues to Zeus and Athene as saviors (Benoit, 1981, p. 22)? Or if the Greek peasant, before putting his hand to a plough, asked Zeus and Demeter to 'give heaviness to the ripe corn of Demeter' (Hesiod, *Works*, pp. 335-340 and pp. 465-469; quoted in a French translation by Benoit, 1981, p. 21), could this be described in English as *praying*?

There can be no doubt that the prototypical usage of this word applies to a unique God of Christian, Jewish, or Islamic religion (especially, of course, Christian); but sentences in which it is applied to the ancient Greek gods, as in the examples above, are not unacceptable to native speakers of English (although they may evoke religious concepts rather different from those accepted in ancient Greece).

Certainly, most speakers of English would recognize as *prayer* Chinese texts such as the following one, which (according to Dyer Ball, 1918, p. 170) "was used by the Ming emperors at the solstice worship of Shang Ti [the Supreme Ruler]":

---

3. The question whether prayer involves 'saying something' or 'saying something to someone' is as interesting as it is difficult. The intention is, no doubt, to say something *to someone*; it is less clear, however, whether or not the actual words are necessarily addressed to someone. One argument in favor of just 'saying something' (without 'to someone') could be based on the prayer of people who don't believe in God and who nonetheless try to reach him. This applies, for example, to Levin's prayer in Tolstoy's *Anna Karenina* (at his brother Nikolai's deathbed):

"During the sacrament Levin prayed, too, and did what he had done a thousand times before, unbeliever as he was" (Tolstoy, 1982, p. 522).

The same scene, however, could also be interpreted as yielding support to the opposite hypothesis, for Tolstoy continues as follows:

"Addressing himself to God, he said, 'If Thou does exist, heal this man (it would not be the first time such a thing has happened) and Thou wilt save him and me.'"

"All the numerous tribes of animated beings are indebted to Thy favor for their beginning. Men and creatures are emparadised, O Ti (Lord), in Thy love. All living things are indebted to Thy goodness, but who knows whence his blessing comes to him? It is Thou alone, O Lord, who are the true parent of all things . . . The Service of Song is completed but our poor sincerity cannot be fully expressed. Sovereign goodness is infinite. As a potter Thou has made all living things. Great and small are curtained round. As engraven on the heart of Thy poor servant is the sense of Thy goodness, but my feeling cannot be fully displayed. With great kindness Thou dost bear with us, and notwithstanding our demerits dost grant us life and prosperity."

But it is equally clear that old Babylonian 'prayers' addressed to their different gods like Marduk, Ishtar, or Nebo, such as those quoted below (from Langdon, 1918, pp. 159-160), also qualify, intuitively, as *prayers* in the modern English sense of the word:

[to Marduk]
"Oh lord, not wilt thou reject me, not, oh lord, will thou reject me.
Oh lord, divine ram of heaven and earth, not wilt thou reject me.
Oh lord Marduk, not wilt thou reject me."

[to Nebo]
"Oh lord open-hearted that puttest an end to sorrow
Thou of wide ears, that holdest the writing tablet,
Oh Nebo open-hearted, that puttest an end to sorrow
Thou of wide ears, that holdest the writing tablet,
Oh wise lord, thou has become angry against thy servant
Upon him have fallen woe and suffering.
In the billows of the flood he is thrown, the deluge [mounts] over him.
The shore is far from him, far away is the dry land.
He has perished in a deep place, upon a reef he has been caught.
He stands in a river of pitch, he is caught in the morass.
Take thou his hand, not shall thy servant be brought to naught
Cause his sin to go forth, lift him from the river of pitch
Oh Nebo, take his hand, not shall thy servant be brought to naught."

It would seem, therefore, that the word God, with a capital G, may be too specific in its semantic content, too culture-bound, to account for the whole range of use of the word prayer. It may be more justified to spell out in the explication certain basic assumptions about the addressee, or the target, of prayer, without including in it the word God, with its monotheistic implications and with its rich implicit theology.[4]

---

4. One could argue that *God* (with a capital G) is part of the meaning of *prayer*, and that all other uses represent marked extensions of this basic use. But in fact, a sentence such as:

Ancient Greeks (Sumerians) offer prayer to their gods.

Towards a definition

But what *are* those basic assumptions about the addressee (or target) without which the word *prayer* is felt not to be applicable (in the literal sense)?

Trying to find a linguistically justified answer to this question, let us consider the following, fairly characteristic statement by an anthropologist (Farnell, 1905, p. 165-166):

"According to the modern definition of prayer, man addresses uttered or inaudible speech to a divine power conceived as Spirit or God, but always as personal, in order to obtain material, moral, or spiritual blessings . . . Though the formulae contain much positive statement and are by no means confined to the optative mood, the attitude of the supplicator is always reverential and self-abased."

Farnell's "modern definition" allows him to draw distinctions which on the whole correspond reasonably closely to the ordinary usage. For example (p. 175-176):

"When the New Caledonian says over the fire that he kindles to increase the heat of the sun, 'Sun, I do this that you may be burning hot,' it is obviously not a prayer that he utters to the sun-god but a formula expressing the suggestion of his magic. And when the Karens of Burma at the threshing of the rice call out to the corn-mother, 'Shake thyself, grandmother, Let the paddy ascend til it equals a hill, equals a mountain; shake thyself, grandmother, shake thyself,' we have surely a command rather than a pure prayer; for primitive vegetation-ritual works by compulsion rather than entreaty. On the other hand, we have record of a genuine Karen prayer addressed to 'the God of heaven and earth, God of the mountain and hills,' on the occasion when a sin of unchastity was supposed to have sterilized the earth: 'Do not be angry with me, do not hate me, but have mercy on me and compassionate [sic] me . . . Now I repair the mountains, now I heal the hills . . . Make thy paddy fruitful, thy rice abundant . . . If we cultivate but little, still grant that we may obtain a little."

According to Farnell's definition, prayer has to be addressed "to someone"; this 'someone' has to be a "spirit or God"; the goal has to be to obtain some 'blessings' (that is, presumably, something good); and the attitude has to be "reverential and self-abased."

This definition seems clearly on the right track, but it cannot be accepted as is, since in some respects it is too restrictive, and in others, too vague. What is too restrictive is, in particular, the alleged goal of all prayer: to obtain some blessings. All three religions which are prototypical to the concept encoded in the English word *prayer* (Christianity, Judaism, and Islam) agree that prayer doesn't have to have such a goal: even though the so-called "prayer of petition" is no doubt the most common type, prayer can also consist in thanksgiving, praise, or adoration, unadulterated with any element of

---

sounds perfectly acceptable in English—unlike, for example, the following sentence: Thai villagers offer prayer to tree spirits.

'petition.' Thus, a semantic component such as "I want you to do something good for me" cannot be regarded as part of the semantic invariant of *prayer*.[5] On the other hand, some feeling of dependence, need and expectation of 'goods' does seem to be relevant to all types of (what is normally called) prayer. As a first approximation, this can be formulated as follows:

if you want, good things will happen to me

The idea that the praying person's attitude needs to be "reverential and self-abased" requires clarification, as both words (*reverential* and *self-abased*) are of course language-specific (not universal), and as the second of them has unjustified pejorative overtones. Trying to extract the healthy kernel from the biased and culture-bound form, we could propose (as a start) the following:

you are not someone like me

There is also in Farnell's definition (and in most other definitions devised by anthropologists) the word *power* (and the phrase *divine power*). Again, trying to disentangle the universal from the culture-bound, we can start by rephrasing this as "you can do things." But what things can the divine addressee do? *all* things? Presumably not, if we want to regard omnipotence—as I think we should- - as something that is predicated of God (with a capital G), rather than as something that is implied by the very concept of 'prayer.' On the other hand, *some* 'power' is indeed implied by it; and (I would argue) it has to be power to do good—to the speaker, but also to other people. This leads us to the following component:

you can do good things for everyone

Of course, the scope of the concept 'everyone' is a matter of interpretation. But, for example, an ancestral spirit, conceived of as someone who can do good to the speaker personally but not to other people, would probably be disqualified on this basis as a possible addressee of prayer. Perhaps this is part of what the phrase *divine power* is in fact intended to imply: the ability to do good, and a kind of universality.

The statement that the intended addressee has to be "a spirit or God" hints at the 'immaterial,' 'extraterrestrial,' or 'supernatural' character of that addressee. If the lexicon of universal human concepts included the concept 'world' we could state the idea in question as follows:

you are not part of this world

Since, however, the evidence available so far suggests that 'world' is not a universal human concept the following phrasing seems to be more justified:

---

5. See endnote following this chapter.

one can't think: 'I know where you are'

The underlying idea is that the addressee of prayer cannot be located in space—not because his or her whereabouts are unknown but because they are, as it were, outside ordinary space, and are not bound by it. I think this is precisely the idea behind the opening phrase of Our Lord's prayer: "Our Father WHO ART IN HEAVEN." 'Heaven' is not a place but, as it were, a denial of any ordinary location, with an additional implication that it is an ideal (imaginary) place. I would explicate this phrase as follows:

> . . . *who are in heaven* =
> one can't think: 'I know where you are,'
> one can think: 'if you are in a place, nothing bad can happen in this place'

The concept of prayer doesn't necessarily imply that the addressee is in an 'ideal' sort of place, but it does imply that He or She is not to be found in any ordinary earthly location.

It is interesting to note in this connection that apparitions can hardly be *prayed* to (as the word is normally used). For example, in descriptions of Bernadette Soubirous talking to the Virgin Mary at Lourdes, the word *praying* is normally not used: Bernadette *prays* when the Virgin Mary is not there, but when she *is* there, she *talks* to her rather than *prays*. All these considerations lead us to the following (interim) explication:

> Person X is praying =
> X is doing something,
> sometimes a person wants to say something like this to someone:
>> I want to say something to you,
>> I think of you like this:
>>> you are not someone like me
>>> one can't think: 'I know where you are'
>>> you can do good things for everyone
>>> if you want, good things will happen to me
>> because of this, this person says something (to someone)
> person X is doing something like this

I believe this explication is essentially correct, but it is incomplete and it requires further justification and discussion. It is incomplete because it still does not account sufficiently for what is metaphorically called the "raising of mind and heart (to God)." We must remember Chrysostom's definition: "Prayer is loving conversation with God" or St Teresa's comment that "prayer isn't a matter of a lot of thinking; it's a lot of loving." On the other hand, many religious books insist that praying does not require the presence of any feelings, and urge believers to persist in prayer even at times when they are unable to feel anything whatsoever.

My own solution to this dilemma would be this: one can certainly pray without feeling anything, but when one prays, one wants to feel something good towards God (or, more generally, towards the supernatural addressee); the feelings in question—not necessarily felt but necessarily desired and intended—do not really have to be 'loving,' but they have to be 'good.'

In fact, it is these good feelings (as well as the assumptions on which they are based) which are expressed in the typical praying positions: kneeling, prostration, folded hands (cf Wierzbicka, forthcoming). A person can wrestle with God (while making all the assumptions about him that Christian—or Jewish—religion expects one to make). A wrestling of this kind would not be called *prayer*—and a person wrestling with God would probably not kneel or prostrate himself/herself. Mephisto or Lucifer kneeling or prostrating himself before God is simply inconceivable (unless in an unexpected act of 'conversion').

Thus, a fuller representation of a *praying* person's attitude would include the component,

> because of this, I feel something good towards you
> as well as those mentioned above

A full explication of a sentence of the kind "X is praying" would describe a person as doing (saying) something that expresses this attitude:

> X is praying =
> X is doing something
> sometimes a person wants to say something like this to someone:
>> I want to say something to you,
>> I think of you like this:
>>> you are not someone like me
>>> one can't think: 'I know where you are'
>>> you can do good things for everyone
>>> if you want, good things can happen to me
>> because of this, I feel something good towards you
> because of this, this person says something (to someone)
> X is doing something like this

One important feature of this definition which requires some comment is its prototypical structure: the formula does not seek to enumerate obligatory and sufficient features of any speech act which would be legitimately called *prayer*, but the obligatory and sufficient features of the conceptual prototype; and it predicts that whatever is seen as 'doing something like this' can also be called *prayer* (if those who see it in this way wish to call it *prayer*). In this way, the definition predicts a measure of fluidity in what different people may or may not recognize as *prayer*; and yet it does not give up the goal of capturing the necessary and sufficient features of 'prayer' as a concept.

Looking back at various key terms recurring in the literature on prayer (such as 'communication,' 'communion,' 'address,' 'encounter,' and so on) it will be noticed that the proposed explication supports the idea of an asymmetrical 'address' (or 'purported communication') but not the ideas of a symmetrical relation or event such as 'communication,' 'communion,' or 'encounter.' (Compare, for example, E. B. Tylor's definition, "the address of personal spirit to personal spirit" quoted in Gill (1987, p. 489) with Gill's own definition (ibid.) "the human communication with divine and spiritual entities.") A religious person may believe that a genuine 'address' to God (or to a 'higher spirit') will always result in 'communication,' but the word *prayer* as such does not imply that. This is why praying people can ask God to hear them (as, for example, the Psalms often do).

This 'address,' however, has to be taken in a semantic, not in a grammatical sense. Grammatically, a prayer does not depend on vocatives and second person forms of the verb, and for example, a psalm such as "The Lord is my Shepherd" can be, and often is, used as prayer in contrast to second-person formulae such as those quoted earlier: "Sun, I do this that you may be burning hot" or "Shake thyself, grandmother, shake thyself." As Fallaize (1918, p. 154) notes, with special reference to Rivers (1906), "some writers have endeavored to distinguish between spell and prayer by assigning to the latter those formulae which contain a vocative." But it is not the "surface vocative" which counts. The crucial point is that the praying person says something (in the broadest possible sense of the word *say*), and that this saying something is motivated by a 'want' to say something to God (or to someone like God).

One can of course take the view that an attempt to say something to God (especially when accompanied by 'good thoughts' about God and 'good feelings' towards God), constitutes by itself an act of 'spiritual communion' with God (cf. Brandon's, 1970, p. 508, definition of *prayer* as "spiritual communion with eternal and divine source of all good"). It is essential, however, to distinguish our views *about* prayer (its value, its efficacy, its consequences, and so on) from the meaning of the word *prayer* itself (established on the basis of linguistic evidence).

Let us consider in the light of the explication provided here a few characteristic definitions which have been proposed in the scholarly literature on prayer. For example, Alexander (1918, p. 158) writes this about American Indian religion: "Any ritual observance designed to bring man into nearer relation with the unseen powers of nature is prayer." This is certainly at variance with the normal English usage: there are many ritual observances which do not involve speech and which would normally never be called *prayer*. One can see, however, why Alexander felt the need to define *prayer* broadly because he continues: "In this broad sense prayer includes not merely the spoken or chanted word, but also dramatic and symbolic ceremonies, and above all, for the American Indian, the 'dances' in which most of his cults center." Clearly, Alexander's concern was to allow for dances and other symbolic acts to be included, even though they do not involve spoken or chanted words. This is entirely proper, since nobody could doubt that, for example, a deaf person can pray using a sign language. The main point is that one can 'say' things with one's body as well as with one's voice. But not all 'ritual observances' involve 'saying' something.

Alexander writes further (ibid.):

"American Indians have two kinds of prayer: (1) spells and oaths and pleas addressed to the lesser, the environmental, powers of nature, expressed in a magical or hortatory mood; and (2) true spiritual supplications directed to a power variously interpreted as the Great Spirit, the Master of Life, the Heavenly Father."

According to the definition proposed here (and, I would say, to English usage), the first kind of 'prayer' is certainly not *prayer*: first, because local, environmental 'powers of nature' are linked to a particular place, and therefore are incompatible with the component 'one can't say of you: I know where this person is'; and second, because the 'magical' character of such speech acts is incompatible with the subcomponent referring to the addressee's will ('if you want'). On the other hand, Alexander's category (2) certainly does sound like *prayer*, and its existence appears to establish that prayer does have a place in American Indian culture.

As a second example, let us consider Anesaki's (1918) discussion of "Buddhist prayer." He writes (p. 167): "As an expression of faith, Buddhist prayer pays homage to Buddha, to his truth and community, mostly in adoration and exaltation." Like other writers on the subject, Anesaki finds it necessary to stress that "Buddhist prayer" is not a petition, and for this reason he does sometimes hesitate to regard it as proper prayer; but he is highly inconsistent in this respect, and at times uses the word *prayer* quite happily, apparently untroubled by the contradictions in the phrasing of his comments. For example (p. 166):

"In the Buddhist religion there is not room for prayer, in the sense of a petition or solicitation addressed to a god. . . . But, when prayer is understood in a broader way, there is the Buddhist prayer as an expression of earnest faith, determined intention, as a means of self-perfection in Buddhist ideals . . . the practice of expressing the earnest intention of realizing Buddhahood gradually took the form of solemn vows taken to commit oneself to practise Buddhist morality. . . . Many of these vows are in reality prayers, addressed to Buddha as well as to the universal truth revealed by him."

The issue of 'petition,' frequently raised in comparativist discussions of 'prayer,' is really a red herring, because, as we have seen, the concept of 'prayer' is by no means linked with the idea of 'petition' either (we will return to this point later). It is significant, however, that when the word *prayer* is used in English-language discussions of Buddhism, this is normally done with reference to religious speech acts "addressed to Buddha." (Cf in this connection the following comments by Klausner (1985, p. 140) on Thai culture: "It is true that the villagers may in certain circumstances pray to the Buddha image in their temple for calmness of spirit, wealth, and the like. However, in general, the villagers conceive of Buddha not as a god but as a great teacher; not as an all-seeing, all-powerful being who can give immediate help but as a religious sage who reached perfection.")

I would suggest that if the expression "Buddhist prayers" does not sound unacceptable in English it is mainly because ordinary speakers of English don't know what exactly is involved in Buddhist religious practices, and because they tend to project on Buddhist religion ideas common to their own culture. When one is told, however, that (in higher Buddhism, at least) Buddha is supposed to be "out of contact," and that the religious speech acts in question represent "an expression of earnest faith, determined intention, [and] a means of self-perfection in Buddhist ideals" (Anesaki 1918, p. 166), then I think one must conclude that acts of this kind do not represent *prayer* in the ordinary sense of this word. I concur, therefore, with the conclusions reached in this respect by Gill (1987, p. 491):

> Various traditions of Buddhism present a test case in the considera-tion of prayer. . . . For those traditions that are not theistic, like Theravada Buddhism, prayer understood as human-divine communication is not possible. . . . However, a number of kinds of Buddhist speech acts, such as meditational recitations, scriptural recitations, *mantras*, and *bodhisattva* vows, have certain resemblances to prayer, especially in terms of many of its functions. . . . Commonly the distinction between prayer and these Buddhist speech forms has simply been ignored and they are considered as forms of Buddhist prayer. It would be more valuable to comprehend specifically the similarities and differences of the various forms and func-tions of these Buddhist speech acts compared with prayer acts of theistic traditions. In their similarities lies the nature of religion, in their differences lies the distinctiveness of Buddhism among religious traditions.

Finally, let us consider the complex issue of the presence or absence of prayer in Australian Aboriginal culture. I have quoted earlier Stanner's (1976, p. 28) statement that in that culture "there was no element of direct peti-tion, so that to speak of 'prayer' would be to go too far, just as it would be to speak of 'worship.'" We have seen, however, that the word *prayer* is by no means restricted to "direct petitions," so the conclusion doesn't follow from the premise. In the same article, however, Stanner states more generally that "there is no justification in the evidence we possess for dealing in concepts of 'prayer,' 'worship,' 'sin,' 'guilt,' 'grace,' 'salvation,' and so on" (p. 30). He continued as follows: "but there is a half-explicit concept of man co-operating ritually with unseen powers at holy places and on high occasions, to further a life-pattern believed to have been ordained by its founders, and of doing so under an assurance of a continuing flow of benefits."

That concepts such as 'grace' or 'salvation' are absent from Aboriginal cul-ture can hardly come as a surprise, given their highly culture-specific nature. But why is Stanner so sure that the concept of 'prayer' is absent too? Stanner himself tells us that "the Aborigines acknowledged that men's lives were under a power or force beyond themselves" and "that they venerated the places where such power or force was believed to concentrate" (p. 28). Elsewhere, too, Stanner emphasizes that 'powers' or 'spirits' care for people: "In several parts of Aboriginal Australia one met the fundamental belief that great guardian-spirits (Baiame, Kunmanggur) existed—whether as ancestral or as self-subsistent beings—to 'look after' living men" (Stanner 1984, p. 148).

What is missing, then? 'Communication' or 'purported communication'?

In fact, communication is not absent either. For example, Maddock (1984, p. 87) describes "extraordinarily experienced communications from the powers (as when new dances, songs, or rites are conveyed, or magical ability conferred while men are in special psychic states like dreams or trances)." He comments (ibid.):

"That the powers cause signs to appear to men, who have learned what they mean, and that powers communicate directly with men, but only while they are severed from ordinary experience by their psychic state, suggests the paradox that powers are withdrawn but omnipresent."

Of course, these are cases of communication from powers to people, not from people to powers. But in some cases, people, too, can talk to powers. For example, "Elkin describes the experiences of the 'clever-man' or 'doctor-man' who is able to communicate with 'other worlds' and who has spiritual or mystical powers not given to ordinary people" (Morphy, 1984, p. 217). In this case, however, nothing is said about the clever-man's attitude to the powers with which he is communicating and one suspects that this attitude is not exactly 'prayerful' (in the sense of the proposed explication).

Let us consider in turn the question of communication with totemic heroes, discussed, for example, by Eliade (1973). Relating Spencer and Gillen's journey to an important totemic center in the company of a small group of natives, Eliade writes (p. 56):

"Finally they approached the famous water hole where the mythical snake Wollunka lived. Near the sacred pool the natives 'became very quiet and solemn,' and 'the chief men of the totemic group went down to the edge of the water and, with bowed heads, addressed the Wollunka in whispers, asking him to remain quiet and do them no harm, for they were mates of his' (Spencer and Gillen, 1904, p. 252)."

Is this prayer? I think not, and I believe native speakers of English would normally not describe it as such. For one thing, Wollunka has a specific location, whereas the addressee of prayer has to be conceived of as someone who is not 'part of this world' (that is, as someone of whom one cannot say: "I know where this person is'). Nor is he conceived of as a truly supernatural being in the sense of not being 'someone like me'" (from the speakers' point of view). On the contrary, they tell him that they are "mates of his." Furthermore, Wollunka is not conceived of as "someone who could do good things for everyone" and as "someone who is good." All these reasons are sufficient to explain why the speech acts in question would normally not be described as *prayer*.

And yet there are cases where some scholars talking about Australian

Aboriginal beliefs and rituals do use the word *prayer*. For example, Eliade uses this word with reference to the spirit Nogamain, "a sky-dweller, who lived (according to some) 'of his own will,' or 'in his own fashion'" (Stanner, 1963, p. 264, quoted by Eliade, 1973, pp. 38-39). When asked of his abode, Stanner's informants "raised their arms towards the whole sky and said in a single word: 'on high.'" Eliade writes:

"Thunder and lightning were attributed to 'the people of Nogamain.' He was also responsible for sending spirit children; Stanner heard many times: 'Nogamain sends down good children.' But he also received the same information about other 'pure spirits.' The most important cultic act was *prayer* [my emphasis] for food in case of distress. One of Stanner's oldest informants remembered that, as a child, he had heard the oldest men 'calling out to Nogamain at night when they lay in camp short of food.'"

Eliade regards Nogamain as "a celestial god" who is on the point of losing his religious significance. He points out that according to Stanner "only one of the oldest informants remembered, from his childhood, the *prayer* [my emphasis] of the oldest men." We must conclude, then, that even if appeals to beings such as Nogamain do constitute *prayer*, prayer would be fairly marginal in Australian Aboriginal culture. But do such appeals really qualify as *prayer*?

Stanner himself doesn't seem to think so since (as we have seen) he has denied the applicability of the term *prayer* to Aboriginal culture. Speaking of sky-beings in general, he describes them as "self-existent beings, beginningless, underived from anyone, and self-responsible" (1977, p. 23). He comments: "So the conception deepens to one of transcendent and eternal beings, other than men but not wholly other, living an unconditioned life, but characterized by disinterest in true men and an absence of power over them" (ibid.).

Stanner's view that the term *prayer* is inapplicable to Australian culture is consistent with the idea (developed in the present chapter) that the concept of 'prayer' is complex and specific, and that it cannot be reduced to a handful of undefined global labels such as 'communication,' 'dependence' or 'divine character.' More specific and more clearly articulated components are needed, such as for example, "if you want good things will happen to me" and "(because of this) I feel something good towards you." The literature on Aboriginal religion offers no evidence for the applicability of such components to Australian religious practices. It seems, then, that we must conclude (with Stanner and others) that 'prayer' is not part of Australian Aboriginal culture.

Conclusion

To speak about prayer in a cross-cultural perspective we must know what we are talking about. Different people have different ideas about prayer, and these different ideas cannot offer us a firm, stable point of reference. The only thing which can offer us such a point of reference (as a first step) is the word *prayer* itself, as it is actually used in ordinary English. For example, the question "Is prayer a universal human phenomenon?" makes sense only if we are using the word *prayer* in its normal sense, as it has evolved in ordinary English. Otherwise, different authors will use it in a different sense, and their answers, whatever they might be, will be simply incommensurable.

On the evidence discussed in this chapter we must conclude that prayer (in the ordinary sense of the word) is not universal; and if this is true of prayer as an activity, it is, so to speak, even more true of 'prayer' as a concept. For example, it could be argued that in Thai society prayer as an activity is not entirely absent, and that some Thai people do on occasion address Buddha in the spirit of prayer (that is, in the spirit of what in English could be called *prayer*), even though such an attitude is incompatible with the doctrine of 'high Buddhism.' Nonetheless, the Thai language does not have a word corresponding to *prayer*, and this fact shows that the kind of activity categorized in English as *prayer* is not a salient part of the Thai culture and society.[6]

Of course the concept of 'prayer' (as encoded in the English word *prayer*) is not uniquely English (or Anglo). All other European languages appear to have words encoding the same concept (*prier* in French, *Gebet* in German, *preghiera* in Italian, *molitva* in Russian, and so on).[7] Furthermore, many non-European languages appear to have words encoding the same concept (*hitpalāl salāh* in Hebrew, *guido* in Chinese, *negau* in Japanese, and so on). Whether or not, however, the concepts encoded in such words are really the same, is a matter which requires serious semantic investigation. The fact that bilingual dictionaries provide supposed equivalents of *prayer* in countless languages of the world does not mean that countless languages of the world do not have words encoding exactly the same concept. It is interesting to note that, for example, ancient (Homeric) Greek did have words reserved specifically for addressing gods, *euchos* and *eugma* (cf Corlu, 1966). But whether the meaning of either of these words can be identified with that of *prayer* remains a matter for further investigation.

Given, however, that the concept of 'prayer' is culture-bound (although we don't know to what extent) does it provide an adequate tool with which to approach different religions of the world? Of course not; but it provides the necessary first step. In fact, this word (and the concept encoded in it) is widely used as such a first step—but usually without the full awareness that what is being relied on is an English word, and that this word has its own def-

---

6. For information on Thai words for various religious and quasi-religious speech acts, I am indebted to Tony Diller. Among these words the one closest in meaning to *pray* appears to be *suat*, which Christians in Thailand have adopted as the word for their concept of 'prayer.' But in ordinary Thai this word (glossed by Diller as 'to chant, usually in Pali, to make merit') does not have the meaning attributed here to *prayer*. In particular, it doesn't imply any desire to 'say something to someone,' that is, to reach an addressee.

7. The assumption that the English verb to *pray* has exact semantic equivalents in other European languages (e.g. *prier* in French, *beten* in German, and *molit'sa* in Russian) may be something of a simplification. The matter requires further investigation.

inite value which cannot be twisted at will (at least not without leading to conceptual confusion and communication failure).

It is only when we realize that the concept of 'prayer' is culture-bound that we will become fully aware of the need to analyze it from a truly universal perspective, that is, in terms of concepts which are independent of language and culture. Having done this, we can raise similar questions with respect to other cultures, that is, we can undertake that careful cross-linguistic study of "the terminology that designates acts of human-spiritual communication," which Gill (1987, p. 489) has justly called for. Ultimately, we can ask about, and seek to formulate, real universals of religion (bearing in mind, however, that even the concept of 'religion' is culture-bound—as are the concepts of 'cult,' 'worship,' 'ritual,' and so on); and if our perspective on those universals is not to be distorted by the conceptual artifacts of our own culture, then, I submit, we must seek to formulate them too, at some stage of our enquiry, in terms of universal human concepts (such as 'someone,' 'good,' 'say,' 'want,' 'feel,' 'know,' and so on).

Finally, it is important to note that (as the evidence suggests; cf Goddard and Wierzbicka (eds), 1994) in all languages of the world people say things such as 'you are not someone like me,' 'you can do good things for everyone,' or 'if you want good things will happen to me,' because both the lexical and grammatical means for saying so are there. Consequently, even if the concept of 'prayer' is not actually universal (in the sense of being readily available in all cultures) it is potentially so: all the necessary building blocks are there, and there appears to be a widespread tendency across human cultures and societies to put these blocks together in ways not unlike the way they are put together in the meaning of the English word *prayer*.

Endnote

The fact that many authors writing about prayer appear to identify prayer with 'petitions to God,' could be regarded as evidence that *prayer is* semantically linked with "asking for things" (as the older meaning of the verb *to pray* would suggest). For religious believers, however, this is certainly not the case, since for them the term *prayer* can apply to adoration, praise, or thanksgiving as well as to 'petitions' of any kind. Should one assume, then, that there is in English a second use of the word *prayer*, restricted to unbelievers and linked specifically with petitions? To my mind, such a conclusion would not be justified. It may be true that many nonreligious people believe that prayer consists mainly in asking for things, but generally speaking, for them, too, there is no sense of contradiction in sentences such as the following one:

Overwhelmed by happiness and gratitude, he knelt down to pray.

It is not, then, that this meaning of the word *prayer* is necessarily different but that this idea of what prayer normally is, is narrow and one-sided.

In his work *The Varieties of Religious Experience*, William James, himself not a religious believer, wrote (1902, p. 444):

"Petitional prayer is only one department of prayer; and if we take the word in the wider sense as meaning every kind of inward communion or conversation with the power recognized as divine, we can easily see that the scientific criticism leaves it untouched."

Significantly, James' own definition of prayer does not include any reference to petitions (ibid.):

"This act is prayer, by which term I understand no vain exercise of words, no mere repetition of sacred formulae, but the very movement itself of the soul, putting itself in a personal relation of contact with the mysterious power of which it feels the presence."

It should be noted, however, that the English verb to *pray* can occur with the preposition *for*, in a construction which, roughly speaking, implies 'wanting' and 'dependence':

X asked/begged/implored/appealed/applied/prayed *for* Y.

(This construction must be distinguished from other for-constructions, such as, for example, "X thanked/apologized/criticized [Z] *for* Y," and for a discussion, see Wierzbicka, 1987, 1988, and in press) This syntactic fact appears to support the view that *prayer* is somehow linked, semantically, with petitions. On the other hand, it should also be noted that *pray* can occur without any *for*-phrases (or any other complement phrases), whereas *ask* or *implore* cannot:

X was praying/*asking/*appealing.

It could be argued that in order for to *pray* to occur with a *for*-phrase points to *some* 'wanting' component ('I want something') in its semantic structure, whereas its ability to occur without any complements points to the absence of a 'petitioning' or 'directive' component ('I want you to do something for me'). As it stands, the explication proposed in this example does include a 'wanting' component: 'I want to say something to you.' Whether or not this component is sufficient to explain all aspects of the syntactic behavior of the verb *to pray* is a matter for further investigation. Furthermore, if a verb can take a *for*-phrase (of the kind in question) this usually implies an inability to achieve something by oneself (cf Wierzbicka, 1988). This would suggest one further component, along the lines of 'I can't do this,' or 'I want something—it cannot happen if you don't say: I want it.' The syntactic behavior of *pray* and its equivalents in other languages, and its semantic implications, require further investigation.

Chapter Three

Early Approaches to the
Psychology of Prayer

Although Leuba (1925) made no specific reference to prayer in his study of mysticism, he distinguished "objective, business-like transactions with God (which could involve prayer) from communion or union with God or even in an absorption in the divine" (p. 2). A major assumption surrounding prayer, which I shall approach only indirectly, is some belief in the existence of God and in characteristics that might allow one to pray to God. This is also a problem for other features of religion, and such matters of belief and practice must be decided by each person for themselves. The grounds on which those decisions are made, and how firm they might be are, however, questions that psychologists should be able to clarify. Yet Leuba noted that mysticism (and we might add prayer) "has suffered as much at the hands of its admirers as its materialistic enemies" (p. ix), and that his study "represents an effort to remove (mystical religion) as part of inner life from the domain of the occult . . . to incorporate it in that body of facts of which psychology takes cognizance" (ibid.).

Heiler's (1918) *Prayer: A Study in the History and Psychology of Religion* (originally in German, with only parts of it translated to English in 1932, cf Wulff, 1991, p. 528 ff) is the classical analysis. Earlier books on the psychology of prayer were by Anna Louise Strong (1909), published under the pseudonym "Anise," and by Stolz (1913, revised in 1923). Hodge (1931) attempted a "vindication of the Christian gospels in terms of modern psychological thought." Despite other defensive or prescriptive analyses of prayer (e.g. Ulanov and Ulanov, 1984), no recent book has been specifically concerned with the psychology of prayer, although Godin's (1985) "dynamic psychology of religion" deals with prayer and religious experience.

Ames and Coe
Finney and Malony's (1985) bibliography of papers on prayer divided the field into definitions and empirical studies of the development of an

47

understanding of prayer, the reasons for praying, and the effects of verbal and contemplative prayer. They stress the importance of any psychological processes that are 'active' in prayer, and the need to study its specific effects on religious and spiritual development. The annotated bibliography in the Appendix lists the ones they mention and other papers in this field.

Passing references to prayer can be found in the general psychologies of religion, so Ames (1910) devoted his Chapter XIII to the 'racial' origins of prayer, which he thought was "almost as universal as sacrifice in primitive religion and persists in later faiths in refined and ideal forms when sacrifice has ceased" (p. 134). He stressed the evolutionary importance of gestures and of language, when talking to oneself and in communication with others, including the spirits. Like language, prayer does not presuppose "some theory concerning the nature of that to what it seems to be directed" although it "satisfies itself immediately as an impulsive expression and at other times as a factor in establishing contact with sacred objects or in otherwise controlling them" (p. 139). Furthermore, since "speech is imbedded within the ceremonial rites" but subservient to them, in "songs, chants and prayer formulae the words seem quite incidental accompaniments" (ibid.). Simple prayer formulae were therefore identified as "exclamatory or descriptive," and it is necessary that they should be expressed through language.

Edward Scribner Ames (1910) noted that prayer seldom occurs by itself, since it is "always part of some ceremony or, at least, accompanies an objective act of some kind. Even in the most rationalized and ethicized religions, the bodily attitude of kneeling or bowing, that is, the action, is maintained with scrupulous care" (p. 143). Prayer also "has power and does work. It exerts magical influence" (ibid.). This is seen in "the charming of a bone, stick, or spear by 'singing' it," which Ames supports with reference to Spencer and Gillen's work among the Australian Aborigines, and with a quote from Marrett's (1903) argument that "prayer proper involves the process of personification" (p. 144).

So prayer is involved in religious ceremonial and shares what was assumed to be in part magical, although in "more advanced religions" that occupies a relatively "secondary and dependent place," since prayer is not necessarily an "expression of direct, personal need" or a search for "spiritual blessings" (p. 146). Ames' theory of prayer stresses that as the 'superstitions' of animism and demonology "give way before the scientific conception of nature, the magical element in prayer is gradually eliminated, and prayer becomes increasingly meditation and communion" (p. 148). As a form of thinking, prayer therefore preserves "the interlocutory, and conversational form."

That analysis has a modern ring, because it captures a sense of skepticism that those who are themselves committed to the practice of prayer might express if they were pursued by questions that looked as if they would expose what might appear to be primitive beliefs about its power to change the world. Yet there are many, especially if they are religiously conservative, who hold that prayer has some material efficacy and does change the world, while others believe that it can only change those who pray. These beliefs are seen most clearly among young children and have been found to change with age (Godin and van Roey, 1959, Brown and Thouless, 1964). Whether any material effects of prayer can be empirically detected is doubtful, both in principle and on methodological grounds, although there are empirical claims on the positive "power of prayer on plants" (Loehr, 1959), and on patients in hospital (Byrd, 1988). Whether such studies are legitimate remains a problem because of their explicit challenge to God's will, so that one is reminded of the koan, "Show me God."

George Albert Coe (1916), on the other hand, noted that the "history and psychology of prayer would be almost equivalent to a history and psychology of religion," since religion focuses life's values, "and prayer is the vocal expression, or at least bringing to mind, of the value focus." This takes a personal form when prayer is described as "talking to or with a god" (p. 302). Coe also contrasted "interior prayer" and contemplation "without word images," against ritualism, in which "vocal formulae are exactly repeated" in connection with "the sacrifice, under an impression that the formula has some efficacy in itself" (p. 302). Coe aligns the use of such efficacious words with "magical spells (however magic be defined)" and he found a single lineage in which "prayer in the 'proper' sense . . . springs, as the gods themselves do, out of earlier anthropomorphisms" (p. 303). That does not depend exclusively on supplication, being found in praise and flattery, thanksgiving, and fellowship, "to help the god in some vicissitude of his career," and in fault-finding, compulsion, submission, or "enlistment with the divinity in a social enterprise" (ibid.). This analysis seems to cover most of the problems that might surround prayer.

Coe also noted the need to identify the structure of prayer and its functions in terms of "what has moved men so persistently to pray, and what advantages have accrued therefrom" (ibid.). He identified the natural cues to prayer in thunder and lightning, as a "divine language" in which answers were sought, and in "opening the Bible and placing a finger upon a text at random in the firm belief that in the text thus indicated a divine message will be found specifically intended for the individual concerned" (p. 304). While the abodes or realizations of the gods have great antiquity, most of our contemporaries who are committed to Christian beliefs are likely to resist the suggestion that such a linear continuity applies to their belief or practice of prayer. Furthermore, Coe's theory can not be directly tested so that we must interpret the apparent or surface manifestations of prayer against the plausibility of an evolutionary explanation, which makes the argument circular. The traditional conclusion that "ontogeny recapitulates phylogeny" in the developing thought of young children has, however, been recently undermined by the evidence from careful questioning of very young children who were presented with subtle problems to solve. They do distinguish human intentions about movement or action from those of animals, and from that of objects like billiard balls (Wellman and Gelman, 1992). Conventional perspectives on religious development (Godin, 1968) and on the acceptance of prayer as a 'primitive' response or as "primary speech" (Ulanov and Ulanov,

1982) might now be aligned with this work on children's theories of mind (Astington et al, 1988).

Recent historical studies of the medieval mystics emphasize the contextual pressures to which these "unquiet souls" (Kieckhefer, 1990) were reacting. Yet Coe found support for his views in the early anthropology of the Australian Aborigines, which he then generalized to the early Christian forms or structures. It is noteworthy therefore that the parallels chosen in most of this early work on prayer followed fashion and were highly principled, with little systematic empirical or concurrent support, although Starbuck's (1897) reliance on survey 'questionnaires' to unpack the bases of conversion, and several surveys about prayer were reported in Hall's *American Journal for the Psychology of Religion*, including one by Beck (1906) which has been replicated by Shackle and Brown (1994). So data were available that might have helped to clarify some of the psychological problems surrounding religion in this early period. The hesitation to refer to them could have shown deference to prayer, or a greater interest in the objective meanings that prayers were expected to carry than in the attitudes to them, or in their subjective significance and use by individuals, and how they came to know about prayer.

Coe placed the traditional "modes of divine approach to man (and) . . . divine responses to man's approach" within a hierarchy that stretched from reading omens to "rewards and punishment, divine discipline or divine self-revelation" (p. 307). To use a modern term, this involved an 'attribution,' shown by Coe citing "a Mormon lady" whose farm had been spared a destructive frost "in recompense for care bestowed upon the husband's aged parents" (p. 307). While the detection of divine purposes is well-recognized (whether seriously or ironically), the rules that govern it have only recently been studied systematically (Proudfoot and Shaver, 1975, Proudfoot, 1985, Furnham and Brown, 1992), beyond the assumption that they were subjective and "dependent on evil or good impulses" (as Coe, 1916, p. 309 put it), or on external cues.

It is important to note, however, that Coe recognized prayer as a "form of internal conversation," and that the "direction of thought and desire Godward is what makes the act of prayer." He did not look for causes, or think that God could be their cause, "since the meanings are directly accepted as mine as in conversation with a friend" (p. 310). Having turned away from any assumptions about the mysterious or transcendental expectations there, Coe emphasized that "in conversation with a friend, I deal with meanings directly as mine and his without stopping to think of him as producing certain of my sensations and chains of ideas" (p. 310). This analysis brought prayer into the everyday world and stressed the extent to which the models through which it is interpreted draw on potent attitudes to make attributions, without trying to identify how widely those meanings are distributed. We can find two levels of interpretation there. One is religious and the other is social (or social psychological) and interactive. Within this context, prayer was constructively understood in terms of its possible alignments with our internal worlds and external realities.

Coe defended his stance with reference to a structural psychology that argued in terms of "physiological conditions, neural processes, and dispositions" as well as instincts and "ordinary laws of ideation, emotion, and so on." But as he put it, "Persons are not simply residual causes" (p. 311). Notice that intentionality and cosmological beliefs are beyond that level of analysis, and can not be deduced from it without reference to the beliefs that support the practice of prayer. When Freud asked what one might believe about the world, he assumed that a dynamic process was operating which itself produced or carried a sense of 'reality' that might be independent of the social or religious traditions from which such constructions would take their meaning. Coe coped with this problem by referring to 'suggestion' which, during the nineteenth century, was as robust a process as 'association' having grown out of an interest in hypnosis once "animal magnetism" became unfashionable, and it was applied to mass phenomena and the assumed irrationality of crowd behavior (Le Bon, 1895) and to individuals' 'imitation' (Tarde, 1898) of others as a form of suggestion (cf Chertok, 1986).

The immediacy of those processes contrasts against evolutionary accounts of a uniform (and linear) development, in which primitive (or traditional) societies (and young children) were assumed to embody the precursors to a sophisticated, scientific understanding. Those arguments read or interpreted the content of thought (as Freud also seemed to do) rather than trying to identify the psychological processes that made thought possible (cf Dennett, 1991).

Nevertheless, Coe also acknowledged that "he who prays begins his prayer with some idea of God, generally one that he has received from instruction or from current traditions. He commonly retires to a quiet place, or to a place having mental associations of a religious cast, in order to shut out the world" (p. 311). Such 'concentration' was said to exclude "a mass of irrelevant impressions, with a posture" that "may favor extensive relaxation" so that "memory now provides the language of prayer or of hallowed scripture, or makes vivid some earlier experiences of one's own." Coe even stressed that a worshiper adopts the role or stance of the Other (cf G.H. Mead, 1934) as he presents (to himself) his needs or interests that seem most important, and "brings them into relation to God by thinking how God regards them" (p. 311). This changed perspective (cf Piaget, 1931) alters "their relation to the organizing idea upon which attention has focused" (p. 312), and as a dynamic or cognitive process (as we might call it) it was aligned with the will, although "when organized toward unity" Coe said it is "simply auto-suggestion" (p. 312). A careful reading of Coe's views shows his evident sophistication. He deferred to terms current at the time, although psychological interpretations now straddle academic or scientific, and 'commonsense' solutions (cf Kelley, 1992).

Coe noted that 'faith' is not a prerequisite for 'success' in prayer since, as he said, "Faith-healing and mental-healing cults often win adherents by producing physical relief in the as yet unconvinced" (p. 312). This process might now be understood as a form of "cognitive therapy," although Coe stressed that "what introspection reveals, therefore, is not God but one's own idea of God" (p. 313). And he was as well aware as Galton (1873) that skeptics were concerned about the validity of prayer. To test that, Galton had studied the efficacy of prayers for the longevity of the British Royal Family prescribed in the Book of Common Prayer, finding that they did not live longer than commoners. In a footnote, Coe noted that, "A skeptical student was advised to determine for himself whether or not there be a God by the experiment of praying. Being of a scientific turn of mind, he decided to vary only one circumstance at a time. So he offered the same prayer first to the Christian God and then to the Buddha. His introspective account of the effects showed that in each case he got the same results, such as peace and a feeling of elevation" (1916, p. 314).

Coe therefore agreed with Strong (1909) that prayer is not a unique activity, but an instance of a general mental procedure that, like conversation, carries its own meaning. As he put it, one does not have to postulate or discover the other as "an additional item in the succession of states, any more than I myself can discover myself as one of my own states" (p. 315). But our sense of self-consciousness makes it hard for us to avoid some conception of an inner self, perhaps behind the eyes, immune to age and bodily changes yet morally responsible, even when moods sway our decisions. This Cartesian or divine theater makes claims on our intuition that injury and bodily malfunction does not easily compromise (cf Sacks, 1986a and b). Dennett's (1991) alternative to that view depends on a word-processing model in which the self is like the "multiple drafts" of a document which can be generated, and then edited out of existence in a word-processor.

Coe found the functions of prayer in its coherence and in our capacity to beget "the confidence that tends toward victory over difficulties," and enables "self-renewal largely by making one's experience consciously social, that is, by producing a realization that even what is private to me is shared by another" (p. 315). As he said, the prayer life may be "the organization into the self of the very things that threaten to disorganize it" (p. 316). But prayer is also shared as a "social form of personal self-realization" and of self-assurance (p. 317), maintained through conversation and in the contemplation by which faith is generated. It involves "voyages of exploration" along with "much traditionalism and vain repetition" (p. 318). Furthermore, the "evolution of prayer" entails what Coe called an "immense change" that can start with "any desire" and "ends as the organization of one's own desires into a system of desires recognized as superior and then made one's own" (p. 318). In current terms, Coe seems to have advocated a form of decentration, in which reciprocity was important. As he put it, "a primitive group feeds its god in order to make him strong and rejoices and feasts with him as an invisible guest, so in Christianity God and men stand in mutual need of each other" (p. 320). Dodds (1951) made a similar point about the Greeks' attitude to religion when he distinguished divine temptation or infatuation among humans from "the communication of power from god to man" (p. 8) that can come suddenly into one's head.

James Bissett Pratt

J.B. Pratt in his *Religious Consciousness* (1921) is the most 'modern' of the early psychologists, in using anthropological and phenomenological approaches that looked across traditions. He cited the results of several surveys from Hall's *American Journal of Religious Psychology* that must have been known to Ames and Coe. Perhaps they had preferred their principled arguments without empirical support, although data, as opposed to casual observation or informed conjectures about the meaning of current practices are an essential feature of any contemporary psychological analysis. Referring to the anthropological theories, Pratt said he saw "small reason to suppose that (magic and anthropomorphism) were related as source and outgrowth" of the belief in prayer (p. 310). Yet he deferred to the "Melanesian concept of *mana*" (also found in Polynesia) as a socially sanctioned spiritual power, and accepted Marrett's (1903) view that religious development proceeds "from spell to prayer," which Godin (1968) later translated (perhaps ironically) as "from cry to word." Whether the development of prayer is embedded in cultural evolution, it seems hard to escape the assumption that for any individual their primitive, naive, or even spontaneous prayers are different from the 'adult' and sophisticated or mature forms. This could be so because it is easier to criticize alien practices of prayer, whether in a Samoan village, in a household, or in a local church, even if they are accepted 'naturally,' than to give conceptual accounts of how such prayers are possible, and what they might mean.

But Pratt tried to be even-handed, and he noted that "the external aids of ritualistic prayer, the bent knee, the closed eye (sic), and other bodily postures commonly used in worship, have on many a worshiper a decidedly helpful effect in bringing about the (sic) religious attitude of mind" (p. 314). (In a linked footnote on the same page he writes that "Not all feel this influence," citing "respondents to a questionnaire of mine" who were evenly divided, and a book that seems to have escaped later attention by Segond on *Le Prière*, published in Paris by Alcan in 1911.) Nevertheless, Pratt noted (on page 314) that "bodily posture" is more important for Catholics than Protestants, and he accepted direct readings of gestures like "attitudes of kneeling or lying prostrate" as "natural expressions of humility." In this analysis he deferred to McDougall's instinct of self-abasement (in his *Social Psychology*, 1908, pp. 62-66).

A serious question therefore concerns the extent to which 'old' psychological concepts lose their force and are replaced, unless they can be translated and change their meaning. If Jews and Moslems are questioned about the relevance of psychology to their traditions, it seems that, like some Christian psychologists, they follow their own traditions to ensure good mental or physical health (cf El Azayem, 1993).

Pratt also included associative processes in his analysis, noting that because across "millions of human beings, the experience of kneeling, closing one's eyes and clasping one's hands has from earliest childhood been associated with the emotions of reverence and religious awe, it is but natural that they should continue to support and incipiently to produce these emotions throughout life" (p. 315). Young children are certainly taught about prayer. Whether it produces a sense of awe is a moot question.

Pratt (1921) wanted to distinguish the prayers of adults that are said habitually from those that are '*real*' (p. 318), supporting this with reference to a study in which 5 of 185 respondents mentioned that they pray from habit, and to Beck's (1906) study in which 2 percent had said that they pray from habit while 98 percent were said to have said they pray because they "feel the need of prayer." It is hard to decide how valid such explanations might be, although Pratt noted that those who continued to pray said, for example, "I pray because I can't help it," or "I pray because God hears" (p. 318).

Such findings might argue against the evidential usefulness of what anyone says about the reasons for their actions, but it is unlikely that our sense of prayer, like our "sense of God" (Bowker, 1973), is for others rather than for us to identify. We are likely to continue whatever practices suit us, regardless of judgements about their validity, although we are expected to be able to justify them. Pratt, however, suggested that we might look for changing rather than stable attitudes, because change was significant for twenty-five of thirty-two adults in another of his studies (p. 318). We might notice that Pratt looked for independent evidence to confirm his conjectures, and he found that twenty-five said that prayer meant more to them as adults than it had in childhood, with only two saying that it had meant more to them in childhood. The reasons they gave included "development of prayer from habit to a real source of strength; more universal things asked for; greater earnestness; greater desire to pray; more confidence in answer to prayer; greater realization of the limitations of prayer and fewer things, consequently, asked for; communion substituted for petition; need substituted for duty; shorter and less formal prayers. Sixty-six percent of my respondents pray more than they did as children, twenty percent pray less, and fourteen percent neither less nor more" (pp. 318-319).

Pratt continued, "Morse and Allan report (from their study of adolescents) that of their twenty-four respondents who had ceased to pray, five stopped praying because of 'negligence or indifference,' nineteen because of 'disbelief in the power of prayer.' Perhaps twenty influences are named by my respondents which in their experience have made prayer difficult or impossible, but they all may be reduced to the following three: (1) ill health, or exhaustion; (2) the sense of sin; (3) discouragement and skepticism. The last of the three is probably the one most commonly at work during the adolescent period. Seventy-nine per cent of Morse and Allan's respondents who had ceased to pray had done so because of their disbelief in the efficacy of prayer (p. 180). . . One-third of my respondents testify that there have been times in their lives when they were convinced that prayer was useless, and in all of these cases this conviction was dated somewhere between the thirteenth and the twenty-first years. The cause of it is regularly some form of adolescent doubt, either as to the existence or nature of God, or as to the reasonableness of prayer, and this skeptical view in many cases has its source in some antiquated teaching as to the nature of God or the purpose of prayer. Another of the causes referred to above for the abandonment of prayer has its source also largely in theological teachings which should long ago have been outgrown. I refer to the sense of sin. And by this I do not mean actual sin, but the feeling of guilt, often of the Bunyan type, which makes the young man or woman regard himself as 'lost' and too vile to come into the divine presence (which had been the case with twenty of his respondents)" (p. 184). Although I have not attempted to replicate those studies, casual enquiry suggests that similar responses might be found now, although the proportions in each category are likely to be different.

Having noted that "skepticism and the sense of sin are the chief obstacles to prayer during adolescent years," Pratt identified (on page 320) a "rather small class of *virtuosos* in prayer if such a phrase may be permitted . . . who seem to have great 'power in prayer' and in whose lives prayer is unquestionably a source of genuine efficiency." In this vein, Shackle and Brown's (1993) study compared responses to the questions that Beck (1906) had asked, with those of twenty-six Roman Catholic secondary-school girls and twenty adult women who were either in an ecumenical prayer group that had met together in the north of England for several years, or at a conference on Christian spirituality. While any comparisons between these sets of data are likely to be unfair, Table 3 shows our results against those that Beck (1906) reported.

While nearly all the adults in our study said they felt a need to pray regularly, most of the schoolgirls said they only needed to pray occasionally. Yet both groups said that prayers help them. While most of the adults said they prayed more in their maturity, find their prayer answered, and that prayer is easy for them to talk about, the prayers of the school girls are more self-directed, reactive, and urgent. A particularly striking difference in attitude was shown by the schoolgirls' emphasis on their own petitions and the adult women's stress on finding God's will in their prayer. It is also interesting to note that earlier uses of 'attitude' refer to posture and that many of the adult women in our study said they had a preferred place or position for prayer. The similar responses of our women and in Beck's data support the coherence of prayer.

Questions about the needs that prayer can satisfy are pervasive, as if in some sense they are expected to show one's dependence on an external support, rather than on oneself. But as Emerson noted, "What we pray to ourselves for is always granted" (cited by Pratt, 1921, p. 321), although he did not go on to say why that might be so. Pratt held that petitionary prayer, which implicitly asks questions and solicits answers, is the original form of prayer, and "for many people probably almost the only conceivable form" (p. 321). In another of Pratt's studies, among the sixty-five who replied, forty-two said their prayer consisted largely of petitions, while the rest said that petitions were "very subordinate" for them. That seventeen of those respondents "believe that God's actions are changed by their prayers" (p. 321) while twenty-six did not "feel sure" that that was the case raises unresolved

Table 3

A comparison (in percentages) of school-girls' (N=25) and adult women's (N=20) answers to direct questions about prayer, together with Beck's (1906) results from an unspecified sample.

	Girls	Women	Beck
Feels a need to pray			
regularly	28	95	98
occasionally	72	5	-
Prays alone			
daily	32	100	'majority'
weekly	40	-	-
monthly	24	-	-
Says grace before meals			
daily	0	50	n/a
never	84	16	-
Adopts a particular position	8	60	'very few'
Has preferred times for prayer	60	60	25
Believe prayers can have an effect on those who pray	80	95	83
Was taught to pray	84	90	n/a
Regularly uses formal prayers	68	75	24
A mistake to pray to change the weather	40	50	>75
Prayer depends on their mood	72	20	n/a
Prayer depends on what has happened	72	40	n/a
Relieved to confess sins in prayer	36	70	19
Remarkable answers to prayers noted	20	65	'few'
Communion more important than dependence in prayer	10	45	22
Prayed most in their maturity	n/a	65	68
Prayer is easy to talk about	12	70	n/a
Prayers oriented to God	12	65	n/a
or to self	64	15	-
Prayer most need in bad times	96	45	n/a

questions about the expectations that either group can impose on God (cf Furnham and Brown, 1992).

Studies of God's characteristics, which have been expected to be a staple in the psychology of religion, rely on the judged appropriateness of the nouns or adjectives that describe 'God.' Despite the Trinitarian nature of Christianity, these results still converge on the solutions reported by Gorsuch (1968) and Vergote and Tamayo (1980), and it is typical to recognize God as Father. Whether the nature of the God to whom one prays impacts on explanations of any successes or failures in prayer, and whether our understanding of God develops or can be validated through prayer remains to be established. While communion might bring peace through confession (which Pratt aligned with psychiatric cures and therapy, on p. 331) because of the expression of "needs and longings," he stressed that the "pragmatic value of the God-idea" may be more important than God as Creator or Giver, since the Great Confessor "sees us as we really are, and with whom alone of all beings we may be utterly frank" (p. 327). Pratt quoted Hocking's (1912) view that through prayer we can achieve "a purity of selfhood" (p. 327) when "self assertion is combined with consciousness of absolute dependence," and he cited C. S. Myers' assertion, quoted from James's *Varieties*, that "if we ask to *whom* to pray, the answer (strangely enough) must be that *that* does not much matter" (p. 328). Pratt asserted that "it seems plain that among the more intelligent (sic), appeals for 'spiritual blessings' largely predominate" while "material blessings and particular ends play a relatively subordinate role" (p. 321) in prayer. He identified spiritual blessings with a better disposition, firmer resolution, and a redeemed inward nature, noting as exceptions crisis, grief, and danger, where the 'wish' itself drives the form of prayer for those who are "in the habit of praying at all." Pratt (pp. 322-323) also mentioned that several Catholic and Evangelical groups had published lists of successful prayers around 1919, so "The *Messenger* for August 1919 announced, 'Total number of Thanksgivings for the month, 4,876,932,' and he noted that 'The blessings asked for are largely 'spiritual.'"

Advice about what is to be prayed for seems to be more explicit than what it is not appropriate to pray for, so asking for divine help contrasts against heaping misfortune on one's enemies. Negative claims on prayer are likely to be disregarded or excused, and Pratt found that sixty of his ninety respondents believed in "special answers to prayer and are convinced that they have had such answers in their own experience" (p. 323). Such "successes" are usually handled more cautiously than 'blessings' sought or received, except by those in 'enthusiastic' traditions (Knox, 1954), and petitions for such spiritual ends as deepening one's faith are more likely to be approved than those for trivial or explicitly material benefits.

If a psychology of prayerful successes was thought important, one might look for them in the Bible and in the confidence about the healing power of particular shrines, and in the natural cues to divine support found in thunder and lightning as a "divine language" (Coe, 1916, p. 303), or in prayers for rain. But there might be only a short distance there between wishes and prayers, especially in the written petitions that can be left in some churches.

Some written petitions

A sequence of 227 cards on which petitionary prayers had been written and left at the back of a country parish church in England was classified in terms of the content of the petitions they contained. These cards, which were lent to me by Professor Leslie Francis, were headed "St Bertram's Prayer Card. Please pray for . . .," and they had a space at the bottom for a signature and date. An analysis of these cards will not capture the traditional contrast between verbal and contemplative prayer, and it gives no indication about their hoped for effects, or the age of those who completed them (apart from unreliable judgments about the handwriting). But it supports the classification in

Table 4		
A content analysis of 227 prayer requests that had been left in an English parish church.		
For family or other named individuals (e.g. "For my mum, dad and brother and all my relatives," and "for my Gran, Mum, Dad, and James, Clare, Tom, also Alice and Tony")	86	(37%)
For those who are sick (e.g. "My Nan and help her through this bad patch and she will soon feel well again," and "Dick who has lung cancer. Please pray for his wife and two little boys too.")	47	(21%)
For those who have died (e.g. "for Albert, may his passing to his loved ones come with peace and love," "Michael, who died almost a year ago in a car crash. We'll never forget you, Michael," (and one person prayed for) "all those people who lost their lives to save others in the 1st and 2nd world war.")	45	(19%)
Generic prayers (e.g. "for everybody to have peace in the world," "for the third world," "for revelation")	23	(10%)
Non-specific religious prayers (e.g. "Peace, understanding, your light and your love for us all. The Lord's peace is upon this Church," "All who need the love of Jesus"	20	(10%)
Prayers for themselves or their pets	6	(3%)

Table 4 of the petitions that were made, showing that most of the prayers involved specific requests, hopes, or wishes, with no explicit demands (cf Vergote, 1988). Cancer was the most commonly mentioned illness, and there was a contrast between direct and indirect messages to, for, or through God, or some other person.

Only one person gave "thanks for healings wrought," and the nature or the urgency and innocence of most of these prayers is shown in the following unselected petitions set out in the order in which they were received.

Charlotte: A baby of 10 months who is deaf: that her hearing may be restored.
All who do not yet know the love of Christ.
Anthony: Grieving bitterly at the death of his son. Please help him to accept this suffering.
The repose of the soul of Jim. Please give consolation to his friend Greg in his loss.
The people of Kings Heath, B'ham — Pray for laborers to enter His harvest field. Mt 28:16-20.
Love and happiness throughout the country.
Us, to come to terms with the possibility of not being able to have our own family.
Robert and Mandy as we prepare for marriage and a life together with Jesus as our guide. Also for St Philip and St James' Church, Ilfracombe, N. Devon that we may continue to grow more like Jesus.
The clergy, priests, and all who minister unto others. Support them, give them health and strength to carry out your teaching in the world.
All these people that their prayers may be answered.
My Nan who is going into hospital. Also all the poor and starving everywhere.
This time Lord, for me. That I may live a little longer to enjoy this snatch of happiness.
My mother — in her trying times — with drink.
All of my family and especially my grandad who is quite ill. Also for my little dog and goldfish. Amen.
All my lost friends, also especially my Gran and Grandad, and Mum and Dad. Also for Stuart who I care deeply for. Please pray for anyone who needs help right now!
Peace, Understanding, Your Light and Your Love for us all. The Lord's Peace is upon this church and it should be cherished.
All who need the love of Jesus.
Me. Please take the bitterness from my heart towards my family!
Thomas 22.4.84. It's been a long hard struggle Dad to get through these two years but we would like to tell you something so there won't be any doubt, you are wonderful to think of but so hard to live without. Lots of Love.
Thanksgiving of a good holiday for the people of St Stephens URC Milnrow who have stayed in the youth hostel and had a good time. We thank you Lord.
My family may soon stop arguing.
Peace and happiness to my family.
My whole family and friends. I love them so much. Please let them know.

Our family and us and hear my prayed [sic]. Thank you.
Good health, peace, and happiness for my family and for peace and goodwill
   in the world.

Few of these prayers have the specificity that seems to have been implied
by those who have argued for a belief in the material efficacy of prayer,
rather than to articulate specific wishes, and sometimes fears.

Pratt (p. 323) disclaimed the relevance of 'objective' answers to prayer,
not on the grounds of faith, as one might expect, but because firm beliefs
about special answers were, he thought, "one of the great reasons why they
pray" (p. 324), although "most religious people would pretty certainly continue to pray even if they lost all faith in special answers." The question
there is, "What sustains prayer?" Is it faith, hope, social support, religious
sanctions, or a behavioral mechanism like Skinner's partial reinforcement
effect (Jenkins and Stanley, 1950), which shows that actions are maintained
by occasional rewards or reinforcements? These phenomena were captured
traditionally by the idea that hope "springs eternal" or that we have "habits
of the heart."

Pratt identified the other kinds of prayer, beyond those that are habitual or
routine and petitional (p. 324), in joy and thankfulness, and in the prayers of
communion that were acknowledged by 65 percent of his 170 respondents,
and by 70 percent in Beck's study. Nevertheless, only 36 percent of Morse
and Allan's adolescents had had such a "positive — sometimes almost a
violent — experience . . . indigenous to every religion and to every social class,
and (one that) *seems* to arise spontaneously among all sorts and conditions
of men" (p. 325). In a more recent study, Back and Bourque (1972) suggest, however, that states of emotional arousal (on which prayerful experiences
may depend) are not necessarily identified as 'religious,' finding that those
who are better educated tend to identify them as 'aesthetic.'

The subjectivity of prayer

Pratt noted (on page 327) that Miss Strong (1909) calls "the mystical
conscious union with the All" 'aesthetic,' and as only one tendency in the
"completely social type" of prayer.

Questions about experiences of communion with God or the transcendent, and about what can produce them are closely related to the practice of
prayer or meditation. Pratt identified a sense of communion with God as
"one of the most interesting things in the psychology of religion" (p. 325),
holding that it is "very positive . . . indigenous to every religion and to every
social class, and *seems* to arise spontaneously among all sorts and conditions of men." It is common to religions, "transplanted by deliberate effort,
. . . experienced in its freshness, inculcated as a duty and its appearance
watched." Some are persuaded that they too have 'felt it.' But it comes, he
says, "as near to being a social convention as so purely private and personal an experience can come to be." Because it is induced and cultivated it
contains "so large an element of invitation and auto-suggestion, the temptation

to the psychologist is strong to explain it all by means of those light-bringing terms" (p. 325).

Evidence for the potent immediacy of our communion with God is necessarily subjective, and identified with awe and quietness, feelings, faith, the imagination, or in pious words and talking about it to oneself, others, or to God. Those processes are quite different from the experience of mystics who might catch "God's response."

An important source of ambiguity about prayer therefore centers on the metaphors by which prayer is identified, despite its wordless character. These are set between a mystical response that realizes the Other and a meditative hope for self-realization. It is odd, therefore, as we shall see, that the effects of prayer have only recently been looked for empirically in subjective states and coping skills (cf Pargament, 1992). Perhaps, as Godin (1985) argues, one reason for this is that those whose prayer is 'mature' have given up any belief or expectations about its specific or external effects. This stance is congruent with modern views about self- or 'learned efficacy,' self-appraisal, and the importance of coping with or controlling our environment and preparing for action. This makes the effects of prayer dependent on our states of mind, and therefore reflexive, which could be an example of what Jacks (1911) called "*The Alchemy of Thought*," with the principle that "to interpret experience is to change it" (Pratt, p. 336).

It is hardly worth continuing to pursue questions about the validity of external claims on prayer (although they will reappear), which have been its major criticism, and not only among its adversaries. We could, however, explore the ambiguities inherent in the subjective value of prayer, and the claims that are made there, despite St Augustine's puzzle: "What then is time? If no one asks me, I know: if I wish to explain it to one that asketh, I know not" (*The Confessions*, Book XI:XIV). The psychological problem is not to decide if there is a God to whom we can pray, but to ask how prayer is understood. That task is in principle open to theists and atheists, to prayers and to those who have never prayed, although some knowledge of the dominant traditions with which anyone might pray is necessary, to ensure that their expectations have some validity or sanctions. Firm interpretations of the prayers within other, and especially non-Christian traditions, are beyond us, without inside knowledge of what talk of prayer means there. Written prayers similarly depend on the meanings that are set by their traditions, and by those who 'use' such prayers. That does not depend on their truth or verifiability, but on their meaning and on what it is that makes them 'religious.'

To ask if God hears our prayers moves us towards a "religious psychology" the validity of which depends explicitly on a religious tradition, rather than on subjective or broadly societal and cultural reference points. We have seen that Phillips (1965, p. 52) points out that different relationships are entailed in saying "Lord, hear our prayer, and let our cry come unto Thee," from those in "Master speak, thy servant heareth." And if one expects that God comes to 'know' anything through prayer (following Kierkegaard, 1962, p. 44), is that like telling someone what they know already, or is it useful to give them another perspective? God's properties are a problem, and so the German poet Rilke in *The Book of Hours* (1:275, written between 1901 and 1903) insisted that God is a creation of the poetic imagination. "What will you do, God, when I die?," he asked, to emphasize that this concept gives coherence to a fragile notion of self in relation to the world, such that the balance tips from an objective-world towards the subjective (cf Ryan 1991, p. 54). This view was consistent with that of the "new psychologies" in the late nineteenth century in which the self was "constituted through the senses rather than rationality" (ibid. p. 51). The subjectivity of such perspectives can still release us from the drive towards positivism that William James reacted against through his pragmatism. While arguing against supernaturalism, James postulated a "wider world of being than that of our everyday consciousness" (1902, p. 412) which may involve overlapping consciousnesses, within which subjectivity can expand ecstatically, with its certainty expressed in art, literature, music, or religion. None of that need be reduced to the scientific positivism that is increasingly seen as an uneasy Procrustean bed (Fox Keller, 1987).

When we pray we might talk to ourselves and express hopes and fears. If so, public and private prayer could involve different states of mind, and we should distinguish worship from mission. While it is our awareness of self and of a societal (or traditional) consciousness that makes us human, the doctrine that prayer is inspired by God entails a similar reciprocity between self and Other. This is expressed in the 1662 *Prayer Book's* collect for Trinity X: "Let thy merciful ears, O Lord, be open to the prayers of thy humble servants; and that they may obtain their petitions make them to ask such things as shall please thee." Trinity III similarly asks "that we, to whom thou hast given an hearty desire to pray, may by thy mighty aid be defended and comforted in all dangers and adversities," and the collect for Trinity XII appeals to "God, who art always more ready to hear than we to pray, and art wont to give more than either we desire, or deserve."

Models of prayer

Phillips (1965, p. 3), wrote of "struggling with a mass of contradictory accounts" of prayer and turned to the "actual usage itself," not of the word "prayer" but through Wittgenstein's assertion that "the meaning of prayer is in the activity of praying." We can find that in religious contexts, although there are also secular prayers to summon support. We will see later that the secular uses of prayer seem straightforward, although the deconstruction and implicit criticism of 'prayer' makes one wonder when its use in a religious sense first drew criticism, although Cruden's *Concordance of the Bible* noted that "revisions frequently change (pray) to beseech." Psychologists might also agree with Phillips' opinion that philosophy "does not provide a foundation for prayer, it leaves everything as it is (at least beyond our attitudes) and tries to give an account of it" (p. 3). Whether any account is accepted then depends on our attitudes and beliefs.

These are not trivial questions and could point, as Coe (1916, p. 315) argued, to prayer as "a way of getting one's self together . . . by making one's experience consciously social, that is, by producing a realization that even what is private to me is shared by another." Coe also held that the prayer of confession "helps us to see ourselves as we are but it also shares our secrets with another (which) has great value for organizing the self" (p. 317). William James held that "it corresponds to a more inward and moral stage of sentiment" (1985, p. 364).

In his essay on "*The Technologies of the Self*," Foucault (1988) stressed the role of confession in religious and penal institutions, through the obligation there to tell the truth. In more general terms he held that these technologies "permit individuals to effect by their own means or with the help of others a certain number of operations on their own bodies and souls, thoughts, conduct, and way of being, so as to transform themselves in order to attain a certain state of happiness, purity, wisdom, perfection, or immortality" (p. 18). This reads like a comprehensive description of prayer, or even of spirituality, within the religious life, and the argument is strengthened by its alignment with technologies of production, language (or semiotics), and power, with its injunctions to "Know yourself" and "Take care of yourself." These self-technologies are justified by medical, political, and religious models in which a classical emphasis on martyrdom gives a model for penitents who are committed to obedience and the contemplation of God (p. 43). To decipher inner thoughts is therefore part of the practice of prayer and more recently of psychotherapy. The fields of psychosomatic medicine and psycho-neuroimmunology similarly occupy an uneasy ground between medical and psychosocial factors when coping with stress and illness, in which we find an increasing recognition of the role (and use) of religious and prayerful practices, at least within traditional concepts of 'prayer' in the West.

A study by Krause and van Tran (1989) among older blacks found, for example, that "although life stress tended to erode feelings of self-worth and mastery, negative effects were offset or counter-balanced by increased religious involvement." Their analysis of religion distinguished organizational involvement from nonorganizational (or subjective religiosity), in which prayer and a 'religious' identity are paramount (cf Table 5, p. 64).

Wheaton (1985) identified three stress-buffering models, which Krause and van Tran (1989) have aligned with the effects of religious involvement that include prayer. In their 'moderator model' they predict that the impact of stress on self-esteem and coping depends on the level of religious involvement (and on other variables that are not identified). With low levels of religious involvement, stress is expected to have an impact on self-esteem, because coping would be less effective and prayer would not have a direct effect on self-esteem in the absence of stress. Their second model assumes a suppressor effect, so that the level of religious involvement would depend on the amount of stress, and that as stress increases, so does prayer or some other form of religious involvement. In that model it might not be the amount or frequency of prayer that changes, but its fervency, since it is unlikely that prayer would alter without some other changes in religious

Table 5. Krause and Van Tran's (1989) Exploratory Factor Model of Religiosity[a]

Questions	Organizational religiosity (Factor 1)	Nonorganizational religiosity (Factor 2)[b]
1. Are you a member of a church or other place of worship	.378	.193
2. How often do you usually attend religious services?	.831	-.001
3. How important is going to church or a place of worship to you?	.881	-.062
4. How often do you pray?	.033	.552
5. How important is it for Black parents to take or send their children to religious services?	.107	.341
6. How religious would you say you are?	-.088	.711

a   The fit of the model to the data was: ^{2} = 17.358 (4df): ^{2}/df = 4.340: Hoelter's Critical N index = 292.289.

b   The correlation between factors 1 and 2 was .542.

involvement, unless that can be resolved by increasing the level of involvement to counter-balance other deficiencies, including one's minority status for example (cf Taylor, 1989). This suppressor model assumes that a balance is maintained between religious involvement and life stress, which might operate chronically or only when it cumulates beyond a threshold. In either case prayer or religious involvement becomes a moderator variable in an analysis that does not distinguish the manner in which the cycle is set up from how it is maintained, although some dynamic balance is assumed since "stress increases religious involvement, which in turn tends to bolster self-esteem and mastery, thereby diminishing the overall negative effects of life stress" (Krause and Van Tran, p. S6).

Their third, distress-deterrent model, places less emphasis on religiosity by assuming directly additive effects on mastery after stress, with prayer or religious involvement having an effect on self-esteem independently of the effects of distress. Krause and Van Tran's survey data supported the distress-deterrent model, suggesting that "although life stress tended to erode feelings of self-worth and mastery, these negative effects were offset or counterbalanced by increased religious involvement."

These models have been described in detail because they emphasize that the early direct tests of the efficacy of prayer are inadequate, not only on religious but also on theoretical grounds. They oversimplified both the religious and secular variables and assumed that prayer could have simple or linear effects on almost *any* target. That can not be so, not because of what is expected from prayer itself, which is controversial, but because of the contextual and secular influences that interact with it to produce a range of outcomes. The effects of prayer should not be oversimplified or disregarded.

Beyond that, however, we ought to be able to specify a model that articulates what might be involved in prayer and the ways in which it and other religious processes might produce any outcome. On general grounds, there are likely to be more indirect than directly causal effects. With William James we should distinguish what *is* from what *ought to be* and find more about what is involved by 'disaggregating' the variables before setting up a study that is necessarily limited in its breadth, recognizing that intervening variables like commitment, the fervor and frequency of prayer, religious experience, and informal or institutional support should be controlled. That the Krause and Van Tran study relied on a secondary analysis of data that were already available emphasized the importance of the adage that there is nothing as a good as good theory.

To expect that something or somebody might be changed by prayer is, however, an over-generalization that cannot be accepted without investigation or clarification. It is made more complex because prayer can be understood too literally, when it might simply express a concern, wish, desire, or hope. So Christ prayed in the Garden, "if it be thy will, let this cup pass" when he was already resigned to what would happen. To say that someone spoke of, or hoped for, a miracle carries an inappropriately apologetic flavor, just as a priest prays, not *for* anything or anybody, but in "union with them." It is in this way that mature Christian prayer renounces efficacy (Godin, 1992, in correspondence).

We might therefore understand prayers of thanksgiving in terms of the way they help to construe outcomes within a religious context, although this view does not resolve differences between a "religious sacrifice" as a formal token, and those who take it to an extreme, by risking a diagnosis as psychotic or deluded in seeking martyrdom, for example. Wittgenstein said that it is "Not *how* the world is, is the mystical, but *that* it is" (*Tractatus*, 6,44, cf Phillips, p. 102). The theological concepts of 'grace' and 'hope,' which have been disregarded by psychologists, might handle these problems and those of social equity, although when Simone Weil asked "Why these things rather than others?" she resisted a final answer. That such questions are not worth pursuing independently of their meaning within faith (or the Faith) returns us to the importance of our received ideas, ideals, and attitudes, and how their meanings develop or change. Osgood's semantic differential, which has been used to explore the concepts of God, is not easily applied there because it disregards the frames through which meanings are filtered and explained. So Kierkegaard's story of the feast for cripples and beggars, which an observer assumed was a charitable gesture, rather than a 'feast,' stresses a difference between compassion and condescension.

If prayer reflects our attitudes to what happens in the world, and not to specific events in it, an attribution of construal is involved. Those who never pray might, according to Phillips (1965, p. 106f), have ruled out the possibility of prayer by that action itself. Alternatively they might be unwilling to appear deferential or to accept that tragedy could *ever* have a purpose. Such unresolved but empirical questions are supported by stories, folk mythologies, and experiences. Our task here is to bring them towards psychology. One way to do this is to consider our reactions to religious practices that are foreign or alien. That is the aim of the next chapter.

Chapter Four

Reaching In and Reaching Out
Prayer in Anthropological Perspective

DAVID H. TURNER

"Listening stops with the ears, the mind stops with recognition, but spirit is empty and waits on all things. The Way gathers in emptiness alone."
(The Complete Works of Chung Tzu, p. 38.)

An anthropological perspective is essentially ethnographic, comparative, and reflexive, and it is in this spirit that I would like to approach the question of prayer as a religious phenomenon. I have prayed with persons of a variety of faiths in a variety of contexts: Christian, Buddhist, Hindu, and Muslim. I am not at all certain that what I was doing was what they were doing, though I did record what they told me they were doing. It may be instructive to begin by recounting what I was doing in each instance, as it was something I had learned to do in a society which really does not pray in the conventional sense, namely Australian Aboriginal society. First, though, what do I mean by "prayer in a conventional sense"?

According to the Oxford English Dictionary prayer is a "solemn request to God or object of worship, a formula used in praying, a form of divine service consisting largely of prayers, an entreaty to a person." Insofar as the Australian Aborigines recognize no God—no superpersonal or suprapersonal force, writ in the singular and capable of intervening in human affairs—to whom they could issue requests or entreaties, this definition would not apply. Is there, though, an 'object' they 'worship'? The answer to this is "yes and no." If by 'object' we mean "something detached and removed, outside one's self" then no. Nothing in Aboriginal society is detached and removed from one's self and others. Everything is in a "part-of-one-in-the-other" relationship, whether person to person or person to the spiritual. But

67

if we qualify 'object' to mean "something *relatively* detached" from oneself, we can proceed.

The Oxford Dictionary's definition of worship is "recognition given to the worthiness and merit of something or someone, to honor and respect; reverent homage or service paid to; adore as divine, pay religious homage to; idolize, regard with adoration." What Aborigines do is venerate with deep respect or warm approbation the spiritual prototype that 'enForms' the person and all those in the same spiritual line of descent as him or her self. Images or abstract representations of that prototype are carved and displayed before initiates while they are taught the Law. When they view the image, each Aborigine feels in touch with an en-Formed part of him or her self that extends from "this side" over to the "other side." Through singing one can reach inside oneself to summon up one's in-Formed spirit and project it along this en-Formed prototypical pathway to glimpse the "other side," or the so-called Dreamtime existence.

Besides this, Aborigines also venerate manifestations of the Dreamtime in nature, that is, the prototypical Forms of nature. I am sure anyone who has ever lived with Aborigines in the bush for even a short space of time will have observed persons sitting for hours on end, gazing out over an ocean seascape or desert landscape, apparently doing nothing. And that is exactly what they are doing—'Nothinging.' They are emptying themselves in order to see/hear the Scape emptied of its content and so exhibiting its Form(s). That is, they are emptying themselves—primarily by singing—in order to apprehend a non-material 'aesthetic,' ultimately a spiritual plane of existence. I have learned to do this myself. It is what I do when I 'pray.'

I have recounted an instance of 'Nothinging' while with the Aborigines of Groote Eylandt and Bickerton Island in 1986, in my book *Return to Eden: A Journey Through the Promised Landscape of Amagalyuagba* (pp. 169-171) and in my "Incarnation of Nambirrirrma" paper, and won't repeat it here, except to say that my adoration was directed at waves laughing. Or perhaps it would be more accurate to say that adoration was the result of opening myself up and letting waves laugh within me.

I would now like to share five personal experiences of praying in other religious traditions: the first in a Trappist monastery in Canada, the second in a Balinese healing temple, the third in a Hindu mountain temple in north India, the fourth in a Tibetan Buddhist monastery/temple, and the fifth on a ridge in the Himalayas with Gudjar Muslim nomads.

Notre-Dame-du-Calvaire

The dictionary definition of prayer recounted above, emerges, of course, out of the English-speaking Judeo-Christian tradition. 'God,' "God as an object of worship," "an entreaty to a Person," "a part of divine service," are all aspects of Christian worship. In Christian worship, prayer may be a reaching out to God or it may be an opening up of oneself to allow God in. In the post-Pentecost tradition it may even be a reaching in, to find God inside oneself. Whether reaching out or reaching in, the object of Christian prayer is generally to petition God for something, or for his guidance. In a monastic context, though, reaching in and out to God can be an end in itself.

In May of 1989, Fr. John Lokko, then a graduate student in the Department of Anthropology at the University of Toronto, invited me to accompany him on retreat to the Trappist monastery of Notre-Dame-du-Calvaire near Moncton, New Brunswick.

The Independent Order of Cistercians of the Strict Observance or Trappists was established by Don Armand Jean Le Bouthillier de Rance at La Trappe in Normandy, France, in the seventeenth century. The 'Observance' in question is the *Rule* of St. Benedict, a sixth century Roman hermit; the 'Cistercians' are the monastic order that emerged in the eleventh century to follow his Rule. One of these Rules is silence for "in much speaking, you should not escape sin" (Prov. 10: 19). Virtually the only means of verbal expression available to the Cistercian Trappists is chanting the psalms during the Divine Offices or prayer services. In 1967, however, this rule was relaxed to permit brief conversations outside the places of worship to facilitate sociability among the monks.

On entering a monastery the monks renounce their material possessions and submit themselves to the authority of the Abbot who in turn (in theory) submits himself to the authority of the *Rule* and, ultimately, to Jesus and God. Life inside the monastery as set down by the *Rule* is a regular routine of collective prayer (the Divine Offices) broken by periods of work, meals, and rest. The Offices are eight in all: Night Office or Vigils, Lauds, Tierce, Mass, Sext, None, Vespers, and Compline.

Notre-Dame-du-Calvaire was founded in 1902 by six monks from the Abbey of Bonnecombe in the Diocese of Rodez in France. In the spring of 1904 they were joined in a separate establishment by the Cisterciennes-Trappistines-de-Vaise from the Diocese of Lyon in France. Since then the monastery has supported itself from the sale of produce from its dairy farming enterprise.

The Trappists see themselves as "men and women of prayer." The main object of the Trappist way of life is to achieve "inner silence," as the absence of inner speech so that God may "come in." Outer speech is banned because it acts as a distraction from the achievement of inner silence. As one monk put it in *Voices from Silence: The Trappists Speak* (p. 13):

> In true meditation the inner voice is stilled. Rather than talking to one's self, the person becomes quiet and thus open to the softer voices of God. Mystics and meditators sometimes speak of 'becoming a receptacle' and this state requires this inner silence.

What do the monks experience in this inner silence? *Voices from Silence* provides some accounts. One monk reported that God "sets the man's heart dancing with a deep interior joy that no one else can produce" (p. 126). He went on to describe "the way of darkness . . . He draws a man as by a magnet . . . But there in the darkness is the presence of God." The nature of this

Presence seems the most difficult thing for the monks to define. It is usually described as being 'enveloped' by something while feeling awe and
joy.

At Calvaire I decided to follow the monks' routine as closely as possible,
including attending the Divine Offices, performing manual labor in the barn
and fasting. I soon began to feel the effects of this routine on my being. The
tension in my body began to unwind and preoccupations began to slip from
my mind. I began to feel very relaxed:

> I woke on Monday Morning, calm and refreshed but too late for Night
> Office and Lauds. My anxieties seem to have subsided. Another month here
> and I might just be back together again. I made my way down to the
> chapel for Tierce and Concelebrated Mass. The monks filed silently in. As
> they stood to chant the Psalms I suddenly had an impression of robeForms
> over and above the contents of the robes—the monks—themselves. The
> chapel seems to bifurcate down the middle, the forms on one side appear-
> ing to mirror those on the other. I recalled Jaleh Jam's painting of the
> Last Supper I have at home. I remembered my experience of Laughing
> Waves on Bickerton Island with the Aborigines.

Later I talked about my experience to one of the monks. It wasn't what he
would consider an experience of God, he said. That was rather an inner
experience, or rather an inner experience leading to an apprehension of
something outside oneself. But it was like an experience he had recently
had himself. He had just come from one of the Offices and was in the refec-
tory sitting opposite another monk at a table. Suddenly there was a kind of
transparency in the other monk's face. It seemed to take on a different look,
and he began to see it in a different way, he said. It was a more beautiful
look. It was like looking at a deeper level of his person. He felt a sharing, a
communing. It was as if he had let his own barriers fall and become transparent too. But the other monks had not seen the same thing in him. In fact
when he recounted his experience to them, the other monks said he had felt
threatened.

An experience similar to that of mine and the monk's is recounted in
Voices from Silence:

> I remember one evening last fall. I had finished feeding the cows. I
> came outside. The sun had gone down, the moon was out, the clouds
> were passing over the moon, and the moon was shining through the clouds
> and the breaks in the clouds. It was a beautiful sight. I just sat and looked
> for a long time. The presence of God became so strong that it seemed
> that everything all of a sudden stopped. The clouds stopped moving, and
> there was a sense of awesomeness, beauty, joy, and peace that overflows
> into the soul. I knew that God was there, that He was profoundly present
> at that moment (p. 132).

He goes on,

> It's so strange, as though there is something that you had never seen before shining through this perfectly common sight. It's at times like this when I feel the presence of God so strongly. These are moments of real communication.

What the three of us seem to have experienced was not so much 'God' as some special quality of something very tangible in the realworld outside ourselves, though the source of that something could very well be attributed to 'God.' We experienced fixed Form or Forms behind which moved variable content. This is the way reality is, assert the Australian Aborigines. They would not attribute its source to 'God' but rather to a pre-differentiated spiritual substance.

Chaumarga

Later that summer I was off to the island of Bali in Indonesia to study the role of religion in economic life and to take a break from my Australian Aboriginal studies. Bali is a Province of Indonesia some 172 miles long by 102 at its widest point, with a population of 2.25 million.

Bali is the last remaining outpost of Hinduism in Indonesia, the remainder of the state now being predominantly Muslim. Hinduism entered Indonesia in the first millennium C.E. from India through Burma, Cambodia, Borneo, and Java, to Bali and beyond. By the tenth century Hinduism was firmly established in Bali, and when the Muslim faith swept through the region in the fifteenth and sixteenth centuries, somehow Bali escaped conversion and continued on its own peculiar path. Today Bali boasts some 20,000 temples, several dozen in each village, dedicated to thousands of deities associated with a myriad of occupations, localities, and functions. These are generally grouped in the conventional Hindu fashion under Brahman (the Creator), Vishnu (the Preserver), and Shiva (the Destroyer).

As Lansing describes it (1983, p. 7), temple festivals form a link between the human world and the unseen world of Indic cosmology with a view to maintaining a balance of forces between them. This is the Middle World of human existence, the Upper World of the gods, and the Lower World of demons. The temples are common points of reference for people within each caste and village, and between castes and villages. According to Lansing it is through the temples and their festivals that social and economic life flows. For instance, the ritual calendars associated with the water temples determine the opening and closing of the irrigation canals that coordinate water-flow from the mountaintops down through the rice paddies to the valleys.

While the Balinese recognize the four varna 'caste' system of Hinduism, there is much more flexibility here than in India. One reason is historical accident. When the Dutch captured Bali in 1908 virtually the whole Balinese ruling Kshatriya aristocracy enacted Puntun or 'the finish' and marched, unarmed, into the gunfire of the Dutch soldiers, stabbing themselves to death if they were not immediately killed. The loss of this stratum of society saw the Vaishya or farming class and the Sudra or artisan class rise in ascendency, while the temples filled the vacuum left by the disappearance of the royal courts. Another reason for flexibility in the Balinese caste system is the emphasis on place (temple) over function (caste). All people who worship at the same temple are regarded as belonging to the same caste, including in-marrying women. One may change caste membership by changing temple affiliation. One merely needs to sense the presence of his or her ancestral spirits there, in a manner acceptable to the temple custodians.

Though there was a noble caste in Bali prior to the European occupation there was no king or queen or overarching authority. The island was divided into a number of independent principalities linked through religion and festivals, the major one being Eka Desa Rudra held once every century to ensure the well-being of the Middle World. As Lansing (1983, p. 142) describes it, its purpose was to "bring together all of the forces at work in the life of an institution, so that they may reach whatever accommodations are necessary in order for the institution to prosper through another cycle of its existence."

Balinese religious practices are based on the Rg Veda or on hymns to the gods dating from the second millennium B.C.E. in India. This tradition emphasizes petitioning and sacrificing to the gods in order to ensure order among humans. The tradition spawned the great Hindu epics, *Mahabharata* and *Ramayana* which the Balinese have elaborated to an extraordinary degree with fantastic costuming and elaborate *gamelan* musical accompaniment.

My first few days in Bali were spent in the tourist haunts of Kuta where I met a young Balinese fellow introduced as 'Ketut.' He was acting as a tour guide for a group of Australians I had met. His real name was *I* (boy), *Ketut* (third born), *Guday* (big), *Ginastra* (name on the fire arrow of Arjuna), *Wiyaya* (winner). I told him of my interest in Bali and he invited me to his home village of Chaumarga in central Bali off the road to Lake Bratan. Chaumarga contains some 4,000 people sub-divided into seven districts or local communities. The village has three major temples dedicated to Brahman, Vishnu, and Shiva respectively and each temple consists of an outer courtyard for meetings, a middle space for musical performances, and an inner sanctum for prayer. Offerings are made here every day, as they are in each room of every private home. Periodic festivals are held to honor the major deities or lesser deities related to them.

Offerings consist of three ingredients: fire to take the prayers that accompany the offerings to the gods, water to purify the sacrificer, and flowers for fragrance to concentrate the mind. Prayers follow a definite form: the first is an "excuse me" to the gods for interrupting them; the second is a prayer "decorated with flowers" so that the gods will notice the supplicant; the third is a prayer without flowers to say thank you and goodbye. Temple prayers and offerings are set within the following form: music is played to summon the spirits to the temple (Balinese temples are empty of spirits except during festivals); the spirits are then 'washed' and an image of the deity embodying its spirit is brought to the temple as an object of worship; a Brahman priest then makes an offering to the gods; finally, holy water from the washing ceremony is used to cleanse or purify the participants. This purification rite has three phases: supplicants dip their hands in the water and then rub it through their hair three times "to clean the brain," then on the mouth three times "to clean the body inside," then on the face three times "to clean the eyes and face."

I attended a number of festivals during my stay in Bali which followed this outline, but I did not myself participate. Then one day Ketut asked if I would like to see a temple no outsider had ever seen before. He said it was a healing temple. We were to travel by van as far as the road would take us and then walk overland through the rice fields to reach our destination. Before we departed, Ketut's mother made a special thanksgiving offering which included a r1,000 note. On the way we picked up a man from one of the villages who had some authority over this temple. It was hot, and I began to doze off. In between sleeping and waking I suddenly had a vision of someone close to me who had recently died. It was so vivid I thought he was real. The pain of grief returned.

After driving for perhaps twenty minutes we parked the vehicle and set off across the rice fields, walking for about half an hour until we came to a small ravine. As we descended the ravine I noticed a small structure on the hillside below us consisting of a platform, supporting posts and a roof. There we met the head keeper of the temple, Madi Kumbu, not a Brahman but a Sudra whose line had been entrusted with the responsibility of caring for the temple. He took us down another level to a cave-temple built into the rock. In it was a spring and a pool. We put down the offering we had brought and descended another level to a fountain to wash. Then we returned to the cave. Ketut, our guide and the keeper prepared to pray in front of the pool and beckoned me to kneel beside them. I did, and the keeper sprinkled water on us and began chanting prayers to summon the god of the temple, and as he did we took up flower petals and held them between our fingers letting them flutter to the ground as he finished. Then he put a flower behind each of our ears. We wet our hands from a bowl and washed in the prescribed manner. Then we prayed to say thank you to the gods. The keeper then opened our offerings and placed them on the wall around the pool and beckoned us over. We were to take the boiled eggs we had brought with us (which I had thought were for our lunch!) and place them in the pool. I bent over the edge of the wall and dropped in the eggs. Suddenly two large eels were moving toward them and swallowed them whole. It was a shock, but for some reason it seemed rather funny. I laughed. The pain inside me vanished.

I asked Ketut about the eels. He said they were holy fish, the reincarnation of people who had suffered from skin diseases when they were alive. If a person touched an eel in the fields he or she would become very sick, but if he or she makes offerings to the ones in the pool they get well. This is the eels' way of making karma so they can be reincarnated as humans. There are crayfish in the same pool with the eels, but unlike in the fields, the eels never eat them. I told Ketut about my vision in the van on the way to the temple and how the pain I had felt was now gone. He seemed profoundly moved and asked me to say a prayer of thanks to the spirits of his ancestors when we returned home for telling him to bring me here, even though he didn't know why at the time.

Aborigines would have no difficulty understanding how spirits could be summoned to a place of worship. They would have some difficulty though, in comprehending how making offerings to these spirits could make one well. Aborigines hold that the spirit-world is neutral in this respect. Healing comes through human inter-activity and music.

Brahmaur

I continued my interest in comparative religion the following year with a trip to north India to examine Hinduism and Buddhism in their original setting. I had been invited to join a trek organized by Professor Harjit Singh of Jawaharlal Nehru University of Delhi and a group of graduate students in cultural geography. We were to proceed to Dalhousie in northwestern Himachal Pradesh and from there to Khajiar, Chamba, make a side-trip to Brahmaur, return to Chamba and proceed north to Bairagarr from there crossing the Sach Pass at 4,800 meters. We would then descend to Kilar and the Pangi Valley and make our way to Rooli, Shansah, Tande, Keylong, and finally Manali before returning to Delhi. This suited my purposes perfectly as it would take us from a conservative Hindu area in the west, through a 'tribal' area in the center to a predominantly Buddhist region in the east. One of the most memorable experiences on the trip occurred at Brahmaur.

Brahmaur Village is located at a height of 2,215 meters on the cliffs flanking the Budhal Nala river. From the seventh century it was the capital of the sovereign state of Brahmaur and today it remains an important religious center with some eighty-four temples—most of them dedicated to the Lord Shiva—in its Chaurasi or holy sector. Adjacent to the Chaurasi is a small market area providing caste-specific services such as barbering, tailoring, shoemaking, and merchandizing. The lands surrounding the village are terraced for agriculture where maize, barley, and wheat are grown. Most of the village's inhabitants are Hindu Brahmins, reflecting the center's religious significance, although there are some 'tribal' Gaddis in the area who tend goats or engage part-time in agriculture.

In post-Upanishadic Hinduism the belief emerged that images could be fashioned to contain the spirits of the gods (or the spirits of parts of the gods). The god enters the world in an unformed state and is formed by the matter available there "as fire becomes varied in shape according to the object it burns" or "as air on entering this world becomes varied in shape according to the object it enters" (*Katha Upanishad II*, 2.9/10). As a result of this belief, temples proliferated throughout north India as sanctuaries for these images. Rites developed to order the fashioning, installation, and animation of these images. Priests or *pujara* became permanently attached to the temples to perform these rites. These were the spiritually oriented *gurus* and the secularly oriented *acarya*. Remaining aloof from this development, however, were the ascetically oriented *sunyasin* or renouncing individuals.

The three large pagoda-style temples in Brahmaur Chaurasi are dedicated to Shiva, Narsingh, and Nagabada and date from the tenth or eleventh centuries. The temples are built in pagoda style to represent steps to the gods, really steps up the mountains to the gods. An older wooden temple dating from the seventh century is dedicated to Lakshana Devi, the mountain goddess of Brahmaur.

The morning after we arrived I rose at dawn and walked from our rest house up to the Chaurasi to view the temple complex in more leisurely fashion. No one was there except for a young man in robes and another who seemed to be his assistant. I sat down and watched with interest. First they walked over to a shrine which I judged to be relatively new. The young man rang the bell near the entrance and opened the door. Inside was the moulded image of a man seated in the lotus position. This turned out to be Guru Maharaj Jee who had recently died. The young man in the robes was his pupil Jay Krishin Maharaj Jehla or Praimahil Mahara. The purpose of constructing this shrine was not merely to house an image of the deceased guru so that he could be remembered and worshiped, it was also to house his spirit so that the young guru could continue to learn from him after his death. The young guru now began to chant prayers while ringing the bells, ostensibly to summon the spirit of the old guru here for the day.

After the prayers were finished the young guru's assistant motioned me to join them in the guru's dwelling to the left of the shrine. I took off my shoes and entered. Directly in front of me was a small table-shrine and to my right there was a mat on which were some flowers, a dish of incense, some offerings and a photo of the old guru. At the table the young guru took some water and sprinkled it over my head which I then applied to my hair, mouth, and face in the prescribed manner. Then the guru marked me on the forehead with his thumb and beckoned me to sit on the mat in front of the photo of his guru. I assumed this was to say a prayer of thanks, which I did. Then his assistant led me outside. No words were spoken through any of this, nor was I asked for money. It was a very moving experience.

While I was inside the guru's dwelling I noticed a small window in the form of a triangle facing west. I didn't think about it again until later that evening when I again visited the temple complex. The sun was setting and as I looked toward it from a vantage point beside the guru's dwelling I realized that it was setting very near the top left of the V formed by the inside slopes of two adjacent peaks that dominated the visionscape. I suddenly felt very excited. It was June 12th and nearing the summer solstice. I realized that the setting sun would soon meet the top left of the V and then start back in the other direction, probably meeting the top right of the V formed by the slopes at winter solstice on December 22nd. More than this, I also realized that when the sun set on the summer solstice point its rays would shine through the window in the guru's dwelling and fall on the photo of his guru. Where it would shine when it set on the winter solstice I did not know. Even more to the point, the combination of the shape of the window and the slope of the peaks visible through it would be a mandala design, sacred to Hindus.

It was a moment of heightened awareness emerging out of my earlier experience with the young guru that morning. I may have seen the very reason why this site was chosen for the Chaurasi and the positioning of the temples a thousand or more years ago.

The experience reminded me of one I had of South Bay on Bickerton Island in northern Australia in 1987. I had not been able to relocate the place where the culture hero Nambirrirrma set down on the island after having visited it with an Aborigine the previous year. Nambirrirrma had incarnated and reconfirmed the Law to the local Aborigines. He then married, had a child, and was buried in the very place at which he had originally incarnated. I was walking along the beach feeling very frustrated with my loss of direction when I turned and looked out toward the bay. All of a sudden the Bay took on the Form of a horseshoe—a perfectly symmetrical, illuminated horseshoe—over and above the water itself. After that impression subsided, I turned 180 degrees and walked inland, arriving almost immediately at the site of his incarnation. He had landed at a point of perfect symmetry (or at least a point of perfect symmetry was where the Aborigines had located his landing).

Aborigines would have some difficulty accepting the Hindu notion of Brahman as a Creator, less difficulty with the notion of Brahmana as a creative principle of the universe, and no difficulty understanding how an image could embody a prototypical spirit. The idea of hierarchical stages of reincarnation to be climbed by making merit would be foreign to them, though some Aborigines believe that one has to proceed through all the stages of the life-cycle before proceeding on to the spirit world. If he or she does not, they come back in bodily form until they do.

Manali

As we made our way from the Pangi Valley to Shansha, Tande, and Keylong the now-familiar Hindu road shrines began to give way to *chorten* and *mane*, indicating that we were entering a Buddhist sphere of influence. *Chorten* are small pagoda-like Buddhist shrines containing a scroll on which is written a *mantra* or sacred utterance repeated hundreds or thousands of times. *Chorten* are usually constructed on the outskirts of a village or near a *gompa* or monastery in order to ward off evil spirits. *Mane* are walled piles of sacred stones on which are carved or painted *mantras*. Travelers deposit the stones there for good luck on their journey, or if they have recently had a child or a good crop. Some of the walls extend for as long as three kilometers. To steal a stone from one of these walls, as some tourists do, is to occasion the death of someone close to you.

Manali, for us, was a place to recover from what had been a grueling journey over the Pass and through the valley. The place was much frequented by Indian tourists, and it had all the appropriate trappings. But it was also home to a group of Tibetan refugees in exile whose monks operated Gadhan

Thekchhok Ling monastery and Himachal Nyinmapa temple.

Sakyamuni, Gautama, Siddhartha, the Buddha, or Enlightened One, was born in northeast India about 560 B.C.E. and died about 480 B.C.E. Son of royalty he renounced his titles and family ties and set out in search of enlightenment, rejecting the path of extreme indulgence or pleasure and of extreme asceticism or pain, finding it instead in the middle path of moderation, and quiet, detached, contemplation. Sakyamuni taught until his death, and a hundred or so years later his sayings and teachings were compiled into the Pali and Sanskrit Canons. The Canons are made up of the *Sutras* or sayings of the Buddha, the *Vinaya* or monastic laws and the *Auhidharma* or spiritual laws. The Buddhist path is not to God or to the gods because there is no God or gods. But there is a Way out of the misery of this world to a state of Enlightenment and, ultimately, non-being.

Buddhism holds Four Noble Truths: that there is suffering in the world, that suffering has its origins in desire, that there is a cessation to suffering, and that there is a Path leading to the cessation of suffering. The path or Way (*Marg*) has three stages: *Svarga-marga* where one is on the Way but is still held back by desire; *Phyanaloka-marga*, the eight stages by which one rises above the phenomenal world of forms (*Rupadhata*) and the world of the absence of forms (*Arupadhata*); and *Nirvana-marg*, a state beyond description. At the eighth stage of *Phyanaloka* one reaches *Bhavagra* or the Summit where even the desire to reach that state is absent. It is at this point that one passes into *Nirvana*, non-being.

The Way is a combination of morality (*sila*), wisdom (*prajina*) and concentration (*samadhi*). It consists of right faith, right resolve, right speech, right action, right living, right effort, right thought, and right concentration. Concentration is the Way to 'rightness.' It is a means of so enlarging one's consciousness that it transcends the boundary of ego and consciousness and, in effect, dissolves them. Both *samadhi* and *yoga* as methods of concentration predate Buddhism in the Indian tradition but were given a different focus by Buddhism. In Buddhism the object was no longer to achieve union with or understanding of Brahman. Through concentrating on the image of Buddha, Buddha quality or any auspicious thing (a lotus) the object is to enter a state of trance in which there is neither perception nor non-perception but only non-being—including the non-being (soul-less-ness) of oneself.

Tibetan Tantric Buddhist deities, sometimes mistakenly called gods, are not images of spiritually constituted individuals as they are in Hinduism, but are rather bundles of qualities representing the various kinds of *dharma* leading to Buddhahood. The core deity is the Buddha, not as Gautama the man, but as a three Divine Bodies representing Truth, Glory, and Incarnation. In concentrating on images of these qualities in the proper fashion the supplicant realizes these qualities in him or herself. The Buddha as a historical person is of no interest to Buddhists. It is what he represents that counts.

Prayer, then, cannot be petitionary for there is no one to whom a petition can be addressed. Prayer is rather a means to furthering the devotees' way along the path.

On entering a temple or shrine the supplicant makes obeisance before the image of a Buddha-quality with toes, elbow, and head—and sometimes the breast—simultaneously touching the ground so that he or she prostrates or humbles him or herself before the altar. Though there are no sacrifices in Buddhism, there are offerings, both material and mental, consecrating the five senses to the attainment of enlightenment. On the material side, incense, silk, flowers, fruit, and even money may be offered; and on the mental side, comprehensions of self and the universe.

In Buddhism the person cannot be loved for him or herself because there is no real self to be loved. The object is to dissolve self into non-being. Love and compassion, though, are a 'negative' consequence of detachment (identity with others seems to be an intrinsic aspect of detachment from self). From this negative detachment six positive, if temporal, Paramitas or Virtues flow: *dana*, giving; *ciba*, morality; *ksanti*, patience; *virya*, energy; *samadhi*, ecstasy; and *prajina*, wisdom.

It could be said that Buddha speculated on the Void, not love, but in the process discovered love; whereas Jesus speculated on love, not the void, and in the process discovered the Void.

For those Buddhists who wish to pursue Enlightenment as a vocation there is the monastery or Sangha. Buddhist monks, like the Trappists, generally follow the path of poverty, chastity, and renunciation but, unlike the Trappists, generally do not perform manual labor but subsist on offerings (though some Buddhist orders do permit monks to marry and work).

Tibetan Buddhism forms part of the Mahayana Buddhist tradition which emerged in north India from 100 to 150 C.E. holding that some truths remained implicit in the Buddha's teachings which it was their task to discover and explicate (as distinct from the Hinayana tradition which was more literal in outlook). The Mahayana school established Buddhology as a field of studies, developed the doctrine of the Bodhisattva or the continuing reincarnation of Buddha or his qualities and speculated further on the notion of Emptiness (whether or not it could be described) and the Unlimited (the possibility of boundless compassion).

On the morning of July 1st I rose at dawn and made my way from our rest house in Manali to the Nyinmapa temple on the other side of town, hoping to catch the monks at morning prayer. I arrived at the front door, took off my shoes, rang the bell, turned the prayer wheel to my right and stepped inside. There before and above me was an enormous golden statue of Buddha-form. Below the statue was an altar and seated on a mat to my right, facing across the altar was a solitary monk holding a cymbal in one hand, a drumstick in the other, chanting *mantras*. I thought I had interrupted something and turned as if to leave. The monk raised his head and held me with his eyes, bidding me to sit down without speaking and without losing a beat in the rhythm of his chanting. I bowed before the altar and sat down on the mat opposite him.

The monk was chanting a sacred *mantra* in Tibetan. The chanting of *mantras* runs deep in the Hindu tradition as well as in the Buddhist. Mantras harmonize the inner consciousness with whatever it is the *mantra* symbolizes or represents whether this be a sacred text, a deity, or the powers of the cosmos. The *mantra* or utterance itself, though, is form rather than content and many of them, like OM, are meaningless in a linguistic sense. OM, for instance, is the *nada* or original soundform of *brahmana* before the creation of the universe. It is a generalized symbol for all possible sounds.

Fritz Staal in his seminal paper on "Vedic Mantras" likens *mantras* to music and posits that their power lies in the repetition, inversion, counterpoint, and interpolation of sacred elements rather than in the meaning of the sacred elements themselves. Correct recitation is all-important with particular attention paid to loudness, pitch, and pace.

One of the explicit functions of *mantras* is to cleanse and purify the temple sanctuary of negative or evil elements and transform it into a sacred space. Because it has a foot in two dimensions of existence—the phenomenal and the transcendent—recitation is also a means of 'animating' the deity or object of contemplation. But another function of the *mantra* is to cleanse the performer of "obscuring phenomena," enabling him or her to see the essential nature of the deity or the object of contemplation. In short, *mantras* both effect 'release' and reveal truth.

I did not understand the meaning of the *mantra* that the monk seated opposite me was chanting. But given the nature of *mantras* it did not matter. I could participate in the form regardless. What I did was simply relax as much as possible and let the chanting enfold me and permeate my being. I'm not sure how long I remained seated there—it could have been half-an-hour, it could have been an hour. The effect was mesmerizing. The chanting proceeded slowly and deliberately, gradually quickening in tempo. As it did I began to lose awareness of my surroundings and focus more and more on the visage of the monk. I began to feel very peaceful and at ease, almost like I was floating. Then, abruptly, the chanting stopped. The monk rose and left. I followed, hoping to catch him outside and express my gratitude. But he was gone.

Ranikot

During the course of our trek through north India we happened upon a group of Muslim Gujar nomads in the mountains at Ranikot just before we crossed the Sach Pass into the Pangi Valley. Two of them accompanied us safely over the Pass and I became good friends with one of them, Abdul Hamid Khan. He invited me to return to India the following summer and spend some time with him at Ranikot. The Gujar are one of India's Scheduled Tribes occupying the northern part of the state of Himachal-Pradesh and neighboring Jammu-Kashmir. Their tradition holds that they were converted to the Sunni sect of Islam during the reign of the Mughul ruler Aurangzeb (1658-1707). They had been part of a Sythian migration into north India about 100 B.C.E. and had integrated into the local Hindu culture. At the time of their conversion they were being pushed westward into the mountains by the Mughul invaders.

Today the Gujur of Himachal-Pradesh lead a semi-nomadic existence moving from the Punjabi plain in the winter to the mountains in the summer with their cattle. Each Gujar *gotra* or 'clan' has an eternal homeland (*dabar-rda*) on the plain associated with its conversion and an hereditary pastureland or ridge (*dhar*) in the mountains where it grazes its cattle. In the mountains the Gujar have formed a symbiotic relationship with the 'tribal' Hindu Gaddi people who cultivate the lower slopes and provide the Gujar with maize and pulse in return for dairy products. The two peoples do not intermarry unless one partner converts to the faith of the other, which is rare.

On principle the Gujar are non-violent and eat little or no meat—certainly no beef—out of respect, they say, for the Hindus (though I sensed an element of self-preservation in this). Their religion is a modified form of Islam, modified I take it by the persistence of features present prior to their conversion. The theological basis of their passivism is quite simple: "Allah could not possibly sanction violence against his own children." What matter if one prays in a Muslim mosque, a Hindu temple, a Buddhist *gompa*, or a Christian church? All lead to the same source. The Gujar believe that when a person dies his or her spirit does not go to God but remains in the mountains. They return to the mountains each year not just to graze their cattle but "because that's where our fathers' and mothers' spirits are." The Gujar also believe that the water and trees contain spirits.

The Gujar pray in the prescribed Muslim manner, the more devout five times a day, the less two, at sunrise and in the evening. The Quoran prescribes morning and evening prayers, tradition decrees private prayers during the night. The tradition of five was set at Mohammed's ascension (632 A.D.) by the angel Gabriel, also the mediator through which the Heavenly Book containing the speech of God was read to Mohammed over a twenty year period. The word Quoran means "something to be recited," namely the 114 chapters or *surahs* that Mohammed wrote down. The revelation to Mohammed did not exhaust the contents of the Heavenly Book, though it was regarded as the most complete revelation to date after the Hebrew prophets and Jesus. Interestingly, the revelation came to Mohammed in a form resembling the ringing of a loud, clear bell. This perhaps explains why the Quoran is chanted rather than spoken or sung. Chanting is somewhere between speech and music.

Islam means submission—to the will of God. God is master, humankind his servant. God's grace is bestowed on those who serve God, do good works, pray, and give alms. Prayer is an essential religious duty and is referred to variously in the Quoran as *salat* (inclination), *du'a* (appeal), *dhrkr* (remembering), *tasbih* (exaltation), *inabah* (returning) and *tabattul* (attachment). Prayer is to express thanks for benefits received, a supplication for more favors and fewer misfortunes, to ask pardon for the past and guidance for the future, and it is an expression of submission. *Ibadah* or worship is from the root *abd* which means slave.

Prayer may be undertaken alone or with others in a mosque under the direction of an *imam* or person well-versed in scripture with the supplicant seated on a mat with the head covered, facing toward the Ka'bah at Mecca.

Prayer begins with ablutions where the supplicant washes his face, hands, and arms to the elbows; head, ears, and feet to the ankles. At each stage of prayer a recitation is made beginning with, "Praise be to God who has made water pure and purifying." The supplicant asks God to brighten their face, employ them in good deeds, teach useful knowledge, enable them to listen to his word and the word of his messenger, and set their feet on the path. Prayer consists of a number of 'bowings' each in seven movements with accompanying recitations. The first movement of the first bowing is recitation of the phrase 'Allahuakbar,' "God is most great" with the hands open on each side of the face, then comes a recitation of Fatihaha or the opening *surah* of the Quoran while standing upright. The supplicant then bows from the hips, straightens up, and following this glides to the knees and performs a first prostration with face to the ground. Then the supplicant sits back on the haunches followed by a second prostration. The second and subsequent bowings begin with the second movement and proceed likewise. After each pair of bowings and at the conclusion of the prayer-sequence, the supplicant recites the *shada* or profession of faith. With these repetitions the supplicant passes into the heavenly atmosphere and enters the presence of God whom he or she salutes, receiving in turn an answer to their greetings.

The first morning I arose at Ranikot I discovered Abdul's brother, Sakhi, seated on his mat on a stone platform in front of the hut facing west and chanting from the Quoran following his morning prayers. Thereafter I joined him in my own version of praying—concentration on the form of the landscape in order to empty myself of presuppositions and preoccupations and open myself to whatever the day would bring. Though Sakhi never questioned me, Abdul did. To him I wasn't praying. I wasn't uttering speech sounds. During prayer, he said, the spirit of the words flies to God, and he sends angels down to give one spiritual strength for the day. No words, no communication.

One morning as Sakhi was chanting and I was 'emptying,' suddenly the form of his chant coincided with a form with which I was already well familiar—a section of the sacred *mardaiyain* song cycle I had recorded amongst the Aborigines of the Groote Eylandt area in 1969. The coincidence was unmistakable, a kind of musical *deja vu*. Somehow at the level of sound-form the two traditions—the Muslim and the Aboriginal—intersected. Circumstantial or the effect of Macassan contact with Muslim Indonesia in the pre-European past? I wasn't sure.

Aborigines would have difficulty not only with the Muslim idea of petitioning God but also with the notion of God Himself (or Herself, or Itself for that matter). Anything, whether empirical or spiritual, that is writ in the singular and is autonomous without qualification is an anathema to Aboriginal people. But they would have no trouble understanding rites of purification before sacred chanting (to them a realization of Form over content), nor understanding the function of chanting itself. Nor would they find puzzling the Gujar notion that the spirits of the dead returned to their homes in the mountains to join their ancestors—though orthodox Muslims certainly would.

Conclusion

In his paper on *mantras*, Fritz Staal likens Agnicayana Hindu mantra-chanting to an aria in a Bach oratorio. Both employ the forms of theme and variation, inversion, interpolation, and counterpoint. Bach's music represents the culmination of a polyphonic tradition in European music which originated in mediaeval plainsong and Gregorian chant. Australian Aboriginal music is polyphonic. In mortuary songs I recorded over twenty years ago on Groote Eylandt I hear inversion, interpolation, and counterpoint (epitomized by Bach's "Art of the fugue"). In Aboriginal sacred songs connected with *mardaiya:n* I hear correspondences with Muslim chanting. Balinese *gamelan* music, like Aboriginal mortuary music, is arranged into a set of separate but interlocking parts (*kotekan*).

Perhaps it is on the level of music and musical form—and this level only—that there is any real correspondence in the diverse religious traditions considered here. In each tradition at least some praying involves a process or reaching out, and/or in reaching through music. My own experience is that music helps to dissolve the self of its 'contents,' thereby opening the senses up to more acute levels of awareness. The end reached may be secondary—whether 'God,' 'non-being,' or "one's Self on other side."

The principal thing may be that at least one form of prayer in each tradition does provide a common point of reference—an ecumenical moment if you will—for a comparison of what seems incompatible from the point of view of dogma. To proceed from this moment is to assume an articulation rather than the disarticulation of traditions, as is the case if one proceeds with a comparison from the vantage point of 'content' or dogma. Perhaps this point of articulation is the be-all and end-all. Perhaps in the inversions, counterpoints, interpolations, and variations that inform this moment we can discover new bases for articulating the various ends perceived, and the faiths predicated on them. Perhaps we will discover differences of content that mutually reinforce rather than confront one another.

Perhaps the world's oldest continuing religious tradition, in Australia, has much to contribute to this enterprise.

Chapter Five

Theological Guidance About Prayer

The central place that prayer has in any religion should be enough justification for an examination of the psychological factors surrounding it. While it is said that psychologists interested in the study of religion have disregarded prayer (e.g. Finney and Malony, 1985), the Appendix shows that that is hardly true, although recent general psychologies of religion (e.g. Spilka, Hood, and Gorsuch, 1985, but not Wulff, 1991) deal with prayer only in passing, and usually restrict their discussion to petitionary or intercessory prayer. So the accepted framework for this area of work is not as extensive as that used by Appleton (1985) for his ecumenical collection of prayers, which shows "the astonishing variety of Christian personal and occasional prayers" (p. 51). It is structured on the phrases of the Lord's Prayer, each being identified with specific psychological attitudes:

"Our Father": Dependence
"Who art in Heaven": Affirmation
"Hallowed be Thy Name": Blessing and thanksgiving
"Thy Kingdom come": Longing; Seeking; Doing; Serving; Peace
"Thy Will be done": Dedication; Obedience
"As it is in Heaven": Guidance; Acceptance
"Give us this day": Daily Graces
"Forgive us our trespasses": Penitence
"As we forgive": Relationships
"Lead us not into temptation": Right living
"Deliver us from evil": Protection; Suffering; Compassion
"For Thine is the Kingdom": Devotion; Contemplation
"For ever and ever": Death and eternity

Innumerable sources within and beyond Christian traditions help to define other stances from which a psychology of prayer might be written. Appleton notes, however, that since "Eastern religions emphasize meditation, whether

83

of mind or silent stillness" (p. 269) there is a smaller body of prayers there from which to identify its models. The problems of whether other traditions pray in relation to "our God" or to a generic "Transcendent Reality," with whom one hopes to "enter into a loving communion," and whether that is a "Supreme Absolute" or a figment of imagination cannot be solved here, since that also involves an attitudinal construction. I must therefore side with Laplace, the French astronomer who, when asked by Napoleon why he had not mentioned the Creator in his large book on the universe, said, "I have no need for this hypothesis" (Sills and Merton, 1991, p. 124).

Against that stance are the religious psychologists who are more likely to be directly concerned with the "evidential force" of prayer and its effects, than are psychologists of religion who work within psychological assumptions, and not with a specific religious or theological perspective. Neither of those orientations seems to have been directly concerned with whether, or how it is possible to persuade God to give us what we want when that ought to be known by an omniscient being, or the nature of a God whose will might be influenced by *our* requests. Resolving those problems reflects attitudes embedded in the language that is used and psychological issues about the dissonances or the logic of religious belief, as well as doctrines about the silence of God (cf Carse, 1985) and readings of Jesus' statement, "Ask and you shall receive." To experience prayerful guidance, salvation, inspiration, or resignation involves attitudes that are as patent as the doubt or uncertainty about whether one is likely to encounter God or only oneself in prayer (Godin, 1985, p. 228), and the ways in which spontaneous expressions of religiousness might differ from those prescribed by specific traditions.

A psychological perspective

Definitions are as crucial here as anywhere and Godin argues (on page 23f) that the concept of Providence "generalizes the animist reaction attributing intentions (sometimes punitive, sometimes protective or benevolent) to certain inexplicable or fortuitous happenings" and blocks (or replaces) the "category of chance" when assigned to "happenings that are the product neither of blind determinism (known or knowable through science) nor of intentional decisions (free or not)." Michotte (1946) argued that to identify causality is a 'natural' cognitive process, and Heider's (1958) analysis of interpersonal behavior applied that principle to personal relationships, when we attribute a deliberate intentionality to the actions (or causes) that help to make the world controllable, at least among those with a sense of their own competence, for example. This effect is increased by accepting that we are causal agents and not pawns on an unpredictable cosmic chess board.

Kelley's (1971) analysis of these causal schemata relies on the extent to which the implicit matrices that link causes with effects are shaped by past reactions and experiences, and by the well-defined beliefs that structure ambiguous or minimal information. While the social-psychological mainstream in attribution theory has given some attention to religious explanations, the difference between internal and external events is crucial for analyses of religion (Lalljee et al, 1990; Furnham and Brown, 1992). Spilka, Hood, and Gorsuch (1985) used those concepts as the theoretical hinge in their account of religion, applying it to a range of interpretive options from God's mercy and justice to incorrect rituals and ineffective prayers, distinguishing between the attributor, events, and their contexts. They suggest that the popular theories of prayer account differently for the successes and failures of others' prayers and that individuals rely on their own experiences to establish the plausibility of their prayers, or on the support and precedents set by the classical accounts, especially of mystics and visionaries.

In writing of *The Parson in Sacraments* in the seventeenth century, George Herbert admonished that prayer should be said "with great devotion," implying an attitude of careful self-presentation. That analysis can be contrasted against the religious psychology of prayer in Myers and Jeeves' (1987) chapter on *Superstition and Prayer*, in which they note that we are inclined to "perceive relationships where none exist, perceive causal convictions amongst events that are only coincidentally correlated, and believe that we are controlling events that we are not" (p. 89). They add to that list, "finding order in random events," interpreting them through preconceptions, recalling instances that confirm rather than disconfirm beliefs and neglect statistical 'realities.' These principles led them to note the 'temptation' that prayers can change the course of events and that warnings about false prayer come more often "from believers than from skeptics" (p. 90). They also advocate moving away from a "preconception with ourselves and towards God-focused prayers . . . of adoration, praise, confession, thanksgiving, dedication, and meditation, as well as prayers of petition." They criticize exaggerated claims and requests for "fair weather for Battle" because a superstitious magic might be involved there.

In resolving those problems they refer to the biblical perspective on God and "a hope that out of defeat and suffering we, like Jesus, may gain new life" (p. 91). They reject tests of the efficacy of prayer, citing C.S. Lewis who noted that the "impossibility of empirical proof is a spiritual necessity" to avoid corruption, since "all events without exception are *answers* to prayer in the sense that whether they are grantings or refusals the prayers of all concerned and their needs have all been taken into account." Myers and Jeeves note, however, that some believers think that if the thing prayed for happens, it is proof that prayer works, and if it doesn't that it is God's will, while non-believers attribute apparently successful prayer to natural causes. If it fails, it is further "proof that petitionary prayers don't work" (p. 93). They do not cite any evidence which shows how common such prototypical solutions might be, unless they believe that such confirmation is irrelevant.

Tversky and Kahneman (1974) similarly stress that "many decisions are based on beliefs concerning the likelihood of uncertain events," and that we rely on "a limited number of heuristic principles which reduce the complex task of assessing probabilities and predicting values to simpler judgmental operations." They also note that "In general, these heuristics are quite useful, but sometimes they lead to severe and systematic errors." The heuristics they identify include representativeness and insensitivity to the prior probability of outcomes, accepting a small sample size, misconceptions of the rules of chance, insensitivity to predictability and the illusion of validity. The last of these has particular relevance to judging people, since we are likely to "express great confidence in the prediction that a person is a librarian when given a description of his personality which matches the stereotype of librarians, even if the description is scanty, unreliable, or outdated." A similar heuristic assigns feminine characteristics more readily to someone who is said to be 'religious' than to a person described as 'not religious' (Gaston and Brown, 1992), which could be an example of the "availability heuristic," since a greater proportion of women than men are involved in religious activities, and are thought likely to pray.

A crucial feature of Tversky and Kahneman's argument is its reliance on cognitive heuristics or habits and not on motivational effects like wishful thinking or distorted judgements about the payoffs or penalties that common sense has expected to sustain (or drive) many prayers. As they put it, "A person bets on team A rather than on team B because he *believes* that team A is more likely to win; he does not infer this belief from his betting preference." Parallel intentions or expectations about prayers can over-interpret their effects, although I have only casual observation to support that conclusion, which is of course what most people rely on in forming their attitudes to prayer and the wisdom of its practice. Those who pray regularly must, however, resolve these problems to their own satisfaction and might become more committed in their understanding and practice if they can find (or prove?) that their prayers succeed. This could be as self-fulfilling (Merton, 1948) as Oskamp's (1965) conclusion from a study of the confidence of clinicians in their own judgements in which he questioned the "evidence for the validity of clinical judgement in diagnosing or predicting human behavior."

George Herbert on prayer
Advice about the prerequisites for prayer include George Herbert's (1652) stringent cautions to a country parson.

> The country parson, when he is to read divine services, composeth himself to all possible reverence, lifting up his heart and hands and eyes, and using all other gestures which may express a hearty and unfeigned devotion. This he doth, first, as being truly touched and amazed with the Majesty of God, before whom he then presents himself; yet not as himself alone, but as presenting with himself the whole congregation, whose sins he then bears, and brings with his own to the heavenly altar to be bathed and washed in the sacred laver of Christ's blood. Secondly, as this is the true reason of his inward fear, so he is content to express this outwardly to the utmost of his power; that being first affected himself, he may affect

also his people, knowing that no sermon moves them so much to a reverence, which they forget again, when they come to pray, as a devout believer in the very act of praying. Accordingly his voice is humble, his words treatable and slow; yet not so slow neither, as to let the fervency of the supplicant hang and die between speaking, but with a grave liveliness, between fear and zeal, pausing yet pressing, he performs his duty.

Besides his example, he having often instructed his people how to carry themselves in divine service, exacts of them all possible reverence, by no means enduring either talking, or sleeping, or gazing, or leaning, or half-kneeling, or any undutiful behavior in them, but causing them, when they sit, or stand, or kneel, to do all in a straight and steady posture, as attending to what is done in the church, and everyone, man and child, answering aloud both Amen, and all other answers which are on the clerk's and people's part to answer; which answers also are to be done not in a huddling or slubbering fashion, gaping, or scratching the head, or spitting even in the midst of their answer, but gently and plausibly, thinking what they say; so that while they answer, *As it was in the beginning*, etc. they meditate as they speak, that God hath ever had his people that have glorified him as well as now, and that he shall have so forever. And the like in other answers. This is that which the Apostle calls a reasonable service, Rom. 12., when we speak not as parrots, without reason, or offer up such sacrifices as they did of old, which was of beasts devoid of reason; but when we use our reason, and apply our powers to the service of him that gives them.

An important feature of prayer is the different ways in which it can be interpreted (and endangered), depending on what is emphasized, the tradition within which it is understood, and the assumptions about that. Each of these factors limits the generality of whatever conclusions might be drawn. Furthermore, to modify Blaise Pascal's wager, should we accept the possibility of influencing the future by prayer, or prepare ourselves for death and other inevitable consequences of whatever will happen? There can be no sound test of those expectations, except within the context of faith itself, and with reference to Christian doctrine or practice. Although there are empirical questions about beliefs in the efficacy of prayer, they are all necessarily circumscribed by uncertainties that are only resolved by the "eye of faith." Prayer is not like the evolution of a scientific hypothesis which is expected to be independent of subjective probabilities and the closure that is demanded, or upset by surprising or unexpected events over which we have little control. We must therefore adapt to events over which we have no control, perhaps with the help of prayer. That we are uncertain about a fact expresses a different state of mind from uncertainty about the existence of God, for which we are expected to rely on evidence, our own judgement, or on a consensus that entails social desirability or deference to some agreed 'truths.'

A test proposed in 1872-73

Because of a lack of systematic data about these questions, my arguments are more principled than I had hoped would be possible. It is, however, important to identify the questions that should be asked, despite the absence of criteria by which to adjudicate about them in specific cases, or about general beliefs and opinions, and other challenges to prayer. Yet a "prayer test" was proposed in 1872-73 (Brush, 1974) in an attempt to resolve the debate between science and religion by establishing whether prayer might help particular people to recover from sickness. That test was, however, never carried out because of crusading debates about its propriety and how it should be done. The issue therefore turned towards 'purifying' the belief in prayer of any dependence on 'superstition,' granted an acceptance in the mid-nineteenth century of a molecular-kinetic theory of matter, and uncertainty about what would count as an answer to prayer, whether group prayer would be better than individual prayers, whether God might refuse to accept all the patients who would actually be prayed for in that study, and whether prayer should aim to build spiritual rather than physical strength. An important conclusion from this debate itself was the difficulty in finding persuasive evidence that prayer would have *any* physical effects, beyond principled moral questions about the propriety of such tests, as opposed to an expectation of their success.

Brummer (1984) identified other questions that an empirical test of the efficacy of prayer must confront, including whether it should be understood as a form of meditative therapy performed on oneself, whether any petition presupposes an anthropomorphic or a persuadable God, why the questions about it focus on petitionary prayer anyway, and whether prayer is "a perpetual exercise of faith" (as Calvin put it), or defines a relationship between 'man' and God in which there may be reciprocal rights.

Myers and Jeeves (1987, p. 94f) tried to resolve (and avoid) those questions by favoring prayers that express praise and thanksgiving for God's infinite goodness (whether as resignation or dissonance resolution). They accepted the Lord's Prayer as a model because it makes no attempt to manipulate God and expresses a mystical relationship in which *we* can be changed. Prayer could then produce changes when we surrender to it as a means of grace. In that view, prayer is inherent to the flow of life and, as Gordon Allport might have said, "functionally autonomous." In their analysis, the goal of prayer could be to "seek inward peace and the strength to live as God's people" (Myers and Jeeves, p. 96), with the psychological consequences of its religious character supported by tradition, example, and its specific forms or models on which prayer is based.

One doctrinal solution

A more detailed theological perspective that supports a psychological analysis of prayer can be found in the *Report of the Doctrine Commission* of the Church of England (1987), entitled *We Believe in God*. It begins by stressing the Trinitarian nature of Christianity, which psychological studies of God have not tried to defend, since 'God' typically refers to the 'Father above' (as in 2 Corinthians 13:14). Although a doctrine of the Trinity was enunciated by the end of the fourth century, when they are asked to describe 'God' it is common for people now to mention only the Father, accepting a common usage rather than necessarily supporting the psychological critiques of 'religion' as a projection of parental images. Despite that, formal Christian prayers end by making reference to "the grace of the Lord Jesus Christ and the love of God and the fellowship of the Holy Spirit." Although Pentecostal traditions accept contact with the Spirit as an experience of God with (or within) us, as the Doctrine Commission puts it, "a good deal of modern Western theology disposes people towards the undifferentiated monotheism that has been detected in twentieth-century Christianity" (p.107) so that the assertion that the Trinity is not "verifiable through religious experience" (referring to Schleiermacher) "calls for careful enquiry" (ibid.).

If one asks about the nature of an experience of God in prayer, the Doctrine Commission stresses the received and "cherished concepts of prayer that derive from the Bible, liturgy, and tradition," and the "competing interpretations" of contemplative practices. To identify them as forms of prayer might entail "waiting on God," with its "strange lack of obvious content," except for the relationship of absolute dependence that Schleiermacher identified as the basic religious experience (ibid., p.108), which Proudfoot (1985) interpreted as "the activity of another." Whether or not this involves a dissociation is inevitably a vexed question, captured by the idea that we are being "prayed in," and "do not know how to pray as we ought" (Romans 8:26).

Classical statements about coming to prayer "empty-handed, aware of weaknesses," inarticulate, and in fear and trembling convey a similar attitude of dependence that has been misunderstood, and criticized on rather psychological grounds by those with 'muscular' attitudes to life. This is captured theologically by the Holy Spirit, not as a separate person but mysteriously in a "divine response to a divine self-gift in which the one who prays is caught up and thereby transformed (see again Romans 8:9-27, 1 Corinthians 2:9-16)" (p.108). Wittgenstein spoke of keeping silence about that of which we cannnot speak and, we could add, of what we do not know or do not have the language to describe.

But the pervasive drive toward reductionism aligns unknown or unusual concepts with whatever is familiar—including psychological assumptions that become theological when those who pray find that the Spirit leads them to the "true mystery and richness of the Son" (p.108). The Doctrine Commission therefore stresses the "experience of participation in a divine dialogue as an experience of God, who actively and always wills to be amongst us" (p.109). That experience is different from the sense of dependence that calls for help in the depths of despair and need, and makes petitionary prayer its prototypical form, while recognizing that we would be shaped differently if we were to rely on other forms of prayer.

While some believe that if there is no one 'there' to pray to, all forms of prayer are meaningless, unless the experience of prayer is described in terms of God having deserted us. The Commission's Report emphasizes that this causes "disturbance, deep uneasiness, the highlighting of sin, and even the fear of insanity" (p.109). Such "dark nights" are crucial, despite their implied egocentricity which can be changed by the perseverance that breaks 'through' our individualism into corporate (sic) and social prayer as members of the "body of Christ." That form of justification is quite different from everyday conceptions of what prayer entails, and escapes the convention that prayer is immediate and directly authenticated. We should therefore be prepared to explore the attitudes that support prayer and clarify when it is directed to the self, or to an Other (or just another), or becomes a cry from the 'heart' or the mind.

Prayer is surrounded by controversy, being defended (and attacked) by passionate claims, demands, and counter-disclosures. The regular practice of prayer is not necessarily pious, since a requirement to pray is imposed on those who have been baptized, which can be met by conforming without a commitment beyond accepting "the flow of the eucharistic action" (p. 114). While many find it hard to describe their responses to nature, to other people, or to God without cliches, accepted descriptions of those experiences can obscure doubts and scruples.

But how do people begin their prayers? The Doctrine Commission says that most do it "in simple obedience" (p. 126). But to whom? Parents, teachers, and church leaders define that, as Francis and Brown (1991) have shown, although experiences of challenge, bewilderment, or need could suggest that prayer is a 'natural' response. One way in which children are taught to pray is explained through facile advice about saying 'sorry,' 'thank you,' and then 'please' (as the Report suggests on p. 128), and not in inarticulate silence or distress. Unanswered prayer is judged to be a more important problem than any criticism of those who do pray. That issue involves maintaining one's "religious integrity," not by being conformed or orthodox but transformed by acting "in the knowledge and love of God" (p.146) and within the "Christian experience of being," as Havel put it. This takes us back to the beginning, and our uncertainty about what (or who) God is, and where God can be found.

Prayer for the departed

The 1971 Report of the English Archbishops' Commission on Christian Doctrine therefore argued that "the basis of all prayer is a fellowship with God and one another, so that prayer is (at least in part) an expression and instrument of communion and solidarity." Nevertheless, "there must be a considerable liberty in both doctrine and practice allowed to individual consciences concerning the practice of prayer for the dead" (p.13), since the "safeguards imposed in any given circumstances belong to the realm not of theology but of pastoral expediency" (p.17). When looking at the "multiform character of prayer itself," they held that "The matter is partly (though not exclusively) semantic. At its deepest level, and always in one of its aspects, prayer is

God-directed, and therefore adoration, worship, love, and humility are appropriate. But prayer also includes the wider business of the articulation before God of our human anxieties, hopes, and desires, which form the "new material of petition and intercession" (p.17).

The issues they examined about prayer for the dead apply to other petitionary prayers in which God is asked to do things that might have already been determined. So prayer might have no evident external effects unless asking God to change 'his' mind assumes that without our prayer God will not act or that there could be no outcome unless we intervened. In those terms it may be impossible to petition effectively without a detailed knowledge of specific situations and the desirable changes (p. 18).

These questions can themselves imply the wrong logic, reducing God's action to our own scale. Whatever the 'correct' solution might be, these problems form barriers that prayers must cross, if they are to be plausible for at least *some* people, and it can be hard to distinguish those who accept any prayer with reservations from those who reject it. Identifying these groups is a phenomenological task avoided by those who speak of the necessity or advantages of prayer and leave aside its difficulties. Intercessory prayers for the dead focus these problems acutely, unless such prayers can only express our thoughts, wishes, and hopes about others, or a 'simple' and trustful confidence in God's care and 'mercy' because "all Christian prayer aims at being prayer that God's will may be done" (p. 19).

The Archbishop's Commission argued for the 'unworthiness' of any cult or prayer that compromises the reality of "the love of Christ and the activity of the Spirit" (p.21). They excluded non-Christian prayers from that argument and noted that prayers for the dead have in the past had "pernicious moral consequences in that they minimize Christ's victory and undermine Christian assurance" (p. 22).

These problems involve the conflict between a *knowledge* of God that expresses subjective feelings, or confidence about the (objective) effects of prayer. Because of the absence of evidence, some agnosticism is needed there since, as the Commission said, the future life has been described as "an unknown world with a well-known inhabitant" (p. 23), presenting us with a mystery rather than a problem. It is impossible to know what effects intercessory prayer might achieve, except through faith, and the Commission agreed that no defense of intercession is a substitute for action, especially if prayer is based entirely on promise.

A 'natural' basis for prayers for the dead was, however, attested by Reginald Heber (1783-1826), a Bishop of Calcutta who, in correspondence with Frances Williams Wynn, wrote that "Few persons, I believe, have lost a loved object, more particularly by *sudden* death, without feeling an earnest desire to commend them in their prayers to God's mercy, and a sort of instinctive impression that such devotions might still be serviceable to them." Heber went on to note that prejudices surround any prayer, citing "The Roman Catholics, (who) by their doctrines of hired masses for the dead, and by their unwarranted and melancholy notion of a purgatory to which the good are liable, have prejudiced the great number of Protestants against this opinion." Yet he remained optimistic, since such prayers "*May*, and I hope *will*, be of service to them" (quoted by Legge, 1914, p. 332). Prayer might therefore be conditional and perhaps reflexive.

Pusey put it more strongly: "We have no doubt that we *may* pray," deferring to the communion of saints and the Eucharistic prayer which asks that "by the merits and death of the son . . . and through faith in his blood, we and all thy whole Church may obtain remission of our sins." This social perspective suggests that prayers might be offered with collective rather than individual intentions. As Pusey said, "It is so odd a thought that we have for the time no more to do with those who loved us here, and whom we loved, that it must needs, on that ground alone, be false (that we should be afraid to pray), because it is so contrary to love." Such principled arguments seem more useful than looking for evidence about the specific successes of petitionary prayers.[1]

Language, prayer, and the self

The relationship between *I and Thou* (Buber, 1958) does not have to be reciprocated if a generalized Other is addressed because a personal bond is established when the speaker's 'I' or self becomes a listener's 'you.' This can occur in prayer or in a conversation with oneself, with one's conscience, or when preparing for a later interaction with another, when a grammatical 'subject' is found in the discourse from which a subjective I is constituted. It then acquires a meaning beyond the speaker's own specific utterances, so that the language supports its own reality.

While performative utterances can influence our immediate social reality, they transcend it by being embedded in talk that refers back (anaphastically) to what has already happened (which Halliday describes as 'endophoric'). The language of prayer similarly moves between the past and the future, referring to an 'I' in previous utterances, with a yet to be experienced future showing a prospective 'I.' In that sense the self-other system within which prayer is cast is *open-ended* and, because prayers are not contingent they are always incomplete, since the future is never 'finished.' If one were anxious until the outcome was known, prayer might be an important way to reduce that uncertainty because of the particular structure it gives; and a good narrative is constructed to sustain suspense. Yet some find it hard to master anxiety in their everyday lives, which others seem to create deliberately. It is not clear, however, whether a closure will ever be found for prayer, unless it is existential, through a hope that offers its own solutions.

---

1. As another solution to this problem it is worth recalling that Dr. Robert Thouless (whose copy of *Prayer and the Departed* I have), an empiricist to the end, left messages in a sophisticated code with the Society for Psychical Research in London. As a specific test of the "survival of death," he had hoped to be able to communicate the key passage to decipher the codes, after his death in 1984. Despite the sophistication of his method and the reward that the Society offered, no successful 'hits' in this project have been forthcoming (Brown, 1989).

We are born into a world of words and cannot avoid them since they help to make us who we are. The language of religion invokes symbolic or constructed orders that are as potent and intangible as grammar, or as culture itself. Prayer lies within the language that expresses it and is used to describe its meanings, and we talk about prayer in ways that focus its performative features, with synonyms like meditation, concentration, 'centering,' and the sense of transcendence. While postures, gestures, and other 'attitudes' indicate when someone is praying, so do the places and customary times for prayer. But they are not good indicators of personal meanings beyond whatever has been prescribed for them, especially since postures and places can generate the attitudes they signify, although the actions of someone who is praying in conformity to prevailing social norms can also be over-interpreted. Religiousness cannot therefore be reliably identified from what is done in public.

Cupitt (1988) argued against the validity of private prayer, through an analysis that locates consciousness in the structural manipulation of signs with language its prototypic form. As he put it, "human reality is primarily outward, interactive, and communicational. It is only secondarily, and as a kind of specialized by-product, inward, mental, and soulish" (p. 88). Support for this view can be found in developmental psychology, where a child's "mental skills" in doing arithmetic, planning a course of action, or building an object are done outwardly, but from the child's own perspective. Whether these operations are judged to be egocentric depends on how the performance is interpreted by its observers and commentators.

The self in prayer

Augustinian ideas about the reality of the self being found in one's privacy, especially at prayer, have been largely replaced by the impact on us of our actual social relationships and our communication with others who are not immediately present, even if by letter, e-mail, the telephone, or only in our 'thoughts.' That a primitive form of prayer could be found there is supported by the pleas and wishes that identify (and establish) a relationship between the one who prays and the 'object' of their prayers. This is the primitive 'cry' that Godin emphasized, which comes to express the coherence of a community and helps to bind it together. If the 'public' God embodies and expresses communal or corporate values, that relationship could be rather feudal, when absolute power is given to the One who must be approached. This attitude might have been appropriate for an absolute monarch but now makes us feel embarrassed or foolish because of its extravagance, especially since Western traditions are expected to have produced a genial collegiality. Only in times of weakness or need does a traditional religious language seem appropriate (Welford, 1946).

Cupitt (1988, p. 90) identified the God he used to address in prayer as "out there," "over against me," an embodiment of everything he was committed to, "my values," super-ego, ego-ideal, reference point, "my Lord" who "made me conscious of myself," so that "I developed myself through the drama of my relation to him . . . (as) a real, a natural and a necessary personification." It is not clear how much of this Cupitt accepts when he goes on to argue for the emergence in the seventeenth century of a "modern individual-self" with the ethic of individualism (called the "protestant ethic") that was needed for the market economy and bourgeois culture developing then. Yet public prayer has remained corporate and "in the office," with its set times for reflection and meditation.

Prayers in private probably have a different status from prayers in public, because of the urgency of the requests or thanks that might be expressed there. Those unable to believe in the existence of God might accept the social benefits of corporate worship while finding private worship irrational, without examining what (or if) we need to believe before being able to offer any prayer. That our own prayer is expected to be intense and private compounds the problems of gathering information about the beliefs and attitudes that might support it, or that could establish whether prayer is simply habitual, playful, a controlled and comfortable fantasy, or an act of deluded arrogance or a path to enlightenment.

Our sense of freedom entails neither predictability and control, nor a capricious God playing dice (or hide and seek) with the universe, until we try to intervene in what we do not understand. Whether those who do pray worry about how it works or find that it gives them strength takes us towards pious questions that lie beyond psychology. So Heiler held that prayer is not 'psychological,' because of its transcendent qualities. Yet we are expected to be able to comment on our prayers. Whether the theories about prayer are inclusive or limited seems irrelevant for those who pray, perhaps being analogous to our inability to control another's understanding of what it was we wished to say. Poloma and Gallup (1991) argue that "Americans not only [have] religious experiences but that these experiences are at the heart of their relationship with God . . . as the vital link between pray-ers and the God to whom they pray" (p. 65). Their data show, for example, that "80 percent of those who were low on the prayer experience scale noted their relationship to God as being 'distant' . . . (while) only 13 percent of those who felt very close to God were low on prayer experiences" (p. 63). These experiences were, however, more common among the older evangelical females.

Poloma and Gallup (1991) also found prayer to be the most important factor in explaining why some are better able than others "to forgive those who have wronged them" (p. 102), which they use as an example of the positive effects of prayer. In terms of whether religion will comfort or challenge, they found that a more passive attitude to meditative prayer is related to a mature challenging faith, by setting "a time of intimacy with the Divine" (p. 122). That prayer does offer comfort supports its common practice, with 88 percent of Americans saying they pray to God and 76 percent accepting it as "an important part" of their daily lives (p. 3). While a major component involves "rote and ritualistic prayer" (p. 129) this can be transcended by a sense of intimacy with God that sets presence against demand. An Anglican Home Mission Society study in Australia found in a sample of 2,300

Protestants that "the chances are the more you pray the less you drink, and the less you drink the more you believe" (*Sydney Morning Herald*, 11 November 1992).

That existential problems can be resolved by prayer is captured by Coles' (1990) account of Anne, an eleven-year-old Catholic girl in a suburb of Boston, who said, "When I start praying, and when Jesus does answer, when He tells me that I've got it good, and I should stop and take it easy and try to put on a smile with people, and not turn my head away from them—that's when I'm all better, and the day seems sunny again. Rain has been pouring on my whole life—that's how I feel—a real heavy rain, and I'm wet and shaking, but then the clouds just go away, and it's warm and I can hear those words the priest says, and the ones my aunt says, and I've learned them: 'I am the light of the world; if you follow Me, you won't walk in darkness, but you'll have the light of life.' I hear that, when I hear Him, when I pray to Him as hard as I can, and I need to hear Him, and I do" (p. 87).

This account contains constructions that could be translated into psychological terms, but however we interpret it the statement "declares her membership in a confessional religious community that has extended over continents, centuries, and denominations—a community that includes children" (ibid., p. 88). This is central to the practice of prayer, and of religion itself. That it might also involve superstitious or urgent demands for material efficacy emphasizes the polymorphous ambiguity of private prayer. Whether we need a God who torments us or one whom we can get close to may be less important than the fact that 'God,' like other features of our social life, can be used.

We should look for, and expect to find, other features that can be described, but how people pray might be less important than the way they construe what they are doing. At the same time, these meanings are not independent of the attitudes, doctrines or interpretations we accept. Wherever we now look for a fixed moral order, we cannot solve existential problems more effectively than our ancestors. And why should religion not give consolation? Our lives would be impoverished if aesthetic and other creative imaginings were abandoned. Even Freud noted that, "religion has spared many an individual from a neurotic disorder" (Vergote, 1988, p. 10). Whether we are incomplete without recognizing the religious dimension is answerable only in principle, and the criteria of mental health are profoundly ambiguous (ibid., p. 16) because of the interaction there between whatever is interior to each person and their world views, which depend on indoctrination or training, and their actual environment.

Freud (1933) therefore identified the functions of religion as
    1. giving information about the origin of the universe (and of ourselves),
    2. ensuring protection and the hope of ultimate happiness (as in Pascal's wager),
    3. directing our thoughts and action by precepts laid down with authority,

4. through existential truths that depend on a constructed or wish fulfilling process, which embodies a 'psychological' truth.

The modern search for innovative techniques and models that can interpret the mechanisms by which these personal, social, and religious worlds are structured make some people restive about *any* received theories. Yet it is unclear to what extent our experience of the social world and what it conveys depends more on reality itself or institutional pressures than on what can be called to mind or imagined. Some religious people find those pressures oppressive and express their individuality in protests against them, although Bowker (1987, p. 143) noted that Christian resources can be made available "without being too dictatorial about the forms of their appropriation," even when they stress corporate rather than individual believing. But that is another way in which Buddhism differs from Christianity, because their 'enlightenment' has no content, and it is not transmitted by dogma or doctrines. Psychology is, however, constrained by its traditions, as are artists and composers. We must therefore depend on *some* content. As Stravinsky put it, "in music as in everything else, one can only build upon a resisting foundation" (quoted by Bowker, on p. 138). In reading earlier and principled work on prayer, it is essential to recognize the context within which it was produced and the extent to which its 'subjects' were themselves bound by the responses they believed they were expected to give. Despite that, William James granted the autonomy of private experiences, and von Hugel took them to be part of a wider tapestry that extends into philosophical issues like those examined in the next chapter.

Chapter Six

The Real Me is the Me at Private Prayer
A Philosophical Perspective

CHARLES CREEGAN

In religion . . . we have to give up the old Augustinian idea that the real me is the me at private prayer. My reality is first and foremost relational and linguistic. I am the sum of all my communicative interactions with other people. That being so, I can just about see how public prayer makes sense—or at least, might make sense. In expressive and symbolic ritual action and language, public prayer binds the community together in mutual support and in the affirmation of common values. In times of communal disaster and at moments of transition in life, even the most secular people in the most secularized societies still instinctively gather in the ancient way. Private prayer is more puzzling but may perhaps be viewed as a secondary derivative of and substitute for public prayer, an internalized ritual like the 'spiritual communion' sometimes practiced by Catholics.

Don Cupitt, *The New Christian Ethics*

It may be that man's talking to God can be understood in terms of the role which such talk plays in a religious community, but what of God's talking to man? It seems that one does not need to refer to a religious community in order to understand what is meant by divine speech. Is not God's communication addressed directly to the believer? Does not God speak 'to the heart'? Calling God a person seems to endorse this view. When God talks to man, we are often told, there is a 'meeting,' a 'direct confrontation.' I should not want to deny that religious believers talk in this way about their experiences. What I am asking is whether such talk is adequate as a philosophical *account of religious experience.*

D.Z. Phillips, *The Concept of Prayer*

What does it mean to speak of prayer as a private experience, a relation between the believer and God? The passage from Don Cupitt, cited above, is one of the most recent, and surely among the most radical, suggestions on this subject within philosophical theology. He argues both that it is illegitimate to speak of 'private prayer' or any private experience, and that the very idea of such experiences is pernicious. D.Z. Phillips' *The Concept of Prayer* approaches many of the same issues from the point of view of the philosophy of religion. The parallels and divergences in their approaches and conclusions provide an interesting cross-perspective on the question of prayer as a private experience.

Cupitt's project

It is important to note at the outset that the problem of prayer is not central for Cupitt (1988). His book *The New Christian Ethics* is a wide-ranging theological investigation of the status of Christian practice in light of the 'death' of the realist frame of reference for Christian belief. He begins by noting that theological realism has been gradually demythologized—certainly it has been socially relativized—since the Enlightenment. Cupitt claims that the increasing human consciousness of the social construction of reality has led to the impossibility of maintaining this realism. Given that meaning is pure social construction, theological realism is rendered a dead option—yet Christian ethics (if not other ethical systems as well) is still stated in the 'residually-theological' terms of a platonic-realist framework.

Cupitt, while he asserts that "all modern philosophies of language" agree that the world is a human creation, with the human world a communication network in and by language (ibid., p. 6), he consistently fleshes out this claim with reference to structuralist and post-structuralist ideas; indeed he remarks that French structuralism is much the most advanced tradition in carrying the ideal of 'world-as-language' to its utmost conclusions (p. 85). So he cites structuralist theories of language and meaning-creation as furnishing the description and effecting the culminating result of the process of demythologizing realism.

Structuralism insists on the social construction of meaning—that there is no reality beyond what is said in language. The Saussurian term *langue* refers to the total linguistic framework within which utterances take place. Language does not express or point to an external reality; it actually forms this reality. Different linguistic constructions thus name and hence 'create' a difference in reality.

Cupitt uses this framework to mount a general attack on the concept of private experience.

I cannot experience a thing unless I have been pre-programmed by culture to be capable of experiencing it . . . If a meaning is not already imprinted upon my constitution, it cannot become excited. There is no experience which is not the firing of a meaning, and therefore, . . . all mystical ideas about extraordinary experiences about the ineffable and about pure unconditioned awareness are dead (p. 87).

One might of course participate in a culture which has mystical ideas as part of its framework. Such ideas would merely be human constructions, with a natural history like any other concepts. But to those who claim to have private unsocialized experiences of the ineffable, Cupitt replies:

What makes it seem so important to you is just what makes it mean nothing at all to me. For, necessarily, the only common meaning is linguistic meaning. *Experience does not exist;* can you understand that? Only the public is real, and experience is not public (p. 82).

Given the death of realism and experience as its base, Christian ethics is challenged to invent a new decision-structure not dependent on them. But to do so requires rooting out the residual theological realism inherent in a host of Christian practices and beliefs, replacing this with forms tenable in the face of a self-conscious social construction. Consistent with his denials of realism as regards the external world and of private experience, Cupitt goes on to claim that the metaphysical self is a necessary casualty of this rooting out of realism, and with it the idea of internal action and thought as a locus of 'truth.' From this it follows that private prayer, construed as the ultimate metaphysical connection between the metaphysical self and the real though hidden God, is an unedifying, mistaken or perhaps even ontologically impossible practice.

In short, Cupitt's project is to consider prayer from a theological viewpoint, as one part of Christian life which needs to be changed. The framework of this task is the contemporary structuralist-influenced understanding of meaning as socially constructed and changeable.

Phillips' project

The aims that Phillips (1965) states at the beginning of *The Concept of Prayer* are somewhat different. First, he is taking prayer as the central phenomenon under discussion in his book. His contention is that investigation of the practice of prayer can lead to a better understanding of the nature of religious belief and practice in general. What believers do as they pray shows the nature of their belief

Another important difference is that Phillips approaches the problem from the direction of philosophy and from the point of view of a Wittgensteinian conceptual investigation. The key to such an investigation, as Phillips understands it, is to be found in the following passage from *Philosophical Investigations,* which Phillips quotes on the first page of his book:

"A philosophical problem has the form: 'I don't know my way about.'"

Philosophy may in no way interfere with the actual use of language; it can in the end only describe it.

For it cannot give it any foundation either.

"It leaves everything as it is" (Wittgenstein, 1958, pp. 123-124).

Phillips' understanding of this famous methodological pronouncement depends on the primacy of observation of the 'actual' or 'depth' grammar of practices and language uses, as opposed to the 'surface' grammar. For as Phillips (following Augustine in his account of time) points out, we may be perfectly able to use a concept without being able to give a conceptual account of the logical grammar of our usage. It thus behooves the philosopher to accumulate concrete examples of the activity in question (in this case prayer) in order to come to an understanding of the deep grammar involved.

Phillips' understanding of this Wittgensteinian methodology also allows for the possibility of mistakes even by those who are the paradigmatic users of a concept. Religious practices are not incorrigible, at least at this level; however, they are corrigible only in light of other, well-established religious beliefs and practices—which constitute and show the grammatical rules of the belief-structure (Phillips, 1965, p. 8).

Thus for Phillips correcting religious beliefs and practices in the light of their grammatical structure is no part of the philosopher's task. But philosophy is not thereby limited to sociological description. For a 'perspicuous presentation' of how things are, leaving them as they were, does not necessarily leave philosophers or their audience where *they* were. At least it may help them to get clear about religion, and it may even reveal inconsistencies between believers' practices and their reflective constructions. But though a philosopher may perhaps advance observations on the apparent inconsistency of various sayings and practices, the ultimate determination of mistakenness can only come from a religious community's own criteria.

Thus while Cupitt as a (philosophical) theologian may by Phillips' standards quite properly call for change in religious practices, Phillips as a philosopher (of religion) must leave things as they are. He is limited to showing how a set of such practices might be coherent, where they fail to be coherent, and what this coherence or incoherence logically implies about other religious concepts.

A final difference between Cupitt and Phillips is that they use slightly different linguistic frameworks. Phillips' notions of language and meaning are taken from the Wittgensteinian tradition. Cupitt, while noting the substantial congruence between all linguistic philosophies at many key points, nevertheless takes his categories from the structuralist tradition.

There is indeed considerable similarity between Wittgensteinian and structuralist viewpoints as they apply to the current problem. The notion of meaning to be gleaned from Wittgenstein's later work derives from the ideas of 'meaning as use' and 'no private language.' The best-known expression of the first idea is the following entry from *Philosophical Investigations*: "For a *large* class of cases—though not for all—in which we employ the word 'meaning' it can be elucidated thus: the meaning of a word is its use in the language" (p. 43). But language cannot be private—it depends on reference to publicly observable phenomena. Thus Phillips (1965, p. 9) criticizes philosophers who "speak as if there were a check on what is real and what is unreal which is *not* found in the actual use of language, but which transcends it."

This reliance on language clearly connects with the structuralist emphasis on *langue* as the defining public framework of distinctions. But it would be as well to note here that structuralism, at least in Cupitt's Feuerbachian application of its tenets to religion, gives the social construction of language even greater power than that accorded to it by Wittgenstein. Cupitt apparently regards language as completely generative of meaning within an essentially formless continuum. Wittgenstein is enough of an empiricist to limit the place of language to the ineluctably social categorization of phenomena, which may exist outside language but cannot be described without it.

To sum up Phillips' project: he considers prayer from a philosophical viewpoint, as a point of entry for understanding the grammar of Christian religious life. The setting of this task is the Wittgensteinian understanding of meaning as intimately connected with use, and of the task of philosophy as understanding and elucidating forms of life.

Community and communication

Perhaps the most striking similarity between Cupitt's work and that of Phillips is that they are interested in prayer as communication and in the limits of this communication. Other philosophers have considered how far the phenomenon of prayer might serve as a proof of God's existence or attributes (cf Mavrodes, 1966, Alston, 1985). But these investigations apparently assume that prayerful communication is a possible religious practice, and that given the existence of God it would be a way of communicating meaning. Phillips' and Cupitt's project is therefore more fundamental.

Despite differences in their specific conclusions, both Cupitt and Phillips are agreed that privacy in prayer finds its limits in the social construction of language and forms of life. Phillips discusses three apparent counter-examples as cases in which God might be thought to be communicating directly to individuals, and in which the community is not needed to guarantee or authenticate the communication: prophecy, the Incarnation in Jesus Christ, and miracles. In each case, he tries to show that communal expectation and authentication has a fundamental part to play.

In the case of prophecy, be it the Old Testament tradition, New Testament witnessing, or even present-day speaking in tongues, Phillips points out that there are recognized traditions which govern the possibility of the gift and the limits of the message. There are true and false prophets, and which is which can only be decided by the religious community through the application of traditions and rules (which may include criteria available to nonbelievers, such as the accuracy of prediction). The message or the gift might be for one person: the authentication of the message is social (Phillips, 1965, p. 141).

The case of the Incarnation is in some respects simply an extension of that of prophecy. Jesus can be accepted (or rejected) as the Messiah only within an understanding of the Old Testament Covenant; his transformation of it into something personal, a *new* covenant, is parasitic on the old. Indeed, Phillips claims that the existence of four gospels and of various higher-critical discussions (such as Form Criticism) appropriately reinforces the impossibility of escaping historical contextualization, even in the case of Jesus' message (ibid., p. 143).

In a recent paper, Phillips (1991) goes even further. Following some remarks of Wittgenstein printed in *Culture and Value* (which themselves are apparently influenced by Kierkegaard's position in *Philosophical Fragments*), he suggests that the radical contextuality of the Gospels functions to drive believers away from the attempt to achieve historical 'truth' altogether, and to provoke a spiritual interpretation. Here he goes beyond the legitimization of form criticism, to claim that even the everyday practices of believers actually rely on a rejection of the surface grammar (the apparent historicity of the synoptic gospels) in favor of a deep grammar based on communal interpretation. (In fact, Kierkegaard suggests that this need to reject historicity is part of the Divine plan.)

Finally, Phillips claims that although miracles might seem to be objective evidence (and so perhaps not subject to communal approval), in fact what counts as a miracle is socially determined. Thus authentication of the apparently most public religious experience follows a grammar broadly the same as that of the apparently most private, prophecy. Of course the private experience component of 'miraculous' phenomena is often negligible. What is at issue here is an individual's ability and right to decide without reference to social norms. Phillips (1965, p. 147) claims that there can be no private decision about miracles. Substantially following Lessing, he argues that "what is held to be religiously significant by the community determines what is and is not a miracle." The determination of what is miraculous—the specific determination of a miracle—will depend on the particular time and the community.

Cupitt's argument for the limitation of prayer by the public sphere is based on his structuralist-influenced understanding of language. He begins with the idea that language is fundamentally a system of differences and relations. He claims that if this is so, proper names are a secondary and misleading linguistic structure (part of the surface grammar which does not accurately reflect the depth grammar). He understands the metaphysics of substance to derive from a mistaken reliance on this misleading surface grammar: substance metaphysics is improperly reified from talk of things. Metaphysical talk should take relations as primary.

Cupitt approaches the same point from the notion of language as necessarily public. Meaning is generated through a system of differences, and such a system cannot come into existence without being agreed upon by a group. Thus he claims that individuals cannot have meanings—and indeed if meaning is central to existence, as he believes, then individuals cannot exist without society. So any metaphysics which makes individuals primary components of existence is confused: social relations and communities are logically prior to selves.

Granted this background, Cupitt argues that public prayer might make sense as a particular kind of affirmation of community. He notes as support for the social value of public prayer that even the most secular people gather for mutual support through symbolic affirmations (one thinks of pep rallies, political conventions, and the like).

A difficulty with such an account of public prayer is that it apparently eliminates the specifically religious tenor of the practice, lessening the distinction between religion and other kinds of social bonding. A danger here, of which other theologians often speak with concern, is what Phillips (1965, p. 58) refers to as the 'debasement' of religious language. Bonhoeffer (1959, p. 67), for instance, refused to admit as religious another prisoner's muttering "O God" during an air raid. Instead he responded in a matter-of-fact way, preserving minimal social contact. So Cupitt's reliance on verbal language and social utility as criteria may make the distinction between orthodox and heterodox public use of religious language more difficult. In Wittgenstein's words (1970, p 144), "how a saying is understood is not told by words alone." This point also applies to private prayer, as will be seen below.

At any rate, Cupitt can give an account of public prayer. But he finds private prayer virtually impossible to explain coherently. The linguistic considerations outlined above ground his refusal to interpret literally the surface grammar of prayer as a communication between metaphysical individuals, since there are no such beings. Private prayer might still survive as a kind of symbolic participation in the absent public realm. But in this case it would of course not be *essentially* private.

Essentially private prayer, insofar as anyone would try to practice it, Cupitt (1988, p. 91) regards as a pathological survival of the need for metaphysical reality over against our public lived world. Because it entails this reification of the Other, as the Source of moral demands and judgment, he finds that it amounts to "systematic self-deception, alienation, and repression." He concedes that private meditation (on the outer world and our relations to it) may be helpful; however we must always remember that this outer life is primary and 'real' and "avoid like the plague any suggestion that our real life is the inner life."

The possibility of privacy

In considering the two points of view summarized here, I want to begin by conceding the main point on which Phillips and Cupitt, despite their differing projects and presuppositions, are in agreement: that our natural language (including religious language) is a social construction which in some important sense of the term 'makes' our reality. I want, however, to consider a major point on which Phillips and Cupitt differ, though perhaps less than their different presuppositions might lead one to suppose. This is the degree to which some 'privacy,' a component internal to the individual believer, is nevertheless operative and appropriate—perhaps even necessary—in prayer and other forms of religious experience.

The first important task is to clarify what is meant by privacy and what the rejection of privacy implies in this context. The best-known philosophical treatment of this point is the 'Private Language Argument' found in Wittgenstein's *Philosophical Investigations*. It is well known that Wittgenstein rejects private language. But it is important to realize that his rejection is based, not on a factual disproof, but on a proposed 'dissolution' of a conceptual or grammatical confusion. For instance, in rejecting the possibility of a private diary recording the occurrence of a sensation Wittgenstein is asserting, not a factual inability based on the public and relational character of naming, but the conceptual impossibility of such a relational process occurring within an individual's subjectivity. One cannot privately *name* one's sensations, since naming is an ineluctably public and relational process; equally, one cannot be privately *mistaken* about them, since mistaken recognition is a practice parasitic on the public practice of naming and recognition. Only by (wrongly) taking sensations as the sort of things one could name and recognize does one face a dilemma about the recognition of private mistakes in naming. Thus Wittgenstein in rejecting private language is not criticizing those who think in terms of a report within the subject for making a factual mistake (wrongly identifying something as language which is not); his point is that they are conceptually confused (see[k]ing a distinction, and a place for error, where there is none).

What is important about this distinction in the present context is that Wittgenstein is not concerned to deny the presence or the importance of an internal, private component to human experience. He is concerned to claim that this private experience is not like public relations; it is not a linguistic transaction, or, to use one of his favorite negations, it is not a 'mental process.' (In the index of *Philosophical Investigations*, the list of actions under the heading 'not mental processes' includes intending, interpreting, knowing, meaning, mental multiplication, naming, reading, remembering, thinking, and understanding.)

A further clue as to what could be meant by denying that human psychological internality ought not to be thought of as 'process' may be found in the collection of his remarks posthumously published as *Zettel*. In a series of paragraphs (on pp. 603-615) discussing psychophysical parallelism, Wittgenstein goes so far as to suggest that causal efficacy is a concept which it is inappropriate to apply to psychological connections. At any rate it is clear that he has a positive notion of the 'private' dimension of human experience quite incompatible with behaviorist or other reductionistic frameworks.

Phillips' (1965, p. 39) discussion of putatively 'private' communications between God and believers is compatible with this account of Wittgenstein's position on 'privacy.' He recognizes the believers' experiences as genuine private events (not hoaxes or logical impossibilities) but claims that their categorization must draw on the public realm. Prophetic, messianic, or miraculous experiences can only be so categorized within the traditions incarnate in public language. Furthermore, the communal interest is not in the internal states of any believer, but in what is said to communicate experiences, and in how these sayings interact with the received traditions of the community.

It should be noted that nothing Phillips says prevents religious categorizations from legitimately being made *in private*, and even by those having the experiences. After all, having learned to perform arithmetic, I may do so privately with some confidence of reaching a result which will prove publicly acceptable (the level of confidence depending on my skill). Similarly, having learned to make theological distinctions—knowing the grammar of religion (Wittgenstein, 1958, § 373), I may classify experiences according to this grammar in expectation of agreement with others. In exceptionally important cases I will no doubt confer with others before placing full confidence in my decision; but this procedure is no different from that followed in other fields. My level of experience and training will also influence the amount of trust others put in my categorizations; this too is how things go in mathematics or biology.

Cupitt's position on privacy is harder to state. It is clear, however, that the difference between Phillips as philosopher and Cupitt as theologian begins to tell at this point. For sometimes Cupitt speaks as if he wishes to deny the *logical possibility* of private prayer (which by Phillips' rules a philosopher might also do); sometimes he speaks as if he wishes to deny the *theological legitimacy* of that practice (which according to Phillips only a theologian should do). Indeed it sometimes seems that he wishes to deny the legitimacy of what is clearly an existing practice, based on its logical impossibility.

The structuralist background to Cupitt's position on the logical possibility of privacy renders that position difficult to accept as a philosophical claim. In the terms of a thoroughgoing social relativism such as Cupitt apparently embraces, it would be odd to say that traditional Western substance-metaphysics by itself is a logically impossible position to hold; after all, as Cupitt himself stresses, this structure has been the long-time dwelling place of many people. His claim must instead be that acceptance of substance-metaphysics is incompatible with twentieth-century theories of the structural mechanisms of meaning-creation, and presumably that acceptance of the theories concerning these mechanisms should lead to a rejection of substance-metaphysics. He must further claim that substance-metaphysics is an essential foundation of the 'privacy' inherent in private prayer, and that rejection of the first implies rejection of the second.

In writing the above paragraph I encountered a telling problem: for the phrase "acceptance of the theories concerning these mechanisms" I originally entered "awareness of these mechanisms." The danger is that another sub-

stance-metaphysics, this one concerning meaning-creation on the structuralist model, may replace the first. After all it is logically possible, no
matter how unlikely it might seem now, that the multiplicity of meanings
and language-games characteristic of the twentieth century in the econom-
ically developed world should eventually turn out to be naming aspects of a
single reality. But having granted that structuralism ought at least to be the
dominant social paradigm of the twentieth century, and that anyone accepting structuralism should, as a logical consequence, reject substance-metaphysics, one might well ask just how many religious believers (even in the
West) know of structuralism, accept its tenets, and have the ability to apply
them in their lives. Certainly lay people who have never been exposed to
structuralist theories can hardly be criticized for failing to grasp the logical
consequences of those theories.

The second claim which must hold for Cupitt's philosophical position to
be viable (that rejecting substance-metaphysics eliminates the dimension
of 'privacy' needed for private prayer) is equally open to question. However,
the question in this case is a conceptual one. Like the structuralists,
Wittgenstein stresses the linguistic foundations of meaning; nevertheless he
recognizes that substance-metaphysics is thoroughly embedded in natural language. Relations may indeed be prior to things, but thing-talk is one of the
widest spread and most deeply embedded structures of language. Wittgenstein
sharply points out the dangers of reification (the application of thing-talk
where it is inappropriate), but he does not believe talk about the internality
of the self to be an example of such inappropriate reification. He merely
claims that talk of the self is subject to confusion, and that attempts to divide
the self into parts are often a source of inappropriate reification. Yet some
notion of the self seems inevitable for any relational language to exist, given
that one kind of relation will inevitably be between individual language
users, which we know as 'selves.'

It may be more productive to think of Cupitt's position as a theological recommendation. This would also be more in keeping with the general purpose of his work, which is to create a theological ethics of action. But then
it is appropriate to ask whether the development of this 'new Christian ethics'
is better served by eliminating from theological grammar the self at private
prayer, or perhaps by reinterpretation of this phenomenon in terms other
than those of substance-metaphysics.

Kierkegaard on relations

Another theological author who struggled with the question of the grammar of the self and the relation of religious inwardness and outwardness is
Kierkegaard. His position on this subject reflects a certain tension. But before
considering how this tension is played out in specific examples it will be
useful to understand how he thinks of the self in general.

Given that Cupitt's reflections on prayer are part of a chapter entitled
"Remaking the Christian Self," it is worth noting that Kierkegaard (1980, p.
13) also has a theory of the self which is fundamentally epistemological and

relational rather than metaphysical. However, he stresses the *internal* relating ability of the self. "A human being is spirit. But what is spirit? Spirit is the self. But what is the self? The self is a relation that relates itself to itself or is the relation's relating itself to itself in the relation; the self is not the relation but is the relation's relating itself to itself."

Cupitt rejects the 'inner' mental and soulish self in favor of the 'outer' and relational self. But attention to Kierkegaard (and to Wittgenstein's philosophical psychology) suggests that this is a false dichotomy. From the point of view of one who wishes to reject metaphysical realism, the inner/outer distinction looks peculiar. 'Inner' and 'outer' are metaphysical terms which must be rejected, and which imperfectly name two fuzzy classes of relations.

Kierkegaard's construction of the self as relational stresses this point. As language users we are constantly involved in the process of relation; and while the world around us controls what kinds of selves we are to some extent by its relation to us, we are at the very least not passive observers of this process. We may choose how to value and integrate the various relations in which we are involved; we may even seek new relations.

Kierkegaard deepens his relational analysis by denying that the self is self-constituted, claiming instead that it is constituted by another, on which it is thus dependent. Inevitably the question then arises of the self's relation to this constituting other. In *The Sickness Unto Death* Kierkegaard runs through the typology of possible relationships between the self and its constitutive other. He finally defines the state of spiritual health thus: "In relating itself to itself and in willing to be itself, the self rests transparently in the power that established it" (p. 14).

So much might be said simply as a matter of philosophical psychology. Even Cupitt's structural-social account of the self might be phrased in these terms, if the constituting power were understood to be the language-using community as a whole. But Kierkegaard of course claims that the establishing power is God. A reliance on God as establishing power certainly appears metaphysical. Still it is significant that God comes into Kierkegaard's discourse as a necessary postulate of relationality, rather than as a metaphysical idea. As Phillips (1965, p. 12) points out, in the everyday grammar of religion, the relation between the believer and God is primary, and theological or philosophical attempts to take as foundational the project of "proving God's existence" metaphysically tend to ignore actual religious practice. Kierkegaard's existential method at least has the merit of not ignoring practice.

Kierkegaard's (1983) understanding of what is implied by the transparent relation of outward relations to the inward (and where it can go wrong) can be seen at work in four distinct contexts: in his imaginative construction and theological category of the 'Knight of Faith,' in his critical remarks on 'hidden inwardness' in Christianity, in his self-evaluation of his own maieutic project, and most directly in his comments on the relation between hidden and visible 'works of love.'

The best known of these contexts is that of the 'Knight of Faith' who represents the ideal of Christianity, in *Fear and Trembling*. The Knight of Faith represents a stage beyond that of the Knight of Infinite Resignation, who has visibly given up the world. The Knight of Faith, having given up the world, nevertheless acts 'by virtue of the absurd' as though the world were his. "He resigned everything infinitely, and then he grasped everything again by virtue of the absurd. He is continually making the movement of infinity, but he does it with such precision and assurance that he continually gets finitude out of it, and no one ever suspects anything else" (1983, p. 41). Kierkegaard's two paradigmatic examples of this stage are Abraham and an invented modern figure who is to all outward appearances a tradesman or a tax collector. What they share is a faith so 'inward,' so subjective, that it does not show at all in their everyday lives. Thus is it impossible to determine what they are: whether the contemporary Knight is not perhaps actually the perfect philistine he appears to be, whether Abraham is not perhaps the heartless automaton the narrative allows.

But while stressing this inwardness as the essence of Christianity, Kierkegaard (1967-78, § 2123) is also acutely aware of the potential problems of hiddenness. He makes fun of the 'starred and beribboned' personage who declares that he is ready to give all if it should be required of him, but in seventy years he has found no challenge requiring him to give all. "This amounts to making a fool of God; it is like a child playing a game of hide-and-seek so that no one shall find him. One says aloud—if it is required, etc.—and then says very softly—look, not even Satan himself will be able to get hold of me—so cleverly shall I hide."

Kierkegaard, always sensitive to the use of language and its relation to other actions, in one passage from his journals makes outward context the test of spiritual sincerity:

> All speaking with the mouth is a kind of ventriloquism, an indeterminate something. The deception is that there is, after all, a definite visible figure who uses his mouth. But take care. Language is an abstraction.
>
> In order for speaking actually to become human speech in a deeper sense, or in a spiritual sense, something else is required with respect to being the one who speaks, two points must be determined: the one is the speech, the words spoken, the other is the situation. The situation determines decisively whether or not the speaker is in character with what he says, or the situation determines whether or not the words are spoken at random, a talking which is unattached" (ibid., § 4056).

Thus geographical or cultural 'Christendom' is composed of those who claim 'inwardness' but do not ever show it outwardly, who effectively avoid ever being put to the test. Kierkegaard claims that both inwardness and its expression are needed: neither will suffice alone.

Kierkegaard's rejection of hidden inwardness might seem to be at odds with his own case, in which he admits to having hidden his inward Christianity.

Indeed he confesses that this "is and continues to be an awkward matter." But he notes that he has not remained hidden in order to avoid the 'Christian collisions,' nor has he in fact been spared them. Furthermore, he claims that the task which he took on, that of prodding others' false 'hidden inwardness,' could only be achieved by the method of indirect communication, which requires its author to hide his purposes (ibid., p. 2125).

Finally, the first section of *Works of Love* addresses the problem straight on in dealing with "love's hidden life and its recognizability by its fruits." Here Kierkegaard (1962, p. 23) maintains that the spring of Christian love and action is to be found in God's unseen love. Yet "if it were true—as conceited shrewdness, proud of not being deceived, thinks—that one should believe nothing which he cannot see by means of his physical eyes, then first and foremost one ought to give up believing in love." If one did so then one would lose faith in the internal relation which grounds those external relations that are conventional works of love. Religious inwardness and social outwardness are here seen as intimately connected, so much so that the spring of the individual's outward relations is to be found in inwardness. More than that, in speaking of the primary importance of looking toward one's own fruits, rather than those of others, Kierkegaard is foreshadowing Cupitt's (1988, p. 91) exhortation to "meditatively question ourselves, read quietly and think about our lives, our friends, our values . . . if they help us with our real life, which is our life with others." But he goes beyond Cupitt in suggesting a touchstone by which one might actually determine something about values, a relation which is valued above all others and in turn serves as a standard of valuation for all others—in short, a transcendent relation.

This notion of transcendent relation, which arises naturally from Kierkegaard's understanding of the self as relational, in both 'inward' and 'outward' aspects, is the foundation of an analysis of religious practices (including private prayer) which does not depend on a substance-metaphysics. Of course, religious believers often refer to these practices using an expression which has the surface grammar of substance-metaphysics, speaking of relations between individuals and 'the transcendent.' But Kierkegaard (1967-78, § 4550) consistently tries to subvert this surface grammar and center his work on the deep grammar of relation, as in the following passage: "When the question of the truth is raised subjectively, reflection is directed subjectively to the nature of the individual's relationship; if only the mode of this relationship is in the truth, the individual is in the truth even if he should happen to be thus related to what is not true."

Yet, as Kierkegaard claims in a gloss on this passage found in his journals, this emphasis on relation does not give the believer a blank check. The tendency which he exhibits in his more theoretical works to keep from direct talk of Divine reality is driven by his "epistemological modesty" (this appellation is due to C.S. Evans) and does not arise out of any doubt on his part about the truth of God. He believes that there is such a truth, but this truth can only be grasped in the course of transcendent relations; it cannot be established ahead of time. For "the remarkable thing is that there is a How with the characteristic that when the How is scrupulously rendered the What is also given, that this is the How of faith. Right here, at its very maximum, inwardness is shown to be objectivity" (ibid., § 4550).

In short, the only person with whom one can have a God-relationship is God, and the only way to the truth of God is through a God-relationship.

Private prayer as a relationship

What can be elucidated about the idea of private prayer by examining its place in religious language or, since the notion is an abstract distillation of practice, by examining the function in religious life of the practices involved? Even at the surface level prayer is a relation; but as Phillips (1965, p. 50) points out, even where it involves language, this relation does not follow the rules which apply to relations between finite language users. Perhaps the most important way of differentiating this relation from others is to note that private prayer is not a 'conversation' between two language-using equals. Phillips argues persuasively that God is not a participant in the relational and communicative use of language which is paradigmatic of such conversations.

Yet prayer may (indeed in the Christian tradition it usually does) involve a use of language by the person praying. This language, and other prayer-behavior, is among the religious behaviors which form part of the grammar of belief. As such it is socially taught and regulated. One main function of this use of language is to set forth and clarify the relation of the individual believer to God—and if we follow Kierkegaard's suggestion, of the individual believer to herself. Insofar as this relation is central to and regulative for the believer's life, it must be the spring of action. So for a Christian to assert that "the real me is the me at private prayer" helps to make clear which relation is central to and regulative for this life.

This assertion has a clear-cut grammar and appears to be as fully related to the public realm as other assertions about what is important to one (for example, "my children are the most important thing in my life"). The truth of all such claims can only be established by observation of the believer's life to see whether this relation is actually regulative (do I always make my children's welfare central in my decisions?). The main difference between assertions about prayer and other regulative assertions, namely that claims about prayer refer to a relation privately experienced, is irrelevant to their testability. The relation of self to God is constituted in publicly established categories, and by its own grammar it must bear a relation to public actions of the individual.

From a philosophical point of view, then, the foregoing analysis suggests that the notion of private prayer is not logically vacuous, even within a primarily linguistic and relational universe. This remains true despite the fact that private prayer is an essentially private experience. From a theological point of view, the same analysis suggests that private prayer may yet serve as a suitable focus for an ethics of action. For a Christian to claim that "the real me is the me at private prayer" does not seem so far-fetched after all.

Chapter Seven

Traditional Analogies to Prayer

The Western world's cosmology has at least three decks. Religion is expected to involve the top level, and some (although there are no estimates of the proportion) accept 'heaven' as more real than the natural or built environments in which they live. Others regard heaven as a metaphor, to be talked about but not verified. McDannell and Lang's (1990) *History of Heaven*, emphasizes the virtuous role of spirit, so that "the proper act of the Spirit is prayer" (p. 36) and the Biblical Revelation to John has a heavenly liturgy with pilgrims "devoutly approaching the divine throne who would offer their prayers and presents" (p. 43). The psychological correlates and implications of those beliefs have not been explored, although an other-worldly perspective is expected to influence our attitudes to this world (cf Swanson, 1960) since the way heaven is built derives from cultural stereotypes. They are embellished by defined fantasies, with prayer having an unknown impact on those 'haunted' fictions. But when Wallace Stevens (1952, p. 24) wrote of "the magnificent cause of being, the imagination, the one reality in this imagined world," he stressed the extent to which all our realities are constructed. That idea was developed by Berger and Luckmann (1972), although Shelley Taylor (1989) has shown that, while a sense of well-being involves optimism, those who are depressed have a more accurate awareness of the reality of their own context.

While fewer people now live a completely enclosed religious life than was the case even fifty years ago, this lifestyle still carries a sense of virtue that those who live "in the world" find it hard to generate or display; and it is rejected out of hand by secularists. But most people are expected to deal with more than one level of reality and with the multiple 'selves' that we need as we move between home and work, or school, church, and leisure activities. Flexibility is necessary to cope with those separate 'cultures' and their demands or constraints, while preserving some sense of one's own coherence.

A similar mixing of perspectives distinguishes sacred from secular

111

demands and reflects another important ambiguity that has relevance for the ways prayer can be construed or appealed to. The closest psychologists seem to have been to that problem is through urban/rural contrasts in religiousness, although those differences could depend on whatever these social contexts can support or offer. The size of a congregation might also be important, since anonymity is harder to maintain in a small community. These issues fall towards sociology rather than with the psychology of religion and may relate to a conservatism that generates strong religious feelings and attachments.

Modern society, however, stresses an independence or decenteredness that respects its members' stance and attitudes, expecting them to grant a similar independence to others. A correlate of this is the shifting boundary between public and private domains, which recently seem to have made religion more private, and sexual preferences less so. Furthermore, the tolerance of others' differences has itself reduced our search for absolutes and it may now be easier to keep sacred and secular worldviews apart, resorting to religious solutions in times of crisis, with illness or death marked for the consolations of religion. That may have been captured by Batson and Ventis (1982), who added a quest dimension to Allport's extrinsic and intrinsic orientations, when questions such as, "Are you religious?" became harder to answer.

Related debates about personality, coping skills or situational determinants as predictors of the way individuals will act in a crisis are resolved with reference to training or prior experience, or they are referred to the etiquette for domestic, work-related, and social or religious problems more than to control through money, prestige, or one's secular roles. But major life crises demand more than control, although several years ago they were thought to hold a key to stress reactions (Holmes and Rahe, 1967). It is now accepted that coping strategies moderate those effects, and that prayer can be an efficient coping device. This is a comparatively recent discovery, as we will see, that contrasts with earlier interpretations and attitudes to medieval religious practice which assumed a tremulous piety and unlimited credulity. During the late nineteenth century, this was deconstructed in terms of 'suggestion.' As Lecky (1893) put it, "Nothing could be more common than for a holy man to be lifted up from the floor in the midst of his devotions, or to be visited by the Virgin or by an angel. There was scarcely a town that could not show some relic that had cured the sick, or some image that had opened and shut its eyes, or bowed its head to an earnest worshiper. It was somewhat more extraordinary, but not in the least incredible, that the fish should have thronged to the shore to hear Saint Anthony preach, or that it should be necessary to cut the hair of the crucifix at Burgos once a month. . . . All this was going on in Europe without exciting the smallest astonishment or skepticism" (pp. 141-142).

Devlin (1987, p. 1), however, argues that modern 'man' is "a realist concerned with the material, with the world that is; historical man lived in an exotic world of fantasy, and nowhere is this seen to be more evident than in his devotion to religion" (the sexist language is in that text). What might seem to be a mysterious account of prayer for us, integrated outward and inward realities, aligning earlier Christian practices with medieval alchemy. When alchemy held that it was possible to alter the properties of base metals, for example, it was spiritually fruitful for Christianity to have found there a way by which the contemplation of nature itself could lead to a true gnosis. That process required initiation by a master, and set parallels between subject and object that also ran between a knower and the known. Other problems that were confronted then and are still being resolved refer to the mind/body problem, models or metaphors of mind, how mental processing is to be understood, and the validity of our concepts of reality within mental or social constructions, and not as an independent reality.

But even the wildest of magical or compulsive imaginings had to accept that stones were hard, fire was hot, and that natural laws were inexorable. So, like those that surrounded prayer itself, their deeper explanations were constructed from transcendental assumptions. In a similar way, at the turn of this century the 'New Psychologists' looked for fields to which their science might be applied, finding one in psychical research and parapsychology (Leary, 1987). This sequence of development from magic and religion to science offers, as we have noted, an analysis that has been used to explain the development of prayer in general, and within individuals. We are only rescued from those principled analyses when they are clothed by data.

Although the alchemical precursors to modern science are primarily of historical interest now, interpretations of the links between magic and divination might still be found in psychical experiences, and perhaps in the fashionable transpersonal psychologies where expanding consciousness plays an important role, and in alternative healing and medicine. Continuing questions about the meaning of life and the independent control we have over ourselves and others might also be found hiding in those current interests.

Analyzing attitudes to prayer without recognizing their doctrinal and practical constraints, and without some information about what those who pray expect of their prayers, and how prayers might differ from the thoughts of those who do not pray, commits one to arguments that can seem as highly principled as those that aligned prayer with magic.

Those who would study prayer might therefore consider the arguments surrounding "the anomaly called psi" (as "the apparent ability to receive information shielded from the senses (ESP) and to influence systems outside the sphere of motor activity (PK)"), and especially the commentaries about it in *Behavioural and Brain Sciences*, 1987, *10*, 539-643. The first paper there by Rao and Palmer (1987) argues against reductionist interpretations of those experiments, favoring the view that in ESP the 'information' behaves "like a weak signal that has to compete for the information-processing resources of the organism, (so that) a reduction of ongoing sensorimotor activity may facility detection." The next paper, by Alcock (1987), argues that any reasonable definition of paranormal phenomena is dualistic, so that the use of "experimenter effects explains failures away, making the psi hypothesis unfalsifiable, since doubt is suspended."

In a way that seems to make it comparable to some attitudes to prayer, the psi phenomenon and its effects are still accepted by some psychologists and the explanations of its mode of operation interpreted, or offered in terms of a signal detection or similar task that involves 'central' processing in which there may be a bias either towards or away from the hypothesis that there is a valid phenomenon there (cf Blackmore, 1990). While the attitudes of cynics, skeptics, or true believers in prayer have not yet been carefully distinguished, those papers on psi show a core from which other likely explanations of the 'effects' are eliminated, including the role of 'ganzfeld,' hypnosis, relaxation, meditation, and dreams. But it seems that the reactions to psi are either credulous, or skeptical and rejecting, and suggest that we must look for other methods if we are to subject them to scientific investigation. Mary Gergen (1987), on the other hand, supports the confidence of those who risk the propriety of their scientific expertise by accepting psi, who attend religious services in their own 'free-time,' or snort cocaine, since "mystical attractions find eager audiences among the Western educated elite."

While psychical researchers have been more interested in 'religion' than prayer, their concern with thought transference, extra-sensory perception (ESP), and psychokinesis (PK), has found that those who believe in these effects (the 'sheep') are difference from those who do not (the 'goats') (Schmeidler and McConnell, 1973). A similar effect might be found for prayers that can be offered informally and "without a firm hope of success," as Dr Johnson said. Wittgenstein is quoted as saying, "Pray for me and God bless you! (If there is such thing)," while Sydney Smith said, "I am going to pray for you at St Paul's, but with no very lively hope of success." Although the words of prayer are crucial, while spells are in principle expected to work, prayers need not. Yet spells and prayers as well as curses are deeply embedded in our cultural awareness and may have an indirect power, especially for those who believe in their efficacy. Pratt (1916, p. 313), however, argued that prayers become spells when powerful 'spirits' or saints are named or appealed to. This could show another prejudice against Catholic practices, or it might have been a step on the path from spell to prayer that Marrett identified.

It is odd that while the ways prayer might work are commonly questioned, fax machines or the modern telephone system, as well as physiological or brain processes, and even consciousness are accepted and their modes of operation go unquestioned by most people, or they are explained in metaphorical terms. Because prayer involves a state of mind, and perhaps its modification, the typical psychological explanations of prayer have appealed to habits, stereotyped or obsessive rituals, fantasy, suggestion, and so on, while disregarding its public features and the support its practice is given.

Devlin (1987) accepted that the 'primitive' forms of thinking were aligned with a lack of education and that even when the doctrines of prayer were revised they "preferred self-interested supplication and festive celebration to introspective piety and devotion" (pp. 6-7). Indeed, she notes that the "supernatural was a fact, more often than not, assimilated to the natural and harnessed to its needs" (p. 7). We can know little about the way that was understood in earlier times, although both orthodox and unorthodox prayers were accepted, and Devlin (p. 8, quoting from Cambry, 1838) could say that "in church, people . . . used to recite, without understanding them, prayers which they thought capable of curing every ailment, making the fields fertile, procuring mistresses for themselves, making their enemies waste away. The hope of meeting with success in these projects inspired them with a frenzy of enthusiasm."

Folklore
Folklorists, especially in Europe, have collected many such prayers, including one quoted by Devlin (p. 9) from Nisard (1864).

"Kyrie, I should like
Christie, to be married
Kyrie, I pray to all saints
Christie, that it may be tomorrow . . .
Saint Frederick, may I have a good husband.
Saint Bartholomew, may he be handsome . . ."

Devlin uses other examples to stress that "the functionality of official religion in its collective manifestations hardly encouraged the development of a refined appreciation of spirituality" (p. 11). There is a grave danger in overinterpreting these examples, although they do convey a sense of the reality of prayer in the material concerns they express, even for animals.

"And if I have a good crop of flax
I'll give clothes to the unfortunate
I'll not do as my neighbor does,
Who prefers to cover his horses
Than go and give alms.
For this reason, I think him a cruel man,
And therefore he doesn't deserve
To have his flax preserved.
As for me, I have my word,
If it's given unto me, I shall give" (Devlin, 1987, p. 39).

Devlin finds that "not only are God and his saints neither remote nor confined to elusive spiritual realms, but they are fully involved in the daily problems of ordinary people. Gratuitous praise is not offered to them: few protestations of loyalty, subjection or devotion—such as we find in official prayers—are made. Instead, their attention is directed to man's practical needs and the physical dangers that beset his life. Indeed, the prayer is more like a list with which a doctor or an insurance agent might be presented, so preoccupied is it with the banishment of earthly worries and so indifferent to the grandeur of God. The same absence of awe is noticeable in night prayers" (p. 40).

These analyses emphasize a realistic perspective on prayers that did not need further explication or analysis, because they addressed the world as it was seen to be, with simple if sometimes urgent pleas about the identified needs, even in the late nineteenth and twentieth centuries. One wonders how these prayers were 'meant' and accepted by others, and whether they were surrounded by awe. Devlin remarks on the absence of awe from the nineteenth-century night prayers (on p. 40), although I have found it in Samoan family prayers, where a sense of reverence during those prayers is an accepted feature of their traditional social life. Perhaps it is the case that, as Devlin observes, "popular religion was at once more eschatological and more practical than authentic spirituality, and this paradoxical character has inspired accounts of it which have insisted either on the boundless credulity which it implied or on its materialism" (1987, p. 42). Her analysis does, however, emphasize sorcery, which some take as a precursor to prayer, although prayer has also been used to combat it.

So "Rocal described the appearance of a sorcerer at the deathbed of an old man called Jendon. On entering the room, the sorcerer threw some salt on the fire, to keep the devil away. He then listened to the dying man's chest, recited a prayer to secure his entry into paradise, then prayed silently, drawing signs of the cross on his patient, placing a sachet on his chest and removing it. Next, he put a bowl of water in each corner of the room, so that the man's soul could wash in the water and, thus purified, go straight to heaven. As the death-rattle sounded in the dying man's throat, the sorcerer recited the *patenotre blanche*, accompanying the prayer with mysterious signs made with his left hand. When, finally, the old man died, the sorcerer threw the water out (so that the soul would not dally in the house). The sorcerer's incantations—which expressed the desire that the man be purified of the evil incarnated in his illness, and so go to heaven—accompanied a ritual which mimed this intention. Both fire and salt are age-old symbols of purification, and the preliminary gesture set the tone of the act to come. The sachet placed on the man's chest seems to have been intended to draw the illness out of him" (Devlin, 1987, p. 50).

She also notes that "prayers and pilgrimages were habits, inculcated at an early age as a way of expressing intense wishes." That "they betray a lack of curiosity, amounting to indifference, about the mechanism whereby the devices were fulfilled" (Devlin, 1987, p. 55) contrasts with more recent efforts to interpret their (hidden) meanings, finding models and analogies for their modes of operation and assuming that it is unreasonable to understand them simply or directly. It is not necessary to go to a Pentecostal Church to find people who wish to be prayed for, but as Henry Miller wrote in *The Tropic of Capricorn* (1961, p. 76), "It is a pity that he had to use Christ for a crutch, but then what does it matter how one comes to the truth so long as

one pounces upon it and lives by it?" The search to interpret these processes could be a product of the Enlightenment which is supposed to have eman-
cipated us from ignorance or superstition (Martin, 1985). A completely different sense of 'enlightenment' is found in the prayers of Tibetan Buddhism,
which aim to understand the meaning of life and death, to make us more
human.

Devlin noted the extent to which commentators risk overinterpretation, "in
the light of their own understanding of causality." She continues, "They
have been forced to the conclusion that peasants, ignorant of the mechanical
interdependencies of nature, attempted to explain and control the world by
postulating supernatural beings like man in all things but power, and that, consequently, they lived in a world dominated to a large extent by the extraordinary and fearful. But the aims of many of the religious gestures which we
have been examining seem to have been pragmatic and the implied view of
the universe was probably beside the point for most pilgrims. Method, in
these areas where man's impotence was a function of his ignorance, was
not a calculated adaptation of means to an end or a reflection of a theory of
natural causality (as it was in technical matters like husbandry), but a rite seen
to be tenuously connected with the desired result, and that partly in the mind
of the performer" (1987, pp. 56-57). There is a freshness and simple direct-
ness in these attitudes of folk-lorists, that contrast against the complex interpretations favored by psychologists and other theorists or commentators
who find it hard to accept the mind-sets of others.

The ambiguity of magic

Kieckhefer (1990) argues in *Magic in the Middle Ages* that magic is a
point of intersection between religion and science, although there are several
kinds of science and at least two kinds of magic. *Demonic* magic "invokes evil
spirits and rests upon a network of religious beliefs and practices while *natural* magic exploits 'occult' powers within nature and is essentially a branch
of medieval science" (ibid.). Within religion, prayer stands at a crossroad
of processes that support or realize religious traditions and orientations themselves, and expectations about their benefits. They include healing, which may
be supported by folk or modern medicine and other ritual practices. Prayer
also mixes popular religious ideas with theological and philosophical opinions among those who would use it to influence reality, God or the gods, or
only themselves. Like magic, prayer could therefore be "where religion con-
verges with science, popular beliefs with those of the educated classes, and
the conventions of fiction meet with the realities of daily life" (ibid., pp. 1
2).

Kieckhefer also stressed that "humor and seriousness converge (in the
magic of medieval Europe)" (p. 2). He illustrated this with reference to the
amusing or frivolous nature of many recipes for magic although, as he puts
it, "the judges who sentenced magicians to death did not take it lightly." We
might draw the same conclusion about the classical accounts of mystical
visions which, like spells, depend on the language in which they are described

for their effect. Early manuals of prayer include blessings and conjurations (or salesman-type appeals and incantations) as well as everyday household and medical advice that now reads like spells. So a remedy for fever in a manuscript from Wolsthuan Castle in the Tyrol recommends taking the leaves of a particular plant, but before using them, "one is supposed to write certain Latin words on them to invoke the power of the Holy Trinity, and then one is to say the Lord's Prayer and other prayers over them" (ibid., p. 3). Kieckhefer continues, "There is no scientific or religious reason, however, to repeat the procedure before sunrise on three consecutive mornings."

We can take it that both science and religion in medieval times were enhanced by magic. Although they supported each other, there are problems about who was being addressed, and whether the formulae were generally intelligible. One remedy for menstrual problems is, however, fairly straightforward, with the recommendation that the words from the mass, "By Him, and with Him and in Him," should be written out before "laying the slip of paper on the afflicted woman's head" (ibid., p. 4). In a treatment for epilepsy, "first one puts a deerskin strap around the patient's neck while he is suffering a seizure, then one 'binds' the sickness to the strap 'in the name of the Father and of the Son and of the Holy Spirit,' and finally one buries the strap along with a dead man" (ibid.). Other prescriptions cited contain no spoken words and had nothing religious in them. There is no way to examine the meaning or support that magic or prayer received then, or how it was understood, although Kieckhefer mentions a marginal note beside the cure for menstrual problems that said, "This is utterly false, superstitious, and practically heretical" (p. 5).

Recasting sympathetic sorcery into explicit appeals to demons produced exorcism to dispel demons or the diseases they cause through 'conjuration,' as in the early thirteenth-century formula, "I conjure you by the Father and the Son and the Holy Spirit, by Mary the mother of the Lord, by Mary Magdalene and Mary (the mother) of James, and Salome (cf Mark 16)" (Kieckhefer, 1989, p. 167). They were also adjured by the Trinity, God as creator, or by Christ as the Word.

"Why God should consent to this use of his power is obscure. One possibility is that the necromancers held an amoral conception of God, as a being who could be influenced (if not coerced) by prayer to bestow his aid in all sorts of dubious enterprises. Alternatively the necromancers may have persuaded themselves that their causes were in fact holy: that if they were destroying their enemies they were righteous in so doing, that if they sought hidden treasures they would use them only for noble purposes, and that if they won the love of married women God would at least wink at their misconduct, even if he did not smile" (p. 168). He also notes that "the mentality of the necromancers is in any case difficult to penetrate, but certain of their writings are utterly 'baffling'" (p. 170). Kieckhefer's conclusion is, however, that those who prosecuted and condemned the ones who continued to use natural magic recognized "the threat of demonic magic in the clerical underworld" and were educated men, "theologians, preachers, lawyers, inquisitors, and other judges who themselves became the greatest of magicians" (p. 201). Persecution by Church authorities continues, if not against magic and its derivatives, but against the "minorities" (especially women) who threaten their hegemony over the orthodoxies they claim (Deconchy, 1991).

Procedures in a Munich handbook include sprinkling a circle on the ground with holy water while reciting Psalm 51:7 to conjure up spirits in the name of God to do one's bidding (and become invisible) (p. 7). Indeed 'magic' derives from the magi, the Zoroastrian priests of Persia, although its character changed when natural (or alchemical processes) became available and magic was used for healing as much as for divination. While Roger Bacon (1214-1292) believed in mysterious and awesome powers within nature, he restricted 'magic' to fraud and deception. Yet the idea of a diffuse power in the universe that could be harnessed was probably as commonplace as our assumption that young children hold primitive or animistic beliefs that the natural world is impelled by an active process, although Wellman and Gelman (1992) have shown that to ask better questions allows young children to show more subtle knowledge or understanding than Piaget had uncovered.

Kieckhefer identifies 'magic' with "the type of power it invokes: if it relies on divine action or the manifest powers of nature it is not magical, while if it uses demonic aid or occult powers in nature it is magical" (p. 14). But he also notes that sixteenth-century religious debates and late nineteenth-century anthropology stressed religious supplications of God or the gods, while continuing to accept that to coerce spiritual beings and their forces was the main characteristic of magic. As he puts it, "Religion treats the gods as free agents, whose good will must be won through submission and ongoing veneration." From that perspective magic and prayer are both coercive, if the rituals are expected to work mechanically.

The expected power of prayer can hardly be doubted, judging by the material available in books of prayers for public, corporate, family, or private use, which suggests that prayer continues to have a strength of its own, despite the ambiguity inherent in an epistemology that contrasts personal piety against an expectation that the Mass, for example, can produce 'substantial' effects. It is perhaps for this reason that the current psychology of religion has placed more emphasis on the characteristics of religious practice, belief or experience, their functions or implications for development or change (cf Spilka, Hood, and Gorsuch, 1985) or on the mythological, ritual, experiential, dispositional, social, or directional *dimensions* of religion (Capps, Rambo, and Ransohoff, 1976), than on prayer, hymns, or even the Bible. It should again be emphasized that the psychology of religion has been primarily concerned with Western religious traditions, especially Christianity, leaving the analysis of other traditions to anthropology, or sociology. Some of that imbalance has been redressed by Wulff (1991) who examined national differences in the ways different features of religion are identified theoretically and the extent to which biological, behavioral, laboratory-based, and correlational approaches can themselves drive or focus on specific features, in the manner of theories like those of Freud, William James, the German phenomenologists, or humanistic psychologists in the USA.

Although historical material is of great importance in understanding the growth of psychologies of prayer, that work sometimes tells us more about the prejudices embedded in the conclusions that were reached than about the evidence on which they were based, or the expectations that are imposed on any prayers. These interpretations are no longer couched in terms of magic, and prayer seems to be easier to talk about than has been assumed. Nor is prayer generally thought to be pious or foolish, in the sense of "lacking good sense or judgment" (as the *Concise Oxford Dictionary* defines that word), unless it is used to excess and without the appropriate sanctions. Yet prayer may necessarily be ambiguous, since Christ promised to do anything his followers asked in His name (John 14:14), and 'common' expectations of it include the "wondrous things" that were done through Christ's miracles, whether by touching the fringe of His garment (Luke 9:43-48), by using his saliva to anoint and cure, or speaking a word like 'be clean' or 'arise' (Mark 7:32-34; John 9:6ff). And exorcism, as the paradigmatic healing miracle in the New Testament, is still practiced in some fundamentalist traditions. Yet the Biblical miracles appear to be direct interventions, or they are interpreted in that way.

Like healers, diviners and geomancers identify the powers (or spirits) in nature that can be controlled, claiming that those powers are no more mysterious than electricity, radio, or television are to the commonsense understanding that judges on practical rather than theoretical criteria. So technicians and scientists, or the 'orefactors' and 'orefictors' in early Chinese science identified by Joseph Needham, are still in conflict over their respective access to the skills of practice and theory.

Language itself is crucial in prayer and magic with apparently elusive meanings that can make those forms seem to be incantational. In that context, prayer directed to a religious figure, whether God, Christ, Mary, or a saint, contrasts against the blessings or wishes addressed to patients themselves, and against the 'adjurations,' exorcisms, or commands directed to the sickness itself or to an agent responsible for it (Kieckhefer, p. 70). Those forms of healing are directed towards a source of power, although repeating the Pater Noster or the Ave Maria, for example, can provoke prejudiced responses among Protestants about the magical or superstitious practices of Catholics. These attitudes depend on what is believed, whether those beliefs are justified as magical, as an act of devotion, or as part of a liturgy. Similarly, wearing a pyx or a cross *could* have magical, devotional, symbolic, or a decorative significance, and to be anointed with oil, or asperged with holy water may be 'merely' symbolic, 'deeply' meaningful, carrying its own effective power, or over-interpreted.

As Kieckhefer says in relation to such ambiguities, "The danger for the historian (and for any psychologist) lies in the temptation to strip away the religious context by a process of abstraction and then take the magic remainder

as the essence of popular piety. Similar difficulty surrounds popular veneration of the Eucharist" (p. 79). That practice can be accepted at face value and
encouraged for its actual or assumed religious or psychological benefits. It
can also be dealt with reductionistically or cast in terms of an attachment theory (Kirkpatrick, 1992) that identifies the relics of the childhood (if not
childish) attitudes it might contain as an archetype, or with a person's own
psychological development.

Attitudes of faith, trust or hope, fear, awe, humility, and devotion have been
thought to be at the core of a religious stance, although William James suggested that we should be more concerned with the fruits than the roots of religion and with the ethical or moral implications of worship than with trying
to unpack the hidden meanings of its practice. While spiritual disciplines
that are designed to control or calm the soul are criticized for the weakness
they suggest, they can also be accepted as a part of a tradition and its folklore.
A spiritual perspective on them can amplify the effects of fasting or sleep
deprivation (Bell, 1985). A major difference between the religious significance
of prayer and the conjectures about its magical efficacy depend on what is
expected of it. From being concrete or specific, the attitudes to it can become
increasingly spiritual, even if the relics of saints or pilgrimages to their
shrines and other sacred places, and favored forms of prayer, devotional
reading, and penitential or meditative practices are used as aids to devotion.
While such practices can be understood at face value, they are also expected to hide (or express) symbolic meanings like those identified by Carroll
(1988) in his analysis of "praying the rosary."

When William James (1902) looked at the efficacy of petitionary prayer,
he said, "As regards prayers for the sick, if any medical fact can be considered to stand firm, it is that *in certain environments* prayer may contribute to
recovery, and should be encouraged as a therapeutic measure. . . . The case
of the weather is different" (p. 365, with the emphasis added). He also identified prayer as "the very soul and essence of religion" (p. 365), because it realized the soul's intercourse with God. That definition places prayer within a
context that meshes "an inner fact" with the "ecclesiastical or theological" to
produce the consciousness of "an intercourse between themselves and higher powers with which they feel themselves to be related" (p. 366). The sense
of tradition when "*something* is *transacting*" ensures at least some efficacy
and stops prayer from "containing elements of delusion" (p. 369) as the
"materialists and atheists have always said it was" (p. 367).

Hopes and expectations

An expectation that material effects cannot be produced through prayer (or
by magic) occurs, as James put it, "when the direct experiences of prayer were
ruled out as false witnesses," although there can still be "some inferential
belief that the whole order of existence must have a divine cause" (p. 367).
James then noted that "this way of contemplating nature, pleasing at it would
doubtless be to persons of a pious taste, would leave to them but the spec-
tators' part at a play, whereas in experimental religion and the prayerful life,

we seem ourselves to be the actors, and to act, not in a play, but in a very serious reality" (p. 367). This shift of emphasis presents another paradox,
although James released prayer from any magical connotations by remark-
ing that, "It may well prove that the sphere of influence in prayer is subjective exclusively, and that what is immediately changed is only [sic] the mind
of the praying person" (p. 367); as he put it later, the answer to questions about
to whom we pray "does not much matter" (p. 368).

To balance literal against metaphorical interpretations of prayer is only one
contrast we can make. Others involve self - other, inner - outer, naive - expert,
spontaneous - liturgical, close - distant, individual - communal, immediate
- eternal, proper (for an occasion) - ordinary, sacred and profane, vertical - horizontal, or mental - physical. A simpler view identifies prayer as an intentional
relationship in which subject and object are indistinguishable. In this sense
subjectivity, which was a major focus of psychology around the turn of the
century (Ryan, 1991) was largely eliminated by the acceptance of behaviorism through the first half of the twentieth century. It is now being rehabilitated with a reformed subjectivism that recognizes "verbal reports as
data" (Ericsson and Simon, 1980), "the experiential dimension" (Richardson,
1984), "private events" (Jacobs and Sachs, 1971), mental imagery (Shephard,
1972), expectancies and self-efficacy (Bandura, 1972), reactions to situational demands (Ross and Nisbett, 1991), placebo effects (Frank and Frank,
1991), and even magical thinking (Zusne and Jones, 1989), as aspects of
main-stream psychology. Cognitive science (Gardner, 1987) aims to simulate some of these processes with computer models. The prejudice that psychologists continue to disregard subjective states and introspective data is only
true for those working within the behavioral traditions that developed in the
1920s and lasted in a strong form for about thirty years. They were criticized even then, but had deliberately avoided 'other minds' or the expectation that they might be known by observing what can be done. Their methods, which derived from studies of animals and of the biological features
of human behavior have, however, contributed immeasurably to modern
psychology.

But when Zusne and Jones (1989, p. 248) observed that "much of the
magic associated with religion is word magic, and names form an important
part of it," they recognized the importance of language, especially, in what
curses, blessings, oaths, and incantations, as well as "the pivotal practice of
the church, which is healing through prayer, [as] another form of word
magic" (ibid.) can do socially. They go on to say that:

> Prayer is the prime example of verbal magic associated with the prac-
> tice of religion. In terms of the intended purpose, two kinds of prayer are
> distinguished, supplicatory prayer and intercessory prayer. In terms of
> their effectiveness, these two forms are rather different. Praying for a
> physical event to occur, an event outside oneself, such as the occurrence
> of rain, the nonoccurrence of a disaster, the cessation of a disease, is pure
> word magic: An informational event in the agent is assumed to be capa-

ble of producing an energetic event outside the agent. Supplicatory prayer that addresses a need for change within the person praying may, however, be quite successful: Whether through self-suggestion or visualization, it may bring about both subjective and objective changes by altering one's emotional state or attitude. These, in turn, may correlate with a change in the physiology of nerve cells, cardiovascular system, the immune system, or overt behavior. Magic of the self can be real enough.

Even intercessory prayer may on occasion be reinforced, either by chance or because praying has occurred just before the prayed-for-event would have occurred anyway, such as praying for rain toward the end of a prolonged period of drought when the rains are bound to come anyway. Also, whether intercessory or supplicatory, praying in itself can have a beneficial effect on those who pray in that they may feel soothed and comforted because the burden of solving a problem has been passed on to a higher and more powerful authority. For all these reasons empirical research on the efficacy of prayer, such as the classical study of Francis Galton on the efficacy of prayer for rain (Galton, 1883), is of little use in convincing a believer that prayer does not work.

Religious injunctions that one should pray may be accompanied by the injunction that prayers be said hard and repeatedly. One consequence of this is that the time during which the desired-for event may occur is extended and the probability that it might occur by chance alone is increased. Another outcome is that praying may become so routinized that not only are prayers said without paying attention to the meaning of the words but that devices that substitute for speaking or thinking may be resorted to for the production of the requisite number of repetitions of a prayer but without the drudgery that such repetitions entail. Rosaries, prayer wheels, and prayer flags are examples. This is word magic once removed from its origin: The words are still there, but they are now in a written form, and the sending forth of them is accomplished via muscle, wind, or water power. A similar distancing between the spoken word and the speaker is seen in the use of prescribed numbers of recitations of the Lord's Prayer or Hail Mary to achieve specific magic aims.

Prayer may be uttered and word magic engaged in not just vocally but also subvocally or mentally. This is the connection between religion and psychology that was made in the New Thought movement. The "power of positive thinking" was to bring about all those positive things that one would wish for, notably health, wealth, and happiness. The theology of it was simple once the philosophy of idealistic monism was accepted: If the fundamental substance of the universe is mind, then God is mind, and the human mind is part of it. Hence, to use mind is to partake of God's power and perfection.

Because God is perfection and therefore perfect, to think God's thoughts is to bring about perfect health. The same goes for wealth: If God is abundance, thinking God's thought will lead to abundance. The health magic of New Thought, Christian Science, or Unity is real to the extent that mental states can affect bodily states (or at least this is how it appears). The relationship between thinking and wealth, however, is somewhat more problematic. Changed mental states do correlate with changed behavior, hence 'thinking abundance,' that is, becoming motivated to seek wealth, may in fact lead to greater actual wealth. This, however, is not the sort of connection that leaders of New Thought were thinking of. The connection was rather more magical: Thoughts were things that generated physical effects directly, and wealth could be obtained by circumventing physical causality (e.g. hard work). It could be obtained by just thinking about it, 'as if by magic.' In other words it was the notion that information processes internal to the thinker could bring about physical changes external to him (pp. 248-250).

This extract states some classically critical, or reinterpretive opinions about prayer that focus on one aspect of its phenomenology. Religious practices are themselves not necessarily built on, or understood through, assumptions that recognize it as 'magical.' Whether they are depends on one's stance and attitudes.

Language

Language is a flexible tool of communication tied to social needs, with a major role in maintaining and communicating religion. Although prayer is not set entirely within language, formulations of belief or doctrine and liturgy or ritual are, and the transcendent is often described with reference to narratives, whether in literature, mythology, or personal experiences. An early theory of the origin of language ascribed it to a divine source (Ogden and Richards, 1923, Chapter II, Exodus 31:18), and appeals to the written 'word' pervade the Bible. Writing itself can be used to achieve mystical effects in some traditions, and there are special languages for some sacred rituals. Naming animals and people enabled control over them, and words give a reality to religious images and to the characteristics of God. Alphabets were interpreted mystically and cabalistically: the archetypal fusion of words and meanings is captured in St John's Gospel: "And the word was God ."

That words are things and can "do things" lies at the basis of verbal magic, with a distinction between the quantity and the quality of words. Yet Jesus is reported to have said, "But when ye pray, use not vain repetitions, as the heathen do: for they think that they shall be heard for their much speaking" (Matthew 6:7). We have seen that medieval practices included fanning a person with pages of the Bible, or making a sick person eat paper with a prayer on it, since words can themselves induce a sense of awe and mystery, and exorcists cast out spirits in the name of the Lord Jesus (Acts 19:13). Praise is given to the name of God, as in Psalm 9:2, "I will sing praise to thy name, O thou most High," and can bring a blessing, produce a favor, enlist the power of God, support a plea, and be a reward: "If ye shall ask any thing in my name, I will do it" (John 14:14). Then there is blasphemy, as "a thing evil spoken of," in uttering impiety against God.

Language is therefore a social process, with a pervasive influence on the signs and symbols that carry or express the religions of individuals and groups. The religious statements that form a faith are explained or exegeted so that we may understand what religion means. By studying beliefs about God (Brown, 1987) we might determine why statements that refer to God can themselves license some linguistic formulae while banning others (cf Ferre, 1962, p. 93).

If we ask how language can validly express the inexpressible, this can be done in anthropomorphic terms (in the Old Testament), analogically with reference to a set of indefinable terms, or with reference to established and received statements whose meaning is accepted or explained within a social context. The features of God referred to in the Old Testament were decreed in oral traditions or forms of communication. The genre changed in the New Testament, with teaching through similes, symbols, metaphors, quotations from the Old Testament, and in parables or narratives about religion that continue to be glossed for their meaning, relevance and imagery.

The sound of words, especially when they are repeated, can 'hypnotize' or move us with their metrical beat and increasing familiarity (Zajonc, 1980). Repetition in religious worship, and in the prayers of those who believe, can motivate others to have recourse to prayer. Hence the statement that "God resides in the details," which has been variously ascribed to Flaubert, Einstein, and Le Corbusier. Those who accept this theology will realize that there are both macro *and* micro perspectives on one's own and others' prayer (and on those who pray). We also know that when prejudices become 'facts' it is hard to have them rescinded. So it is with beliefs about prayer (cf Burnam's [1975] *Dictionary of Misinformation*).

A continuing question might therefore ask whether it is prayer that shapes our minds and religious attitudes, or whether *we* shape the prayers we use and that move us. As an instance of the "chicken and egg problem" it must be left aside here. But there is point in understanding how prayer is used and what those who use it expect it to achieve and the prejudices surrounding it, that we might hope to defuse without recourse to Whorfian prejudices about the importance of the size of our vocabularies (Pullum, 1991), although the Oxford Dictionary's CD Rom has 221 separate references to 'prayer.' Systems of thinking or praying carried by language may be associated with particular cultural or religious traditions, and with individuals, while the spiritual meaning of a text is usually different from its literal meaning, despite the claims made by fundamentalists.

While prayer is defined as raising up the mind (and heart) to God, there are also public and shared prayers. The range of private prayer covers momentary, impulsive offerings, and the intense if apparently simple contemplation of a mystic that may or may not be formed in words. Public, especially liturgical, prayer is explicitly prescribed, and in the Free Churches the services, if not their language, are well-structured. That language and its accompanying activities and gestures support each other points to an underlying spirituality in "acclamations, responses, psalmody, antiphons, and hymns, as well as by actions, gestures, and bodily attitudes" (Constitution on the Sacred Liturgy, translated by C. Howell, p. 7, quoted by Crystal, 1965, p. 151).

Recognizing that there are colloquial or everyday and formal as well as sacred forms of language, their use is an important feature of religious practice. Accepting that religious language has correctness and archaism as its stylistic features, the recent and profound changes in English translations of the Bible and prayer books have divided conservative traditionalists from those who believe that revisions were needed for the Church to maintain its relevance. Those contrasting opinions seem, however, to have been more often based on principled argument than data, although vernacular forms are now widely used, if not universally accepted.

Welford (1946) showed, furthermore, that such preferences can be readily investigated, and that they were then rather conservative. Adams Smith (1989), however, notes that the new forms of worship that use inclusive language have involved lexical changes, "relating to connotation, reference, diction, and image" with unintentional semantic implications in the syntactic simplification.

But what can we *do* with words, beside using them to mean, or for "phatic communion" in which "ties of union are created by a mere exchange of words" (Malinowski, 1925). That will be examined later (on page 127), but the social function of words may carry little meaning beyond that embedded in everyday conversation, with polite remarks about the weather as opening gambits for greetings that may not allow a relationship to develop. The language of prayer appears to be conventional, and other meanings must be assigned if it is "to fly." And if communication is to be maintained, we should recognize the "atmosphere effect" (Woodworth and Sells, 1935) and the deliberate use of sounds that can achieve aesthetic or literary effects by alliteration and rhyme, for example. The understanding of any language is not necessarily immediate or self-evident and its suitability for different occasions must be learned. Contexts will also change meanings and we recognize whether someone who says, "Oh God," utters an explicit prayer or a gasp of fear.

Similarly, the logic that supports "God made man" is quite different from that supporting "He made a sand-castle," although they have a similar grammar, and to ask, "Where was God before the universe was made?" is meaningless since 'where' and 'before,' as terms about time and space, can have only a metaphorical relevance for some timeless Being. An important problem for understanding the uses of prayer therefore centers on attempts to cast it in contexts with transcendental implications that are realized only within that domain itself. Scientific or psychological analyses of behavior are similarly restricted, being models of the 'real' processes they purport to describe. Religious statements are therefore limited by their logic, their existential force and the beliefs and traditional meanings assigned to them, with the semantic differential offering a method by which such meanings can be accessed psychologically (cf Snider and Osgood, 1969).

So miracles and visions do not have to be understood simply in terms of the specific claims that can be made for or against them, since they must also be understood in relation to their own frameworks of belief, and not as exceptions to a normal course of events, or as veridical 'appearances.' Any language system or 'genre' therefore has its own uses and specific limitations, whatever confrontational or striking paradoxes might be imagined or examined through it. An important problem in coming to terms with prayer (or magic) and its language therefore involves the ways it is used. Private facts about one's hurts, pains or faith that are not observable are hard to display non-verbally in public, and their 'existence' can be misunderstood, with many conclusions about other people based on situational cues that may not be correctly interpreted, given the "fundamental attribution error" (Ross and Nisbett, 1991).

Prayer can therefore be understood within at least three separate contexts. The first is the religious tradition that prescribes or assigns meanings to 'prayer' (or 'prayers'), and to the legitimacy of their particular forms, whether they are wordless, involve glossolalia or speaking in tongues, a natural language with free or prescribed formats, or are associated with defined postures. Then we have those who pray, the language they use and the plausibility and values they find in whatever practices of prayer they accept. We need not assume that anyone who does pray has been primed for its practice by an implicit or personality-based predisposition, although they are likely to have been trained or socialized into some set of established prayer forms that are unlikely to be immutable. Then there are the accepted situations or contexts, and the recognized purposes for which prayer can be used as a deliberate practice, or to display and share one's religious ideas with others. Malinowski (1925) described this in the following terms: "The festive and public character of the ceremonies of cult is a conspicuous feature of religion in general. Most sacred acts happen in a congregation; indeed, the solemn conclave of the faithful united in prayer, sacrifice, supplication, or thanksgiving is the very prototype of a religious ceremony. Religion needs the community as a whole so that its members may worship in common its sacred things and its divinities, and society needs religion for the maintenance of moral law and order."

Although social norms and the language in which prayers are couched may change, they are supported by the traditions from which their primary meanings are assigned. Nevertheless, language can be misleading, when, for example, it divides the color spectrum, or identifies the properties of mind or body. Austin (1962) similarly identified a class of performative utterances which use words "to do things," as when we say 'I do' in a marriage, "I name this ship," "I give and bequeath," or 'I bet' (p. 5). Such utterances are not descriptions. They are actions that are neither true or false. As he said, this "needs argument no more than that 'damn' is not true or false: it may be that the utterance 'serves to inform'—but that is quite different" (p. 6).

If we accept that 'prayers' are performative in this sense, we remove from them abstract claims about where they are directed. That is made clear by their context, and by the beliefs or intentions that support them. Like actions, they are to be performed and then evaluated as contractual ('I bet') or declaratory ('I believe' or 'I pray that . . .'), with reference to the circumstances in which the words themselves are uttered. As Austin put it, they "should be in some way, or ways *appropriate*, and it is very commonly necessary that either the speaker himself or other persons should *also* perform certain *other* actions, whether 'physical' or 'mental' actions or even acts of uttering further words" (p. 8), in reaction to them.

That prayers have this character, and not only in relation to God, makes them immune to reductionistic criticisms of the meaning of those actions, which is limited by their context. So, in marrying, for example, "it is essential that one not be already married with a living spouse and undivorced" (p. 9), and a bet must be accepted by the taker. In that sense it is possible for prayers to lapse, when they are not taken seriously by someone from another religious tradition, for example. The validity of a prayer depends on its being spoken 'seriously,' although it is also commonplace to joke about prayers and to find them being used in plays. Perhaps a sacramental attitude (following Godin) is needed, when the outward and visible sign is accompanied by an inward and spiritual grace (or attitude), so that the "outward utterance is a description, *true or false*, of the occurrence of the inward performance" (Austin, 1962, p. 9). Austin reinforces that with reference to Hippolytus who said "my tongue swore to, but my heart (or mind or other backstage artiste) did not." Thus "I promise to . . . obliges me - puts on record my spiritual assumption of a spiritual shackle" (pp. 9-10). This turns a false promise (or prayer) into one given *in bad faith*, although it will not void it, and Austin points out that while we might not speak of a false bet or a false Christening, we do speak of a "false move" in a game (p. 11). So he notes that the laws of evidence do not recognize what is hearsay, accepting what is to be said as an action, and he recognizes that failures when "things go wrong" are infelicities. This approach emphasizes that prayers are governed by rules or conventions that specify the appropriate effects that can be claimed for them.

Although it was not cast within the context of Austin's analysis of performatives, an early study stressed that the appropriateness of petitionary prayers are prescribed, because of the consensus about what can be prayed for, while their efficacy remains a matter of judgment (Brown and Thouless, 1964). That study did not examine the consequences of good and bad (or infelicitous) prayers that might be flawed by being misapplied or insincere, and not merely inappropriate. So an old New Yorker cartoon shows a stockbroker kneeling by his bed and reading the stock-market reports. This emphasizes the conventional nature of performative utterances, through Austin's principle that "there must *exist* an *accepted* conventional procedure having a certain conventional effect, the procedure to include the uttering of certain words by certain persons in certain circumstances" (p. 26 with the emphasis added). When that is not satisfied, the 'prayer' becomes a 'joke,' which allows us to distance ourselves from it, or to reject codes of procedure about prayer, marriage, responsibility, and so on, when *the* 'rules' are not satisfied. So in some traditions it is 'impossible' for a woman to recite the prayer of consecration.

Questions about what we (or others) can and cannot do acceptably with (and through) prayer can only be answered by specifying the conventions or rules that govern its practice. That the essential ambiguity of religion itself inhibits only one prepared or received interpretation is paralleled by the fact that to say, "There is a bull in the field" may or may not be a warning, since it could describe the scenery. "I shall be there" may or may not be a promise, since "there may be nothing in the circumstances by which we can decide whether or not the utterance is performative at all" (Austin, 1962, p. 33). The persons involved, as well as their circumstances, must be appropriate before a prayer can be 'prayer' and not part of a game or a play. The limitations that Austin identified for any performative also include its intentionality, not having the requisite thoughts or beliefs, and advising a course of action that it is not thought to be expedient. Yet none of those factors makes it void, so Austin notes that these distinctions are all loose and not easily distinguishable (pp. 40-41). We might, therefore, accept that prayer could help to repair breaks in real or transcendental social relationships, in a manner that is similar to making an apology or giving thanks.

Austin further refined his concept of performative utterances by contrasting locutionary acts that carry conventional meanings against illocutionary acts that inform, order or warn, and the perlocutionary acts that we use to "bring about or achieve, by saying something, such as convincing, persuading, deterring, and even, say, suppressing or misleading" (p. 109). Perlocutionary acts might cover different kinds of prayer, by referring to intentionality or purpose, and what can be expected beyond any (specific or general) meanings the words might convey.

To approach prayer at its face value shows continuity in the language if not in its apparent meanings, with reference to the images and overt signs (or 'gestures') that express our attitudes. At a social or cultural level, habit, custom, and public opinion (which can be at variance with practice) provide interpretations of prayer that do not seem to answer the questions that psychologists are expected to be able to answer about it. Yet those problems when interpreting religious devotion or practice will remain as long as skepticism about any religious point of view appeals to its magical, superstitious, or irrational implications, and neglects its social and performative value.

It is unclear why social scientists have not aligned prayer with other social activities. Work and sport, for example, are self-validating, and although there could be similarities between the 'exercise' (or competition) that sport entails and the "spiritual exercises" of St Ignatius, it is the validity of the latter rather than the former that is questioned. Perhaps such questioning aims to rationalize processes that are not well understood, although in both sport and prayer individuals are engaged in a social activity, which in one case is directed at physical health or well-being, and at spiritual or mental health in the other. Their consequences may not be the same, although in both sport and prayer a goal could be to influence or control the self and others in social or natural environments with reference to a transcendental order. Beyond those practices lies a logic and reasoning about the results or the efficacy and appropriateness of any 'training' procedures, with close analogies between 'fitness' and success in each case.

Nevertheless, few people seem to think about prayer in those terms, perhaps because we have been dogged by problems about "how natives think" (Lévy-Bruhl, 1926) that accept the thought of 'religious people' as pre-scientific or traditional rather than 'modern.' While Lévy-Bruhl contrasted affective, poetic, and mythical thought forms against 'civilized' thought, which is rational, logical, and scientific, the primitive (or disordered) thought forms became a focus for psychiatric investigation and for developmental studies of the thought of children (Piaget, 1931). Those approaches neglect the differences between adults' deliberately playful and their serious uses of language, especially in the thought-forms that are found in art and literature. Scientism and political constraints have, however, presented severe barriers that imaginative work must cross, even after it has been socially approved or sanctioned, as the censorship of Joyce's *Ulysses* and Rushdie's *Satanic Verses* show.

Our current 'modernism' has exposed those prejudices by emphasizing the role of cultural contexts and the effects of deliberate training on the gender differences that were previously assumed to be 'natural' rather than cultural. 'Supernatural' cosmologies are socially constructed, even if their ideas are objectified, and dreams seem to be realistic, even when we accept them as only an 'experience.'

Halliday (1985, p. 30) makes a similar point about representing experience in talk or in writing, since talk accesses 'processes' and writing represents 'products.' Each of those codes finds "reality as being like itself," so that written language has the "form of an object, and depends on nouns." So when we talk, we are doing or acting, and use verbs. To express an event from the point of view of a reader requires a synoptic view because the text is spread out on the page, with a tableau of meaning standing behind it. A listener, on the other hand, is given a 'text' dynamically, with things happening. As a visual metaphor of these processes, Halliday contrasts a painting with a film, although he notes that modern technologies are blurring that distinction. Academic analyses defer to the textual and synoptic versions, and the practitioners fail to recognize themselves there.

The boundaries between spoken and written language can be as fluid as those between what is living and animate or dead, which could itself account for some of the current argument about when death occurs, and human organs can be harvested for transplantation, or whether abortion interferes with the finger of God, and if young children have an awareness of their own intentionality, in relation to that of 'other minds.'

Recent evidence supports the claim that the mind is in some sense compartmentalized or modularized, with our understanding of space, for example, quite different in character, structure, and development from our understanding of language. Developmental psychologists now claim that infants are predisposed to attend to faces *versus* speech, and that older children have "specific islands of expertise, about dinosaurs, physics, and chess" (Wellman and Gelman, 1992). They go on to note that "Various serious claims have been advanced: that human concepts are entrenched in larger naive theories; that conceptual change and thus important aspects of cognitive development are akin to theory change in science; that cultural worldviews are instantiated in folk theories; and that theories supplant similarity-based conceptions both in current scientific thinking and in the individual's own learning or development" (p. 338).

Scientific understanding

The earlier developmental psychology of mind assumed that it changed (or developed) in a generic sequence that moved from enactive to iconic and then symbolic modes (Bruner, 1964). This view replaced Piaget's (1950) theory of development from concrete to formal mental operations. It is now thought that either form of development is likely to be domain rather than process specific. If that is a robust finding, it could explain why some children appear to be interested in religion, in the sense that Chi (1978) found that "children who were chess experts outperformed adults who were chess novices in memory for chess board positions" (in Wellman and Gelman, p. 339), although it did not reflect a better overall memory. The relevance of such findings to religious development warrants further investigation for its application to conventional theories about the sequenced nature of religious judgment (Oser and Gmunder, 1991), to decide whether such development might depend on modular abilities, cognitive modes of processing, an explicit knowledge base, or on other implicit psychological theories, and their understanding of causality and coherence.

Similar problems surround scientific knowledge, with the assumption that our developing understanding of the world has formed the ground for the histories of science, and differences between serious and playful uses of words and ideas, or prayers. Langer (1951) illustrated the development of scientific thought through the dynamic evolution of understanding shadows. She found four stages in the descriptions of what happens when a shadow is cast on a table. "The first stage is characterized by a sort of reasoning by participation, akin to the manner of the primitives. The child declares, for example, that this shadow produced on the table comes from under the trees or from the sky, that is to say, from night, or from the depths of the room. In other words, for him there is not only identity of substance between the shadow produced and all the other shadows in the universe, but also direct action one with the others. It is sufficient to put a book above the table for a piece of the sky or a fragment of shade hanging under the trees to rush to take up a place under the book.

"During the second stage, the child renounces these participations, but, for all that, does not abandon the idea that shadow is a substance and that this substance moves about by itself. For the child the shadow comes from the hand, or from the book, and it can take its place on either side, no matter which. The relation between the shadow and the source of light is not understood at all.

"During the third stage, this relation is, on the contrary, distinctly perceived. The child realizes that the shade is always on the side away from the window or the lamp. But the child still continues to believe that the shadow is a substance issuing from the book or from the hand. If this substance makes for the side away from the daylight it is because the shadow is black and flees from the day.

"It is only during the fourth stage, that is to say at about nine to ten years, that the shadow is clearly understood as an absence of light, and that the object, the cause of the shadow, is considered as a simple screen. We thus see how these various actions converge to show the progressive abandonment of dynamism in favor of a rational and mechanical explanation" (p. 546).

That description encapsulates in another domain a well-developed account that is relevant for understanding the intangibility of prayer, which helps to counter bald criticisms of the formal logic and the psycho-logic that has been used to describe, and then explain prayer.

To personify the world and express its nature through myths and stories does nothing to change beliefs in the causal efficacy of spells, wishes, or commands. To assume that those who pray have an 'unreal' (meaning 'religious') attitude to the world, expecting their prayers to be concretely or causally effective is a prejudiced over-generalization. While we might question those beliefs, anyone who prays can be asked about their expectations and successes. But if such questions are direct and not carefully phrased, strongly implicit or social demands can shape the answers, and 'mature' religious attitudes must come to terms with the realization that although one's prayers might seem to be effective, if in unknown ways, they are not necessarily so, even when they appear to be expressed in a simple or naive way. The concept of 'causal efficacy' can never capture the breadth of attitudes to prayer among Christians. To believe that God hears and explicitly answers petitionary prayers does not preclude the answer being "No!" or that the prayers may be self-directed. And as Brown and Thouless (1965) showed, adults find it hard to decide if a bush-fire is 'alive.'

If this chapter had also referred to popular, 'naive' or commonsense interpretations of prayer (cf Kelley, 1992) one might go on about the 'diagnostic' (and prescriptive) uses of psychological theories that depend on personality types, perhaps using the Enneagram (Rohr, 1991) or Myers-Briggs systems that would identify a person's 'true' character and their resistance to confronting that, when approaching God or themselves through prayer, and in a way that identifies the 'true' balance between their tendencies to think, feel, or act.

But those approaches are closer to a "religious psychology" than to the psychology of religion. Yet those procedures are widely used, and focus popular forms of spiritual direction that seem very close to those advocated by humanistic and transpersonal psychologies, while relying on theories that are too prescriptive for most empirically trained psychologists.

Chapter Eight

Anti- And Other Prayers

Mark Twain said in his Notebook, *"Let us swear while we may, for in heaven it will not be allowed."*

The nature of prayer from the stance of someone who prays may, like the rest of religion, carry either extrinsic or intrinsic meanings and goals, following Allport's (1950) contrast between the instrumental and expressive uses of religion. Those who *use* their religion might regard it as a ritual, or as a form of incantation for religious rather than secular purposes. Others who may have 'purified' their religious motives of concrete or immature wishes, hopes, or fears might be expected to align themselves with the will of God. The Collect for Trinity XIII hopes, "That we ask those things that will be good for us." In this sense the 'wish' in that prayer is to be able to change oneself.

This counterpoint between a focus on self and on other (or the Other), and between private or personal, and public, social, or societal demands and needs is readily identified, but not easily resolved without guidance (if not 'direction') about the attitudes that *should* support prayer. Psychologists are in danger of making gratuitous interpretations about this that reflect cultural stereotypes and may not support religious perspectives. One problem here is, of course, the range of religious perspectives that is available, which need not share a common core.

Those global perspectives are different from confronting the efficacy of any actual *words* that can be used in prayer, independently of the meanings carried by them, or the attitudes that might support classical spells and incantations, for example. So "abracadabra" is identified in the *Concise Oxford Dictionary* as a "spell, magic formula; gibberish - [cabalistic word supposed when written triangularly, and worn, to cure fevers, etc.]." That the cabbala "refers to a Jewish oral tradition; mystic interpretation, esoteric doctrine, occult lore" emphasizes the religious ambiguity of such signs or usages. We

133

might also enquire why a cross is being worn, or whether someone would agree with the joke in *Punch* about a man who took his car to a garage for servicing, and is reported to have said, "Never mind the brakes, just polish up the St Christopher badge"?

In this connection it has already been noted that Phillips (1965, p. 115) remarked, "When men are in danger, or think they are facing death, they sometimes pray a certain kind of prayer which can be summed up as, 'O God, O God.' Bonhoeffer (1959) gives an example of this, in telling of an incident during a heavy bombing raid on a concentration camp where he was a prisoner. 'As we were all lying on the floor yesterday, someone muttered, 'O God, O God'—he is normally a frivolous sort of chap—but I couldn't bring myself to offer him any Christian encouragement or comfort. All I did was to glance at my watch and say: 'It won't last any more than ten minutes now'" (in *Letters and Papers from Prison*, p. 67).

It is not clear if 'prayers' offered in times of distress show an urge to pray that is "latent in everyone," an impetuous outburst in crisis, or whether prayer is available to those who know when, and how to use it. Phillips' criteria that contrast a religious prayer against its superstitious use are to be found crucially in the continuing value of prayer when the crisis is over. The same criterion can be applied to church-going, or stealing Christian "instruments of worship" to use them for "black magic," which again emphasizes the ambiguity of religious 'signs.' A common criticism of religion (after Freud) holds that it involves mere repetition (which is one of the root meanings of 'religion'), so that it is then identified by extrapolation as an obsessive-compulsive disorder. Whether that diagnosis could be applied to those in non-Western religious traditions, without prejudice, requires some knowledge of the inside meanings of those other practices. Prayers for specific favors are always ambiguous and might seem incantational if no other courses of action seem possible, although recent emphases in health psychology on coping strategies suggest that prayer itself has adjunctive and therapeutic possibilities (to use a medical analogy). Our question should not be simply, "Was there a prayer?" but "What else did you do?," and "Does every prayer include that?"

Even if prayers are isolated and not a part of life before or after a crisis, an act of prayer could still be deeply felt. But there seem to be no accepted rules about how often anyone *should* pray, for their prayer to be thought effective, or morally approved. A *reductio* in that argument stresses the concrete thinking of those accepting fundamentalistic beliefs or expecting that prayer is appropriate when looking for a parking place. But we do not know which assumptions about the nature of prayer are shared within, let alone across religious traditions and perspectives. In the previous example, Bonhoeffer stressed that he did not speak religiously, but offered comfort. Perhaps a religious stance, unlike swearing, carries 'added value,' to use an economic or financial metaphor. Prayer should, therefore, be set against swearing and imprecation in the use of religious language.

Crystal (1987, p. 10) notes that the release of emotional tension (or "nervous energy when we are under stress," as he put it) is an important function of language when using swear words and obscenities, but also in our "involuntary verbal reactions to beautiful art or scenery," in conventional words or phrases (like 'gosh'), and in semi-linguistic interjections ('tut-tut') in which the prosody (and especially the intonation) is an important way of expressing attitudes when we speak. Swearing, like prayer, can also be a social marker of group membership and identity. Crystal notes that other uses of language can be 'ideational' and to facilitate social interaction, in the manner identified by Malinowski as phatic communication, when we say "Bless you" if someone sneezes, which draws the answer, "Thank you." English orthography uses punctuation to signal such prosodic emphases and nuances, as in Gerard Manley Hopkins' "(my God) 'my God' ( )." In that context, Hemingway is said to have said of writing that it cannot be taught, but that it can be learned. The same may apply to prayer.

Cursing and swearing use both complex and sophisticated expressions from religious, legal, and other formal contexts, and simplified or taboo forms of speech in the profanities and obscenities that express hatred, antagonism, frustration, or surprise. Crystal (1987, p. 61) therefore notes that "Sex, excretion, and the supernatural are the main sources of swear words," especially through tabooed body parts and the "names of gods, devils, sacred places, the future life, and anyone or anything that holds a sacred place in the belief systems of the community: God, Dear Lord, Heavens, Hell," and 'by Jove.'

Swearing and blaspheming

Since Robert Graves' (1927) *Lars Porsena or The Future of Swearing, and Improper Language* reads like an examination of 'anti-prayer,' it is worth quoting from it directly, for its historical interest alone. Graves began by noticing the decline of "swearing and foul language," and that a "shock to our national nervous system might revive the habit of swearing simultaneously with that of praying." He then writes:

> While obscene and blasphemous tongues are temporarily idle, it would be well to inquire intelligently into the nature and necessity of their employment: a ticklish theme and one seldom publicly treated except in comminations from orthodox pulpits. It is to be hoped that this essay will steer its difficult course without private offense to the reader as without public offense to the Censor.
>
> To begin with a few necessary commonplaces. The chief strength of the oath in Christian countries, and indeed everywhere, is that it is forbidden by authority, and the Mosaic injunction against taking the name of Jehovah in vain must mark the beginning of our research. This commandment seems to have had a double force, recording in the first place a taboo against the mention, except on solemn occasions, of the tribal god's holy name (for so among certain savage tribes it is still considered unlucky to use a man's real name, often only known to himself and the priest), and in the second place a taboo against the misuse of even a decent

periphrasis of the god's name: for the act of calling him to witness any feat or condition, or the summons to curse or destroy an enemy, must involve elaborate purifications or penalties. Any vain appeal to God to witness or punish a triviality was therefore forbidden as lessening not only the prestige of religion but also the legal dues of the priestly commissioners of oaths. Now however that the economic interest has dwindled, and priesthood has been shorn of temporal powers, the vain oath is no longer punishable with stoning or with the stake—it is regarded merely as a breach of the peace. "Goddam you, sir, for your interference," spoken to a railway company official, is not liable to greater penalties than "To the pigs with dirty King William," spoken in Belfast. Though the railwayman is given credit for possible religious fanaticism, and though the goddam-er is formally reminded of the solemn nature of the oath when he kisses the Book in the witness-box, the Almighty is left to avenge the spiritual fault personally.

The taboo on vain mention of God or Gods is also extended to the divine mysteries, to the sacraments and sacred writings, and to the human representatives in Heaven where they are permitted direct communion with the Absolute. In Catholic countries, Saints and Prophets are, therefore, used for swearing in a low key, and it has meant a serious lessening of the dignity of the Almighty in England that Protestantism and Dissent have removed these valuable intermediaries from objurgation as from adoration. In Catholic countries, too, the Bible is not vulgarly broadcast, and an oath by the Great Chained Word of God is resonant and effective; while in England the prolific output of sixpenny-worths and even pennorths of the Holy Scriptures from secular presses has further weakened the vocabulary of the forceful blasphemer. The triumph of Protestantism is, perhaps, best shown by the decline into vapidity of "By George!," the proudest oath an Englishman could once swear; for the fact is we have lost all interest in our Patron Saint. . . .

Undistinguished as the oath by St George has become, he has at any rate had the honor of outlasting all his peers. Where is there an Englishman who, mislaying his purse or his pipe, will threaten it in the name of St Anthony? or blackguarding a cobbler for making a bad repair to his boots will swear by the holy last of St Crispin that, if that cobbler does not do the job again properly, he will have half-a-pound of his own blunt brads forced down his lying throat? And who has England got to match the Pope as a swearing-stock? Once in a public-house a young Italian and a middle-aged Londoner were arguing politics. The Italian paid a warm tribute to the Vatican and its works. "Oh, to hell with the Pope!" remarked the Englishman. "And to hell," replied the furious Italian, upsetting the glasses with a blow of his first, "and to hell with your Archbishop of Canterbury!" The Englishman swallowed the insult agreeably, but expostulated on the waste of good liquor.

Bound up with the taboo on the mention of God, of Heaven His throne, and Earth His footstool, and of all His other charges and minions is the complementary taboo on the Devil, His ministers, and His prison-house. At one time the vain invocation of the Devil was an even more dangerous misdemeanor than the breach of the third Commandment. God, though He would not hold him guiltless who took His Name in vain, might forgive an occasional lapse; but the Devil, if ever called in professionally, would not fail to charge heavily for His visit.

However, since the great Victorian day when an excited working-man came rushing out of the City church where Dean Farrar was preaching the gospel and shouted out to his friends at the public-house corner: "Good news! old Farrar says there's no 'ell,'" the taboo has yearly weakened. "That dreadful other place," as Christina respectfully called it in the death-bed scene of Butler's *Way of the Flesh*, is now seldom dwelt upon in the home pulpit, though the Law still formally insists on it as true because deterrent. One regretfully hears that the threat of hell's quenchless flames and the satyro-morphic view of Satan are now chiefly used for export purposes to Kenya and the Congo Basin, as a cement to the bonds of Empire.

There is no surer way of testing the current popular religious opinion than by examining the breaches of the taboos in swearing. At the present day the First Person of the Trinity is not taken too seriously. "O God!" has become only a low-grade oath and has crept into the legitimate vocabulary of the drawing-room and the stage. The Second Person, since the great evangelical campaigns of the last century overturned a despotism and inaugurated a spiritual republic, is far more firmly established. To swear by Jesus Christ is an oath with weight behind it. The Third Person is seldom appealed to, and makes a very serious oath, partly because of the Biblical warning that the sin against the Holy Ghost is the one unforgivable offense, and particularly because the word *Ghost* suggests a sinister spiritual haunting. "God" to the crowd is a benevolent or a laughable abstraction; Jesus Christ is a hero for whom it is possible to have a warm friendly feeling; but the Holy Ghost is a puzzle and to be superstitiously avoided.

From blasphemy and semi-blasphemy it is only a short step to secular irreverence. Many secular objects where they have become symbolic of deep-seated loyalties are held in the highest reverence by naval, military, and sporting society. The Crown and the Union Jack are for the governing classes enthroned beside the Altar and the Communion-cup. . . . (pp. 5-14).

Tristram Shandy, who was an Elizabethan born too late, treats of contemporary swearing and protests against the connoisseurs of swearing that they have pushed the formal critical control of swearing too far. He speaks of a gentleman, "who sat down and composed, that is, at this leisure, fit forms of swearing suitable to all cases from the lowest to the highest provocation which could happen to him; which forms being well considered by him and such more-over as he could stand to, he kept them ever by him on the chimney-piece within his reach, ready for use." Tristram Shandy finds this practice too far academic. He asks no more than a single stroke of native genius and a single spark of Apollo's fire with it, and Mercury may then be sent to take the rules and compasses of correctness to the Devil. He says furthermore that the oaths and imprecations which have been lately "puffed upon the world as originals" are all included by the Roman Church in its form of excommunication: that Bishop Ernulphus who formulated the exhaustive commination which he quotes (and which later the Cardinal used with such success on the Jackdaw of Rheims) has indeed brought categorical and encyclopaedic swearing to a point beyond which there can be no competition. He asks what is our modern "God damn him!" beside Ernulphus':

May the Father who created man curse him!
May the Son who suffered for us curse him!
May the Holy Ghost who was given to us in baptism curse him!
May the Holy Cross, which Christ for our salvation triumphing over his
    enemies ascended, curse him!
May the holy and eternal Virgin Mary, mother of God, curse him!
May all the angels and archangels, principalities and powers, and all
    the heavenly armies curse him! (pp. 35-37).

As part of its physiological ground, Graves notes the "alliterative emphasis and rhythm of swearing speech," contrasting its indecency against prayer and the places for prayer. He supported his argument by instances from stories and ethnographic accounts. But a PSYCLIT search on 'swearing' shows that the work being published now addresses its social inappropriateness, except for its place in sport and its obsessional or automatic character (Chastaing, 1976). It is worth noting that a physiological basis is suggested for Tourette's Disorder as a psychiatric syndrome that presents with recurrent, involuntary, and repetitive rapid movements or tics, and in which 60 percent of the cases present "an irresistible urge to utter obscenities" (DSMIII, 1980, p. 76). This supports the physiological relief that swearing is widely assumed to offer, rather than the 'sublimation,' as Graves calls it, in swearing, as the "poor man's poetry," although he did note that "in this mechanical age, even our swearing has been standardized" (p. 42) and emphasized the alliterative emphasis and rhythm of swearing which, interestingly, has not been noted as a specific characteristic of prayer.

Swearing must also be distinguished from blasphemy, where there is a definite intention to vilify in a religious way, and from the religious language that involves speaking in tongues or the glossolalia that displays a repetitive, reduced range of syllabic and rhythmic patterns, to signal sincerity of belief, evidence of conversion, or a gift of the Spirit (cf Malony and Lovekin, 1985).

Religious control

Crystal (1987, p. 12) concluded that "all forms of supernatural belief involve the use of language as a means of controlling the forces which the believers feel affect their lives. The various prayers and formulae which are directed at God, gods, devils, spirits, objects, and other physical forces are always a highly distinctive form of language." In relation to that, Crystal (as a Catholic) notes that prayer is "a somewhat abnormal type of communication, for the response is usually appreciated only in the mind or behavior of the speaker, and there may be no evident response at all." Similarly in the Mass, speaking the words "This is my body" identifies the moment when the communion bread is changed into the body of Christ, without a change of substance. As in naming a ship at its launch, we have seen (on p. 129) that this is a performative utterance (Austin, 1962), that is open only to well-defined ('ordained') individuals.

Other varieties of religious language cover liturgical forms that may be spo ken or sung by individuals, in unison or antiphonally, 'acts' of invocation, petition, doxology and praise, intercession, thanksgiving and litany which derive from the Bible or from other sacred writings carried by a tradition. There are defined prayer forms for baptism, confirmation, confession, funerals, meditation, absolution and other cleansing rights, vows, exorcism, and for blessing people, places, and objects. Religious texts are read, doctrines expounded, and affirmations of belief made in public or in private, with mystical or other intentions, in normal or ecstatic states, and to praise, prophesy, or show that one is possessed by a spirit. At the same time, silence is also valued, especially in George Fox's Quakerism, and in Buddhism where thought is paramount and the 'spirit' leads.

Questions about why prayer fails draw formal answers that include inadequate faith, not praying hard enough, or having some measure of blame. A lack of commitment or devotion could also be found, but probably not as a 'superstitious attitude' (Devlin, 1987). When prayers are expressed in gesture, the ambiguity of those signs becomes important and the garland on a statue of the Virgin could be an act of thanksgiving, a request for assistance, or a pious devotion.

Whether such signs are judged to be effective raises attributional questions about their meaning that center on the 'grammar' of prayer, and on interpretations of what are meant to be specific (or abstract) statements about our helplessness or religiousness. If prayer is to be read as a statement of a desire or wish, or to be accepted simply as a statement, William James (1902, p. 463) held that it "should be encouraged as a therapeutic measure."

To ask, "Why do the wicked prosper?" might show an awareness of the inequity of the 'system,' or God's lack of goodness rather than resignation or dependence on a community. Alternatively, to hold that God prays in us (cf Thomas Merton, 1950) is hard to comprehend because it entails a 'religious' interpretation that belongs with faith and not psychology. St Augustine's *Confessions* (Book 1.1) asked, "For who can call on Thee, not knowing Thee? For he that knoweth Thee not, may call on Thee other than Thou art." In that sense there is an inevitable circularity in prayer that many outsiders to religion find it impossible to break into, and from which others find it hard to escape, once they are inside.

Prayer could also be like telepathy if we are asked to pray for those in the "mission field," unless such prayer is only to be understood within a community. This is, however, not a psychological but a religious issue, since in that capacity psychologists cannot know how "divine power is harnessed," which is a matter of belief. As Phillips put it (1965, p. 129), "What is possible stands as the center term between two extremes: the impossible and the necessary. If, in relation to prayer, one confuses the center term with either of the extremes, it leads to untold misunderstandings."

If our prayers 'fail' we have no greater support for blaming ourselves than for blaming God, if an analogy between prayer and a scientific test or experiment is accepted. But if a scientific experiment fails we blame the experimenter, the apparatus, or the experimental design. If God is to blame, no one can expect a necessary connection between the hoped for result, the means to that, and the outcome, since that would deny the nature of prayer. A similar argument can be advanced against those expecting consistent results from an experiment on the efficacy of prayer, which binds God to *our* logic. But do 'instincts' of self-preservation weigh against resignation (or a fatalistic attitude) for *any* outcomes? Can we pray 'religiously' and not have some positive beliefs about God? Is 'praying' to God, for whom all things are possible, to love God whatever the outcome? Are our prayers in any sense contingent? Must we distinguish pseudo-prayer from a *true* 'prayer' or from individual needs and the community within which they are set? Should a focus when examining reactions to prayer be on what it means to "talk to God" in prayer? Issues like these involve concepts about who (or what) God is, and the contexts in which prayer is appropriate. They might all be answered in terms of the ejaculations that are thought to typify swearing. We are also taught to pray by listening to the prayers of others, although their effects are said to depend on God, on some feature of the real, natural or social world, or on some other reality constructed from assumptions about the transcendent, or from our own ideas, imagination, and cultural archetypes, rather than their effect on those who might hear our prayers.

However those issues are resolved, they contrast what is private against whatever is public and social or traditional within both religious and secular domains. To learn to pray is to learn what a community accepts and sanctions as a relationship to God, and to those who guide them through prayer (and blaspheming). So prayer is taught by example (cf Francis and Brown, 1991), and it is not necessarily disclosive, despite being heavily protected (or criticized). How much intellectual content it carries depends on the community that supports it, and the ease with which those who pray can be swept into some state of altered awareness. A 'problem' there is how to prepare one's state of mind for those *other* levels of awareness. That can be achieved chemically, by spiritual exercises, or by the mere repetition of words or phrases.

The classical spiritual exercises of St Ignatius stress the fact that a pre-history of psychology can be found in religious traditions, as much as in philosophy and physiology. Advice by medieval mystics about prayer can similarly be read as manuals of self-help, guidance, or therapy based on an implicit or commonsense psychology that was supported experientially rather than empirically. Modern psychological research began by system-atizing those and other opinions, although none of that science will displace the subjective validity of what can be experienced, even when it is inter-preted with reference to an ideological system that might reduce one's con-fidence in their religion. Some claims are rhetorical, as in the hymn, "I heard the voice of Jesus say, come unto me and rest," without entering the theo-logical debate, a quest for the historical Jesus (Schweitzer, 1913) and for the Jesus of faith must both be driven by prior ideological claims.

The signs by which the actions of God are detected, whether in miracles or other mysterious events, are 'easily' explained through the concepts of attri-bution theory (Kelley, 1992). How they are recognized is another question. Some medical cures are hard to explain when we do not know the mechanisms that might have produced them, and they seem to violate the received laws of nature. We might find some evidence for ourselves, or rely on others' claims on faith or divine intervention. That could be a terminological prob-lem or it might involve a deep mystery that, like an unsolved crime, demands more information. Accepting miracles as evidence for religious truth, or as veridical events, reflects different attitudes to faith, as do 'punishments' from God that could reflect a sense of guilt or a set of religious beliefs them-selves. When those solutions are not grounded in the life or beliefs of a reli-gious community, they could be psychologically disclosive and not part of a web in which the God to whom one prays is at the core.

The psychology of religion that developed at the end of the nineteenth cen-tury emphasized subjectivity and experience, neglecting the social nexus within which meaning was found. In her analysis of that period Ryan (1991, p. 17) remarks that "It would be tempting to imagine that the line of influence from empiricist thought to (literary) impressionism was a direct one, but in fact it proves to be more elusive." Yet it is important to identify the social and psychological influences on our religious thought or practice, independent-ly of such interpretive theories as Skinner's (1989) pessimism which led him to say, "Man's struggle for freedom is not due to a will to be free, but to certain behavioral processes characteristic of the human organism, the chief effect of which is the avoidance of or escape from so-called 'aversive' fea-tures of the environment."

Subjectivity

When we confront the earlier theories that still have scientific respectabil-ity, we should remember that William James (and other academics of his time) had an interest in psychic demonstrations, while admitting that he had never had a mystical experience himself. Drawing on those demonstrations and other confessional sources he advanced the idea that there exist in the uni-verse various types of energies on which our consciousness can draw, under certain circumstances (cf Ryan, 1991, p. 15), giving access to a "wider world of being than that of everyday consciousness" (James, 1902, p. 412). Building theories of consciousness in this way, from the accounts of others, is no longer psychologically acceptable.

The logic or grammars of prayer distinguish its causes from the propriety and attitudes or conclusions about what can be expected from it. Since they are never self-evident we must form our own conclusions about its efficacy, and whether any effects are in the 'real' world, in the mind, or within some ideal or transcendental order. Earlier accounts might have been in terms of "cognitive dissonance" (Festinger, 1957), or with reference to a mental algebra by which values assigned to the elements of an argument would be balanced (Heider, 1946) or made consistent (Rosenberg and Abelson, 1960). The core of Festinger's theory was that "any decision between alternative courses of action (or beliefs) will lead to a state of psychological tension or 'dissonance' to the extent that the net attractiveness of the two alternatives is similar. This state of dissonance, moreover, does not immediately dissipate once the individual has embarked on this chosen course of action. For it to be so, he must usually engage in some 'cognitive work' that evaluates the relevant 'cognitive elements'" (Eiser, 1980, p. 132). In the case of prayer, dissonance resolution could be 'pro or con' when reconstructing its foreseen consequences by saying, for example, "I never thought the prayer would be successful." Such 'rationalizing' is crucial for understanding the importance of our attitudes to prayer. They are not only cognitive (in the sense that they involve beliefs), but they carry evaluations and an emotional stance about prayer as a whole, or about its targets and specific practices. So people may pray regularly and conscientiously or only occasionally, in public or in private, with attitudes that may be consistent or variable. The prescriptiveness and protection of prayer is complemented by a concern that denying its validity can itself draw criticism.

The privacy of prayer allows one to express inner feelings, and constrains what will be said about it, unless we are in a confessional mode. This means that descriptive studies, even when they compare defined groups, offer only limited insight into the psychological processes that might support its practice. The conclusions drawn from those data can be misunderstood, but as Emerson said, "Is it so bad, then, to be misunderstood? Pythagoras was misunderstood, and Socrates, and James, and Luther, and Copernicus, and Galileo, and Newton, and every pure and wise spirit that ever took flesh. To be great is to be misunderstood."

Those who hold that prayer makes it possible to control the natural world rather than the self may show over-belief, in the sense that swearing also can become a habitual form of expression. Yet "the devotees of overbelief seem much like the anchorites William James criticizes in his discussion of saintliness. Systematic thought offers a refuge of order and stability in a disorderly world. In contrast James prefers the instability, incompleteness, and vagueness of the experiential" (Ruf, 1991, p. 66). As James put it, "As soon as we deal with private and personal phenomena as such, we deal with realities in the completest sense of the term" (1902, p. 393). But he also noted that "whenever a procedure is codified, the more delicate spirit of it evaporates" (p. 245), and that "a genuine first-hand religious experience . . . is bound to be a heterodoxy to its witnesses." If it becomes an orthodoxy it can be counted as "a staunch ally in every attempt to stifle the spontaneous religious spirit" (p. 270). In this sense psychology also imposes convergent pressures to be objective, since subjectivity is mercurial.

W.H. Clark noted that, "as a whole, the psychologist's contribution to religion is mainly a rational one. The psychologist is like the music critic, who can analyze and therefore help the hearer to appreciate. And so, as a psychologist of religion, I work to understand when I can. But ultimately I must stand in awe before what, as a psychologist, I cannot match—the authentic religious life. This is the subtlest, most profound, yet puzzling and paradoxical, of the achievements of the human spirit" (1958, pp. 236-237). To stress subjectivity does not, however, allow us to disregard the theological support and justification that religious traditions (and denominations) give to generic religious practices, especially in prayer. And Donahue (1989) notes that "some social scientists project on to conservative religionists in general and fundamentalists in particular the sort of closed-mindedness and prejudice which the scientists *feel* toward the religionists."

Yet it is worth assembling the evidence that has been used to support beliefs in the existence of God, how to detect the will of God, and whether prayer alters the real world, since "the will of God is determined by prevailing beliefs about God. In short, God's nature is the grammar of God's will" (Phillips, 1965, p. 153). Heretics and reformers (as groups about which psychologists of religion have had little to say) and perhaps maniacs, are embarrassing because they question doctrinal teaching, while the unchurched have no place for religion. The less rigid social controls in our own time mean that heresies are infrequently identified now, and appear to have little impact on religious practice. Even Galileo was rehabilitated by the Pope in 1992.

It is therefore difficult to say what a mature prayer ought to be like, without reference to a religious tradition and the attitudes of those who have been influenced by it and its established reference points. The relativity inherent in that might hold that the truth of prayer cannot be distinguished from a readiness to pray in accordance with the grammar or rules of a tradition. Both naturalistic and supernatural fallacies must be avoided in that, because of their implications for what is within or beyond nature, rather than for what permeates it. Since religion tunes human actions to an envisaged cosmic order that was designed before we could know how it was made, the sense of that is maintained through the texts, sermons, and rituals that orient us to words, especially in prayer. It can do this for many people, but as the statistics show, not for everyone. Cassirer (1946) therefore held that religious symbols help to unlock reality, through a world of their own, although, like prayer, their referential value is not transparent and must be learnt. Similarly, the everydayness of poets who may speak to our "streams of consciousness," use a voice that is not easily heard, while those who swear or blaspheme use a language that has been detached from its apparent roots, primarily for its expressive value.

Chapter Nine

Attitudes to Prayer

"Which annoys God the more: to be addressed familiarly as 'You,' or to be invoked in revisionists' bad grammar, as in 'O God, who sees . . .' (the vocative followed by a verb in the third-person singular)?"—Phillip Howard, Winged Words.

Within Christianity at least, prayer is widely recognized as the prototypic religious act. Support for this assertion can be found in the Bible, and in the traditions that derive from it, with the Lord's Prayer its paradigm. But prayer is not specific to Christianity, since it can be found in other religions and in secular, especially legal, contexts. Religiously prayerful attitudes are detected in what is said, in postures and gestures, and in the prayer books and hymnals that contain 'pattern prayers,' through the icons, furniture, buildings, and other places that assist prayer, and in the respect given to those who are thought to be in prayer. They might be praying for specific outcomes, or putting themselves into a prayerful (or meditative) 'attitude,' or into some other mental state.

But none of these modes or other accompaniments of prayer identifies it well, not least because prayer need not be displayed or depend on traditionally set forms, even when it is part of an explicit ritual or liturgy. And we can easily be a spectator who takes part without intending to pray. That 'prayer' is usually protected and regarded as private (and possibly secret) presents a problem for the 'psychology of prayer' if it restricts us to what pray-ers will say while they are at prayer or afterwards, and what they can give access to, whether through psychophysiological recordings or direct questioning, and to whatever else can be observed or conjectured about their actions. The sense of immediacy or need that has been expected to stimulate prayer and give it its potency presents problems for any attempts to gather acceptable data for a psychological account. That could be one reason why Meehl asked (or asserted), "Can any psychological analysis of prayer ever be science or sci-

144

entific, rather than (hopefully) an artful analysis that seems to be a rather soft or 'wet' psychology?" Furthermore, because questions about personal prayers are thought intrusive, most of the direct data we have come from volunteers, unless we rely on detached observations of postures, or the depth of genuflection, for example (Allport, 1934).

If we appear to be in communion (or communication) with God, the respect of others is provoked when we signal prayerful gestures in prostration, kneeling, standing, or bowing, with hands crossed, folded, or raised up, head bowed with eyes closed or with the head raised towards heaven. Special garments may be put on or worn, and ablutions might be part of the preparation for prayer (cf Heiler, 1923, p. 98ff). Bauml and Bauml (1975), in their *Dictionary of Gestures* emphasize the importance of the hands in prayer, across time and traditions (pp. 158-162), perhaps because of their expressiveness and the way they can symbolically display one's identity. Even in the catacombs, "worshipers are portrayed with arms outstretched to the sides in imitation of the crucifixion" (p. 159).

Gesture and posture

In a study of such prayerful attitudes, [1]sixteen males and forty-eight females who had been identified from a large sample of Australian students as actively religious (N=17), not religious (N=28) or 'doubtfully religious' (N=19), were asked to rate eight pictures of people in prayerful postures on each of eight bipolar adjective scales covering 'evaluation' and 'religious orthodoxy,' that had been derived from Osgood's (1952) semantic differential, and were previously used by Brown and Moore (1990). The stimuli consisted of two females and two males who were evidently Christian, two statues of the Buddha and two uncertainly religious males in stereotypically religious postures. (Each stimulus measured 11.5 by 14 cm and was reproduced by a color Xerox process.)

From each subject's eight adjectival ratings of each of the eight stimuli, separate 'evaluation' and 'religious orthodoxy' scores were calculated by summing the appropriate scale-scores. These became dependent measures in a multivariate analysis of variance (MANOVA 1) with a 2x2x4 design that examined the differences between men and women, and between religious and nonreligious subjects. As repeated measures on the third factor, a set of contrasts was planned to test differences between the ratings of (i) the female and male Christian figures, (ii) the Christian and Buddhist males, and (iii) the Christian males and the 'uncertainly' prayerful males. A Bonferroni adjustment was used to control the family-wise error-rate at $\alpha =$ .05 for each contrast and the interactions. Further analyses (MANOVA 2) examined the same differences between the nonreligious and 'doubtfully' religious, and between the religious and 'doubtfully' religious subjects as main effects, testing differences between the stimulus figures with the same repeated measure contrasts as in the first analysis.

---

1. This study was done in collaboration with Dr. Gail F. Huon.

The means and standard deviations of the evaluations and religious orthodoxy ratings for each of the eight stimuli are in Table 1, which shows that
while an image of the Virgin Mary was evaluated as the most positive, and
the most religious stimulus, the two uncertainly prayerful males were seen
as being the least religious. (In these analyses low scores indicate a more
positive evaluation, or a more religious rating.)

Table 6					
Means and standard deviations for the evaluation and religious orthodoxy ratings for each of the eight stimuli.					
		Evaluation		Religious orthodoxy	
Stimuli	Number	Mean	SD	Mean	SD
Christian	1	7.6	4.0	8.4	3.2
females	2	11.3	5.3	14.7	3.7
Christian	3	11.9	5.2	11.0	3.3
males	4	18.3	5.7	13.0	5.3
Buddhist	5	10.9	5.3	9.2	4.1
statues	6	11.8	5.2	9.8	4.3
Uncertainly	7	20.9	4.9	20.5	3.9
prayerful	8	15.8	3.9	21.1	3.7
males					

There was no difference overall between the ratings of the eight photographs made by males and females, or between those who had been identified as actively religious or not religious. The stereotypically Christian
female figures were, however, rated more favorably than were the Christian
males (F < .05; d.f. 1,41= 40.72). The statues of the Buddha were also rated
more favorably than were the Christian males (F < .05; d.f. 1,41 = 6.48),
who were in their turn, more positively evaluated than the nonreligious males
(F < .05; d.f. F,41 = 15.44).

There was also a significant interaction between the religious and nonreligious subjects' evaluations of the Christian males and the Buddhist statues.
While the religious subjects evaluated pictures of the Buddha a little less
positively than they rated the Christian stimuli, the nonreligious subjects' evaluations of the Buddha were significantly more positive than were their evaluations of the Christian males.

When the scores for 'religious orthodoxy' were subjected to an analysis
of variance, there was again no difference overall between the male and

female, or the religious and nonreligious subjects. Furthermore, there was no difference in the subjects' ratings of the orthodoxy of the stereotypically Christian female and male figures. Yet the statues of the Buddha were rated as significantly more *religious* than the Christian males (F < .05; d.f. 1,41 = 6.54) and, not surprisingly, the two uncertainly religious males were rated as less religious than the Christian males (F < .05; d.f. 1,41= 140.77).

While nonreligious subjects' ratings of the religious males were a little more strongly religious than were their ratings of the two females, the religious subjects rated the females as significantly more religious than were the ratings by males (F < .05; d.f. 1,41 = 7.87). Moreover, while the nonreligious subjects' ratings of the religious male figures were more religious than were those of the religious subjects, they rated the 'uncertainly' religious male figures as less religious than did the religious subjects (F < .05; d.f. 1,41 = 13.20).

Subsidiary analyses showed that the 'doubtfully' religious subjects did not differ overall from either the religious or nonreligious subjects, although they rated the religious females more positively (M = 8.5) and as more religious (M = 11.2) than the religious males (those means being 14.6 and 12.3 for evaluation and religious orthodoxy respectively). They also evaluated the Buddhist statues more positively (M = 11.8) and as more religious (M = 10.0) than the religious males, who were evaluated more positively and seen as more religious than were the two 'uncertainly' religious males (these means were 18.2 and 20.4). A significant interaction between the nonreligious and 'doubtfully' religious subjects' religious orthodoxy ratings of the female and male figures emphasize that the nonreligious subjects' ratings of the religious male figures were a little more orthodox than were their ratings of the female figures. But the 'doubtfully' religious subjects rated the male figures as significantly less religious than did the religious females.

This experiment shows that in their detailed responses a group of active Christians reacted differently to explicitly religious stimuli from those who had identified themselves as 'not religious.' The absence of any differences in the overall judgments of these males and females or between those who are or are not religiously active shows a consensus about these icons of prayer, in which an image of the Virgin was judged to be the most religious, followed by the two Buddhist statues, the two male figures, and a pre-Raphaelite woman at prayer. The least religiously orthodox ratings were given to the Christian men in prayerful postures and in contexts that were not obviously religious.

Had the analysis been left at that level, one might have concluded that the religiousness of these pictures is coherent, and perhaps driven by stereotyped reactions. But subtle judgments about religiously orthodox postures and gestures are embedded in these data, when we look for the criteria that might be used to distinguish prayerful from broadly 'religious' actions. To emphasize that such gestures *are* important consider Hamlet's wish to kill the King (in Act III, Scene II, at line 73), whom he finds praying: "And now I'll do't: and so he goes to heaven; And so am I reveng'd. That would be scann'd: A villain kills my father; and not that; I, his sole son, do this same villain send to heaven." So Hamlet then decides to kill him: "When he is drunk asleep, or in his rage, Or in the incestuous pleasure of his bed, At gaming, swearing, or about some act that has no relish of salvation in't."

Evelyn Underhill (1930) appealed to the James-Lange theory of emotion to emphasize the priority of bodily or physical reactions in prayerful attitudes. As she said, "those who deliberately kneel are rewarded by an increase in worshiping love" (p. 26), and she stressed an 'expressive worship,' in which "religious ritual is an agreed pattern of ceremonial movements, sounds, and verbal formulas, creating a framework within which corporate religious action can take place" (p. 32). She thought that repetition itself provokes the "religious feeling of worshipers" (p. 33), so that just as we "abandon ourselves to the dance, lose ourselves in it, in order to dance well and learn by dancing that which is done, so with the religious rite" (p. 35), in which the tune counts for a great deal more than the words (p. 33).

That interpretation goes beyond imitation or modelling to an explicit recognition of the value of prayerful actions, which have been neglected in the prevailing focus on religious beliefs. Prayerful attitudes expressed out of context produce strong, but not necessarily negative reactions, and it is worth noting that our study showed that the religious people (28 percent of whom were Catholics, and 27 percent Greek Orthodox) identified a representation of the Virgin as the most positive and most religious image of prayer. While our study should be replicated, the stimuli had been selected because males at prayer were expected to be judged as less religious than females at prayer. Our finding that the two male figures were judged to be more 'religious' by those who were themselves religious than by those who were not shows the importance of posture in identifying the underlying attitudes of others.

The awe and dread of God is not only expressed nonverbally. The words (Otto, 1917) and forms of address (although 'thou' has become archaic) that carry petitions are, like prayers of praise or thanksgiving, exclamatory, or lengthy accounts that remember God's work and saving history, in song as well as narrative. Liturgical and ceremonial praise and 'services' that shape the prayers of individuals can be supplemented by reciting creeds or confessions of faith, since God is also found within the collectivity (Matthew 18:20).

While the language of religion need not be understood literally, variable meanings are extracted from it (or found there) that can be understood most parsimoniously in symbolic terms. The history of salvation, with which individuals become aligned as they offer "themselves, souls and bodies," is itself a vehicle that expresses attitudes. As a wish for material rather than spiritual benefits, prayer may be treated unsympathetically, even if it looks for union with the divine will, with language itself a divine gift through the 'logos' or 'the word made flesh' (John 1). The nuances of these prayers extend from mystical purification and union to resolving specific problems, from seeking nothing to finding God (paraphrasing St. Augustine), from a lack of response to signs of a favorable outcome. McKenzie (1988, pp. 167-8) nevertheless identified the central characteristic of Christian prayer in the Bible as a request for the Kingdom, with intercession supporting an appeal to God's promises.

Our preferred forms of prayer and the content of spontaneous or free prayers are expected to be psychologically disclosive of needs and wishes. As Appleton (1985) put it, we are likely to show our "religious psychology" in the way our prayers are made to make sense. But it is hard to establish how valid that can be beyond the claim itself, although Romans 8:26 notes that "we do not know how to pray as we ought, but the Spirit himself intercedes for us with sighs too deep for words." Appleton writes that most of his own prayers "came out of experience, in situations in which I found myself, in struggles for faith, sometimes in travail of spirit, occasionally in moments of deep communion with God. They were written down . . . as recording a new insight to tranquilize, guide and strengthen my own spirit." This description suggests a 'deep' sense of struggle or confidence, rather than immediate or superficial wishes.

We should also distinguish popular forms of religion from the orthodoxies against which reformers have tried to reshape their traditions. A paradox there entails the move from a belief in magic, with its assumptions of inevitable success, to the docility of 'true' prayer, and the tension between an external or spoken 'word' and the (inner) mystical insight that is required for its understanding, or between a revelation and its reception, which potentiates an awareness of God's absence or silence. This silence is acknowledged by a refusal to utter the name of the Deity, or by only sharing that secret with those who have been initiated. Silence can also express reverence, adoration, a state of receptivity, or an expectation of disclosure. It may concentrate internal physiological or psychological processes and facilitate our external awareness. These contrasts pervade the meditative practices, even among those who may not be 'religious,' that are different from an ascetic silence connected with the desire not to be distracted from worship or devotion.

If the ineffable is beyond understanding, silence and gesture could be its 'language,' unless irrepressible prayers take precedence over whatever leads to a "prayerful state of mind." The *via negativa* or path of denial identifies what God is not, among those in the classical traditions for whom God, Nirvana, or the Tao are inexpressible. While the 'law' constrains, 'prophecy' stresses mystical knowledge with the divine Word expressed in silence. Wittgenstein also held that we must keep silence about what cannot be said.

We have seen that the early psychologists of religion offered cosy and rather prescriptive interpretations of the psychological processes that support or explain prayer, typically relying on conversation, suggestion, or reflexivity to explain the help it gives "in the practical and emotional life" (Pratt, 1907, p. 278). A little later Freud's 'new psychology' made reference to unconscious wishes, and anthropologists had already postulated an evolutionary process from spell to prayer, detecting religious intentions in the wish, "My will be done," then that "Thy will be done," to the hope, "Thy will be done with my active help." This sequence, like that from 'cry to word' (Godin, 1967), entails a development from the primitive, or egocentric, intentions that were thought to lie behind magical formulae, through 'spontaneous' pleas for help, to accepting one's own responsibility when petitioning for favors.

These steps are hard to detect in prayers of praise and thanksgiving, or in contemplation and meditation. But the early psychologies of religion were from Protestant traditions and seemed to assume that we are called to be 'in the world' and that material needs are primary, distinguishing attempts to make objective changes from any subjective effects of prayer and worship. Western mystical traditions were, however, not innocent of the broadly psychological and therapeutic analyses of the prayerful practices that aimed for union with God, with defined techniques to overcome the weakness or lack of enthusiasm that was called 'acedia' (Haré and Finlay Jones, 1986, p. 220f), depression or 'the dark night of the soul' (Dudley, 1992) that drew people away from the mystical path.

Surveys

Except for questions about the frequency of prayer which accept it as a form of religious behavior, and the developmental work that Godin stimulated in the 1950s, there is less work on the attitudes to prayer than might have been expected. The twenty year index to the *Journal for the Scientific Study of Religion* up to 1981 has no entry for 'prayer' in its subject-list, although six papers are listed under 'Occult, magic, and astrology.' That none of the four papers under 'Liturgy, worship, and ritual' concerns prayer further emphasizes its marginal role then. The unevenness in this field continues, although the annotated bibliography in our Appendix shows the body of psychological work on prayer and related topics that is now available.

Van de Kemp's (1984) bibliography of 'Psychology and Theology' includes nineteen books on "The psychology of prayer and worship" published between 1901 and 1961 with longer sections on "Spiritual Healing and Pastoral Counselling." With a few exceptions they are early and principled or oriented towards pastoral or 'religious psychology.' The only specifically empirical work she includes is Moore's (1956) questionnaire study of the prayer life of Carmelites in the Roman Catholic Church, which can be put alongside Beck's (1906) paper reporting a study of Protestant attitudes to prayer in G. Stanley Hall's journal. But a recent attempt to replicate Moore's study in England (Shackle, 1988) failed because the pre-Vatican II piety of its questions met strong opposition, even among those in a Religious life. Only two of the sixty people who were approached agreed to complete that questionnaire, which shows that the stance of any enquiry is itself a crucial determinant of what can be uncovered about prayer. I have already noted that the early books that explicitly link prayer and psychology are all theoretical or interpretive. They include Heiler's (1918) German text, translated into English in 1932, Anna Louise Strong's (1909) doctoral thesis, and Stolz's (1913) book on *Autosuggestion in Private Prayer*, revised as *The Psychology of Prayer* in 1923.

Pratt (1907, pp. 271-279) reported a questionnaire study of how sixty-eight (or perhaps seventy-two) respondents 'pray,' from which he argued that prayer begins as a habit inculcated in children and maintained for 'active reasons' (presumably because it is found to be useful). While William James believed that we cannot help praying, Pratt thought its value was pragmatic, for the "strength and insight and comfort that He gives" (1907, p. 274), asserting that even 'doubt' does not destroy "the efficacy of prayer" (p. 275). Godin (1967), on the other hand, found a basis for prayer in the belief that "natural phenomena can be swayed in favor of those who pray in a spirit of biblical trust." With developing awareness or 'maturity,' that assumption can be purified of its superstitious implications so that the attitudes to prayer become more sacramental and 'symbolist,' emphasizing 'spiritual' states of mind.

The most widely accepted paradigm for psychological, as opposed to religious studies of prayer, involves questionnaire and survey methods (cf Poloma and Gallup, 1991). The results are usually interpreted through social or sociological theories. Piagetian theory has, however, been widely used to interpret the developing understanding of what prayer involves among children and young adults (cf Godin, 1967, Long et al, 1967, Oser and Gmunder, 1991). While the psycho-physiological work in this field has focused on the correlates or consequences of (usually) Eastern meditative practices, a current interest in the role of prayer in health-related coping (Parker and Brown, 1982; Pargament et al, 1990) suggests that this is the new and developing model.

As an orientation to the practice of prayer, and to the social representations (Farr and Moscovici, 1984) that make it intelligible within, and beyond religion, I gathered data from 421 Freshman students of psychology who, early in their course at the University of New South Wales in 1988, completed a brief questionnaire that had been distributed to a large class of 832 people. Because of the required anonymity, an unknown number of those who did not reply are likely to have withdrawn from the course or were absent when the questionnaires were distributed, so I can not calculate the proportion who refused to reply. This questionnaire was in two parts: a set of open-ended questions and sixteen closed Likert-type items. Those who completed it ranged in age from seventeen to fifty (mean age 22.6 years), of whom 69 percent said they pray now, with the majority of them saying that they pray at least weekly (cf Table 7). Answers to the question, "Why do some people not pray?," that were given by those who said they do not themselves pray referred to their nonbelief or lack of belief or faith (by 62 percent), wanting to control their own life (17 percent), and having 'no need' of prayer (16 percent).

That and seven other open-ended questions were content-analysed in terms of the respondents' religious affiliation, sex, and whether they said they prayed or not. These questions elicited surprisingly consistent replies which suggest that prayer is well-recognized and typically understood as a normal correlate of religious belief, or as a plea for help. Specific answers to the question, 'What is prayer?,' included 'conversation with God,' 'talking

Table 7

Percentage frequencies of prayer for males and females separately

		Daily	Weekly	Monthly	Less often	Never
Do you pray now?	yes	49	18	9	23	1
	no	-	3	5	19	73
Males	yes	44	21	10	21	4
	no	-	-	4	17	79
Females	yes	51	17	9	23	
	no	-	5	5	21	69

to God about your hopes and disappointments,' 'talking to God, listening to Him, just being in the presence of and aware of someone who loves you unconditionally,' and 'the silent communication between yourself and God.' Very few people mentioned that such talk involves asking or thanking, and the God talked to was identified as 'a higher being,' or they said that prayer is 'talking to oneself' and that 'God is within us,' although the fact that prayer can be helpful when 'asking for guidance' was another common reply. The dominant theme in these answers linked prayer to communication with God, for example as "A relationship and form of communication between oneself and the Church or God, where God = belief" (to quote one respondent). Perhaps the early psychologists Coe and Pratt who identified prayer with conversation or communication had generalized their commonsense understanding, unless they directly interpreted the forms of address that are common when opening prayers.

Another question asked about the kinds of people who are most likely to pray, which only two people did not answer. Specific characteristics were mentioned by 86 percent, and 13 percent said that 'All kinds' pray. Apart from emphasizing that 'Believers' are most likely to pray (given by 71 percent), other answers referred to those who 'have faith,' 'regularly practice their faith' and 'believe in God.' An emphasis on those who are 'lonely or in need' was given by 14 percent. One person said that those most likely to pray are "people who need help. People who pray have been brought up with a religious background. They have been taught to pray and hence fall back on this when need be." Those in desperation or serious trouble seem to have almost been expected to pray, which suggests that instrumental prayer, perhaps as a 'last resort,' should be distinguished from prayers that are expressive or worshipful.

That prayer continues to be recognized as 'religion in action (or) real religion' (to quote Pratt, 1907, p. 217, from Sabatier's *Philosophy of Religion*) is shown by those who said that 'anybody with a religious awareness' or 'people who believe in God and have an inner spiritual life and believe in life after death' are the ones most likely to pray. There is, however, little information in this study (or elsewhere) about how most people have been taught to pray. That children are probably introduced to simple (and sample) prayers when they are young, for solace, to express gratitude, or wishes, is shown in the recent collections of children's prayers and letters to God (e.g. Durran, 1987).

Two questions in the study about when and where people are most likely to pray were answered with reference to home, church, situations of danger, pain, sadness, or 'when faced with a traumatic experience' and at night. It is worth noting that 8 percent said that prayer is likely 'at any time' (with 20 percent of the Baptists giving this answer). That young people are taught to pray at home and at church is emphasized by Francis and Brown (1990), whose path diagram is shown in Figure 1.

When asked why people pray, most of the answers recapitulated earlier replies. That 'comfort,' 'strength,' and 'guidance,' as well as 'to give thanks' were stressed reinforces the solace or support that prayer is expected to carry. The question, "What do they usually pray for?" produced a broad range of answers from 'the impossible,' to 'self-satisfaction,' 'petitions,' 'reparation or forgiveness,' 'relief,' 'strength,' 'thanksgiving,' 'praise,' to 'derive an immense sense of peace and inner tranquillity,' for 'reassurance,' or 'in desperation.' One person said, "They pray for forgiveness, for help, for thanks, for faith, and for strength." The coherence of these objects of prayer needs to be further established, although most of the language that was used implies an attitude of transcendence, rather than a search for material goals. No one gave specific or concrete answers, nor was there a difference between the pattern of answers from those who did or did not pray.

The common answers to questions about how people know 'if their prayers are answered' included 'belief,' 'by faith,' getting 'what they are looking for,' or 'peace.' Twelve percent said that those who pray don't know if prayer is answered, and another 5 percent said they had 'no idea' how people might know that. The person who said that if they 'don't get what they want, everything still works out' captures the common attitude that prayer is not expected to produce material successes, but that it works reflexively and ensures or supports religious practice, thereby maintaining a religious attitude, and perhaps offering solace.

There are few surprises in this material. That 'prayer' is used in crisis and to restore stability and confidence seems consistent with the conventional religious training most in this group of students are likely to have been exposed to. That very few answers were critical of prayer suggests that prayer is accepted 'matter-of-factly,' as an essential component of a religious perspective, shared by those who are and who are not themselves actively involved in religion or prayer.

Figure 1

Path diagram from Francis and Brown, 1990

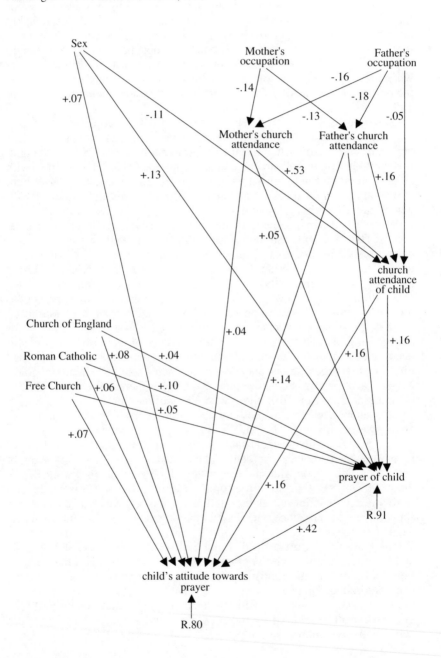

The closed alternative questions in the second part of that student questionnaire contained sixteen items relating to the practice of prayer, its believed
efficacy, and the socio-demographic characteristics of those who had answered
it. While 69 percent of the sample said they now pray by themselves and
31 percent say they do not, only 24 percent, when answering a separate
question about how often they pray by themselves, said 'never,' and 19 percent who had said they never pray by themselves also said, when answering
that other question, that they pray occasionally. These findings not only
show the pervasiveness of prayer, but that 'not praying' does not mean 'never
praying.' An estimate of the unreliability of these answers is, however, given
by the 4 percent who said they never pray in one question *and* that they
prayed weekly or monthly in the other.

An analysis of the answers by sex and religious denomination showed
that daily prayer is more common among women than men (37 percent and
27 percent respectively), and that more of the Catholics (63 percent) and of
those in the small denominations (54 percent) than among the Orthodox
and Anglicans (35 percent) said they pray frequently. These results emphasize acknowledged differences in the practice of religion among those in
the separate Christian traditions that predominate in Australia.

An initial factor analysis of the answers to those sixteen closed questions
yielded five factors with eigen values > 1.00. The first factor, which accounted for 35 percent of the variance, had positive loadings greater than 0.67
for questions that asked directly about the frequency of private prayer (0.88),
the 'need to pray' (0.87), being likely to pray 'in a really difficult situation'
(0.73), and about the belief that prayer will 'have an effect on those who
are praying' (0.79) and on natural phenomena (0.67). This general factor
also had high loadings on questions about the importance of 'religion in
your life' (0.85) and on the frequency of attending religious services (0.77).
That religious denomination, which was scored from Roman Catholic through
Anglican to the evangelical traditions was only weakly linked (0.38) to the
first factor, emphasizes the uniformity of positive attitudes to prayer (and
to religion in general), and that prayer *is* central to a religious stance. Factor
scores for those who do and do not pray were significantly different on this
factor (F=323.9 where F crit = 5.85).

The second factor, which accounted for 10 percent of the variance, involves
the privacy of prayer (0.76) and a preference for praying alone rather than with
others (0.73). These factor scores were also significantly different for those
who do and do not pray (F = 13.0).

The third factor (accounting for 8 percent of the variance) involves having been taught to pray (0.75) and agreeing that prayer depends on one's
mood (0.60). Religious denomination (scored from Catholic through to non-
conformist groups) loaded 0.62 on this factor, and there was no difference here
between the factor scores of those who do and do not pray.

Because age and sex emerged as separate factors, the analysis was repeated with only three factors extracted. Those factors accounted for 53 percent
of the variance, and the factor loadings in Table 8 show that while the first fac-

tor focuses on prayer in general, the second emphasizes the privacy of prayer, and the third draws on a traditional training in prayer and the effects of mood on one's likelihood to pray. Further factor analyses that extracted factors separately for those who do and who do not pray yielded very similar patterns, which further supports the conclusion that social knowledge and beliefs about prayer are not restricted to those who practice it.

Despite the different forms of Christian prayer (from petition to praise and contemplation) the attitudes, practice, and acquaintance with prayer appear from these results to be homogeneous. The demands of particular traditions could account for some differences in its practice, but they have little effect on the attitudes that were measured here, whether because Christian traditions share a common core, or they accept rather nonspecific answers to questions about the efficacy of prayer.

Table 8

Loadings on a factor analysis, restricted to three factors

Factor			Loading
I	Q16	Do you pray by yourself?	0.89
(35.1%)	Q15	Do you ever feel a need to pray?	0.87
	Q11	How important is religion in your life?	0.85
	Q9	Do you ever pray now?	0.79
	Q10	How often do you attend religious services?	0.79
	Q19	Could your prayers have effects on others?	0.77
	Q23	How likely are you to pray in difficult situations?	0.74
	Q20	Could your prayers have an effect on natural phenomena?	0.65
	Q18	Can prayers have effects on those praying?	0.49
II	Q24	Do you prefer to pray alone or with others or is there no difference?	0.72
(9.9%)	Q17	How private do you think questions about prayer are?	0.61
		Sex	-0.46
III	Q21	Were you taught to pray?	0.71
(7.7%)	Q22	Does whether you pray depend on your mood?	0.56
		Age	-0.48
		Denomination	0.45

The attitudes to prayer that were found seem to rest on the assumption that psychological pressures and urgent demands impel people to pray, especially in states of distress, and that prayer accesses religiously sanctioned comfort and guidance. In this sense, prayer fits with the other coping techniques that help us deal with crises and depressive episodes (Parker and Brown, 1984). These instrumental roles for prayer, which will be discussed again later, contrast against its expressive use in worship, with less immediacy because worship is constrained by tradition or conventions that invoke or establish a context for the transcendent.

Testimony

As a feature of religious practice, prayer is shaped through explicit teaching or guidance and supported by innumerable examples that define its character. Expectations about the psychological effects of prayer that are implicit in most teaching about it and in the experience of prayer itself suggest that the answers about prayer depend on 'faith.' This avoids the difficulties inherent in documenting specific instances of success independently of individuals' claims or beliefs about them.

A recent newspaper report in Sydney offers a striking example of such a claim by the Director of World Evangelism for the World Methodist Council. The report says, "When his voice was troubled last year and he sought medical help, it was thought that all the preaching had taken its toll. A speech therapist advised another opinion. A Macquarie Street specialist removed two polyps from a vocal cord and discovered cancer. Sir Alan wrote in his diary: 'Oh God, My Heavenly Father, on this day, the sixth of May, 1992, when dark clouds have lowered over our lives, we cry out for your presence. We, Winifred [his wife] and I, have received the worst news of our lives . . . I place my stricken throat in your hands. Heal it, I pray, that I may still be able to preach your Word . . .' The old preacher looked and sounded so ill that many acquaintances assumed the worst. 'As a Christian, I am not frightened of death,' said Sir Alan. 'I am confident of eternal life and look forward to meeting my mother and father, but I don't want it to happen yet.' His doctor pointed out that the recovery rate from throat cancer was relatively high. And church congregations in various parts of the world got busy with prayers. 'Prayer does two things,' said Sir Alan. 'It sets up a positive, confident approach which aids healing, and it can involve God directly. God does much more healing than this doubting age gives credit for.' Undergoing radiotherapy, he felt he experienced 'a real sense of the presence of Christ.' Sir Alan agrees that spiritual healing is open to charlatans but said: 'We are living beneath our potential as human beings because we are not tapping these resources.' The secular view of what happened to the clergyman is that clever doctors removed the cancer and that his 'spiritual experience' can be explained psychologically—the prospect of death causes powerful emotions. Sir Alan believes that God worked in his mysterious way through the doctors and the speech therapist and that prayer helped. His diary entry for September 10 reads: 'Oh God, my Father, how can I thank you for a wonderful deliverance? All that has happened is a miracle.'"

We have seen that Francis Galton showed in 1873 that prayers for the health of Britain's Royal Family did not give them a longer life, and the Commission that validates cures at Lourdes has accepted very few of them. Even if there were positive outcomes from controlled trials of prayer (Byrd, 1988), or from those that have been conjectured, they could be questioned (or dismissed) as a placebo effect, or attributed to faith alone. Prayer is therefore maintained 'religiously' (whatever that means) or by confidence. The possibility that it might influence natural phenomena, other people, or only those who pray, seems to be recognized by those who do and who do not themselves pray. To hold that prayer is maintained by habit and that expectations about its success show its social acceptance, allows that its specific effects depend on rhetorical claims. As a means of coping, however, prayer is probably no more effective than seeking warmth, listening to music, or spending money on yourself, which are other common techniques of self-consolation (cf Parker and Brown, 1982).

One goal for research could be to compare the attitudes of those who use prayer persistently against those of its casual practitioners, to establish whether prayer is as easily accepted as the data I have gathered suggest it might be. Since it is thought improper to enquire too searchingly into another's prayers, we might compare the attitudes of those who say they pray regularly, occasionally, or who reject prayer outright. In this connection one remembers the study in *The American Soldier* (Stouffer et al, 1949) which showed that during the Second War about 75 percent of men were helped 'a lot' by prayer when the going was tough, and that 72 percent of those who had been most frightened said they were helped by prayer, compared with 42 percent of those who were least frightened. To feel hatred for the enemy or to think about what they were fighting for was said to be less helpful. More of those exposed to stress were helped by prayer, as were those who had seen friends killed, those with poor resources for coping with stress, and those most frightened in battle (72 percent) against 42 percent among those who were least frightened. Stouffer et al (1949) pointed out, however, that the use of prayer might have made some of these men more afraid.

After summarizing those results, Argyle (1958, p. 50) conjectured that to find prayer helpful in battle could lead others "to expect ex-servicemen to be more religious." But the findings in Allport (1948) and Stouffer (1949, p. 187) are equivocal, since similar proportions said they became more, or less, religious, although 79 percent with combat experience and 54 percent without it said their faith had been increased by that experience, while 18 percent in both groups said it had decreased. Allport reported that those who had become skeptical blamed the horrors of war, or after seeing church-goers killed, while those who had become more religious attributed that to the help of prayer in battle. That such contrary effects are still an issue suggests that one's immediate attitudes do not predict how individuals might react to stress. Despite that, there are consistent differences between the prayer practices of men and women, for which Argyle (1958, p. 73) cited a mean ratio between women and men of 1.74 in four of the early prayer surveys.

Those findings can be explained socio-culturally, in terms of what men and women are expected to do, or with reference to experiments which show that we attempt to control uncertain outcomes (cf Jahoda, 1969, p. 134). Whether they are more easily explained by superstition (through charms, amulets, and appeals to luck, for example) than with reference to religion itself is an unresolved issue that depends on one's prior assumptions, and the ambiguity of religious attitudes must again be recognized. We have already noted that mathematically approved strategies for making decisions under uncertainty seldom guide the decisional processes of individuals, because of our preferences for regularity and control. But even they are not consistent, since a tendency to alternate any response sequences was observed many years ago (Tolman, 1925). Systematic analyses of outcomes seem to be resisted in the world of experience, which favors wishes, hopes, and preferences, belief in an inherently just world (Lerner, 1980), telling fortunes, and accounts of paranormal events (from which many religious people distance themselves, cf Zollschan et al, 1989).

The practice of prayer

"Most apt to cite the importance of daily prayer are women (82 percent), nonwhites (90 percent), those without a high school degree (84 percent), persons over 50 (85 percent), and Evangelicals or self-described born-again Christians (93 percent). Groups less inclined to stress daily prayer are men (69 percent), college graduates (65 percent), persons under 30 (58 percent), and Jews (36 percent). Catholics and Protestants at 80 percent each say that prayer is an important daily exercise" (from Poloma and Gallup, 1991, p. 5). They also note that in 1948, 90 percent answered the question, "Do you ever pray?" affirmatively, compared with 89 percent in 1978 and 88 percent in 1988. Inspection of their results shows a few (small) absolute differences in answer to the question, "Do you ever pray to God?" that depend on age, sex, education, race, region, or income. (Because their sample consisted of 1,030 people, and the differences reported have been weighted so that the response patterns match the adult population (p. 138), those differences cannot be reanalyzed, although 822 men (85 percent of the total) and 916 women (91 percent of the sample) did answer that question affirmatively.) There are also differences between denominations in praying from a book of prayers or from memory (for example, among Catholics the percentages were 29 and 72 respectively and among the "Total Protestant" group they were 16 and 40 percent respectively), in asking for "material things you need" (with 37 and 48 percent respectively), but not, it seems, in meditative prayer (cf their Table 5, page 38).

When Poloma and Gallup (1991, p. 3) reviewed other Gallup reports on prayer they found that "although the percentage of persons who report that they, at least on occasion, do pray has been relatively constant for over four decades, there has been a decrease in the frequency of prayer. For example, the proportion of Americans who pray, on the average, twice a day or more declined from 42 percent in 1952 to 27 percent in 1978. The Gallup Reports show surprisingly few differences in the USA between separate groups in the proportion who ever pray. Some differences emerge, however, among those who pray three times a day or more. While the overall national figure for this group is 19 percent, the percentages for women (12 percent), older persons (24 percent), blacks (23 percent), and Protestants (22 percent) are significantly higher than for comparison groups in each category." Later they note that those saying "grace out loud before family meals" moved from 69 percent in 1962 to 57 percent in 1979 (Poloma and Gallup, 1991, p. 3).

Gallup and Castelli (1989, p. 136) reported that while "88 percent of Americans pray to God," 76 percent agreed that prayer is "an important part of their daily lives." They conclude that this "suggests the enormous extent of private piety in the U.S., which coexists with notable expressions of self-reliance" (cf Poloma and Gallup, 1991, p. 3). This illustrates a tendency to interpret data, if not gratuitously, at least with reference to taken-for-granted knowledge of the culture, although their conclusion *is* supported by another survey in which 45 percent claimed "to rely more on themselves than on a higher power to solve life's problems," while 36 percent said they relied on a "higher power, such as God" and 17 percent relied on both self and God (in Poloma and Gallup, 1991, p. 4). The use of prayer for coping is stressed by the fact that 87 percent indicated that their family is the main source of support in a crisis, followed by working a problem through on their own and by prayer, which were tied in the second place, with 80 percent each.

Many other surveys of religion include questions about prayer. Leaving aside why such surveys have become commonplace, the importance of religion for Americans is well illustrated by Gallup and Castelli (1989, p. 45) who note that "94 percent believe in God, 90 percent pray, 88 percent of Americans believe that God loves them, and only 3 percent believe this is not the case, (while) more than three-quarters say their religious involvement has been a positive experience over their lifetimes, with 30 percent saying it has been very positive." Those bold conclusions are supported by the responses to attitude statements like, "You have to go to church or practice religious ritual if you expect God to do anything for you": 59 percent of Americans "strongly disagreed with that statement, while another 12 percent (only) disagreed" (ibid.). Other items in their study included, "a person can be a good Christian if he doesn't go to church," faith is "strengthened by questioning early beliefs," that it "should change throughout life," and that "God reveals Himself through a variety of religious beliefs and traditions" (p. 46).

When those American results were compared with European data, "Only Ireland ranked ahead of the 66 percent of Americans who believe in a personal God," followed by 55 percent in Spain, 40 percent in Norway, and down to 19 percent in Denmark and in Sweden (p. 47). The questions in those surveys asked whether comfort and strength is received from religion, how satisfied they are with religious leaders, and what has changed their faith, including the positive events that reinforce it, although divorce is a negative event that decreases it (pp. 49-50). Consistent gender and age differences show that more women than men are 'religious' (p. 50f) as are those who are married, as well as more of those whose marriages have ended (p. 52).

Survey data like these emphasize that expressions of religion relate to socio-demographic variables and socio-political attitudes (cf Argyle and Beit-Hallahmi, 1975). But what is their religious significance? The answers to these questions show the dominant position of a Christian interpretation. It is unfortunate that we lack comparable data about the religious practices and beliefs in non-Christian traditions and in non-Western countries.

Poloma and Gallup (1991) attribute what they believe to be a lack of interest in prayer among social scientists to their positivist attitudes, the assumption that prayer is irrational, and the extent to which they are themselves "indifferent or skeptical about prayer, (or) simply have no interest in investing time and energy into its study." (p. 3). Identifying prayer as irrational, or as a practice to be 'used' as a last resort invokes a limited set of interpretations that may be independent of one's practice or experience. As H.G. Wells (1934, p. 71) said, "I would pray when I was losing a race, or in trouble in an examination room, or frightened," hoping perhaps for a 'sign' of God's existence or support, which like religion itself, would be ambiguous even if it were socially sanctioned. Despite the difficulties of defining and identifying who is praying, even from the signs, there are in general fewer studies of prayer than of religious belief, orthodoxy, commitment, churchgoing, values, or experience. The work on prayer does, however, focus on individuals' constructions and developmental changes in understanding its meaning, and the interpretations are consensual and even predictable when one knows the stance of the investigators. The meaning is, however, important because it centers on the "emblems and symbols" that generate, carry, or elicit associations that derive from texts, practices, and traditions. The current interest in prayer-related coping has, however, moved these interests away from assumptions about the material efficacy of prayer.

Perhaps that is why Spilka and his collaborators accepted Rothbaum et al's (1982) distinction between primary control, which attempts to change the environment, and secondary control that tries to change the self to accommodate the outside world. While secondary control may be predictive, illusory, vicarious and interpretive, Spilka could not reproduce these factors, although he did find three factors that cover a relationship with God, undifferentiated control and the meaning-giving role of prayer. When those separate measures were aligned with religion as a source of help, through confession, 'ritualistic' and habitual prayers, it was found that the most closely related forms of prayer involved active coping.

David, Ladd and Spilka (1992) have now developed a set of scales to measure confession, petition, thanksgiving, ritualistic prayer, meditation as self-knowledge and knowledge of God, good feelings, and self-improvement as a result of prayer, intercession for others, and the habits of regular prayer. Poloma and Gallup (1991), on the other hand, distinguished between ritual, petitionary, conversational, and meditative prayer, and Calkins (1911) had identified prayers of thanksgiving and penitence as well as petition (which she contrasted against incantation) and forgiveness, confidence or fellowship, and adoration for a spiritual rather than material good. She said of that, "With the whole weary controversy (of material answers to prayer) we have no concern" because it "mistakes the nature of God's answer to prayer," which implicates "God's answer to prayer in God's consciousness of the human self as turning to God. The conviction that prayer is, in this sense, answered is indeed an inherent factor in prayer."

Expectations of an answer to prayer must be set against the religious and other experiences that are made possible through prayer, in the balance between reason and emotion in the sense of other-worldliness that can be found there, and in the forms of prayer that are accepted, or perhaps preferred.

Religious experiences and other responses to prayer are not, however, evenly distributed in any community (cf Harding et al, 1986) and claims on their truth or falsity are themselves data for psychological analyses that have been made, as Wulff (1991) shows, in the context of psychoanalysis, phenomenology, behaviorism, social psychology, personality theory, and even biology (Hardy, 1978, Reynolds and Tanner, 1983). Since people are assumed to *use* their God, and a great deal of pastoral work is built on implicit, rather than overt, psychological principles, different psychologies of religion are involved in their description and interpretation. Gorsuch's "measurement paradigm" for the study of religion, in the *American Psychologist* (1984), suggests a specifically psychological perspective, in which religious phenomena can be taken as dependent *or* independent (and as intervening) variables that draw on, or refer to *this* world, or to the concept of an 'other-world.' This heightens the counterpoint between "science and religion" that some psychologists have tried to resolve in principle, although it is not clear if any data would have helped them in that work.

We therefore need to clarify the boundaries that are set around the perspectives on prayer, and the reasons for studying the links between psychology and religion. They include,

1. The traditional place of psychology in social and personal life. Even before the work of Fechner and Wundt as modern innovators, 'psychology' was linked to religion by Augustine and Aquinas for example, while religious terms like guilt, desire, and sin (which Maslow thought a lesser evil than guilt), referred to psychological states.

2. Psychology as a field has been used to interpret social actions. At the simplest level, knowing a person's religion (or lack of it) accounts for some variance in nonreligious attitudes and behavior about, for example, judgments of sexual or political attitudes, that may be 'found' or derived from other beliefs and attitudes.

3. Psychological interpretations are implicit in the formulations of many religious traditions, in Buddhism as much as in Catholicism. Their implicit psychologies were not necessarily precursors to our formal, scientific psychology, although they continue to have an influence on commonsense solutions.

4. The ways in which religions can sanction altruism or social control, offer social support, and guarantee rites of passage can be articulated and clarified

with reference to psychological theories.

5. Since religious ideologies presuppose a worldview (or cosmology), it is important to contrast the correlates of 'religionism' against those of materialism for example, especially since materialists and positivists explain religion with reference to such concepts as animism, ego-centrism, and socialization, or in terms of psychosis, or projection, rather than accepting it on its own terms. The relevance and validity of those interpretations should be tested systematically.

6. Because the consequences of a religious perspective are variously judged to be adaptive or maladaptive, those consequences need to be examined, especially for their impact on health and its correlates.

7. Since not everyone who has been explicitly trained into a religion sticks with it, the reactions to religious change, in enthusiasm or apostasy, also need to be explored.

8. The implications of 'religionism' as a personality variable have linked it with prejudice, closed-mindedness, and other values.

9. The attitudes and beliefs of those for whom religion is an 'occupation,' are likely to differ from those among religious people who work in secular contexts.

10. The criteria by which any religious beliefs are judged more or less mature may impact on the practice of prayer, and on whether they encourage a false consciousness, or an awareness of the 'real' world.

11. Psychological conflicts surround contrasts between certainty and doubt, belief and disbelief, and positive or negative attitudes involve the coherence of the content that is unique to religion, although those who live within secular contexts must accept the rules imposing decisions that might diverge from what is religiously approved.

While psychological explanations have, for many people, replaced explanations in demonological terms (which killed witches but protected epileptics), understanding the contexts of these (and other) explanations might give a novel focus for the theories and explanations of what prayer might involve or have an impact on.

Chapter Ten

Prayer, Meditation, and Control

"To illuminate the relation of things, as though with a light at once from without and from within—as if reality can be changed . . . (but he said 'by the writer's will . . .')."—Robert Musil *(1880-1942)* The Man Without Qualities.

Beyond the descriptive studies of attitudes towards prayer and its practice is an experimental psychology of prayer, in which *variables* relating to the practice of prayer and meditation are manipulated. Wulff (1991, p. 163f) has summarized these studies, which he identifies with 'the laboratory,' while a different approach is offered by Deconchy (1991) who focused on the basic mechanisms that might support religious modes of behavior. He identified them as 'good' or 'bad' forms of religion, open or closed, intrinsic or extrinsic, and as more or less 'authentic' and adaptive. The psychological mechanisms he found include locus of control, dogmatism, and 'orthodoxy,' and he set them against dependent variables that have religious implications, such as reading a Biblical text or wearing religious clothes, and against their effects on other dependent variables that are not necessarily religious but might differentially implicate religious attitudes through altruism (Darley and Batson, 1973), for example.

The design of those controlled studies is usually correlational, or quasi- rather than truly experimental, although Deconchy (1985) has outlined a way in which an experimental psychology of religion could be developed by experimentally manipulating religious structures (with a false feed-back of results, for example). Yet it is obvious that the participants in an experiment involving religious categories can not be randomly assigned to separate treatment groups. In that sense any religious attachment is, like sex, an 'organismic' variable. Furthermore, to identify the implications of a set of experimental results that involves manipulating religious variables is difficult if they conflict with religiously accepted solutions. Deconchy identifies that as a "functional censorship," when religious systems (or individuals) object to using randomized experimental designs to explore *any* religious effects. Oddly enough, a few apparently well-controlled studies of the efficacy of prayer (e.g. Byrd, 1988) *have* been carried out, although Thouless (1971, p. 93) wondered if Galton's study of the effects of prayers for Royalty involved experimental theology rather than psychology. It is for reasons like these that opinion polls and surveys provide most of the data on which we must rely for our knowledge of the social psychology of prayer.

Wulff (1991, pp. 168-172) summarized Loehr's (1959) study of plants that had had prayers said over them for growth (or no growth), or that had not received any prayer. Loehr estimated the "prayer growth advantage" as between 5 and 35 percent, depending in part on "who did the praying and in what state of mind" although the "no prayer" condition also yielded a growth advantage, according to Wulff. Wulff does not, however, mention another study carried out by Lenington (1979), in which plants were or were not nourished with holy water.

In another study, Parker and St Johns (1957) assigned forty-five volunteers with neurotic and (says Wulff) psychosomatic disorders, to three groups of equal size. One group received "prayer therapy," another was given weekly individual counseling in which religion and prayer were not mentioned, and the third group agreed to pray in their accustomed manner each night before bed, and to summarize a problem the experimenter had identified for them. The dependent measures in this experiment were assessed by the projective tests fashionable in the 1950s, with an "impartial tester" estimating their level of improvement nine months later. "The prayer therapy is reported to have shown 72 percent improvement in both symptoms and test results, and the psychotherapy group 65 percent improvement and the random pray*ers*, no improvement" (Wulff, p. 169). Wulff notes several problems with the design of that experiment, beginning with the non-random assignment to treatment conditions that were not well controlled, since the two groups that showed the effect of prayer had both involved some contact with others, while the group that showed no effects of prayer was exposed only to their own established prayer practices. Furthermore, it is not clear what knowledge of the experimental conditions the participants or the person who interpreted the test results might have had.

The next experiment that Wulff refers to is by Joyce and Welldon (1965) in which prayer groups directed their prayers to forty-eight out-patients with "chronic, stationary or progressively deteriorating psychological or rheumatic disease." These patients were carefully assigned to treatment or control groups matched for age, sex, diagnosis, marital status, and religious tradition. This study was 'blind' since the patients did not know they were being prayed for, and the physicians who made the clinical evaluations did not know which group each patient belonged to. The findings showed a marginal statistical significance, because the results of only sixteen pairs of patients could be traced, four of whom were tied in their change of clinical state, seven showed an advantage for the treatment group and five for the control group—where an 'advantage' could have meant no change rather than a deterioration. A sequential analysis showed, however, that the first six patients to be evaluated who yielded a difference showed an advantage for the treatment group, and the five pairs showing an advantage for the control group had been evaluated five to twelve months after the period for which the prayers had been requested.

In another study, Byrd (1988), noting that intercessory prayer is "one of the oldest forms of therapy (that) has had little attention in the medical literature," therefore designed a "prospective randomized double-blind protocol for a coronary care unit." Over ten months 393 patients were assigned to an intercessory prayer group (N = 192) or a control group (N = 201), while another fifty-seven refused to enter the trial "for personal reasons, religious convictions, or an unwillingness to give informed consent." The intercessory prayer group was offered prayer by 'born again' Christians, actively involved with a local church, who prayed 'outside the hospital' (whatever that means). No patients were directly contacted after the initial interviews and the two groups were said to show no differences at that stage. The intercessors were given the "patients' first name, diagnosis, and general condition, along with pertinent updates in their condition." Three to seven of them prayed daily for each patient until they were discharged from the hospital. The results showed that those prayed for "subsequently had a significantly lower severity score based on the hospital course after entry ($p < .01$). Multivariant (sic) analysis separated the groups on the basis of the outcome variables ($p < .0001$). The control patients required ventilatory assistance, antibiotics, and diuretics more frequently than patients in the IP (intercessory prayer) group. These data suggest that intercessory prayer to the Judeo-Christian God has a beneficial therapeutic effect in patients admitted to a coronary care unit." When their hospital course was rated as good, intermediate, or bad, a 2x3 chi-square had $p<.01$, with 85 percent in the prayer group and 73 percent of the controls rated as 'good,' and 14 percent of the prayer group and 22 percent of the controls rated as 'bad.' There were, however, twenty variables on which the two groups did not differ.

Byrd refers to two other controlled trials of prayer (Joyce and Welldon, 1965; and Collipp, 1969) neither of which showed a significant effect for prayer. In his acknowledgements he not only thanked "God for responding to the many prayers made on behalf of the patients," but he noted that no attempt was made to limit prayers for the control group outside the study, saying that, "This may have resulted in smaller differences observed between the two groups. How God acted in this situation is unknown, i.e. were the groups treated by God as a whole or were individual prayers alone answered?" Furthermore, "whether patients prayed of themselves and to what degree they held religious convictions was not determined."

While that study appears to have been well designed, it emphasizes the epistemological and theological problems confronting any attempt to demonstrate the efficacy of prayer within a Christian context, in a way that, as

Wulff (1991, p. 171) perhaps petulantly notes, limits God's beneficence or power. Wulff asks whether "God intervenes in the natural course of events merely (and only) on request—and that He makes Himself available as an intervening variable for experiments on plants as well?" Even if we accept the validity of those results, they carry implications about our concept of God, which Byrd mentions only in passing, that might be explained in other ways, including the patients' coping skills and the severity of their condition. But a major anthropomorphic problem centers on whether, and if so why, God might have agreed to disregard those who had not been prayed for. Byrd's study reads like part of a search to define or control God, and it leaves those who had no one to pray for them disadvantaged—unless they were being prayed for vicariously by some others who accepted the mystery of faith.

Studies like these may be religiously invalid. Spilka, Hood, and Gorsuch (1985), however, located prayer within their section on "Religion as therapy" (pp. 301-305), in which they also included intense religious experience, glossolalia, and conversion. They accept that the practice of prayer is widespread and that it can be a "deeply meaningful behavior" with great therapeutic potential (p. 303). Its "fundamental element" is the belief that one "has a direct line to the deity, and that God is likely to notice this supplication, allegiance and praise, and will respond accordingly. The hoped-for result is often protection and forgiveness, but subjective well-being and a sense of personal control and strength are important concomitants" (p. 303). They also cite other opinions, that prayer performs a personality-integrative role, that group-prayer ceremonies 'should' be regarded as a form of group therapy, and that "loneliness and conflict tend to be reduced, especially if prayer occurs in a public situation where others are similarly involved" (p. 304). They refer to studies by McCann (1962) which showed that 78 percent of Baptists and one percent of Jews use prayer to reduce stress, and by Welford (1947a and b) who identified "an increase in prayer with frustration as an effort to cope with a trying situation rather than an attempt to escape reality" (p. 304). They note that Stouffer et al (1949) reported that soldiers found praying beneficial in battle. Loveland's (1968) finding that prayer increases and helps the bereaved cope with loss is also cited (p. 304). At the same time they note that a "pathological religious mental content" can inhibit therapists' attempts to deal with the causes of mental disorder— although why that should be so is not discussed, beyond the fact that it has "deep roots in our cultural order" (p. 305). They stress that religious activities can be a substitute for dealing with life, so that "Recourse to prayer may indeed be very personally gratifying, but if it replaces appropriate and necessary action, its spiritual function has been distorted and may constitute a serious psychological problem" (p. 305). It is clear that Deconchy's functional censorship of what it is possible to study in religion interacts with the difficulties in identifying the features of prayer that can be examined empirically or even experimentally, and with the psychologists' own prejudices about what ought to be possible.

Early studies of prayer

Beck's (1906) results from his study of an ill-defined sample include the fact that 73 percent believed that prayers of maturity are for spiritual rather than material things, that 70 percent of those who pray feel the presence of a higher power, that 75 percent think it misguided to pray for a change in the weather or in other people, and that 85 percent believe that the effects of prayer are wholly subjective. One has no idea who those people were. While many in that study who prayed felt they gained access to new sources of energy in this way, they were divided about whether this power comes from within or without. All but one person in Beck's study believed that remarkable answers to prayer can be understood as normal, and not miraculous.

Beck's overall conclusion that "prayer certainly changes the vision of right and wrong, disposition and resolution, because it is such an intense mental occupation backed up by emotions" should be set against the attitudes of those who may have given up prayer or who had never begun to pray. Yet similar conclusions are still likely, and there is no doubt that prayer can have an effect, if only discursively or rhetorically, despite our uncertainty about how many people it might affect, the ways that might happen, and whether positive conclusions about prayer are reached only by those who are themselves 'religious.' Is prayer therefore self-fulfilling only for those who believe in it, and how many will argue that prayers detached completely from a religious context could be effective? If so, is it prayer in particular *contexts* rather than prayer as such that brings about any of its effects? If that were so, a social psychological interpretation of prayer is needed, rather than the more conventionally individual psychological or religious theories about it.

While English survey data suggest that an awareness of a 'higher power' is reported by 75 percent (Hay, 1982, p. 153), and Beck's data show that some of his sample used prayer as a means to achieve a religious experience, there can be no consensus about the objectivity (or the implications) of such conclusions. Beck noted that "it would require the testimony of God to establish this beyond a peradventure."

Religious and other experiences might therefore be self-validating, supporting those who believe they have had such an experience, which they might be unwilling to describe to others. Yet surveys and questionnaire-based studies of these phenomena have themselves altered our social context, bringing to our notice the mere fact that prayer is widespread (Poloma and Gallup, 1991). In that sense, the Kinsey Reports on sexual behavior changed attitudes to sex, helping to make the current public discussions about 'safe sex' and its variants possible. Furthermore, prayer groups talk about how prayer works, and listen to their members' own testimonies, as they pray together. Discussions about 'unanswered' prayers, whether they were for material or spiritual benefits, might alter the context within which prayer is practiced and change the expectations about it, since being able to answer such questions unselfconsciously is an important step towards defusing prior expectations about what prayer involves or can do. When Beck asked people if they were ever disappointed at not getting what they had prayed for, he noted that "very few were ever disappointed in not receiving the mental results they anticipated from prayer, for a willingness to accept any result was a part of prayer itself."

Unanswered prayer presents a continuing problem for those assuming that the Biblical injunction to ask and it shall be given is a fail-safe promise that can only be resolved by asserting that 'no' can be a positive answer (as Festinger's concept of dissonance reduction might expect). But a continuing difficulty with prayer involves our attempts to reduce it to a human scale, as a form of guaranteed communication, or the assumption that it follows its own rules about efficacy, rather than some socially agreed principles. It is also the case, however, that the 'correct' attitudes to prayer are not likely to center on the concreteness of any expectations that might support it, beyond finding that prayer could be vaguely 'helpful,' even if we do not know how that is possible.

Furthermore, it would probably be thought 'quaint' for someone to give up a religious stance by keeping count of the favors that have not been granted, although one hears of people who have turned against God because of an injustice, natural disaster, or the death of a child (cf Furnham and Brown, 1992). But that is an attributional problem, and we usually hear of them at second hand. Others whose prayers 'fail' might redouble their efforts, or change their ideas about God and what they will pray for. As with the failures of prophecy, one's 'basic trust' in a person or their religious and other claims can override a disconfirmation, as in the Biblical statement, 'Though he slay me, yet will I trust him.' Godin (1986) identified those failures as points of resistance in which mature and immature attitudes conflict because we do possess a coherent religious stance and are guided by 'superstition as much as by faith.'

T.V. Moore (1956), a Catholic priest-psychologist, reported a study of a devout life of 'the Catholic' that he hoped would give "a picture of the interior spiritual life from the zero level to its very heights" (p. 391). He gathered 200 completed questionnaires, and in their analysis adopted the role of a spiritual director, with clear ideas about the proper spiritual path. So the scales he used ranged from hardness of heart to relative perfection, from obstinacy in mortal sin to relative imperfection, and from the deliberate suppression of any recourse to God to an habitual life of prayer. Beyond emphasizing that no rating or scoring scale is epistemologically or ideologically neutral and that his results have little general relevance, I have mentioned the attempt by Emma Shackle and me to replicate this study in England and in the USA in 1987. It failed because of the objections even of those in two contemplative religious communities who were asked to complete the questionnaire. As one person wrote on the questionnaire she was given, it "seems to be more concerned with struggling than about letting go, which I see the contemplative life to be about." Schneiders (1986) strikingly shows the extent to which the religious life *has* changed, abolishing many older prejudices.

Moore had used eleven questions that he derived from St John of the

Cross's *Dark Night of the Soul*, chapters 19 and 20, to decide if someone "truly loves God," with other questions that dealt with mental prayer, ascetic practices, the desire to identify with the suffering Christ, and St Teresa of Avila's experiences of the spiritual life through her prayers of quiet and union, ecstasy, locutions, visions (true and Satanic), the spiritual betrothal and spiritual marriage. Moore himself accepted the validity of the Council of Trent's post-Reformation formulation and their divine sanctions, and distinguished Paul's experience on the road to Damascus, which he said was planted 'from within,' from dreams or visual images. He presented this material in a didactic rather than a descriptive manner, and gives an insight into pre-Vatican II Catholic piety when he says, "Prayer includes Grace before meals, the children's 'Angel of God' and 'Hail Mary' and frequent aspirations as 'Dear God help me to be patient,' many times a day" (p. 21).

Cultural and religious change has turned Moore's study into a period piece of religious psychology, in which God is understood as working directly on the mind through an infusion of grace. Its developmental psychology is like that of the sixteenth-century Spanish mystics. While Moore's questionnaire has ninteen references to God and ten to Christ, Beck made no direct reference to either, being concerned with an everyday prayer life, and the beliefs and theories about it, and not with the mystical graces or communion and dependence. While the practice of prayer allows some who pray to cope adaptively with the vicissitudes of life, our everyday language still contains prayerful formulae that are not counted as prayers, until they are *intended* as such, when saying 'God bless' rather than 'Goodbye,' for example.

While we might distinguish novices at prayer from those who are its adepts, Christians are encouraged to persevere well beyond adopting the prayerful postures by which prayer is recognized behaviorally. Although it may be useful to know how often people pray, we should not ignore the content of their prayers, the ways they pray and their use of religious and social contexts for prayer. We must also accept the stereotype that it is unusual if someone prays too frequently, or in the 'wrong' places, unless they are bound by a set of religious rules or demands. And we should recognize the differences between those who pray as petitioners, listeners, contemplatives, prophets or mystics, charismatics, or as followers of a 'law.' Prayer does not need to be justified by its explicit effects, since as Welford (1947) showed, petitionary prayer could reduce frustration and help us adapt to unusual situations. It can be emotionally satisfying.

Spilka et al (1985, p. 97), after citing Gallup poll data from the USA go on to note that "Estimates vary widely regarding the frequency of prayer, probably because most studies are not always clear as to the proportion of church members assessed. Locality, religious group, ethnic heritage, and class level may also be influencing factors. Given these considerations, it is not surprising that Moberg (1971) summarizes evidence suggesting that anywhere from 58 to 92 percent of church members claim they pray frequently. Argyle and Beit-Hallahmi (1975) cite (early) research by Gorer to the effect that these propensities also grow stronger with age. There was an orderly increase in those reporting private prayer, from 32 percent among thirty year olds to 75 percent by age seventy. This observation has been confirmed in other work (Marty, Rosenberg and Greeley, 1968). Regardless of age, more women pray regularly than men (Argyle and Beit-Hallahmi, 1975, pp. 97-98)."

But why do so many studies focus on intercessory prayer, and is it reasonable to try to measure the abstract 'power' carried by such prayers? The experiments I have mentioned certainly assume that others who pray might be able to produce equivalent results. In that sense they embody a material conception of a spiritual process. Perhaps this is one reason why the results are equivocal, even on methodological grounds. We therefore need to look more carefully at beliefs about the kinds of effects that are expected from prayer and its appropriateness for various contexts.

Other empirical studies of prayer in our bibliography show that the focus has moved from petitionary prayer as an independent variable that might produce defined effects, to work on the use of prayer as a means of coping with illness or social disadvantage and perhaps therefore as a dependent variable. The primary questions about prayer do not concern its judged efficacy and what that might depend on. While that question has been asked, and answered in the New Testament with reference to the saying of Jesus that whatever is asked for in his name will be granted, that formulation does not seem to accept failures, unless we lack the proper spirit. That raises unavoidable questions about what prayer could 'be' as a generic phenomenon, with testable outcomes beyond a relationship in which "something is transacting" (as James, 1902, p. 365 put it). The debates between materialists or atheists and religionists continue and can only be resolved through conviction and persuasive arguments, and not by evidence that is simply textual, to support claims or counter-claims that might refer to devotional states or the contexts in which new meanings (or a new life) can be developed or identified. But should we "expect a significant difference in efficacy (however that is assessed) between the outbursts of men and women in a crisis, especially if they do not habitually pray, from that of a saintly devotee" (Muelder, 1957, p. 35—cited by Wulff, p. 172). This quote itself points to the intangibility of any dependent variables in the experiments on prayer. Praying for the stock-market to rise is acceptable as a joke, but probably not as a prayer.

The links between *"Religion and Health"* (the title of a Journal) are set between a pair of constructs that must be carefully defined, beyond bald references to religion or illness. Furthermore, while most people expect to be healthy, those who hope that prayer might reliably (or only rhetorically) bypass the 'laws of nature' find it hard to identify with prayer as "a dynamic harmony within and without that heals conflict and loneliness in renewing one's sense of belonging to a larger wholeness" (Johnson, 1953, p. 35, cited by Wulff, p. 172). But mental states are like electrons and can only be measured after they have happened. And so are physiological responses in heart rate or skin conductivity, and brain states during EEG, CAT, PET, and MRI procedures as evidence for relaxation or an altered awareness. Yet it is those methods that have been used as evidence for the correlates [sic] of meditative practices, but not for comparable effects from petitionary prayer (West, 1987).

Other references to prayer in Spilka, Hood, and Gorsuch (1985) concern the 'respectability' that physiological studies of brain function have conferred on prayer and meditation, noting that "while full-scale theoretical treatments of prayer have yet to emerge in contemporary psychology, the study of prayer is in process although psychologists seem to feel most comfortable in discussing 'meditation' and its infinite [sic] varieties" (p. 165). They align the activities of prayer and meditation with "an apparent withdrawal from normal waking consciousness and a concern with a passive receptivity 'withdrawn' from normal daily activities," holding that prayer and meditation involve a meaningful, if difficult, confrontation with reality, "legitimated and made meaningful in terms of religious interpretations," although "prayer or meditation is a 'different mode of consciousness' than waking or sleep, with different theta/alpha brain wave frequencies since 'persons who pray and meditate clearly recognize that they are 'turned inward.'" (pp. 165-166).

Meditation

Pekola's paper (1987) in West's review of studies covering the "phenomenology of meditation" stresses its "profound effects in terms of reported subjective experiences," and the likely effects on the meditation process of "introspective sensitization (or the training for an act of introspection) compounded by sensory deprivation and experimental demand." No mention is made, however, of the direct effects of cultural or traditional models that sanction these practices and specify what can be expected during and after their practice. So Hendlen (1979) is said to have experienced "an activation of energy at the base of his spine that flowed upward and ended in a 'beautiful display of golden light'" (Pekola, 1987, p. 62). This is reminiscent of a *chakra*-type experience.

In short, the results of those studies are of necessity confounded by previous training, the context and expectations within which they are set, and by the factors that are investigated and the responses that the participants in any experiment are able or willing to produce.

Since 'free associations' are known to be constrained by the relationship with an experimenter and the demands of the experimental situation, it is customary to use nonreactive measures in these studies. But what effects are to be expected from meditation, or from prayer? Do any changes reflect self-directed attention or a longer-term state of tension or happiness? Which other sources of error variance are to be found in the different forms of meditation that are practiced, and to what extent might they fit personality styles or expectations, and the acceptability of specific techniques, of breathing for example?

Pekola disregarded single case studies, summarizing nine studies that grouped data from meditation groups (between 1963 and 1984), and another twelve studies in which meditators were compared against matched controls, that he criticized for their methodological inadequacies and conflicting results, because of a lack of consensus about the mental states that might be modified by meditation, and could then be evaluated. Self-reported changes may be indicative, but they are not soundly evidential, and the characteristics, expectancies, and introspective skills of those who are involved impose crucial limitations on any results. Perhaps we should simply compare naive against committed practitioners, although to control the time in meditation, or the method and content of their prayer is difficult, and if reported effects are a primary dependent variable, they involve expectancies, 'introspective sensitization' (Pekola in West, p. 79) and a willingness to report fairly, which itself reflects demand characteristics.

It is not clear if altered "states of consciousness" or any other effects that flow from prayer might themselves reflect some of the 'reasons' for prayer, since people pray to fulfil an obligation, out of habit, from a compelling need, to express an attitude, or for guidance. Those differences reflect specific attitudes to what prayer is 'about.' While fantasies are now externalized and simulated in computer programs, science fiction, films, virtual realities, and pornography, it is often assumed that these representations are new, although texts and narratives, paintings and sculptures have a long history of being used to capture perspectives on what is "in the mind's eye," or in consciousness.

The early psychologists of religion, especially William James (1902), and Leuba (1925), were concerned with religious experience and mysticism, arguing about its pathological or regressive character. Their mystical categories share a noetic core, giving what has been regarded as valid, if paradoxical knowledge, and pointing not simply to an experience that is hard to describe, beyond a positive sense of the holy. Stace (1960a) also distinguished between an inner or subjective certainty that all things are 'alive,' sharing a unity in their diversity as parts of a whole (which he called 'extrovertive') with the sense of a timeless and spaceless void and a dissolution of the sense of selfhood in a consciousness without content.

Pahnke and Richards (1966) derived their ninefold phenomenological typology from Stace (1960a) to cover a sense of unity that is either within the experiencer who loses the sense of self without becoming unconscious, or with a unity "perceived outwardly with the physical senses through the external world" in a transcendence of time and space, a deeply felt positive mood, a sense of sacredness, and an intuitive, nonrational yet authoritative sense of real knowledge that is paradoxical or logically contradictory, ineffable yet transient.

This can be aligned with what is described in the *bhakti* texts of the Hindu religion, and in the lives of the paragons of *bhakti* who were led to withdraw from the world (Thiel-Horstmann, 1989, p. 129). Their "primordial status of being" involves renunciation, so that as Dumont (1970, p. 56) put it, "One can leave the world from within, and God himself is not bound by his acts, for he acts only out of love."

Other paradoxes in mystical religion include the fact that moments of 'union' are neither producible nor reproducible at will, and they are usually brief. Their brevity and spontaneity is used as evidence of a genuinely religious trait that distinguishes them from all other sensations that might be 'metamorphically' related to them. The Indian literature describes this as a dialectic between *sahaja* (mystic union) and *viraha* (separation). "Even if the mystic slips out of the state of union and resumes his ordinary worldly life, he is unlikely to take a pre-mystic stance in approaching worldly matters" (Thiel-Horstmann, 1989, p. 129).

This evidence or experience, if that is what it is, could help to argue against any alignment of prayer with meditation, although those who pray may find themselves moved by it, on occasions. But people can also be emotionally moved by their experiences of nature, their interactions with 'significant others,' by music, poetry or a novel, and through engagement with social transitions, especially in birth or death.

An almost theological question therefore concerns whether mystical states can be achieved by our own efforts, or whether they are *gifts* from God, or *rewards* for effort or good behavior. In *bhakti*, for example, only God's grace is able to bestow liberation, which may involve a lifelong struggle and not a simple ritual. But in some traditions, merely conforming to the prescriptions seems to guarantee what is promised, which Christians are more likely to find hereafter than in enlightenment now. So, "the reward of *bhakti* is *bhakti* itself, that is, the experience of the divine. Liberation is considered to be of secondary importance." (ibid. p. 130). The deference given in Christianity to saints and martyrs for their holiness and their role in intercessory prayer shows the extent to which a culture or a traditional theological system can shape or guide the contexts within which religious practices gain meaning, although a few individuals might develop that sense autonomously. Thiel-Horstmann (1989, p. 131) argues that "the charismatic influence of an outstanding *bhakta* will rarely prevail much longer than the first generation of a newly emerging sect," and that "both monk and layman have equal access to grace."

Western psychological perspectives give only weak support to the validity of these processes, perhaps because we can 'see' their self-serving nature and the social benefits of making *any* of those claims, while holding that our own Christian perspectives are not like that. Our own experiences have, however, become consensual, not least because of the language and the external events to which they are referred. Their similarity to the experiences of others cannot, however, be guaranteed.

The mental states that accompany other types of Christian prayer slide through thanksgiving (perhaps for specific benefits received) and praise, to confession for sins of omission or commission, and contemplation or the meditation that might be monitored psychophysiologically for transient psychological changes. The 'action' or intentions involved there are usually understood as directed towards the God in whom one believes, and whose nature or character is consequently accepted. Although prayers are constrained by that, they may be precipitated by, and carry or express, personal needs and beliefs (as Welford, 1947a showed in his study of frustration as a precondition for prayer). This gives them a self-reference, especially if we ask for our will to be aligned with God's will.

It is reasonable to look for any evidence that people might accept as proof of the validity of their prayers, but we also need to know what can be accepted as an 'answer' to prayer, which does not necessarily involve expectations about specific material or objective effects. Wulff (1991, p. 172) offers a solution to this problem by identifying prayer with a "spoken, sometimes formal address to a divinity, one element of which is often heartfelt petition." He contrasts that view against James's (1902, p. 365) definition of prayer as "every kind of inward communion or conversation with the power recognized as divine." This aligns prayer with 'meditation' and does not expect it to have petitionary implications, since James is likely to have accepted a mystical union with the divine as the sense of an inarticulate, formless, and passive dependence.

The current psychology of meditation relies more on Eastern than Western conceptions of mind and self (West, 1987, p. 3), whether it is to be used for self-control, training, therapy, to explore experience or awaken one's consciousness (Tart, 1986), or "to achieve a direct experiential knowledge of an absolute such as God, Being, Oneness, Buddha nature" (West, 1987, p. 5). The psychology of prayer relies on Western conceptions. Practitioners of meditation are adamant that it can be explored practically and from the inside; those who pray seem confused by its 'tangible-intangibility.' Since our concern is primarily with prayer (and only secondarily with meditation) in religious contexts, the search for stillness through focused breathing, relaxation, or reduced external stimulation may have more secular or therapeutic than religious connotations for Christians, although some hold that those practices are also prayerful, since the attitudes to them are changing, if only at the edges.

Transcendental meditation (TM) (Crook, 1980), which has come to be widely known in the West, encourages a practitioner to watch their thoughts come and go as they focus on an object, or repeat a mantra (or an action). This aligns with the emphasis on mindfulness, in which attention is focused on all that is "here and now" (Langer, 1988) or with a personal focus on an altered consciousness that may involve trance-like states, inculcated by rhythmical and repeated stimulation. These procedures, which are not novel, have been fostered by some of the "new religious movements" since the 1960s that are either admired or feared (Barker, 1986) because of their political implications, in drawing young people away from their families and previous commitments. They could, however, have similarities with the practices of the nineteenth-century Romantics.

While the practice of prayer appears to be rewarding for its practitioners, many people have been involved with it since they were children because it is expected of them, and not because of independent evidence about the validity or plausibility of those practices. Once it is established, however, the practice of prayer might be found to quieten and strengthen the sense of self or self-worth, and knowledge of a developed tradition (cf West, 1987, p. 12f) is likely to alter the context of one's prayer and therefore its impact on experience. To over-simplify, this might emphasize one pole in the basic dichotomies we have noticed between inner and outer, self and Other, personal and material. Alternatively, one might focus prayer on emptying one's mind through silence rather than with reference to specific formulae, themes, or "spiritual exercises." The physiological effects of Yogic and Zen practices of meditation that aim for a higher consciousness, variously called enlightenment, illumination, or union are well described and undoubted. Fenwick (in West, 1987) contrasts those approaches to the world by analogy with a dusty mirror that is polished by meditation to produce a perfect reflection like that of a universal mind, which reduces the personal self to align it with nature or with mercury on the move that can be stilled and alchemically changed to silver or gold.

The language in which these, or any experiences are couched is always problematic unless we have found agreed and operational definitions of states of mind. While our own conscious awareness might be clear to us, it can be doubted by others who must be, and by convention are the judges of our adjustment. Our own perspectives must be decentered if we are to recognize the complementarity that can combine "a and not a" (cf Oser and Reich, 1987) in the search for enlightenment, through a tradition that has its impacts on a "discursive mind." This is Fenwick's (1987, p. 117) term for the practice of meditation that has "a physiological effect resulting in a change in brain functioning." Another model of those processes rests on a balance between the different strategies of the brain's hemispheres, with the right brain dominant in producing "a three-dimensional view of self as not separate from the world," so that its actions arise in response to prevailing circumstances and not from some individual will.

More data are needed to clarify these processes and their effects, and it is not yet clear if the rapidly developing technologies for brain imaging and increasing sophistication about neuropsychology (cf Shallice, 1991) will improve our understanding of how prayer might impact on the brain. Present knowledge suggests that we are no longer confined to conclusions that depend only on phenomenological claims of esoteric knowledge among "researchers eager to ease their own intellectual doubts about meditation" (West, 1987, p. 15). But the psychological contrasts between concentrative and 'open-up' meditations (Ornstein, 1972), and insight (Goleman, 1977) or in the procedures that focus other attentional strategies that Shapiro (1982) describes as "wide-angle, zoom lens attention," all draw on the elementary fact that when physiological processes change from one steady-state, they reach another.[1]

---

1. When this chapter was being revised I happened to attend a presentation by the French "performance artist" Orlan, whose speciality has been to stage and videotape surgical procedures ("performance operations") that are designed to sculpture parts of her body to conform to the social ideal of the perfect woman. One effect of these proce-

But, as with a great deal of psychological research, demand characteristics and expectancies can bias or invalidate any results designed to test specific explanations. This makes it hard to establish the validity of prayer independently of its societal or traditional value and of the claims or accounts of individuals who explain why they pray or meditate. But what counts as an explanation of prayer, and what purposes can it serve? Social or religious criteria sanction a limited set of explanations, most of which do not refer directly to what is happening psychologically. They simply indicate the possibilities of our own control, not over outcomes but over whatever psychological processes are identified that could be involved.

Explanations

Langer (1983, p. 17) notes that to believe that one cannot control an aversive event because one is stupid is worse with respect to one's sense of competence than believing that one has no control because the event is uncontrollable. If one thought one had control through prayer, and that did not work out, is this more likely to be explained as our fault for not being 'good,' or for not praying hard enough, or because God did not want us to have that control? Explanations of prayer are not trivial, nor are opinions about the propriety of our own or others' prayers. In therapeutic interventions directed to overcoming "learned helplessness" (Abramson, Seligman, and Teasdale, 1978) the focus is on the outcome, which is where control is to be found. But Langer (1983, p. 17) also stresses that our sense of control depends on whether we adopt the perspective of an actor, or as an observer of another's actions who may distinguish behavioral from decisional control, independently of an actor's awareness of what they might appear to be doing.

In applying this perspective to prayer we need to know the forms of control that it allows and whether they are direct or indirect, since the way in which prayer is understood determines how it will be used. By analyzing the repertoires of coping skills and the situations that elicit them, we might ask if offering a petitionary prayer involves a dynamic decision, except among those for whom prayer has become routine or habitual. 'Occasional' prayer reflects specific demands, with expected outcomes that can be part of a course of action, with prayer before major surgery, for example. Langer therefore notes (pp. 19-20) that we "should pay more attention to the way

---

dures is to emphasize a dualistic split between body and mind. The extent to which meditation might aim to achieve that through mental (and perhaps physical control) what is dealt with explicitly by Orlan. One sees with her performances that the intentions of supporting meditation and prayer, and perhaps the forms of our own life are not trivial guides to the meanings that we and the context of those 'performance' assign to what is being done. In a note accompanying her performance she remarks that "For the critic this (intentionality) becomes the crucial question in a context in which real and fake, art and anti-art (and we might add religion and irreligion) vie for attention . . . (since) whatever is said about an artwork (or a prayer) becomes attached to it as an additional meaning."

responses are exercised than to the outcomes that remain after the process is over. Accordingly, when control is viewed as process there cannot be a situation in which absolutely no control is available to the person."

Using prayer to achieve a goal entails "the *active belief* that one has a choice among responses that are differentially effective in achieving the (or any) desired outcome. However, there *cannot* be certainty that any one response will bring about the desired outcome. It is important that there is at least some uncertainty of success, or else the behavior could be performed mindlessly (and mechanically)—it then would be psychologically equivalent to a nonevent" (ibid. p. 20). Unless prayer could *never* make a difference, because the outcome is completely predictable, its use is not necessarily mindless since it could be part of a self-mastering process. Apparently mindless prayer, when reciting the rosary or the Angelus, is, however, likely to be devotional rather than petitionary, and it is to be understood within that tradition and not as a form of self-control. Research on prayer *or* meditation nevertheless presents difficulties because of its mixed goals (Orne, 1962), that may be health-related, spiritual or religious. Their effects could then depend on the secondary gains attached to being (seen as) 'holy.' Positive expectations about prayer could also be like the experimenter's bias described by Rosenthal (1964) in which we look for the predicted outcomes that are hypothesis-confirming.

Chance, skill or luck

Prayer is criticized or dismissed as an illusory form of control, although in this sense it could be similar to taking a 'chance' in a lottery. The development of probability theory can be dated from the early seventeenth century (Gigerenzer et al, 1989) and rested partly on trying to systematize how the will of God might be established, since that had traditionally been determined by casting lots, and to calculate the value of annuities and other risks. While gamblers have many strategies to influence the outcome of wagers, which have also been understood as challenges to fate, Nisbett and Ross (1980), and Kahneman, Slovic, and Tversky (1982) give examples of strategies that are used to find information that supports prior hypotheses. They include ignoring disconfirming evidence, finding 'illusory' correlations when causes and consequences seem to be related, and selective attention to particular outcomes.

Studies of the effectiveness of psychotherapy offer another model that might be taken into account when considering the efficacy of prayer. Prayer and psychotherapy both have been regarded as intangible. Prayer might align with psychotherapy because of their common core of ingredients that can account for the positive outcomes from any theoretical orientation, despite differences in their techniques or traditions that obscure the causal factors that could be involved and the difficulties of measuring psychological change. Lambert, Shapiro, and Bergin (1986, p. 163) stress that all therapies can engender hope in patients with low morale and dysfunctional symptoms, and that it is a commonplace for psychological methods of treatment to focus attention, respect, reassurance, support, modeling, encouragement of risk taking, and efforts at mastery.

Those issues could all be involved in prayer, the effects of which might be like a placebo. This use of a 'placebo' was borrowed from medicine where it is a widely accepted test of the efficacy of drug treatments, by contrasting an active chemical agent against an inert substance. While that is a sensible procedure in drug trials, it may have less value when the effect of some bogus psychological intervention is at issue. Lambert et al therefore speak of the "common factors" in any psychosocial treatment that include the setting itself and "expectations for improvement, persuasion, warmth and attention, understanding, encouragement, relaxation, and so on" (p. 163). In prayer as much as in psychotherapy these factors are not inert or trivial, having an active role in many outcomes and an impact in any evaluation of them. They might also work incrementally over time.

We must therefore accept that prayer could have its therapeutic effect because of beliefs and expectations about those effects, the relationships with other people who are involved and schematic expectations about the commitment of those who pray, the opportunities it offers for self-understanding and the practice it gives in preparing for potentially troublesome problems. Lambert et al also stress that since any therapeutic change will be multidimensional, a sound conceptual scheme is needed if we are to systematize those outcomes. Carefully monitoring one's prayers, and the reactions to them, might be more useful for psychologists than for religious people themselves, although the great manuals for mystical prayer can be read as if self-monitoring *was* required. Furthermore, Claxton (in West, 1987, p. 23) explicitly identified meditation as a therapeutic practice that is rarely taught "in a theoretical vacuum" but involves constructing or accepting a model of what is required. Delmonte (in West, 1987) describes these theoretical approaches to meditation in terms of an altered (and greater) awareness of how information is processed and of one's inner state(s), thereby giving knowledge of 'unconscious' processes in learning to relieve stress through concentrative mindfulness, habituation, and deautomatization. The most notorious study of meditation was carried out at Boston University by Pahnke (around 1963) and involved chemical ecstasy. It will not be described here since inducing a mystical state chemically hardly seems to match our major concern with prayer, although endorphins might be found to have an explicit relevance for prayer or for meditation.

A crucial feature of prayer is the extent to which it allows or helps us to transcend immediate constraints, by reframing them within more inclusive narratives. Despite the idealism inherent in that psychological perspective, religious acts or ideas that involve experiences of the divine may be world-rejecting (as in Eckhart or Hinduism) or world-affirming and expressed through natural, historical, or personal events. They might contrast emotional and practical attitudes in worship that involves words, gestures, or actions, and introspective judgments about their validity that interact with the attitudes that draw a commitment, even with small incentives (Festinger and Carlsmith, 1959).[2]

To follow the rules of a tradition is an important way to enter its 'faith.' This helps to explain why converts seem to over-conform to their new group in tuning their own judgments to conform with those of the group. (Sherif et al, 1958, showed a similar process in the autokinetic effect.) That there is some latitude there is shown in the difference between young people's judgments about the appropriateness of prayer for particular ends, which converge on what their tradition expects, and their beliefs about its efficacy, which must be constructed from experience (Brown and Thouless, 1964). Whether any practice is referred to as religious (in praying, for example) or as sport or work should not interfere with the ways in which it is maintained or structured by a belief-disbelief system in which beliefs are accepted or rejected for their content, or dogmatically structured around an ideal that regulates the knowledge, attitudes, and practice of its 'orthodox' members (cf Deconchy, 1991). It is therefore important to examine judgments about the rationality of whatever ideological statements individuals believe to be true, since reasonableness is a filter that beliefs must pass through before they can be accepted. That process is controlled by group pressures and social expectancies like those identified by Lerner's (1980) model of the just world, which might itself mediate some beliefs about prayer.

If studies of prayer were placed within these contexts, some psychological bases for their differently constructed meanings might be exposed. So Deconchy (1991) refers to the results of experiments by Walster, Aronson, and Brown (1966) and by Curtis, Rietdorff, and Donell (1980) which suggest that those who have been 'chosen' to carry out an unpleasant task will administer more painful shocks beforehand than those chosen for a 'pleasant' task because a "self-administered harm might distance them from an angry fate" (p. 17). This suggests another model by which the penitential practices of religious groups can be understood, if they are built on the generic attitudes (to harm, for example) that are beyond 'rational' strategies of action. But we do not yet know enough about 'prayer,' its practice in particular groups, and how much it is assumed to be 'natural' to embark on such studies. Nor do we know how those who do *not* pray are immunized against its validity or usefulness, and how those who *do* pray justify its apparent failures (beyond holding that 'no' is an answer to prayer). Earlier this century it was agreed that prayer, if not religion itself, is "an essential endowment of the human mind" (Wulff, 1991, p. 523). Whether that implies an absolute or a finite God who "when elevated to the absolute sphere," can become an ideal and not simply another dialectical synthesis, like money or nationalism, is itself defined by a tradition.

---

2. I wonder if Wulff is making an ironic reference to Scheler (1921) when he notes on p. 522 that the interdependence of "theory and practice is reflected in Scheler's contention that "They who pray kneeling have not seen God in the same light as they who pray standing (p. 266)."

Any typecast religious actions contrast specific explanations against some theoretically defined components. So Wulff (p. 523) refers to Long's (1952) distinction between primary and secondary religious acts, the first arising from "religious motives and refers to religious objects," while the other concerns the "effects of religious motives in the ethical, political, and social arenas." This view assumes that religions follow their own rules, and that a primary act involves a core experience, perhaps in an encounter with the holy (which is itself an interpretation) that depends on other preparatory or consequential acts. Those distinctions have little value, however, except to privilege "dramatic encounters with the divine," or to sanction them with reference to a phenomenology that could be within the imagination.

Imaginative solutions in art and literature therefore show where we might look for further insight into prayer, although their idealism has made it hard to bring them into psychology. The contrast between subjective certainties or insights and an 'objective' verification has presented a continuing problem to psychologists whose solutions oscillate between denying the scientific validity of experience, and making claims on 'personal' or 'transpersonal' psychologies that defer to spiritual systems, whether in Buddhism, Yoga, Sufism, or Western magical and alchemical thought, as a basis for the claims on spiritual development or improvement. Other 'psychologies' that look 'outward,' as in Jung's archetypes, have been used to find the meaning of images and dreams in mythologies and folklore that can be matched against psychoanalytic models of mind and social behavior (cf Kirkpatrick, 1992). For whatever reason, no hermeneutic tradition that is more concerned with process than context has found a place in those psychologies, perhaps because social practices are maintained within some social context.

Although biologically based explanations of religious phenomena locate a sense of God in the temporal lobe (cf Persinger, 1987) or in the right cerebral hemisphere (Jaynes, 1976), Bowker (1973) shows the range of other sociological and psychological theories that have been offered. Since it is impossible to verify whether there *are* truly spontaneous religious experiences, because of our (latent) contact with at least some religious ideas, many of the problems that religions set are similar to those confronting social psychology itself.

But what are the psychological consequences of becoming 'religious,' granted the social control of doctrines through traditional or textual authorities and institutional processes, which are of course supported by individuals? Disputes about the ordination of women, prayer in public schools, and the extended opportunities for gambling and Sunday trading are examples of conflicts that must be resolved, or controlled. They are important to insiders because of their implications for the orthodoxy of their religious systems. For outsiders they threaten their freedom of choice. These problems of control are not specific to religionism, since the levels, demands, and kinds of response that can be made anywhere offer recurrent problems. Psychological interpretations of prayer are similarly set between the realities (and for some the hopes) of institutional or social (and natural) control, and within individuals' convictions about the possibility of being free, or controlled by an unseen plan (or agenda). While the 'realities' of religion are intangible, they are realized in signs and symbols, texts and testimonies, myths and metaphors, and in places, buildings and communities, and in social relationships. These structures generate their own support through an awareness and experience that requires (and satisfies) emotional, cognitive, or social needs for stability or change through a prayerful presence, or by a demanding communion. These forms have been variously regarded as substantial or illusory, aligned with early attachments to parental figures and other "internal objects," or with quantum forces and even animism. But religious (and Biblical) models can themselves support contradictory courses of action and solutions that defer to law or to prophecy, for example (cf Dittes, 1969).

The psychology of religion has struggled to escape questions about whether God exists and what 'He' might be like, how to tell who is 'religious,' or what its best forms might be, beyond accepting a creed or claiming a genuine religious experience. The validity of such religious claims are easily deconstructed, although these claims (and counter claims) and their effects will themselves reflect particular religious or secular and scientific orthodoxies that mediate, limit, or contextualize whatever variables are used to understand the religious material that can be supported with reference to experience, objective reality, or social reinforcement (following Dittes, 1969, p. 643).

That psychologies of science are appearing only now, while a psychology of religion has been around from the beginning of psychology, is a surprising commentary on the ideological interests of psychologists, some of whom are outraged by the suggestion that their search for solutions should be more open-ended, or even open-minded. But it is hard for some religious people to accept the claims (or effects) of new religious movements, which seem so alien. Even the data about them and the processes involved in deciding to join such a movement must cross several epistemological and pragmatic barriers. But for any religion to survive it must maintain social structures that organize and protect its knowledge, and balance faith against order.

Religious systems are, however, a resource with alternately constructive or destructive consequences for those who can accept, or join them, even if in some traditions they must give away their independence in doing that. This itself turns any measures of religiousness into continuous variables with wide individual differences in their psychological implications.

As well as identifying whatever genuine processes might support prayer, we need to know the constraints that are specific to particular religious traditions. They could be similar to the constraints on writing atonal rather than tonal music, since in both forms one must stay within its rules of composition. An inherent characteristic that marked religion for psychological analysis focused on its subjectivity (James, 1902) or on the control it exercised over natural or doctrinal processes (Deconchy, 1991). Explanations and descriptions, like that proposed by Koepp (1920, cf Wulff, 1991, p. 524f), who claimed a "purely empirical method of the psychology of religion" that required the insight (or intuitions) of "deep inner piety, the gift of exceptionally accurate self-observation, a good measure of artistic sensitivity, and the broadest possible familiarity with the religious testimony of others from diverse traditions and times" (from Wulff, 1991) seem to define the characteristics of a religious person, rather than of a psychologist. Otto's *Idea of the Holy* (1917) and Heiler's *Prayer* (1918) are classic examples of that approach, both of which depend on a sympathetic understanding of religious practice before it is possible to identify what is hidden in the personal documents and disclosures that describe prayer. Otto used 'numinous,' from the Latin word for divine will or power, to capture a state or feeling that is only comprehensible to those who have had that experience themselves. Despite their analogies with other experiences, they classically convey the irreducible character of an awesome, majestic, and daunting energy (the *mysterium tremendum*) which fascinates yet is dreadful (the *mysterium fascinans*). Those schematic forms are only guides to the essence of these reactions, since our languages give out in the face of them. Yet they can be found in the lives of others, in the art and music that conveys a sense of quiet withdrawal, or in the emptiness identified by Eastern traditions.

Types and preferences

In *The Republic* Plato contrasted the Dorian and Phrygian modes of music in a manner that emphasized those features in religion. He said:

> I'm no expert on modes, but leave me one that will represent appropriately the voice and accent of a brave man on military service or any dangerous undertaking, who faces misfortune, be it injury or death, or any other calamity, with the same steadfast endurance. And I want another mode to represent him in the voluntary non-violent occupations of peacetime: for instance, persuading someone to grant a request, praying to God or instructing or admonishing his neighbor, or again submitting himself to the requests or instruction or persuasion of others and acting as he decides, and in all showing no conceit, but moderation and common sense and willingness to accept the outcome. Give me these two modes, one stern, one pleasant, which will best represent sound courage and moderation in good fortune or in bad.

Heiler's study of prayer relies on similar language, but he defined prayer negatively: "Not in dogmas and institutions, not in rites and ethical ideals, but in prayers do we grasp the peculiar quality of the religious life. In the words of a prayer can we penetrate into the deepest and the most intimate movements of the religious soul" (Heiler, 1932, p. xv). He also identified the diversities of prayer "as the calm collectedness of a devout individual soul, and as the ceremonial liturgy of a great congregation; as an original creation of a religious genius, and as an imitation on the part of a simple, average religious person; as the spontaneous expression of upspringing religious experiences, and as the mechanical recitation of an incomprehensible formula; as bliss and ecstasy of heart, and as painful fulfillment of the law; as the involuntary discharge of an overwhelming emotion, and as the voluntary concentration on a religious object; as loud shouting and crying, and as still, silent absorption; as artistic poetry, and as stammering speech; as the flight of the spirit to the supreme Light, and as a cry out of the deep distress of the heart; as joyous thanksgiving and ecstatic praise, and as humble supplication for forgiveness and compassion; as a childlike entreaty for life, health, and happiness, and as an earnest desire for power in the moral struggle of existence; as a simple petition for daily bread, and as an all-consuming yearning for God Himself; as a selfish wish, and an unselfish solicitude for a brother; as wild cursing and vengeful thirst, and as heroic intercession for personal enemies and persecutors; as a stormy clamor and demand, and as joyful renunciation and holy serenity; as a desire to change God's will and make it chime with our petty wishes, and as a self-forgetting vision and surrender to the Highest Good; as the timid entreaty of the sinner before a stern judge, and as the trustful talk of a child with a kind father; as swelling phrases of politeness and flattery before an unapproachable King, and as a free outpouring in the presence of a friend who cares; as the humble petition of a servant to a powerful master, and as the ecstatic converse of the bride with the heavenly Bridegroom" (p. 353).

Behind that diversity Heiler found nine types of prayer, the first being naive, immediate, and impulsive petitions free of reflective criticism and any traditional formality, precipitated by a sudden threat to the well-being of an individual or a group, or by the practical need for gratitude, directed to a being with human qualities, and accompanied by sacrifice or sacrificial formulae, or by a vow contingent or granting the request. Praise, flattery, and appeals to sympathy are used repeatedly in the prototypical language in Christian prayers, accompanied by gestures and bodily attitudes, and shown in facial expressions.

While the stereotypic and recognizable nature of the postures and gestures that accompany prayer can be investigated systematically, Heiler might not have approved of their study because it forecloses detailed descriptions of the range of gestures he identified, which have been gratuitously interpreted in terms of powerlessness and the dependency of a child reaching for a parent, or in the magical rites to secure or protect someone from a divine power, which Heiler claimed had earlier served as a form of secular greeting or respect. Since we cannot know what might have been the sequence in that development it is safer to note these parallels than to accept their identity.

Another type of prayer that Heiler identified covers prescribed ritual formulae. They are not spontaneous, and he postulated an evolutionary sequence there in "petrification or mechanization" since "acts of worship harden with amazing swiftness into sacred rites" that allay uncertainties as a sense of the divine presence diminishes (Heiler, 1932, p. 66).

Heiler next identified the prayers of Greek religion as simple and spontaneous forms that focused on well-being or happiness through high ideals. Then there were the philosophical prayers of those who could not affirm

the "real presence" of an anthropomorphic god, but produced an ideal, purified form of prayer that aimed to realize the highest ethical ideals for others
as well as themselves, surrendering to their destiny, and contemplating the
greatness of all things including life itself. He found a lack of urgent necessity in this form of prayer, because it is controlled by reason, and he contrasted
those philosophical prayers against the prayers of those with a "religious
genius" which may be spontaneous and involve a relationship with a personal
God. Those prayers require continuous interaction with God in solitude, to
find the gift of God at work in the soul. Heiler also contrasted mystical and
prophetic types of prayer, the first being feminine in their orientation to an
ecstatic union with God, the other being masculine and anchored in the
social world. His other types of prayer involved creative artists and poets, for
whom religion itself is not at the center of their life, so that prayer does not
control but serves as the source of their artistic inspiration in public worship. Creative prayer could be aesthetic-contemplative or emotional-ethi-
cal, the first identifying a pantheistic god and the other centered on an ideal
of artistic creation. Public worship then unites the shared experience of religious communities, lifting individuals to higher stages of devotion through
their congregational participation.

Last come the prayers, not of anguish, but for fear of punishment, with the
hope of rewarded duty aligned with good works, fasting, and giving alms to
accumulate merit. They may be empty of religious value, or they can help to
sustain a spiritual mood and purify the religious life.

Heiler's nine prayer types were then grouped as primary or secondary,
depending on whether they express a profound experience, or are imitative
and cold abstractions. The primary prayer is " a living communion of the religious man with God, conceived as personal and present in experience, a
communion which reflects the forms of the social relations of humanity"
(Heiler, 1932, p. 358). Their common psychological root enhances life (p. 355)
in "the soul of all piety" (p. 362) that others have deconstructed in terms of
an animistic consolation in searching to make sense of the environment.

Pharmacologists refer to occasions when a biological effect can be deci-
sively observed as its "window of opportunity." Times of crisis, need or
when other help fails provide a similar window for religion and prayer that
has been used in recent studies of the use of prayer by those confronting
breast cancer (Johnson and Spilka, 1991), psychological distress (Neighbours
et al, 1983) , cardiac surgery (Saudia et al, 1991), low back pain (Crisson and
Keefe, 1988; Rosenstiel and Keefe, 1983, Keefe and Dolan, 1986, Turner and
Clancy, 1986), or arthritis (Parker et al, 1989). Identifying the role of prayer
in those contexts points up its common use in coping with, or in attempting
to resolve a crisis. This has been criticized for its apparent opportunism,
although Johnson and Spilka (1991) stress a contrast there between praying, knowing that others are praying for you, and having a member of the clergy offering, or being asked to pray for you. That we can use prayer for coping is regarded as a secondary or instrumental use, and not a primary attack
on a set of target problems. Studies that have assigned this role to prayer

then put it with other cognitive or behavioral coping strategies (cf Rosenstiel and Keefe's, 1983, Table 1), as a specific "religious variable" (cf Johnson and Spilka, 1991, Table 2), or as part of religion in general (Pargament et al, 1990).

It is important from this perspective to note that Biblical accounts of prayer contrast its success against failure, suggesting that we might consider how the subjective understanding or confidence in prayer could be improved. But we cannot expect that 'better prayer' would be more 'successful' without specifying what this would mean in religious, pragmatic, or subjective terms. To ask if prayer makes a difference, beyond wanting to satisfy some 'need' to pray, begs questions about how one's sense of well-being can be tangibly influenced. Unless we know what evidence is acceptable and where to look for the effects of prayer, no tests are possible, beyond one's beliefs about its efficacy. This is a question for the studies of coping cited here, and in the vignette methods that involve hypothetical problems that can draw controlled responses (cf Lilliston and Brown, 1991, Lilliston, Brown, and Schliebe, 1982).

In a partial replication of those vignette-based studies I used two religious and two nonreligious solutions concerning a man or a woman who had been given a diagnosis of cancer, or who was told that there was nothing wrong with them.

The results showed consistent differences in the preferred solutions for these targets and their diagnosis that depended on the respondents' religious commitment. Nevertheless, choosing prayer or church-going, rather than considering suicide or reading about the problem is not only related to one's religious background but it is carefully tailored to the demands imposed by the diagnosis. These results are shown in Tables 4 a-d.

Another question therefore concerns what prayer can 'do,' as well as how it is to be 'done,' when articulating or expressing needs in a way that might change our context, or our attitudes to ourselves. This brings us back to the perspectives that have been adopted in attempting to understand prayer, whether among those who pray, those prayed about, and any who observe these prayers. These perspectives do not give equal access to what is involved or intended in prayer, especially when the explanation could refer to biological, psychological, sociological, historical, theological, biblical, or other categories.

If prayer is taken-for-granted, its character is hard to reduce or reinterpret. So the exemplary theories of prayer have themselves drawn more religious attention than their expected effects, which those who teach about prayer seem reticent to examine beyond assuming a reflexive outcome, or by making pious statements about the propriety of prayer.

Table 9a

Showing the raw mean ratings for each question, for each vignette in a replication of Lilliston's et al (1981, 1982) studies.

Diagnosis of Cancer

Solution	Suicide				Read			
Sex of subject	Male		Female		Male		Female	
Sex of target	M	F	M	F	M	F	M	F
1. Effectiveness of the solution.	3.07	4.08	2.21	3.18	6.65	4.46	6.12	5.98
2. Need professional help.	5.93	6.58	7.49	7.15	5.59	6.08	5.68	6.04
3. Would do the same.	2.93	2.75	2.86	3.33	6.71	5.54	6.44	6.45
4. Another possible solution.	1.54	1.29	1.33	1.18	1.59	1.63	1.66	1.62
N =	15	24	43	33	17	24	41	47

Table 9b

Diagnosis of "Nothing Wrong"

Solution	Suicide				Read			
Sex of subject	Male		Female		Male		Female	
Sex of target	M	F	M	F	M	F	M	F
1. Effectiveness of the solution.	3.00	2.88	2.49	2.72	4.59	3.17	3.72	3.86
2. Need professional help.	6.48	6.21	6.87	6.85	5.50	5.61	5.23	5.74
3. Would do the same.	2.22	2.50	2.53	2.49	3.09	3.22	2.81	2.80
4. Another possible solution	1.35	1.21	1.33	1.18	1.27	1.28	1.20	1.21
N =	23	24	45	39	22	18	43	42

Table 9c

Showing the raw mean ratings for each question, by sex of subjects and sex of targets.

Diagnosis of Cancer

Solution	Go to church				Pray			
Sex of subject	Male		Female		Male		Female	
Sex of target	M	F	M	F	M	F	M	F
1. Effectiveness of the solution.	4.68	4.95	4.84	5.80	4.38	4.32	4.86	5.27
2. Need professional help.	5.53	5.68	5.98	5.52	5.08	4.82	5.89	5.58
3. Would do the same.	4.47	3.68	3.89	4.89	4.17	4.73	5.11	4.96
4. Another possible solution.	1.42	1.45	1.41	1.54	1.38	1.77	1.57	1.67
N =	19	22	44	46	24	22	37	45

Table 9d

Diagnosis of "Nothing Wrong"

Solution	Go to church				Pray			
Sex of subject	Male		Female		Male		Female	
Sex of target	M	F	M	F	M	F	M	F
1. Effectiveness of the solution.	4.75	5.38	5.39	5.72	4.73	3.53	4.71	4.64
2. Need professional help.	4.33	4.31	5.02	5.08	4.55	4.67	4.76	5.48
3. Would do the same.	3.25	4.94	4.12	4.38	3.91	3.47	4.71	4.09
4. Another possible solution.	1.38	1.81	1.47	1.59	1.45	1.47	1.44	1.43
N =	24	16	49	39	22	15	34	44

Chapter Eleven

Development and the Meaning of Prayer

Once they made a White man into a Priest of the Bow
he was out there with other Bow Priests
he had black stripes on his body
the others said their prayers from their hearts
but he read his from a piece of paper.
—A Zuni poem, from Gill (1987, p. 89).

The emphasis in any account of prayer can be placed on an inherently developmental process (Godin, 1988) or on social and contextual influences. In a study of the responses of 4,948 eleven-year-old children in England, Francis and Brown (1990) found that after controlling for the practice of prayer of these children, a path analysis (see page 154) showed the direct influence on their predisposition to pray of their own and their parents' church attendance and denominational identity, and of their sex, with girls more likely to pray than boys. When sex was controlled, church attendance had a significant additional effect on their practice of prayer. Furthermore, churchgoing children from churchgoing homes said they pray more frequently than churchgoing children whose parents did not attend church, while Roman Catholic children were more likely to pray than children from other denominational backgrounds with similar levels for their own and their parents' church attendance. These findings support the view that children's attitudes to prayer reflect what they are taught, so that the results of any developmental analysis of prayer should be read in the context of the support that might be given to their attitudes by parents and other explicitly religious influences, and by the experiences that they offer or will support.

Using another vignette procedure, Brown (1966) found that beliefs about the appropriateness of prayer for specific contexts, and the actual forms that were preferred depend on the religious traditions within which they had grown up and had been trained to accept. Because children seemed not to be

189

deliberately taught about the efficacy of prayer, it emerged as an age-related developmental factor in which increasing age from twelve to seventeen was associated with a systematic decrease in the believed efficacy of prayer, which also depended on the problem being prayed for. As with the replication of Lilliston's (1981, 1982, 1991) work, there is considerable specificity in those responses. We have already noted a change in arguments about the stages through which beliefs about any expected success in prayer develops, from "my will be done" through a transitional phase to the Christian view that "God's will might be done with my active help" (Reik, 1955). Whether that reflects a change in insight or some implicit teaching about prayer that moves undifferentiated views about the automaticity of prayer or the existence of God to a more differentiated or abstract view about its efficacy, as a personal conviction, is still unclear. We should expect an interaction between some explicit teaching about how prayer 'works' and beliefs about its psycho-logic which might be understood in a "mature and sophisticated way that does not deprive it of its transcendental qualities, and does not force it to be a panacea for all problems or difficulties" (Long, Elkind, and Spilka, 1967).

The effects of prayer might be seen as acting reflexively on those who pray (and even on those who are known to have prayed). This avoids understanding prayer by contrasting its direct causal efficacy in the natural world against some indirect effects. An example of that approach is found in the Akron area telephone survey of Poloma and Pendleton (1991) which concluded that prayer "like its parent concept religiosity, is clearly multi-dimensional and contributes to a profile of well-being." They classed prayer as colloquial (asking for help, giving thanks for blessings), petitional (for material things), ritual (reading prayers), and meditative (thinking about God), and found that meditative prayer was significantly related to "existential well-being" and religious satisfaction. Petitional prayer was not involved there, although colloquial prayer predicted happiness, and ritual prayer was related to reports of being "sad, lonely, depressed, and tense."

In more general terms, Poloma and Pendleton concluded from their adult sample that "Religious satisfaction was positively related to age, frequencies of prayer, prayer experiences, and the use of meditative prayer." They stress that merely "saying prayers without corresponding experiences is not likely to alleviate unhappy feelings," which shows that the 'self-efficacy' of prayer must be deliberate and 'meditative.' Furthermore, although the frequency of prayer by itself may be a significant predictor of life satisfaction, "When other dimensions of religion were controlled, it may be clear that frequency of prayer is actually a misleading proxy for the religious contribution to general life satisfaction," since "what happens when one prays and what one actually does during prayer" is more important. This argues for accepting the religiousness of prayer and its different models and supports Gill's (in Eliade, 1987) definition of prayer as "human communication with divine and spiritual entities," and as "a necessity of the human condition" if the "material world is accounted for in an act of creation resulting in a cleavage or separation from the divine or spiritual world." Gill stressed the textual nature of prayer, since the forms of communication prescribed by any religious tradition must be distinguished from the performative nature of the acts through which those texts are given some intentionality in being used or expressed as petitions, invocation, praise and thanksgiving, confession, or benediction. Heiler (1932) similarly identified prayer as a pouring out of the heart before God, so that it is the intentions that give meaning to prayer as *prayers* and stops them from being like charms, spells, or other magical utterances, the mere repetition of which might guarantee their efficacy.

Animism

Tylor (1873) had earlier distinguished prayers in 'primitive' societies from those in 'advanced' cultures, and postulated an evolutionary sequence in terms of the ethical character of their message, suggesting that primitive prayer was primarily concerned with personal needs or wants, while prayer in the 'higher' religions was ethical and an instrument of morality. When confronted with rosaries, prayer wheels, and liturgical prayers, Tylor identified them in terms of a mechanical routine to regulate human affairs by a fixed ordinance, which made them formulaic, working like a 'charm' [sic]. Gill (1987, p. 92), however, identified a new pattern of anthropological analysis, following Reichard (1944), in terms of the symbolic and structural characteristics that distinguish invocation, petition, and benediction from "an address to the deity, the reason for the deity coming to the aid of the one praying, the symbols of the deity, and the description of the repetitive ritual acts" (Gill, p. 93). That set of questions has been disregarded by psychologists. The next phase, which I have deferred to, is in Austin's terms performative utterances (cf Ravenhill, 1976), with a textual, or as Gill notes, semantic emphasis that allows him to disregard the rigid or repetitive character, and the specific contexts of prayer, for what it is able to *do*.

Tylor's (1873) concept of animism was readily applied to prayer because it personified the world, attributing a "living soul to plants, inanimate objects, and natural phenomena, thereby making them, at least in principle, accessible to being influenced, even if only by thought." Since the meaning of what is said is expected to be subordinate to the results of a spell or incantation, what is said "matters less than whether what is said works or not" (Phillips, 1965, p. 114). Animism was later used by Piaget (1931) to explain the 'philosophies' he detected when he asked children to tell him about the characteristics of living things. As children grow up, the features they identify change, or develop towards what adults themselves accept. Recent studies suggest, however, that when more carefully directed questions are asked, very young children readily distinguish the intentionality among people from that of animals and objects (Wellman and Gelman, 1992).

The evolutionary process accepted in the developmental sequence of understanding prayer was confirmed by Long, Elkind, and Spilka (1967) who showed that children aged five to seven years emphasized 'things' in their prayers, while from seven to nine they emphasized words and from nine to twelve thoughts. Goldman's (1964) analysis of unanswered prayer paralleled those steps, so that children up to age nine stressed the bad choice of words, and wrong intentions. From ten to twelve they said that prayers failed because of selfishness or greed, and that after twelve or thirteen their answers were more decentered, influenced perhaps by an anthropocentric view of God who might see that the request could harm others. Godin and van Roey (1959) stressed that the causal logic of prayer was "spontaneous . . . after 6 or 7 if the event avoided were painful," and that the concept of a "protective providence" as opposed to a punitive providence was dominant up to about ten, perhaps because of the training they had been given. We have seen that Brown and Thouless (1964) showed that across the period from ages twelve to seventeen, a belief in the material efficacy of prayer decreased, independently of the denomination within which those adolescents had been taught to pray, although it was found that the approved objects of prayer did show a denominational effect. In another study, Brown (1966) replicated the finding that the appropriateness of prayer depends on denomination rather than age, and found that while a belief in the specific efficacy of prayer decreased with age, a nonspecific efficacy depended on the object of the request. This finding was obtained by asking if specific prayers, formulated as conditional requests or as a submission to God's will, would be an appropriate prayer for a football match, a military battle, or for a school examination. The results suggested a residual egocentricity over issues that are personally involving.

In a summary of these studies, Godin (1971) stressed a correspondence between the child's thought and what is expected or assumed about children on one hand, and their own thought on the other, as they process the demands that they believe have been imposed on them. As Godin put it, "educators, even though they have attained a certain spiritual and intellectual maturity for themselves, revert to forms that are much more childlike when they speak to children. They tend to use stories, comparisons, or ambiguous expressions which reinforce some of their (children's) own natural tendencies: the magical or automatic effectiveness of ritualistic signs; a tendency to use prayer to ensure that God will put Himself at their service when they need Him and transform the laws of the material world for their benefit" (p. 136).

He goes on to note that

> psychologically, this training in rites and prayers bears a double weight which can heavily burden its development: (a) Rites and prayers appear at first (to the child) as obligations to which social pressure demands conformity. One must obey as one obeys moral prescriptions. Performed as a consequence of moral pressure, much more than ways of personal expression, these devotional acts are drawn, later on, into the more general crisis of moralism. (b) But rites and prayers, before adolescence, also carry the weight of a magical mentality, marked by superstitious animism, an archaic trait spontaneously at work in all the religions of mankind. The magical attitude relies on ritualistic or imprecatory acts to bring about modifications in the world of phenomena. This is done either

by direct automatic causality (casting of lots, protective talismans), or by exerting pressure on superior spiritual powers whose intervention is thus set in motion, or at least solicited. The magic attitude 'convokes instead of invoking' ('summons instead of praying') (Austin, 1952, p. 227). The ritual or prayer becomes a means of pressure; in this way its worth as religious expression is reduced and even compromised.

The difficulty of studying rites and prayers stems from the psychological ambiguity of these acts. As seen from the outside, they reveal nothing more than conformity or nonconformity to traditions or institutional practices.

Sociologists and especially psychologists who confine themselves to the study of such behavior cannot know these acts as formally Christian; are they the result of a social conformity, of a magical attitude, of a religious expression that seeks oneness with the spirit of Christ? These questions remain without answers as long as the research (Argyle, 1958; Ross, 1950) does not go beyond simple acts in order to discover the motivations and meanings, conscious or at least partly conscious.

Godin emphasized that a magical (and perhaps extrinsic or utilitarian) attitude to religion is closely intertwined with an intrinsically religious perspective since it is only with reference to "an organized religion in a given culture that a devotional practice can be called religious or magical" (and perhaps intrinsically or extrinsically religious, cf Pargament, 1992). He adds that a cultic act in response to a natural phenomenon could be identified as 'religious' in a primitive culture, but not in a modern Christian culture within a scientific tradition (including psychology, I assume). The boundaries that can be drawn between religious and scientific perspectives are therefore not fixed or rigid, but depend, like so many other psychological phenomena, on the constraints, or characteristics of their context. Godin and Marthe (1960) nevertheless identified a 'magical mentality' in a belief in the direct causal efficacy of a sacramental sign as a material, rather than a spiritual process. Godin (1971, p. 133) also interpreted the explanations that children give of any sacramental effects at verbal, epistemological, and religious levels. At a verbal level the right words might be used, although their meaning is not understood. At the epistemological level, the meanings are linked logically, and at the religious level they are explained symbolically or sacramentally with reference to a 'spiritual grace.'

We have seen that the underlying development of attitudes in prayer that Goldman (1964) identified parallel these broad stages from a belief in their magical or automatic efficacy up to about age nine, with a material process mediating their efficacy up to age twelve. After that the efficacy of prayer depends on some spiritual or psychological effects on those who pray. (Granted that sequence, one wonders about the logic that formed the basis of Byrd's (1988) efforts to monitor experimentally the effects of prayer on patients in hospital.) Long, Elkind and Spilka's (1967) study had also looked at the changing conceptions of prayer through three major stages. The first, from five to seven, involves global and undifferentiated or inconsistent responses. Between seven and nine, the responses become differentiated, with prayer being understood in terms of concrete and self-oriented requests, while those who were aged from "ten to twelve identify prayer abstractly and consider it more a sharing conversation rather than a request," with its significance found in abstract goals rather than material objects. That study relied on answers to open-ended questions, like "What is a prayer? Can you pray for more than one thing? Where do prayers go?," and to incomplete sentences such as, "I usually pray when . . ."

The explanations that Long, Elkind, and Spilka (1967) gave for unanswered prayer parallel that development, with the inappropriate words being identified first. The emphasis then changes to the wrong things being asked for in the second stage, because they were selfish or greedy, for example. At the third stage God's point of view was adopted, even if in anthropomorphic terms (since God might recognize that granting the request would harm others) or when religious efficacy depends on the context or object of the prayer.

Oser and Gmunder (1991, p. 19) refer to prayer (and conversation) as processing "life experiences in a religious mode" by participating in "the life of religious communities" as regulative or meaning-making systems that represent a relation to an Ultimate (p. 19). They contrasted subjective interpretations against objective traditions, with construals specific to a tradition drawing on universal cognitive structures. When the success or failure of communication with an Ultimate goes beyond those acts, prayer becomes a consensual and an open process that facilitates the integration of new experiences and fosters freedom (against dependence), trust (against fear) and faith or hope in the sacred within a transparent eternity. The fundamental religious structures they identified are in the meaning of life and the future, and in coping with fate, death, and other contingencies.

The developmental stages they identified reproduce those identified by Piaget and Elkind (1962, 1963), although Oser and Gmunder's (1991) developmental theory of *Religious Judgement* also builds on Kohlberg and Fowler. Referring to results from a semi-clinical interview they explored reactions to moral dilemmas or vignettes that were also used by Scarlett and Perriello (1991). One of these concerned, "Paul, a young physician (who) has recently passed his board exams. He has asked his girlfriend to marry him. Before the wedding, he goes on a trip to England paid for by his parents as a reward for having successfully completed his education. Paul embarks on his journey. Shortly after take-off, the plane's captain announces one engine is malfunctioning and the other one is working unreliably. The plane is losing altitude. Emergency procedures are initiated immediately: oxygen masks and life preservers are being handed out. At first, the passengers are crying and yelling. Then, there is a deadly silence. The plane races towards the ground at a great speed. Paul's entire life flashes before his eyes. He knows it's all over. In this situation, he remembers God and begins to pray. He promises that, if he was somehow saved, he would invest his life in helping the people in the

Third World. He would also renounce the marriage to his girlfriend, should she refuse to accompany him. He promises to forgo a high income and social status. The plane crashes in a field—yet, through a miracle, Paul survives! Upon his return home, he is offered an excellent position at a private clinic. Because of his qualifications, he has been selected from among ninety applicants. However, Paul recalls the promise he made to God. Now, he does not know what to do" (pp. 102-103). The questions begin, "Should Paul keep his promise? Why or why not? Should anyone keep a promise to God? Why or why not? Do you believe that one has duties to God at all? Why or why not?"

Other vignettes that Scarlett and Perriello (1991) used involved requests to change objective, subjective, or spiritual realities, with a contingent bribe or promise, disclaimer, or apology. Confessions, as a request for forgiveness might be accompanied by a promise, thanksgiving, "expressions of thoughts, feelings, and/or questions about objective, subjective, or spiritual reality," loving or angry feelings directed at God, set prayers, or by the tags that end a prayer. Their analysis supports Oser and Gmunder's (1991) typology, as well as similar work by Brown and Thouless (1964) and more recently by Taaminen (1991).

From their material, Oser and Gmunder identify a step-wise development from a pre-religious attitude in which children "only know they are being influenced from the outside" (p. 69) to the assumption that "everything is guided, led, and steered by external forces," the recognition that the "Ultimate is active, humans are reactive" and then to "objectify consequences so that they are able to coordinate them with the power of an Ultimate Being outside of them" (p. 71). After a transitional phase "the perspective of absolute autonomy and deism" is recognized as a perspective on "religious autonomy and the plan of salvation" followed by perceiving the Ultimate "as being mediated intersubjectively" (p. 79). They accept that there is a further stage "revealed as love and absolute freedom" (p. 81) but are cautious about specifying what it may be like.

Nedoncelle (1964, pp. 87-100) was less cautious and defined the forms or stages of prayer among adults, in which we first withdraw into ourselves in the imitation of Christ and in recollection, turning away from external phenomena to pacify "our souls." At the next stage those initial steps are integrated in a movement towards transcendence through communication or conversation with the Absolute, as we expose our minds to the influence of God. We therefore move from spiritual recollection to an inner life, which is, he says, verified by the novelty of the message that the soul receives and in a revision of our moral standards. We must then move outward to find "the intrinsic meaning in the movement of things," and the "God who reveals himself at the heart of the world and of the world's history as an inexhaustible force of new life or of correction" (p. 100). Those stages go across occasions and time, "from without to within, then from within to the regions above" (p. 97). In that analysis, prayer itself becomes a metaphor of the religious life.

These typologies are indicative and should not prescribe what prayer ought to be like, or how it might work. In fact, their main value could be exegetical and hermeneutic, as well as pedagogical, rather than strictly psychological. Because earlier accounts of these recurrent patterns or structures were seldom data-driven, we still need principled guidance about where to look for a knowledge of prayer beyond the major contrasts in religious understanding between concrete or literal, and abstract or interpretive constructions of the myths, narratives, revelations, and practices that constitute religion, and of what they can generate. To do that we need facts and sensible evidence, rather than further theoretical interpretations that pile layers of meaning on top of the earlier ones. Vignette methods offer a constructive procedure by which to gather data to test the earlier interpretations.

The constraints imposed by other systems of practice or belief could be explored in a way that contrasts the conflict between agency and immediacy at human and transcendental levels, identifying what God might influence or control in principle, and then in the beliefs of individuals and in their readiness for closure on traditional formulations. Norbett Elias (1969) identified that as an old problem and said that out of "the interweaving of innumerable individual interests and intentions—be they compatible, or opposed and inimical—something eventually emerges that, as it turns out, has neither been planned nor intended by any single individual. And yet it has been brought about by the intentions and actions of many individuals. And this is actually the whole secret of social interweaving—of its compellingness, its regularity, its structure, its processual nature, and its development; this is the secret of sociogenesis and social dynamics."

This is not a place to advocate educational strategies, but the arguments that Godin (1971, 1988) develops stress that adults are not immune to child-like conclusions and conceptions of God, and that religious demands and expectations frequently accord with our desires. He therefore identified five developmental tasks for Christian education that involve awakening a historical consciousness, recognizing the symbolic nature of events that signify the actions of God, transforming a magical mentality into an attitude of faith, being released from moralism and its preoccupation with obligation rather than forgiveness, and then purifying parental images so that the foundation for a Christian maturity is not an image of the mother (following Klein or Erikson), the law of the father (after Freud), or social solidarity (Fromm) but a reconciliation of those paradoxical images through faith in the 'kerygmatic' core of religion. As Godin put it, "the criterion of a Christian maturity is the distance it maintains from the psychological traits of a purely human religiosity" (p. 149). There are some theoretical problems with this analysis since it presupposes a (correct) psychological analysis of how we 'should' react to, or understand and interpret religious doctrines and practices. Religious people might repudiate that simply because they do not accept it or because they have themselves been compelled or captured by the immediacy and strength of "what the Lord hath done." They may also be (over-) convinced by the validity of a simple faith that is for them, if not for others, compelling.

The attitudes that we attribute to, or detect in anyone else have a crucial effect on what they appear to be doing. In the case of prayer these attitudes form a barrier if prayer is to be understood in religious terms. While Godin stressed the importance of a "progressive reduction in moralism during child-hood and adolescence" (p. 136), every investigator must be wary of the extent to which their own attitudes may not have been purged of, or 'decen-tered' from the implicit prejudices they might carry about the rationality, or the origins of prayer, and the obligations it could entail. It is for this reason alone that some Christians may have difficulty in accepting others' prayers, or in allowing prayer to be studied psychologically. While it can be hard to emancipate oneself completely from deep-seated prejudices, social scientific studies of religion, or of prayer itself, should be as little confounded by reli-gious assumptions as is possible, leaving those within a religious tradition to identify for themselves how any conclusions from sound data might be applied. It is important for this reason alone to recognize that my psycho-logical account of prayer depends on Christian (and even Protestant) per-spectives, with a logic that accepts dualities between self and other, and between spontaneous ideas or wishes and what has been prescribed. Although that view might develop into what Piaget (1931) called 'artificialism,' he said that "Bovet (1925) has shown, in his penetrating studies, that there exists among children, at least among the very little ones, a spontaneous religion: the religion of parents. Parents are omniscient, all-powerful, eter-nal. From this to the idea that man made the universe is only a step. The conviction that his parents have organized the best possible world for him leads the child to conceive all nature as organized according to a plan and con-structed by man himself" (p. 543).

This stance was once believed to be reinforced by the 'natural' thought that must give way to a realism that recognizes the need for complementarity to coordinate the different explanations of particular states of affairs (Oser and Reich, 1990). It *is* possible to reconcile magic with religion, creationism with evolution, fundamentalism with whatever its complement might be, by forming a "religious climate" that distinguishes contingency from neces-sity and that recognizes different styles of discourse, in which the contrast between spoken and written languages is primary (Ong, 1982). This is cru-cial for prayer, especially when we articulate or think about our own prayers and compare them with any others we have heard or read, or as we distinguish between artificial (or formal) and 'true' prayers, for example, the first being in a written or textual form and the other as outpourings before God of praise, wishes, or demands.

The wide individual differences in our hopes and fears suggest that grouped data will only indicate where we might look for the psychological charac-teristics that prayer could involve for each individual. Yet generic meanings continue to be identified in the regressive 'games' that Carroll (1987) held are played out in praying the rosary, for example, and in the prescriptive 'diag-noses' that defer to the Enneagram (Rohr, 1991). If our prayers did develop our own preferred styles, they might be more satisfying or complete. Yet that level of analysis could disregard the extent to which prayers themselves involve situationally appropriate 'speech acts.' Evidence about the meaning of prayers themselves can be found in the personal documents left by its adepts, although even they could have been manufactured for pious or political advantage. While ritual prayers may have been composed to instruct, within the doctrines and conventions of their tradition, they are also performative when they declare, affirm, and promise, transforming the mental states and moods of worshipers through their words, actions, and meanings. That the context of prayer is crucial to their meaning is shown by the daily prayers of Islam that coordinate time, dress, place, and the actions that are needed to prepare for and express them.

Personality and other differences

Another defect of any general theory of prayer lies in the fact that not everyone prays, nor will everyone pray in the same circumstances. It also fails to recognize that individuals and their habits or tendencies to pray are poor predictors of any nonreligious characteristics. The situations in which God can be expected to act are themselves identified as 'religious,' and while some believe that all their actions depend on God's guidance, others distinguish the situations that involve God from those in which they should act independently. It is therefore hard to show whether prayer necessarily involves a need, or a wished-for contact with God, and when prayer defines God in personal terms, as a force beyond nature, or an abstract concept. Such views are sanctioned by tradition, supported by authority, and might be only loosely aligned with ideas about fate or other patterned characteristics of the real world.

Few defined differences in personality have been found between those in different religious traditions and even between those in sacramental churches and those from churches with a sterner theology (Clark, 1958, p. 209). Any differences in their attitudes to prayer could then simply reflect theological and liturgical factors or practices. Yet Clark expected less anxiety in Catholicism because of "confession, the sacraments, and such like," than in the Protestant traditions that emphasize an individual's acceptance of salvation, which William James (1902, p. 202) had used for a typology that was based on the susceptibility to gradual or sudden conversion. Sociologists have made other classifications using 'objective' identifiers (Wach, 1944) that could reflect reactions to theological, rather than to any social or psychological features, including the depth of involvement with a denomination that might be nominal, only on Sundays, or with a life-long vow about a 'religious' life. Fichter (1954) typed Catholics in the terms of an involvement with the Church that could be dormant, marginal, modal, or nuclear. Thouless (1954) suggested exaggerations of belief, as Father, Jesus, or Spirit-centered (and we might add Mother- or Mary-centered), or in terms of one's preferred practices. Detailed studies of groups or individuals defined in these ways might establish the relevance of those classifications, and their effects could reflect in the patterns of prayer, or in beliefs about it. A "primary religion" would then involve an inner experience, while a secondary orientation might cover religious habits and practices that impinge on or modify everyday behavior, with a tertiary stance accepting religious behavior as a matter of routine or convention, on the authority of another (cf Clark, 1958, pp. 23-24). It is probably not sensible to continue to 'type' people for their prayer preferences, especially on the basis of their Enneagram or Myers-Briggs profile, or to privilege intellect or feeling, and not the forms of prayer itself that can be used in particular contexts.

Batson's notion of "religion as quest" (Batson and Schoenrade, 1991) which has been widely used, was developed from Allport's classification of orientations, adding to means (extrinsic) and end (intrinsic) with a focus on quest (Batson and Ventis, 1982). Their goal was to determine "the ways in which each of these three dimensions might facilitate or inhibit psychological adjustment and positive social behavior" (Batson and Schoenrode, 1991) and they argue that those dimensions are "independent, orthogonal, and not interchangeable." If we had sensitive measures of the preferred forms or styles of prayer, rather than of the alignments with Christian beliefs or traditions, we might be able to specify the implications of those varied reactions for prayer. It is interesting, however, that Batson consistently uses 'quest' as an independent variable associated with moral reasoning, prejudice, and altruism, and not as a dependent variable that could have been produced by those or other religious processes. And it neglects the extent to which we may have different 'needs' on different occasions.

We are therefore forced to the conclusion that any psychological defense of (or attack on) prayer is likely to be more principled than empirical (or even existential), since the stance that anyone accepts depends on a set of prior assumptions about how prayer might work that reflects their own forms of maturity and religious attachment.

Towards maturity

A developmental psychology of prayer might hold that, "in the beginning" there were only prayers, and no reasons for them, since children without a purpose of their own imitate adults (or so we are told). If the injunction to pray without ceasing were a reasonable approximation to that 'story,' prayer is a 'natural' thing to do. And we know that some adults pray unselfconsciously. When prayer has not been established in that way, a questioning perspective produces doubts that overtake the innocence of childhood, especially if questions are answered uneasily, or with a logic that seems flawed. Appeals to a received authority will only be persuasive if one has been prepared to accept it.

Questions about the validity of prayer could stem from its apparent lack of efficacy, especially granted the expectation that one will be given whatever is prayed for. Existential questions about why *my* prayers fail lose their potency as our own perspectives decenter and the environment is found to have a 'mind' of its own, or because other people will make contrary requests or wishes that cannot all be granted. Prayer might then be given up, if it has been presented in a way that has made petitions primary. But we know too little about the teaching that lies behind prayer, and the expectations that are inculcated. Phillips (1965) and Brummer (1984) both consider the constraints on how we act or pray if an absolute dependence on God were accepted. This raises problems about the rationality of prayer that take us towards a metaphysic that might align with current views about the "virtual realities" that simulate some actual (or natural) reality. Within that context, personal prayers are self-referenced statements of hope and 'wishfulness' about the "best of all possible worlds."

Claims on prayer do not, however, explain why this perspective developed unless, as a 'natural' religious response it is a means of self-control that calms or consoles. But what discovery process might allow us to find that prayer can work in this way, as opposed to having been taught about that? We need not be pragmatic about that, since the logic of petitionary prayer is easily attacked on the ground that we need not tell or ask an omniscient God what *should* happen. We can only hope that it lies within Providence. Grice's (1975) maxims for conversation made a similar point about not telling others what they know already. His other maxims cover the quality, quantity, and manner of conversation. But prayer is not restricted to communicative speech acts that are 'merely' psychological, since it also expresses adoration or gratitude. And articulating an issue (in prayer) can help us 'see' the possible solutions.

From that perspective we might identify two major attitudes behind prayer. The first is egocentric, as we ask for our own will to be done and the other involves decentration through an attitude in which our own stance becomes detached, with an 'objective' reflection on our place in the world. The early psychological interpretations of prayer did not, however, recognize the role of imagery, self-instruction, self-control in preparing for any action. While those features can be found in meditation, prayer itself is assumed to make more demands than being receptive. Furthermore, prayer appears uniform to outsiders, just as 'religiousness' has been taken to be a single variable by its outsiders and not a nest of separate components (Dittes, 1969).

But a continuing problem, especially for the critics of prayer, concerns what counts as an answer to prayer beyond any customary attitudes and expectations, at least in public when we are told, usually indirectly or implicitly, what to expect. If the communicative context for prayer is horizontal rather than vertical (accepting a traditional view of God 'up there'), antiphonal prayers (in which one side of the choir responds to the other) could realize the dialogue that is inherent in prayer. There are, furthermore, innumerable occasions in ordinary life when we ask for information or assistance, leaving others to answer, or when we are provoked to offer a commentary on what others have said. This conversational mode is common in other religious contexts where one side, perhaps one of the clergy gives an exposition, speaks on behalf of God, gives advice or spiritual direction leaving the others to react.

Interpretations of prayer *can* therefore go beyond accepting it simply as a religious act on *our* part, by identifying its parallels in everyday social interaction, and in current psychotherapeutic practice, rather than continuing to stress its foolishness. Even if prayer were confined within language, giving or sharing information is only one of its functions. We can also *do* things with words, and the fact that as we speak we hear ourselves in the way we hear others allows Dennett (1991, p. 195) to note in a "thought experiment" that, as we hear our "own request, the stimulation provoked just the sound of other-helping utterance production that the request from another would have caused." This allows us to answer our own questions which could have been the beginning of self-awareness, and of the self-control that produces "better-informed action-guidance."

While broadly evolutionary perspectives assume development or change, so that only useful habits or responses are retained, recent evidence suggests that play allows us to develop new skills, and releases us from the restrictive bonds of routine (Csikzentmihalyi and Csikzentmihalyi, 1988). Aleatory or exploratory play and fantasy, whether by ourselves or with others, is also an accepted part of life. This *might* include religious practices in fasting or feasting, repeating prayers, or meditating with a teacher. Those issues might be controversial, but when Dennett (1991, p. 201) lists some basic 'ideas,' he included wheel, clothes, alphabet, calendar, the Odyssey, God, perspective drawing, impressionism, and narrative prayer. That list could be continued, and its contents have become 'second-nature' to us. Dawkins (1976, p. 206) similarly identified the units of cultural transmission or imitation by the French *'memes,'* which derives from a Greek root that relates to memory, since they run in parallel with the more familiar concept of 'genes.'

Contemporary social psychologists are familiar with an elaborated form of these ideas in Durkheim's concept of the "social representations" (Farr and Moscovici, 1984) that shape our thoughts, to express and capture the ideas that support social and scientific explanations. As 'good ideas,' they propagate by spreading from one person to another. Since we accept that ideas can be used, we should recognize that social practices and institutions have a similar value. Prayers and the religious institutions that support them are therefore likely to be retained for their social value, which is readily transmitted to children.

A failure in the early theoretical psychologies of religion was the neglect of its interpersonal or social and cultural dimensions, in a search for the sources of prayer within the religiousness of *individuals*. Father images and private rituals of purification or amelioration seemed to carry a religious significance that Freud aligned with individuals' 'illusions' and obsessive-compulsive disorders. But no one invents all their religious ideas. When the idiosyncratic meanings of received concepts and practices are accessed in single case studies, they have a social focus, as was shown in Rokeach's (1964) study of the *Three Christs of Ypsilanti*, each of whom believed that he was Christ. When these patients were placed in the same psychiatric ward each had to accommodate to the claims of the others. In a similar way private beliefs have a social significance as part of a tradition and so the 'memes' of prayer are accepted or "deemed to be true" (Dennett, 1991 p. 205), and made coherent through the traditions that offer a habitat for them. This process is similar to other kinds of indoctrination that form an identity of the self as Christian or Jew, American or Canadian (cf Elkind, 1964).

While the content of Chinese or French 'minds' are expected to be different, we assume that their 'nature' will be the same. So a religious mind is only likely to differ from a nonreligious mind in its content, unlike the search for differences between normal and schizophrenic brains. Perhaps plasticity or openness to change mimics the differences between those who are unwilling to make an ideological commitment and those finding it easy to stabilize and close on the position in which they have been trained (Deconchy, 1991).

That process could be like a computer program that runs on a 'virtual' machine. The program represents 'reality' by sets of rules that will change the computer as a machine into a word-processor, a calculator, or a robot. Habits or dispositions might then react like a program that can run on different machines. Computer scientists now refer to the "virtual presence" of information in a computer, a library, or in the imagination, that is waiting to be accessed and can supplement a text, in a way that could be similar to the way we 'build' a picture of the characters in a novel, or of religious figures and practices. Understanding how such material is processed in a computer and the 'constructions' they allow depends more on a knowledge of the program than of the computer's hardware.

Similarly, understanding how religious material is processed is not helped by having a model of the brain, although early training and socialization are made possible by the brain's plasticity. This means that the brain's functionally important features are likely to be invisible to neuroanatomical scrutiny, "in spite of the extreme salience of the effects" (Dennett, 1991, p. 219). Despite that, Jaynes's (1973) theory about the *"origins of consciousness in the breakdown of the bi-cameral mind"* suggests that the voice of God was 'heard' in the right hemisphere (in right handed people) generating messages that the left hemisphere of the brain did not recognize as its own (p. 106f). Jaynes supports that theory with reference to classical Greek writing about the gods. The idea that God might involve one part of the brain unwittingly 'talking to' another, as a puppeteer controls the puppet, is one explanation of our 'self-control.' We can do many things unwittingly, subsequently generating accounts of what we have done in ways that make sense within our own context. Taking control of oneself is therefore an essential part of Beck's (1990) "cognitive behavior therapy," and perhaps of a mature attitude to prayer. We also off-load memories to 'buffers' in the environment when we write them down. And we can use the material that has been prepared in this way by others to guide hunches about what *we* might be thinking or feeling.

Religion can be understood in a similar way as a 'program' that helps to reduce our chaos (or complexity) by its doctrinal explanations, so that the practices it makes available allow control, and help to direct the search for information about the world and our role in it. Religious explanations may, however, be over-used and need to be kept in perspective. That their psychological meanings are 'unconscious' can be confusing if it suggests that we do not know what we are thinking, although that could also be seen as a kind of Turing Test in which our task is to decide the validity of apparent answers to prayer. The classical form of that (unsolved) Test involves finding a rule or procedure by which to decide whether typed messages we receive have been sent from a person, or from a computer in another room. To press that analogy, some religious people accept that God answers prayer, while others reach different conclusions.

To consider computer programming and the 'languages' they use (or apply) as a model of prayer stresses that natural languages are an important "source program" to express and help us understand what we know. Those who are 'religious' find that their religious language and its concepts have a powerful role in eliciting emotional reactions, because they have been shaped by it and by the (virtual) realities that are conveyed by texts, doctrines, and the rituals that can be used in various ways. That these processes are not directly accessible to introspection means that the accounts of how we have arrived at what we believe are necessarily principled or theoretical. Prayer has a place there as part of a repertoire for our thinking, problem solving, and reflection on what could have happened.

Differences between thoughts and beliefs contrast transient or episodic against dispositional states. We may believe in prayer but pray only occasionally, when a need, or the thought of prayer strikes. How important that is depends on other beliefs or habits about how to handle crises and day-to-day affairs. Whether we need separate theories to account for our liturgical prayers and for prayers about improving our own prayer adds another layer to this system and to the logic of prayer itself. While we may accept that we have thoughts about thoughts, and can be troubled by those that seem intrusive or unacceptable, we do not expect our thoughts or fears and wishes to have direct effects on the world. Nor should we expect our own prayers, or those used in religious performances to have such effects. Yet cynics are likely to react to the content of a prayer (in the "Our Father" for example), interpreting the words, rather than trying to understand their broader context and its 'spiritual' qualities, the meanings of which must be learned. This could be like thinking of God and religion as a playwright who gives a play to the players and the audience, allowing them to realize it as they will.

But how do we 'see' where God is, unless God is 'everywhere'? Why can't everyone 'see' God? To see God is not like seeing an object or recognizing a person, since the image must be constructed. We learn to do that rhetorically, through statements like "I know my Redeemer . . . .," by an extended argument, or in more realistic terms with reference to 'tokens' as "temporary episodic representations" (Treisman, 1988) created through our semantic memory and which we are trained to use 'correctly.' In that sense, 'God' becomes an identifier that might be a guessed or filled-in construct, rather than a picture, or perhaps a pattern of speech to which information can be added. That this process is not available to introspection aligns it with the 'demons' in our head that would destroy the coherence of our experiences. To pursue those metaphors, just as some people 'neglect' one side of their body for sound neurological reasons, others neglect God or their bank balance when those ideas or phenomena are of little use for them.

Other easily identified interpretations of the properties and effects of God need to be explored for their hidden interpretations, and the basic metaphors or terms on which the shared understanding of what religious texts, mythologies, and institutions will support. And that prayer might be able to access. The 'soul' might then be rehabilitated as an abstraction or construction of the self that, like gravity or mass, has agreed properties and is not a metaphysical entity. If 'God' were primarily a moral force, it would be a social concept, and more like embarrassment than gravity, which involves literal or first order judgments about a 'real' feature of the world. Religious judgments, on the other hand, are at a second order and discriminate features that might correspond to Hunt and King's (1971) distinctions between literal, antiliteral, and metaphorical constructions of the meaning of religious beliefs. That many concepts cannot be defined with reference to the real world, and can only be talked about or discussed (cf Bowker, 1987), does not mean that we live in a dream world, or that we are victims of some mass delusion. There may be no evolutionary or social advantage in believing in God or having access to a large vocabulary of color names. But these features do make the world more interesting. Facts about God or about Locke's secondary qualities are, however, inescapably linked to the *judgments* of a reference class of observers who are usually theologians or evangelists, when religious matters are at issue. Although their judgments might only be aesthetically satisfying, they can still be powerful, as when one 'believes' and begins to 'see' others in a different 'light.' We find there an essential subjectivity that is both consensual and practical.

But what properties are assigned to God? In Christianity it still means "God as Father," creator, and so on, for many people, despite the arguments against chauvinism or paternalism, with the Trinity apparently disregarded by those who have looked at the popular representations of God. Yet these questions can be answered at two levels: one is public and consensual, the other idiosyncratic and harder to access. Psychodynamic theories that defer to subjectivity and an "inner world" of personal meanings offer an accepted explanation, although it is ironic that it defers to generic processes involving character-types that in their turn derive from childhood experiences or are products of other defense mechanisms.

Attachment and loss

Against that view we have Winnicott's (1971) theory of transitional objects that acknowledges the importance of solace, and the internal 'objects' that help to satisfy it. This theory specifies that 'the breast,' pieces of blanket, and familiar toys allow young children to move safely into their environment with a cared-for independence that allows symbolic representations. The capacity to relate to solacing objects, with a correlated sense of being 'at-one' with things, ideas, and objects that are external (or felt to be external) to the self is also inextricably bound up with the development of language (Horton and Sharpe, 1986). The language of prayer therefore involves a 'transitional' relatedness, especially for those raised in a religious context, since it "facilitates engagement with novel, conflictual, even frightening circumstances and mediates or catalyzes psychological growth" (ibid.). When this "internalization is successful, each subsequent life experience with a transitional 'whole object' (which could include well-rehearsed prayers) is, in part, a solace déjà-vu" (ibid.). That the mother is the first transitional object adds strength to this argument, granted the finding that God's characteristics are aligned more closely with mothering than with the father, who is a prototypically 'punishing' figure (Vergote and Tamayo, 1980).

The emphasis given to such attachments extends to people or mentors, activities and contexts. It also allows idiosyncratic words or phrases, ideas, and (doctrinal) concepts to have an arousal value. Winnicott also noted that "an infant's babbling or the way an older child goes over a repertory of songs and tunes while preparing for sleep come within the intermediate areas as transitional phenomena." He might have added prayers to that list, since children are taught night prayers, as in the poem by A.A. Milne:

> "Little boy kneels at the foot of his bed
> Drops on his little hands little gold head
> Hush! Hush! Whisper who dares
> Christopher Robin is saying his prayers
>
> God bless Mummy, I know that's right
> Wasn't it fun in the bath tonight
> The cold so cold and the hot so hot
> Oh God bless Daddy, I quite forgot.
>
> Thank you God for a lovely day
> And what was the other I had to say?
> I've said bless Nanny, So what can it be?
> Oh now I remember it, God bless me."

On the other hand, Isaac Watts (1765) produced a book of *Prayers composed for the use and imitation of children suited to their different ages and their various occasions* in which "The Infant's Evening Prayer" reads, "O Lord God, who knowest all things, Thou seest me by night as well as by Day. I pray thee for Christ's sake, forgive me whatever I have done amiss this day, and keep me safe all this night while I am asleep. I desire to lie down under Thy care, and to abide for ever under Thy blessing, for Thou art a God of all power and everlasting mercy. Amen." In a set of instructions on the "Duty of Prayer," in the form of a catechism, Watts' answer to "What is it to pray to God?" is "To ask the great and merciful God to bestow on me the good things which I want" and he holds that "the chief parts of prayer" are "these eight, (*viz*) Invocation, Adoration, Confession, Petition, Pleading, Self-resignation, Thanksgiving, and Blessing."

Horton and Sharpe (1986) note that "co-actional vocalization" creates "a positive experience of relatedness" and is a precursor to work songs, choral singing, hymn singing, and prayer in a recitative form. Comfort and security are important benefits of such shared and familiar activities. The prayers (and poems) we learn and repeat when we are young also offer solace when we have grown up. New translations of the Bible and of liturgies discard that linguistic continuity, although those translations have been more often resisted on stylistic or liturgical, than on psychological grounds (cf Crystal, 1987). Robinson's (1973) critique of them began by quoting Peter Winch who said that "what a man says or does may make a difference not merely to the performance of the activity he is at present engaged on, but to his life and to the lives of other people." Sharing a linguistic style, or a language itself, contributes to our sense of identity, because of the sub-culture within which we can live with it. This might have been recognized by the Psalmist who wrote, "Thy testimonies have I claimed as an heritage for ever: for they are the rejoicing of my heart" (Psalm 119:111). Robinson's specific complaint about the language of the New English Bible lies in its 'neutrality' and in the problems that confront those who read it in public, since the work of making meaning has to be done by the reader when "it is not in the language of the passage" which "becomes flatly noncommittal" (p. 29).

We should distinguish the reasons for prayer from its 'causes' and from social (or traditional) sanctions and models, and the subjectivity of our reactions to what is offered by any tradition. Stressing a spontaneous impulse to pray makes no attempt to explain what might sustain its practice. Skinner's partial reinforcement effect identifies a specific mechanism that could do that, and any prayer will 'work' sometimes, even if only by coincidence (Koestler, 1972). People also stop praying for many reasons, including a sense of sin, discouragement, or skepticism. That St. John of the Cross urged us to keep praying steadfastly through the dark night of the soul is itself a psychological commentary, if not in conventionally psychological terms. But why should we not account for prayer in religious *and* psychological terms! Believing that one has found one's own way to a concept of God neglects socialization and the logic of any arguments that will drive personal insights.

Each culture has a common core for the psychological world that can break up around the edges because of idiosyncratic experiences that are not readily expressed if we do not want to offend others, or if we find it easier to hold to old-fashioned beliefs that support claims on a romantic nostalgia about what the world could have been like. We also learn to keep quiet in church and follow its other rules. So what we say about God tends to be formal and schematic. 'Seeing' God in that sense could be like Jackson's (1982) thought experiment in which a black and white TV screen is *said* to show all the colors, until the observer emerges into the 'real world' and finds that its 'colors' had not been seen, but were epiphenomenal.

Yet Pratt (1916, p. 319) assumed that said prayers are not 'real' prayers, which would be wordless. If that perspective derived from his interpretation of 'successful' petitions in terms of imitation or suggestion, it shows the *ad hoc* arbitrariness of his and others' psychological analyses, few of which can be independently tested. The data we need for any test of theories about prayer are hard to collect, largely because of the privacy attached to the prayer-lives of most people, their suspicion of those who want them to talk about it, and the dependence of prayer on belief. Whether subjective interpretations give enough support, for theories about what prayer depends on, and whether that is found in emotion and tradition as Pratt suggests (on page 330), prayers entail many attitudes beyond (and including) what is mystical or meditative as we reflect on, or attempt to find our individuality, rather than looking for some reflex effects in our mind or character (p. 334). It is sobering that Pratt's interpretations still stand, although our awareness of the perennial problems surrounding prayer has been sharpened, and some of the newer general theories do help to make sense of some of its aspects.

We should recognize the role of the 'modeling' that is set by the teaching of specific traditions that shape the attitudes and character of those who pray, which then distinguishes them from those who pray within other traditions and from those who do not pray. Related to that are the continuing issues of a pleading egocentricity, and the salience and support given to religious practice in the lives of those who *pray*, in relation to their other religious and secular commitments. Prayer can itself be an anchor on life, despite the problems that were mentioned by Wittgenstein when he identified prayer as a language game, in which the medium itself might be the message (to misuse McLuhan). Whatever conclusions we reach in developing a theory of prayer, we must at some stage specify the measurable variables that it involves and find how its target features impact on social life, if only through the political or polemical claims on it.

Chapter Twelve

Further Explanations

If we assume that prayer is a form of fantasy wherever it is directed, we must remember that at some time we all talk to or about those who are not present and prepare for contact with them by imagining how we, or they will act. While the gods might never be found, their reality is carried by myths, images, and icons (cf Brown and Moore, 1990). So the models that explain prayer in terms of illusion or delusion are impoverished and partisan. That prayer can be a way to share our private life 'safely' does not invalidate it, and it may be described as a "moment of the soul," a contractual relationship with God (since "Whatever is asked in my name will be given to you"), or as the mystery of Presence. McNamara (1981) asserts that we learn to ready ourselves for prayer as we "dispose ourselves for this conversational encounter with the loving Father," reflect on "a passage of the Bible, or an image of Christ or an event in his life, and are led by his meditation into prayer, that is: the loving awareness of God" (p. 421). He goes on to identify contemplative prayer as that in which God becomes active and we are passive. There seems little doubt that prayer can have an effect. The problem is how to account for it. This is possible if we align prayer with other practices that can help us change our mind (sic), including exercise and dieting, martial arts, meditation, and taking counsel. Prayer itself can also be used politically in vigils, and as threats to alleviate injustice or facilitate healing, perhaps with an implied criticism of the care that has already been offered.

Persuasion and healing

Frank and Frank (1991, p. 85) are confident that "successful instances of both psychotherapy and spiritual healing reduce psychologically caused suffering, increase self-esteem, and foster a sense of mastery in persons who seek their ministrations." They recognize the power of "the leader and group" to whom members surrender "control of their decisions and behavior," which they compare with a conversion process. But it is also possible to stand firm and preserve one's position unless, as they are argue, the targets of revivalists and psychotherapists are "in a similar state of demoralization," since "confession, guilt, or frustration springing from personal characteristics or social conditions seems to heighten the attractiveness and enhance the effectiveness of revivalistic religions and cults" (ibid.). Their interpretation of how that works rests on a "susceptibility to emotionally charged methods of influence that arouse hope by offering detailed guides to behavior based on an inclusive, infallible assumptive world" (ibid.) which is assisted by the revivalists' "belief in the existence of beneficent transcendental forces that can be directly experienced through appropriate rituals."

They go on to assert that to recognize supernatural forces gives a more powerful sense of mastery than submission to a secular leader and that shared beliefs and rituals forge bonds among the members of a group. Their analysis of the religiomagical rituals in "non-industrialized societies" (p. 87f) contrasts natural against supernatural causes with reference to the ambiguous roles of a shaman. They do, however, use Lourdes as a Western example (p. 103f) noting that its failures do not shake the "implicit validation of the assumptive system on which the tradition there rests," in which the pilgrimage itself is a crucial accompaniment to the daily procession of the host which results in a "tremendous outpouring of emotion and faith" (p. 105). Although "the great majority of the sick do not experience a cure, most of the pilgrims seem to benefit psychologically from the experience" with the pilgrimage conferring its benefit in a spiritually uplifting "atmosphere" (ibid.). The cures there are, however, seldom spontaneous, being linked to the "sufferers' emotional state" (p. 106).

Frank and Frank (1991) cite two systematic studies of religious healing. "One, based on interviews with almost 200 persons (half members of charismatic groups and half members of groups primarily using meditation), showed that the attenders at healing ceremonies reported significantly higher levels of physical and general well-being when compared with a matched group of patients in primary medical care (Glik, 1986). . . . The other study described seventy-one healings reported by forty-three members of charismatic fundamentalist sects (Pattison, Lapins, and Doerr, 1973). The researchers found that sixty-two of the recoveries occurred in the course of a healing ceremony, about half of them suddenly. Fifty involved moderately severe or life-threatening illness. Although the great majority of subjects reported no residual symptoms, the sense of being healed was related to participation in the healing ceremony, not to a perceived change in symptomatology" (p. 108).

Frank and Frank argue that belief in or acceptance of an ideology is itself crucial for healing and that the actual theory or techniques used are irrelevant, being replaced by the expectant trust that was demonstrated in a study by Rehder (1955, reported by the Franks on their page 111), or by a charismatic 'gift.' "Anxiety and despair can be lethal; confidence and hope, life-giving" (p. 112). Furthermore, the forms of healing that people respond to are made consistent by the conceptual schemes of their assumptive world, which makes sense of their inchoate feelings and heightens their sense of mastery that may be linked with their recognition of supernatural healing forces, and the reassurance offered by them.

The subjectivity of prayer

Perspectives on prayer that stress its subjectivity or immediate persuasiveness stand in contrast to the public displays of prayer that were criticized in the New Testament. They may entreat or placate 'the furies,' involve worship or become separated from life itself. When these processes are described, the accounts must be taken on trust, being beyond objective verification. If their justification is held to be obligatory, guidance is needed to understand those consensual practices and the sense of the holy that they generate.

Most of the religious evidence about how prayer operates depends on claims that are hard to test in a way that is free of residual beliefs or prejudices about what should be said when prayers are not external they are sometimes said to "pray in us." This translation disregards counter-claims about how it is possible to pray and the grounds or the faith on which that rests. This might have been received or acquired inadvertently, like a flash of insight or a moment when an overwhelming and creative force strikes, supporting a sense of spiritual reality. Classical attacks on the validity of that were made by Feuerbach, on the projective qualities of religion, by Marx for the unreal consolation it offers, Freud for its illusory character, Nietzsche for its nihilism, leaving Rudolf Otto and Friedrich Heiler to define a transcendent sense of the holy that prayer or religion carries against any deficiency model. Modernism itself is thought to have made prayer increasingly unnecessary, replacing it with practices that might directly alter the mind or consciousness, with little meaning beyond the practice itself. Yet gentle (social) rituals are an important part of life that may have little instrumental purpose beyond the expressive values they carry, and their suggestion of 'something more' within any cultural practice and the myths supporting it. They include stories about the welfare of the dead and the need to heal that breach, cosmic journeys, and residual practices of alchemy or geomancy that help to structure the world. These processes have deep roots in contemporary streams of understanding, contrasting our materialism against *dharma* or the *Tao* as a natural, universal wisdom which derives a power from meditation to penetrate appearances through mindfulness itself.

But what God can influence or control depends on one's beliefs and readiness for closure, unless that concept is accepted as a metaphor, and as a "manner of speaking." Even if God *is* dead the idea can be taken on balance as part of a "rich tapestry of life," supported by the stories that continue to be told. For example, a man in a Pentecostal church in New Zealand was on a pension, but he would not tithe. One Sunday he agreed to tithe, having been spoken to about Malachi. In the next week he won a car, which validated the prophecy that he would be rewarded a hundred-fold. Accounts of miraculous healing from that Pentecostal group include movement recovered in a shoulder 'frozen' after a fall, the morning after the woman had asked to be prayed for. Stories like these multiply and are confidently used as evidence for specific answers to prayer, with the failures forgotten. They reveal a context in which experiences of prayer are understood through allegorical or interpretive explanations of events in retrospect.

Evidence

The major task of this book has been to show what the social sciences have said about prayer as the realization of an attitude to the most elementary form of religious life (to mangle again one of Emile Durkheim's concerns). Karl Girgensohn stressed that to know how much religion a person has, one must know how and what is prayed about, rather than how often they pray. We have seen, however, that almost by definition an outsider can not access that information, so we must be content with fleeting and distorted insights into the genuinely private religion that is concealed from strangers and the profane. Because answers to survey questions, as the major source of data about prayer, may be acquiescent to social pressures about what is 'proper,' perhaps the only true insight into prayer is gained from its classical practitioners. So William James (1902), in relying on the evidence in spiritual writing, said, "In the natural sciences and industrial arts it never occurs to anyone to try to refute opinions by showing their author's neurotic constitution. Opinions here are invariably tested by logic and by experiment. It should not be otherwise with religious opinions. Their value can only be ascertained by spiritual judgments directly passed upon them, as judgments based on our own immediate feeling primarily; and secondarily on what we ascertain of their experiential relations to our moral needs and to the rest of what we hold as true" (1985, p. 23).

Psychological (or scientific) criteria are inevitably intertwined with judgments about their usefulness in arguing for or against particular interpretations. William James rejected the relevance of Saint Teresa's nervous system (and her mental state) to her theology, which he judged in terms of its immediate luminousness, philosophical reasonableness, and moral helpfulness, as the "only available criteria" (ibid.), despite assumptions about its (psychological) origins through "intuition, pontifical authority, supernatural revelation, a 'higher spirit,' or 'automatic utterances'" (a medical preoccupation at that time) (p. 24). He stressed that 'medical materialists' turned "the tables on their predecessors by using the criteria of origins in a destructive instead of an accreditive way" (ibid.).

The problems with prayer no longer center on the credibility of whatever is being claimed, since it is assumed that that can be tested against the context or a consensus. And we are more suspicious about private devotions in public than in the solitude of one's room or in nature's open spaces. 'Experts,' saints, and mystics who spoke of the prayer life to their disciples, when teaching them how or what they ought to pray for, seldom held *their* intimate conversations with God in public. Recorded prayers, in the *Oxford Book of Prayers* and in confessional and mystical writing are nevertheless part of our religious inheritance. But they exclude the spontaneous cries that convey deeply felt needs and yearning, so we must be content with the *traces* of those events. Yet we expect that when anyone is confronted with an ultimate need there *are* loud cries to God, so that involuntary utterances of joy or distress imprint themselves on those who happen to have been present at the time.

Despite their literary strategies and conceits, written prayers give pastoral guidance (as in the Lord's Prayer), and they are used liturgically. So it is not clear if the prototypic prayer is found in a free and spontaneous 'cry,' in the deliberate words of a liturgy, or in the hymns that can have an evocative power for those who sing them. Mysticism and spiritual direction occupy a special place in prayer and lead back to an inner life and its self-examination. Perhaps it is for this reason that only in the last thirty years or so has an empirically based psychology of religion been developed by Catholics. Before that, Catholic psychology was principled or theoretical, and it was to be found in spiritual direction rather than by detached observations of its practice. Heiler therefore described St Teresa as "the woman psychologist among the saints" (p. xxvi) and in that sense religious psychology belongs with theology and the philosophies of religion to advance the practical and moral points of view that could modify, interpret, and control religious experiences. There is, however, continuing doubt about whether the accounts of such experiences offer unequivocal data for psychohistory, as in Erikson's (1958) study of *Young Man Luther*.

The commentaries on Augustine's Confessions in Capps and Dittes (1990), show how easy it is to write oneself over another's confessional statements. In a similar way, testimonies to prayer, and spoken prayers, as well as rituals, gestures (not only with the hands), and the language in which prayer is conveyed in public are unlikely to parallel private prayer, although some psychological effects can be expected in both contexts. We have seen that the dominant nineteenth-century theory of those causes, advanced by Schopenhauer and Feuerbach, and echoed by Freud, that faith in God arose primarily as the projection of a wish or fantasy, can be found in the classical view that fear itself created the gods. Marx's alternative was that the gods were created by those in power, to bluff and subdue the rest. These theories reject the concept of an ideal order beyond the flux of immediate experience that may be an essential feature of adult thinking, and offering an explanation in terms of compensation for our (own) feelings of weakness or dependence. Since none of those separate interpretations is easily tested, the plausibility of religion rests more strongly on the acceptance (or rejection) of religious doctrines that may be supported by religious experience, than by reducing its appeal to a brain dysfunction, misattribution, or even a social influence. Sceptics or materialists who are not impressed by the imaginative constructions that Heiler (1932, p. 83) set between trust and distrust, dependence and independence discard religiousness outright. There are also dangers in assuming that modern religion has developed directly from a primitive form, whether it is found in magic, the Mass (if you are a Protestant) or Pentecostalism (if you reject enthusiastic religions), since the evidence suggests that most of us have taken over (or rejected) the faith in God of the religious community or tradition in which we grew up (Hunsberger and Brown, 1984).

Most Westerners have some knowledge of prayer and will reject aspects of it as too concrete (or abstract), directed at the wrong targets, uncommitted (or too personal), not spontaneous, too sacrificial or mindless, depending on how religion is understood and the range of emotions it involves, from reverence or admiration to humility or frustration. Prayer has also been criticized by philosophers and moralists as searching for 'happiness' rather than 'divine favor' or for material rather than spiritual benefits. But as Socrates put it, we should pray for whatever *is* good, since the gods know what is good. While the Stoics surrendered to the hands of Fate, Rousseau prayed for "what Thou wilt." Voltaire could only address the God he had made. Others pray in solemn contemplation, adoration and praise, and never for what they might achieve for themselves.

Prayers are abandoned by those who believe in the immutability of natural law, although traditional reasons for retaining prayer include respect for its traditions, and believing that God exists or that God's work is incomplete without *our* recognition or support of it. It is those beliefs and attempts to compromise the demands of rational thought and presuppositions about the objectivity of prayer that make it psychologically interesting, as we develop an attitude to its validity and its breadth. Heiler (1932, p. 353) therefore noted that prayer ranged from the calm collectedness of a devout individual, to the ceremonial liturgy of a great congregation, from the creativity of a religious genius to its imitation by common people, from spontaneous expressions to the recitation of incomprehensible formulae, a blissful ecstasy or a painful fulfillment of the law, an involuntary or deliberate concentration on some religious object, a flight of the spirit or a deep cry of distress, thanksgiving or supplication, from a petition for bread to a yearning for God, from a selfish wish to unselfish compassion, a vengeful curse or an intercession for enemies and persecutors. Such contrasts go on, within the essential distinction between profoundly compelling experiences and imitations or rejection of them. A real experience and its shadow is not, however, illuminated without reference to some sense of innocence, and it is unlikely that that range of prayers could be reduced to a single psychological explanation.

The force of evidence

When Davis (1989) identified challenges to claims on valid religious experiences through an underlying theism, she examined them scientifically rather than theologically, appealing to psychological (or psychiatric) factors and drawing primarily on evidence that distinguishes normal from abnormal states. She asserts that "an argument from religious experience cannot be built on experiences which have therapeutic value but no evidential force; and to say that all experiences are ultimately caused by God only preserves the evidential force of religious experiences (even) if they play a very minor role in a cumulative case . . . Naturalistic accounts of religious experience must therefore be taken very seriously" (p. 194). Traditional appeals to the psychological evidence that might explain religious (and other experiences) have relied on hyper-suggestibility, compensating for social deprivation, sexual frustration, projective identification, maladjustment, or frank mental illness and abnormal neural or physiological states. Yet religious people are identified prescriptively in terms of strongly orthodox beliefs, church-going (especially when it is socially supported), and their conformity to cultural norms about religiousness.

But like 'being religious,' to 'have' a religious experience or find an answer to prayer does not define a single class of persons or psychological states, since those 'experiences' might have been prescribed or offered as rhetorical claims. At the baldest level, as Derek Wright (1976, p. 260) put it, "in cultures where angels, familiars or other non-material objects are expected to be seen by many people (and prayers answered), and this expectation has been fostered in each individual from birth onwards, they are indeed legitimate although they are not necessarily accepted at their face-value." In this sense those experiences and their targets may be like social representations (following Durkheim or Moscovici), collective idea-patterns (Tyrrell, 1953) or socially prescribed *and* sanctioned reactions. They then become part of the social history of the religious tradition that supports them. As Maurice Wiles (1976, p. 38) put it, "Talk of God's activity (in prayer, for example) is . . . to be understood as a way of speaking about those events within the natural order or within human history in which God's purpose finds clear expression or special opportunity." These claims are therefore instances, "where the purpose of God has been apprehended, expressed or put into effect in a particularly profound way" (ibid.), involving and exemplifying a sense of God that is independent of the way they might be interpreted or deconstructed by social scientists (cf Bowker, 1973). Proudfoot (1985, p. 196f) contrasted this as a "descriptive reduction," in failing to identify the emotion, practice, or experience in a subject's account against an "explanatory reduction" which involves an interpretation that might not meet the subjects' approval.

Any gratuitous or *social* interpretation of God's action must nevertheless rely on the cultural knowledge and assumptions we are acquainted *and* aligned with, and that lie behind concepts like 'sacred,' 'harmony,' and 'numinous.' It is therefore the form of the account or interpretation of an experience of prayer that gives it a religious quality by referring to a divine power, union with the "ground of being," or through the intuition or insight it gives into natural or transcendent order. None of those interpretations need touch whether God's existence is, or is not, to be accepted as 'true.'

While divine intervention through the natural order is not logically necessary, social sanctions are needed to support or justify appeals to God's existence, especially if they reflect "psychological and physiological states (or needs), background beliefs, our model of the divine or elements of our (attitudinal) 'set'" or make reference to religiously "significant settings, actions, and people, great natural beauty, and moments of crisis" (Davis,

1989, p. 227). Culturally embedded models of the divine color these reactions and explanations since, as Davis puts it, "divine activity (in that sense) does not *violate* the natural order, but rather works with it and through it" (ibid., p. 227). Concrete and "word-perfect, miraculous revelations of the divine" (ibid.) must be ruled out on those grounds, even when they are sanctioned by a particular group, since apprehensions of God (or anything else) will be "partial and must be understood within the context of the subject's cultural background. Metaphorical descriptions may still be reality-depicting" (ibid.), and although incomplete, they may point to an awareness of "the 'other' of numinous experiences and the unitive 'ground of being' of mystical experiences." Together with other types of experience and belief they support the cumulative case for "a well-grounded picture of the divine aspect of our world and life" (ibid., p. 227).

This constructed perspective must be set against strongly theistic analyses, and against reductionist accounts of religion that purport to explain how people might believe in God's direct intervention. Perhaps more effort should be put into finding how many, and why, people believe in a simple or direct theism (cf Brown, 1988), and how many people find non-interventionist practices (like Buddhist meditation) acceptable, or accept Durkheim's view that religion entails a personal form of control, rather than being a cognitive interpretation that accepts religion as a form of pseudo or primitive science that fills the gaps in our knowledge which are not yet explained 'scientifically.' But religions also deal with nonscientific questions about morality and the purpose of life, to which Davis adds consciousness and creativity (p. 220). She looks to "incorporated interpretations" (p. 144) as an essential component of any experience, perception, or belief. These incorporated beliefs are a part of our cultural knowledge, embedded in the language which, during child rearing, shapes the needs or desires, states, and traits that form our personality.

While we might have been prepared for particular experiences in rituals of purification or relaxation, for example, a problem arises if we have an experience for which no preparation has been given, and which must therefore be interpreted later. The first experience of being 'drunk,' 'stoned,' or transfixed, and some prayers (or the 'answers' to them) could fall into this category. Questions about whether those processes are 'natural' are impossible to answer, and we do not easily distinguish what we do experience from whatever we might have been prepared for.

We must therefore accept cumulative, over-determined models of experience, and of prayer, not least because our experience and knowledge of the world is accumulated with reference to justified beliefs and the information that supports them (Davis, p. 165). There need be no self-authenticating religious experiences, since the knowledge by which an experience is justified can always be challenged, as when a doctor claims to be able to "turn bad news into good," or says that "it was inevitable" or "God willed it." When those problems become troublesome, we might try to pray more, or seek help through counseling or psychotherapy.

Healing and psychotherapy

Assuming that "all psychotherapies are meant to help patients reduce or overcome distress, function better in personal relationships and at work, and concomitantly increase self-esteem and heighten patients' sense of control over themselves and their surroundings" (Frank and Frank, 1991, p. 185), interventions that aim to heal in this way are supported by many theories that focus on psychological, biological, or social processes. Frank and Frank (p. 186) note that "transpersonal therapies" that involve "rituals of meditation, prayer, and, sometimes, mind-altering drugs that are intended to provide experiences of direct contact with healing powers" can also be justified. Those authors comment on the recent explosion of specific forms of psychotherapy, in which novelty, and the "enthusiasm of the inventor" can foster "emotional states analogous to those aroused by placebos, which lead both the therapist and the patient" to overestimate the effectiveness of new treatments making overly optimistic claims for it.

These therapeutic procedures share generic characteristics that may parallel the practices of prayer, although some are more like prayer than others. Group therapy, for example, which accepts that "analysis of communications between patient and therapist is equivalent to study of a stress-producing interpersonal communication system, and internalized reference groups in both patient and therapist affect what transpires in therapy" (ibid., p. 187) is like a dynamic view of prayer. Despite their different "treatment settings," extended 'interaction' is possible in both prayer and therapy within "a relatively protected environment where patients can feel free to express forbidden thoughts, release pent up emotions, or experiment with new ways of behaving without fear of consequences" (p. 188): the success of both prayer and therapy could be measured by its effects in daily life.

That the repertoires of coping skills include prayer, especially during illness, may suggest a one-dimensional view that begs questions about the other processes that could help us to cope, and could help to explain how prayer might work 'psychologically.' Developmental theories and cross-sectional tests show what appear to be spontaneous changes in the meaning of prayer that might depend on a changed understanding of the world and of the place in it as one grows up. As young people turn into adults they are exposed to many influences, and become more actively involved with their environment, making independent decisions. Furthermore, because the Christian God has personal qualities, forming a relationship with God is expected to be helpful. That sense of dependence was identified by the Psalmist: "my help cometh from the Lord who has made heaven and earth."

Current opinion about counseling and "helping relationships" (Janis, 1982, 1983) suggest that "systematic evaluations of a wide variety of counseling treatments generally show that almost all of them are effective to some extent, and no one of them is consistently better than the others" (Janis, 1983, p. 2). The common elements now identified in counseling include providing sound support, giving (or finding) pertinent information about alternative choices, helping the client to clarify their personal objectives and potential "by eliciting cognitive rehearsals of aspiration and images of the future," and "encouraging the client to develop a cognitive structure to organize information about himself or herself in relation to available choices" (Holland, Magoon, and Spokane, 1981, p. 285f). These components of typical counseling interventions are also found in prayer, and not just in petitionary prayer. There is no need to labor those parallels, which extend to the relationship of the clergy with their parishioners and other people. The success of such interactions or interventions may depend on intuitive skills, rather than on an explicit awareness of what is involved. Research on this process-oriented perspective on counseling has not yet recognized that it might also be applied to prayer, not because of a passive sense of dependence or resignation on the part of those who pray when "God will provide," but through an active involvement in the search for solutions when decisions are made within a prayerful context about lifestyle, habits, preferences, and how to change them.

Carl Rogers' (1951) client-centered or non-directive counseling, which put its weight on the relationship between the counselor and their clients, can be set against directive approaches that rely on a counselor's expertise to solve their clients' problems by telling them what to do. That some people expect and look for specific answers to their prayers could, on those grounds, have suggested the interpretation of prayer as a form of 'magic.' That view can be set against attempts to resolve one's own conflicts and difficult decisions, with the help of a counselor who does not give advice about specific courses of action but encourages their clients to use their own resources, while respecting their value system. Increased awareness of those decision-making procedures is an important feature of this newer approach to counseling which expects counselors to identify and improve their clients' decision making, as they resolve realistic conflicts and face the difficult choices about which they have sought help. That such help is "usually nondirective with respect to the substantive issues involved in the decision" (Janis, 1983, p. 9) aligns this process-based approach to counseling with prayer, not least because they both involve self-awareness.

Analogies between counseling and prayer can not, however, be pushed too far since "decision counselors" become directly involved with their clients in suggesting where information can be found, the alternative courses of action, and risks in handling real problems, within what has been referred to as symbolic helping relationships. The current research in counseling therefore aims for a sound empirical base for the practices that are beyond an "illusion of success," placebo effects, and spontaneous recovery. Offering prepared solutions does however, provide a model for prayer.

Table 10 (from Janis, 1983, p. 148) sets out some of the processes that a client must go through before deciding on a course of action, and the difficulties they face in doing so. Granted that the influence processes in counseling are examined through counselor, client, and message variables, and their interactions, a new direction for studies of prayer could draw on those social psychological models and theories to explore the responsibilities that are assigned to God, to the one who prays, and to the demands that might be imposed on them. Reactions to those processes might then depend on the 'clients' (or the petitioner's or penitent's) beliefs about what is possible, and about the other courses of action available. Since counseling assumes that the clients are active processors of and seekers for information, the methods of thought-listing (cf Heppner and Claiborn, 1989), electromyography, and schema analysis that have been used to study the characteristics of counseling could also be applied in studies of prayer.

One could also map the contexts within which prayer is appropriate and those in which God might be expected to act autonomously, without being petitioned. The role of individual differences in prayer, beyond those relating to sex, age, traditional religious affiliations and beliefs, and previous experience or expertise in either prayer or meditation and the support they give (cf Shackle and Brown, 1993) might be expected to show whether the opinions of others help to set the balance between them and the self in the practice of prayer. These bounds might also draw on the social psychological models that have been used to study attitudes and attitude-change, including differences between the central and peripheral routes to change (Petty and Cacioppo, 1986).

A process-oriented analysis

Previous work on prayer has, however, stressed its outcomes, rather than the processes it directly involves. But asking someone to rate their preparedness for prayer is likely to be resisted, and the current counseling literature suggests that the content of specific communications may not be as predictive of an outcome as the quality (and focus) of the relationship that supports them. The forms, and the confidence detected in a prayer-alliance is therefore likely to be more relevant than the specific petitions or images and concepts of God it might involve. Just as there are many forms of prayer and meditation (Goleman, 1988), there is a proliferation of psychotherapies in which the quality of the alliance between clients and therapists (or with God in prayer) is expected to have most effect, so the forms of prayer that are maintained could be more important than the content of any specific requests. Like any social relationship it depends on its demands, and the fit between them and the outcomes or satisfactions that are expected.

Unlike analyses of the symbolic attachments that extrapolate from a person's early development (Kirkpatrick, 1992), the realistic, process-based perspective advocated here depends on contemporary social bonds within which 'help-seeking' is possible, and of which there has been previous experience and contact with others (especially helpers). Crucial questions there depend on whether the goals are for change, to maintain stability or cope with external pressures. We also need to know whether prayer entails an enduring preoccupation with the thoughts and feelings that shape one's experiences, or with situated and specific goals for interaction or involvement with God, or with social, physical, or transcendent environments. The expectations of success that prayer supports are also likely to depend on whether prayer is

Table 10 Predecisional behavior characteristic of the five basic patterns of decision making

Pattern of coping with challenge	Criteria for high-quality decision making							
	(1) Thorough canvassing of alternatives	(2) Thorough canvassing of objectives	(3) Careful evaluation of consequences		(4) Thorough search for information	(5) Unbiased assimilation of new information	(6) Careful reevaluation of consequences	(7) Thorough planning for implementation and contingencies
			a. Current policy	b. New policies				
Unconflicted adherence	-	-	-	-	-	+	-	-
Unconflicted change	-	-	+	-	-	+	-	-
Defensive avoidance	-	-	-	-	-	-	-	-
Hypervigilance	-	-	±	±	±	-	-	-
Vigilance	+	+	+	+	+	+	+	+

Source. Janis & Mann, 1977

All evaluative terms such as thorough and unbiased are to be understood as intrapersonal comparative assessments, relative to the person's highest possible level of cognitive performance.

Notes. +, the cecision maker meets the criterion to the best of his ability; -, the decision maker fails to meet the criterion; ±, the decision maker's performance fluctuates, sometimes meeting the criterion to the best of his ability and sometimes not.

understood in terms of procedural and other skills or satisfactions, rather than in terms of its content, which is easily criticized from whatever perspective is adopted, about the nature of God and religious traditions.

Current research on counseling offers other ways to investigate the effects of prayer, not as a mysterious process but involving warmth, attention, encouragement, understanding, respect, support, and modeling, resignation, mastery, risk-taking, and so on. These are important features of any form of psychological treatment, as is the hope that can be engendered among those with low morale, to help them recast their long-term goals. In the same way a client's own effort is crucial in counseling to broaden their horizons and learn techniques for relaxation, coping, and to gain exposure to their problems. Lambert, Shapiro, and Bergin (1986, p. 171) therefore list the common factors, or "effective ingredients" in counseling, as warm support, reassurance, suggestion (which they thought crucial), the credibility of the procedures, attention, and a demand for improvement, changing expectations, empathy, positive regard, congruence, and genuineness. Those factors can all be applied to prayer and rated directly, without reference to the fantasied or symbolic material that was used in the 1950s when Rorschach and TAT records were used to indicate 'recovery' following a psychotherapeutic intervention. Lambert et al (p. 187) accept that the changes will be global, multi-dimensional, and divergent, although reduced distress, increased self-acceptance, and similar observable differences are likely to be central. Applying those factors to prayer would emphasize the need for better conceptual schemes, religiously meaningful longitudinal studies, and the correspondence between the opinions of those who themselves pray and their observers.

Frank and Frank (1991) distinguish evocative therapies from those that are directive or that prescribe "certain activities or rituals for solving specific problems, or alleviating certain symptoms," that might occur through an "increase in patients' self-confidence and sense of inner freedom" (p. 188). Therapy and prayer can both involve strong emotional reactions as well as persuasion, modeling appropriate behavior, and compliance with relevant doctrines or theories. They can also be person or problem-centered and, like therapy, there are many interpretations of prayer beyond its doctrinal support. Because it can be as hard for a client to find out about their therapist's own life as about God, we might find further similarities in the proverb, "When you cry for others you cry for yourself." Lists of the self-help therapies could well include prayer (Huon and Brown, 1988) just as in the *Meditative Mind*, Goleman (1988) emphasizes the importance of mindful breathing, eating, walking, and he offers meditation "as a useful adjunct to any psychotherapy" (p. 172) for its stress reduction potential.

In the *Politics of Experience*, Laing (1967) advocates psychotherapy as a process that pares away all that stands *between* us, "the props, masks, roles, lies, defenses, anxieties, projections, and introjections, in short, all of the carryovers from the past that we use as our currency for relationships." In this sense prayer could be a way to explore the 'depths' of the self when we are 'alone,' and the internal 'objects' we carry, which include our concepts of God, ancestors, absent friends, and others with whom we have 'lived.' This is consistent with the notion that both social and transcendent relationships involve forms of social exchange, as we tend to the wants and needs of others and for ourselves. William James (1907), on the other hand, held to a sense of the absolute, since "the 'true' is the only expedient in the way of our thinking, just as the 'right' is the only expedient in the way of our behaving."

A revisionary theory

The analysis given by Frank and Frank (1991) integrates and updates terms like imitation and suggestion which they describe as the "process by which one person, without argument, command, or coercion, directly induces another to act in a given way or to accept a certain belief, opinion, or plan of action" (p. 253). Although this carries an implication, as English and English note, that suggestion is "devious and designed to circumvent critical consideration" (1958, p. 535), Frank and Frank define imitation as "an action that copies the action of another more or less exactly, with or without intent to copy" (ibid., p. 253). This sounds more benign, although our understanding of healing processes has changed them into an active means by which patients can improve or develop their own coping skills.

"Auto-suggestion" as a variant of suggestion has also been widely used to account for therapeutic change, with English and English (1958) defining it as "the technique of trying [sic] to improve health or behavior by repeating verbal formulas till (supposedly) the induced belief effects the desired end." The best known example of this was Coué's formula, "Every day in every way I am getting better and better," which has a close link with a common criticism of prayer.

While the concept of 'placebo' may have replaced Mesmer and Charcot's use of suggestion to account for another's influence at a distance, by analogy with magnetism, the faith in therapeutic procedures (or a therapist) may contribute to their success, and both prayer and psychotherapy rely on the power of a "symbolic message" that "changes the patients' (or prayers') self-image from victim to coper" (Bootzin, 1985). That prayer does this with reference to God as a transcendental figure seems less important than the opportunities it allows for self-examination and understanding. While Frank and Frank themselves accept the similarity between prayer and a conventional placebo (p. 138f), a placebo drug "implicitly teaches the wrong thing, that the medication is what enables the patient to cope" (p. 140).

Whether the activity of praying enables problems to be approached with an increased self-confidence which depends on the attitudes and expectations that are brought to it, in line with a "therapeutic alliance" (Bordin, 1979), to stress the importance of a correspondence between the values of therapists and their clients is another development in psychotherapy that is relevant to prayer. Jensen and Bergin (1988) also stress the importance of therapists' values for a positive, mentally healthy lifestyle and for guiding psychotherapy. The themes they identified there include the expression of feelings, responsibility, integration and coping, self-awareness and growth, social relatedness, self-maintenance, forgiveness, and spirituality. The values that are expected to change with age and theoretical orientation include self-awareness and growth, forgiveness, and spirituality. These characteristics are all relevant to a mature perspective on prayer, and the implications of Bergin's (1980) own emphasis on values rather than on specific therapeutic practices has yet to be explored in relation to prayer.

When Frank and Frank (1991, p. 2) emphasize a healing agent's role, and their relationship with those seeking help, this relationship can be direct, mediated by a group, or supplemented by others, so that the healing influence is "exercised primarily by words, acts, and rituals in which sufferer, healer, and sometimes a group participate jointly." This specification also applies to prayer, as do the effects of healing that produce changes in a sufferer's feelings, attitudes, and behavior, whether inadvertently or directly, or through placebo responses in which the efficacy "depends on its symbolization of the physician's healing function, which produces favorable changes in the patient's feelings and attitudes" (ibid., p. 38 and cf pages 132-154).

The Franks' analysis therefore stresses the importance for psychotherapy of particular settings and a conceptual framework that specifies the relationship between healer and patient. Their shared goals emphasize mastery in alleviating the patients' sense of powerlessness or demoralization about change, which are properties of "all forms of religious and secular healing in the West and in the healing methods of other cultures" (p. xiv), so that "psychotherapy (and I would add, prayer) may be more closely akin to rhetoric than to applied behavioral science." This analysis side-steps complaints about the idealism of prayer, since we know that 'talk' about ourselves, others, and the environment will construct meanings and realities that can be as potent as any 'actual' experiences. Those processes do not work automatically, being mediated through our values, personal characteristics, previous experiences, felt confidence, and prejudices. Such factors might allow one method to succeed where another fails.

This alignment of prayer with healing has its roots in religious traditions themselves, which some believe involve attempts to control and explain the natural environment explicitly, or rhetorically (cf Szasz, 1974). The success of empirical or naturalistic healing treatments and claims was codified by Hippocrates in the fifth century BC through rites, rituals, and expertise, despite continuing attempts to demythologize and reconstruct beliefs about the purposeful nature of life and of religious realities. During the nineteenth century Mesmer showed that mental states could be altered by trance, which Freud achieved by helping his patients relive their early experiences. When Pavlov developed laws that relate autonomic or physiological responses to events in the environment through conditioning, he gave a behavioral or biological account of responses that are not consciously mediated. That analysis was supplemented by Skinner's operant psychology, leading to behavior modification and then to "cognitive behavior therapy" (Beck, 1990). The extent to which that procedure operates directly or is itself mediated by rhetoric is still a moot question that should be solved empirically, and which carries existential implications for the moral responsibilities assigned to our inner life.

The continuing criticism of prayer as unreal or subjective is accentuated by the belief that God exists only as a figment of the imagination. But if we take ourselves back to the late 1890s, Judith Ryan (1991) shows that in the "new psychologies" that were developing then, there was little tension between principled and empirical psychologies. Those new psychologies altered the pictures of 'self' and allowed consciousness to be investigated from the inside, "without regard to those logical reconstructions that correct its perversions, fill in its gaps, and amplify its range" (p. 9). This gave a phenomenalist rather than a positivistic understanding of the world, and Ryan notes that proto-phenomenology grew from the dual function theory of a "distorting vision and correcting mind" that "permeated the thought of most of the early psychologists" (p. 10). This view accepted the interaction between subject and object, in which "the object was, in effect, partially 'created' by the act of seeing it" (p. 11). That process was familiar to Romantics like Wordsworth, although "the new empiricists went farther in their explorations of just how this relationship functions" (p. 11). When Brentano (in Vienna) set out to explore the subject-object relationship, as Hilgard (1987) puts it, he held that "all mental phenomena are directed to objects, but not necessarily physical ones, so that the objects are 'intended' but do not 'exist' in mental activity except as imminent or potential objects. The mental acts fall into three groups: acts of representation, acts of judging, and acts of desire, loving, and hating. The objects in psychic phenomena are found in these three kinds of acts: in representation, something is sensed or imagined; in judging, something is acknowledged, accepted, or rejected; in desire, love, and hate, something is always desired, loved, or hated." (p. 73).

There is no need to identify other variant theories from that time, except to note that William James, by linking thought to will and action, "removed a great deal of the fear that resulted from the notion that things might exist only phenomenally, as figments of the imagination rather than as things in their own right. By conceiving of his absent hat as the potential object of an action—being taken by James from the cloakroom before he went home—James avoided the awkward problem of having to think of the hat as going in and out of existence according to whether it was present to the senses at any given moment" (Ryan, 1991, p. 13). That may sound principled and philosophical, but it is pragmatic and, had it been widely accepted, psychology might not have had to be as dismissive or reductionistic about the value of prayer as it appears to have been. While it would be hard to develop a plausible form of argument for the existence of God from that perspective, subjective certainty carries its own conviction, even if it is only about what reality might be like. This subjectivity was found to be liberating in the late nineteenth century, although Boring's (1950) account of the history of experimental psychology fostered positivist ideals that neglected introspection and supported the behavioral paradigm that many academic psychologists aspired to then (and some still hope for).

Contextual pressures

Like other forms of intellectual analysis, psychology is not independent of the context of which it is a part. This is illustrated by Adorno's (1973, p. 5) comment that "the liberation of modern painting from objectivity, which was to art the break that atonality was to music, was determined by their defense against the mechanized art commodity—above all, photography." In a similar way, recognizing the power of the imaginary in the world of the real suggests that thoughts may be no less valid than things. Ryan (1991) pursues this point with reference to a snippet from William James about his brother, Henry. In "The Notion of Consciousness," William wrote that "thought and actuality are made of the same stuff, the stuff of experience in general." Similarly, "anything is real which we find ourselves obliged to take account of in any way," arguing that, although common sense will always see thoughts and things opposed to each other, there is not a sufficient basis for assigning a separate status to them. A room we see, for example, is actually a 'field of consciousness,' and thus not basically different from a room we imagine or recollect, as a 'state of mind.' In essence, William James counted anything we experience as real, the effect of that being to give a new and positive value to things that had previously been seen as 'just in the mind.'

Henry James's "The Turn of the Screw" (1898) demonstrates the same point. "Here the imaginary not only bursts in upon the real, but the two actually seem to change places. At times, the governess is so impressed by the 'reality' of the ghostly apparitions that she loses all sense of her own reality: 'While these moments lasted indeed I had had the extraordinary chill of a feeling that it was I who was the intruder.' The insoluble ambiguity of this story is, in effect, Henry James's response to the problem of demonstrating how anything experienced, however hallucinatory, is yet in another sense as real as anything else. The clashing and mutually exclusive interpretations critics have given of the tale merely illustrate the point James wished to make, that 'thought and actuality are made of one and the same stuff'" (Ryan, 1991, pp. 78-79).

This analysis emphasizes that psychology itself, and the meta-psychology that flows from it dictate the validity of what can be investigated and the meanings of what is found. The impact of this on our understanding of prayer could be as profound as it is for psychology, helping us to recognize that psychological analyses are themselves both culturally and content bound, and making us mindful of others' perspectives in our understanding of prayer and its psychology. While Procrustes, that inn-keeper in ancient Greece, may have had a bed that some found quite comfortable, if they fitted it, it was a disservice for those who did not fit.

That religious values, and the coping strategies advocated by Christians differ from secular values, can be illustrated with reference to the currently fashionable use of 'control' (Langer, 1983). While "taking control" is an accepted technique for improving one's adjustment, there is a religious sense in which giving up control might also be adaptive in situations when a loss is irrecoverable, with a death for example, or when one might save one's life by 'losing' it. The Christian virtue of humility either accepts one's limitations or reframes them in terms of God's will. While it might seem paradoxical to gain control by giving up what one did not have, Christian advocacy for that is strong, and because we are unable to change everything, it is essential to know the difference between what can be changed and what we should accept.

The positivist stance of the social sciences could account for the neglect of naive or lay explanations, although Proudfoot and Shaver (1975) appealed to attribution theory when they stressed that an important role of religious explanations is to account for actions and events. Since then, other studies have shown that an appeal to God can explain negative events, illness and injury, and positive personal or medical outcomes (cf Spilka and Schmidt, 1983).

Gorsuch and Smith (1983) argued that since the God of Christianity is personal, attributions to God's causality are similar to any other appeal to personal causes. Although Spilka and Schmidt (1983) agreed with that analysis, religious explanations must be distinguished from others, since only those who are convinced of the reality of God can be expected to be conscientious when they attribute causality to a divine agent who controls an orderly and just, rather than an arbitrary universe. But for some Christians such an appeal is only a rhetorical formula, or a figurative use of language, the deeper meanings of which are hard to access.

While religious experiences and prayers can carry explicit attributions about God's presence or intervention, parallel explanations of those phenomena could refer to the role of drugs (Clark, 1958, Pahnke, 1966), social situations, mistakes, or some form of madness. Yet children who have been trained to appeal to God as an explanation might readily think of God in times of illness, adversity, or death when they become adults. Spilka et al (1985) therefore advanced their formal theory of religious attributions that separately identified the roles of the context, the event itself, and any attributor's purposes. Those purposes could simply be designed to identify the meaning of an event, attempts to control it or to maintain self-esteem by direct appeals to divine control, or to God's omnipotence, with little reference to their own awareness, conscience, belief in a just world (Lerner, 1980), or to the role of chance. Each of those mechanisms could also operate as a filter to interpret or explain what might have caused an event, unless the explanation itself relies on a stereotyped formula that disguises uncertainty. Other specific explanations could include conformity to God's plan that is revealed slowly, or the belief that God is testing us.

There are as many difficulties in making God's actions appear coherent as there are in identifying the characteristics of God that are not traditionally or doctrinally received (Vergote and Tamayo, 1980). We should also remember that 'divine' itself is not only defined in terms of what proceeds from God, but in relation to the task of finding out by "supernatural or magic insight, hence to interpret, explain, make known" (O.E.D.). In biblical times, casting lots was an acceptable way to assign work, divide land, *and* to establish the will of God.

Attribution theory

Early work on attribution theory in the 1960s (Hewstone, 1989), which was concerned to understand beliefs about the causes or reasons for actions and events, might have found religion a ready target for analysis, had it not focused on person perception and social action. Although the Christian God *is* recognized as a "personal being," those who conscientiously appeal to providence, divine intervention, or just rewards are criticized for appearing to show concrete thinking or dependence, when they do that.

Spilka et al (1985) therefore developed an attributional framework that put religious orientations, belief in God, and personal success or failure "comfortably within a single conceptual framework" that applies generally, yet explains specific events. Their argument might, however, be irrelevant to what people believe, or it could be too principled because no religious explanations are necessarily validated by logic or an appeal to 'reality.' The only ways to test them is with reference to traditional sanctions or a social consensus. Religious explanations might then be like *beliefs* about causes, even for those who accept God as a necessary if intangible being, whose role is to bestow meaning. Nor can we be certain how to invoke God's support. Is that to be done by a confession of faith, purity of heart, lifestyle, or intensity of prayer? This problem might explain why many people seem to believe that good management or responsible action is a better way to get things done than to pray or appeal to God, except when other means have failed.

To clarify these problems, consider classical attribution theory itself. In their authoritative and influential review, Kelley and Michela (1980) divided the area into categories covering the antecedents of any attribution and its consequences. In that sixty-eight page paper, thirty-five pages are devoted to antecedents, fifteen to the consequences of an attribution, with only six pages for the motivational antecedents that form the cornerstone of Spilka et al's "general attribution theory." Before identifying what Spilka et al leave out, it is important to emphasize that the features shared by the psychology of religion and attribution theory make religion the paradigmatic case of a meaning-giving system, if we can assume that the basic function of an attribution is to impose (or find) meaning.

But the major impact of attribution theory on social psychology now rests, not on those issues, but on an information processing model that offers a constructive counter to the accepted fact that lay people are poor reasoners because their needs and wishes distort and impair an efficient and rational processing of information. Opinions are divided, however, as to whether those who believe in a God who intervenes in the world are necessarily mistaken in that belief.

The earliest, and still the most influential model of attribution was put forward by Kelley's model of lay people analyzing information "like scientists." In a 1973 paper he distinguished cases in which an attributor gets no further information about an event, from those in which further information is available. The first condition includes attributions to God, which Kelley suggests are resolved with causal schemata that operate through principles like 'augmentation' and 'discounting.' When further information *is* available, it is assumed that we perform a kind of analysis of variance in producing an attribution.

Spilka et al disregarded those aspects of attribution, although it is worth considering the relevance of Kelley's information processing principles, which have dominated attribution theory, in understanding when attributions to God are invoked.

1. *Augmentation.* This principle states that extreme events need more "causal force" if they are to occur (and to be explained) than moderate events, so that a minor success may be explained in terms of an individual's own effort, which is not enough to account for a major triumph. While this is a reasonably well documented principle (cf Lindzey and Aronson, 1985), recent research suggests that the *number* of causes may be less important than their nature (Antaki, 1986). Doing fantastically well may therefore not be explained by a conjunction of causes, such as effort + intelligence + luck + good working conditions, in the way Kelley suggests, but through another cause, like intelligence, or even God's support. This line of reasoning implies that relatively little causal force is needed to explain everyday events. While the agency of a person or the operation of natural forces might give an adequate explanation, it may not explain dramatic or extreme happenings. Furthermore, to invoke God's agency could simply involve another hidden, supplementary, or moral cause, as when the "wrath of God" is used to explain a plague.

2. *Discounting.* This principle states that the role of a given cause in producing an effect is discounted when other plausible causes are present. If a person behaves in an expected and socially appropriate way in a particular situation, acting like an extravert in an interview for a job in which being extraverted is a desirable characteristic could be explained by at least two plausible reasons. Either they *are* extraverted or they act like that to get the job. On the other hand, if they behaved in an introverted way, the only plausible explanation is that they *are* introverted, because other plausible causes would undermine the attributor's confidence in their validity.

For a discounting principle to predict when God will be invoked therefore depends primarily on the attributor's understanding or knowledge of when God can be a plausible explanation. If God could cause *all* events, so that no event is thought to be caused by particular people or by natural processes, one can be confident that an outcome must be the result of God's agency.

With other plausible causes of an event (whether personal, physical, or divine), confidence in any one of them is lessened if they are not equally possible in the first place. This argument is similar to that about a "God of the gaps" to explain whatever can not be accounted for by other (usually natural) processes, and implies that God's action is an additional cause, especially when God is thought to work through natural events or in the actions of others. This assumption is relevant to the next model, although it places a limit on human responsibility.

3. *The analysis of variance model.* This is a general model, and subsumes the previous ones. Kelley expects that an individual with access to several

observations about an event will rely on the covariation between their assumed causes and effects, to make an attribution. He also specifies that the covariation in this information draws on knowledge of the reactions of others to the issue (as consensus), their reactions on other occasions (consistency), and to other relevant entities (distinctiveness). To explain why "Susan did well on her history test," Kelley's model holds that an attributor draws on consensus information about how well others did on the test, on Susan's consistency in history tests on other occasions, and on the distinctiveness of her performance in other subjects. By processing the covariation across these dimensions, an attribution can then be made to aspects of the person, the stimulus, the circumstances, or to some combination of them. If no one else did well on the history tests, the explanation would refer to Susan and not to the test or the conditions under which it was taken.

This analysis is not readily applied to the occasions or events that might involve God, unless some universal principle or law operates and there is no covariation, but there may be evidence for a necessary relationship, or for God's unique involvement. If something always happened to everyone, multiple observations provide no information about covariation. In Kelley's terms, universal phenomena are high on consensus and consistency, but low on distinctiveness. Universality might therefore predispose an appeal to God's will, unless another principle is more accessible or more likely. On the other hand, God's intervention could explain unique occurrences, so that if Susan usually does badly in history (or her prayers are not answered) and she and everyone else did badly on the other tests, her success in the history test might be explained in terms of God's will, if God is able to intervene in different ways. Although Spilka et al emphasized the motivational aspects of attribution, that is not independent of any cognitive antecedents that might allow God to be used to explain an event. So far as God is concerned, however, social conventions limit appeals to God's intervention to good events, or at least to good outcomes or constructions of events (such as the Crucifixion) that are either good in the longer term, or inexplicable in themselves.

In an unpublished study, I found that not only was God infrequently drawn on to explain misfortune or immoral actions, but that frequent churchgoers were significantly more likely to identify God's involvement than were either infrequent or non church-goers. The vignettes that were used to elicit responses in that study referred to people who were themselves judged to be significantly more likely to be responsible for their good *and* their bad actions, than was any intervention by God, or by luck.

The difficulties in principle and in practice in applying Kelley's (or any other) model to explanations that involve God are compounded by the assumption that lay explainers do not use prior theories about causes, but process each instance in terms of its consensus, consistency, and distinctiveness, to arrive at an explanation (Lalljee and Abelson, 1983). It is hard to see how that model would handle findings which show that medical and social events are explained more often in terms of God's will than are, for example, economic events. Since we are taught how and when to appeal to God for an explanation, such appeals are not spontaneous nor can they be derived inductively from previous experience.

Habits of thought that involve "collectively (ideologically) conditioned patterns of misinterpretations" (Ichheiser, 1943) are, however, not errors but indispensable for the way some societies or cultures work. So the "fundamental attribution error" (Ross and Nisbett, 1991) which assigns success and failure, merit and blame, is based on the ideology that our actions *are* personally determined. But explanations change, and unemployment is now said to be a consequence of social or political conditions, and it is not to be blamed on individuals, unless perhaps they are politicians. Attributions to God's involvement in successful prayers might also be shown to have changed, if we had the data about that.

A societal perspective on attribution can be found in witchcraft and the role of the devil, if not also in the responsibilities of God. Witches have been variously interpreted through scapegoating, projected wishes or fears, but not through their passivity in the face of natural and social calamities (Bains, 1983). They have also been understood in terms of a medieval (and so traditional) theory of causation that held out the possibility of some redress. Conspiracy theories continue to permeate explanations of 'obscure' phenomena and of natural or political disasters, and it may not be unreasonable to invoke God's action or intervention to control them. This is conveyed by Zukier (1986) who noted that "from 1348 to 1350, Europe was ravaged by a bubonic epidemic, or Black Death plague. Over a third of the European population was decimated, and in many places more than half the inhabitants perished. People were stunned by the dimensions of the calamity and, groping for some understanding of what was happening, and for a measure of control over the events, Pope Clement VI declared the pestilence an act of God. But to many people, the Jews soon came to embody the explanation: the plague was but the monstrous unfolding of a Jewish plot to poison Christianity" (pp. 96-97). Similar uncertainties surrounded the early phase of the AIDS epidemic.

Prayer, as a means of control with providential outcomes, cannot be dismissed as irrational or bizarre, since the explanations of it depend on the ideas of the time, that must be expected to change. Even in our scientifically saturated and postmodern society there is a plethora of explanations of any phenomenon, not all of which can be accepted with equal seriousness. Some people do not grasp, or they are not interested in pursuing, the complex causal links that the physical, biological or social sciences trade in, and expect to share their moral judgments and outrage about events and circumstances that might be different if only we were to turn to God, or reduce pollution and "green house" gasses. And poverty (as Feagin, 1972, showed) has been explained in individualistic rather than in societal or fatalistic terms, although there are differences there between racial, educational, income, religious and age groups (cf Hewstone, 1989, p. 28). The variation in judgments about prayer could therefore be self-serving, societal, or religious and evaluative. The important point for us is that an inherent, if obscure feature of prayer and other forms of religious practice depends on the psychology of individuals only as far as it helps them to make sense of, and control experiences of the natural and social world. Prayer only seems magical if one does not have access to other explanations. Psychological analyses have an important role here, in broadening our perspective on the explanations that can be used in understanding the real world, and the religious contexts within which prayer is practised, and the issues it can be expected to resolve.

The general model of attribution proposed by Lalljee and Abelson (1983) can be readily applied to God. They suggest that arriving at an explanation involves a search for information that allows a choice between different hypotheses about the occurrence of an event, that depend on prior knowledge and beliefs about similar events in the past. This emphasis on beliefs about the causes of events recognizes beliefs about God and the conventions about when they are appropriately invoked. AIDS for example can be identified with a virus, carelessness, immorality, or the wrath of God. Although we do not know the appropriate rhetorical contexts for each of those accounts, the search for confirmatory information about likely explanations depends on what any explanation could achieve. To validate an explanation we need some 'evidence,' consensual support for it, perhaps from an expert, and a closure on the most appropriate (if not the most likely) explanation for a particular purpose or context.

Kelley (1973) and Lalljee and Abelson (1983) therefore treat God as an additional causal agent producing particular events or outcomes. In the same way, misfortune can be explained in terms of carelessness or a lack of intelligence (or both) within a particular context. This is similar to the interaction between actors, occurrences, and contexts in fixing the attributions identified by Spilka et al (1985). But we should also be able to explain why God can be invoked, whether as a metaphor of our ignorance of proximate or ultimate causes, or as an additional cause that works through people or natural processes.

It is commonplace to accept that God's agency has been progressively reduced over the centuries, or pushed to a meta-level by increased knowledge and scientific theories about probable causes. That AIDS *might* be caused by a virus sent from God could be a helpful, or a rhetorical account. Someone may do well at school because they are clever *and* have dedicated their work to the "greater glory of God." Such compound explanations could be a matter of detecting intentions, unless people believe that God-type explanations and our personal agency are alternatives. So Pargament and Hahn (1986) found that positive health-related outcomes from responsible actions are explained in personal terms *and* through God's will, and that negative outcomes for an irresponsible action were explained in personal terms, but without reference to God's will, perhaps because God's punishment is regarded as admonitory rather than final, as Lerner's (1980) studies of the belief in a just world suggest. For positive events, explanations in terms of the person and God might therefore be complementary (although we do not know their relative contribution). For other events, those explanations or accounts could be mutually exclusive, especially for those who believe in a punitive God, or belong to a religious tradition that identifies what it is appropriate to pray for. So Roman Catholics but not Methodists accept prayer for a horse-race (Brown and Thouless, 1964).

The motivational processes involved with attributions, which Spilka et al emphasized, add another factor. While any explanation could preserve self-esteem or a sense of control, the specific implications of those explanations have been neglected. If failing an exam is explained by external factors to protect one's self-esteem, that failure might imply a lack of control. Furthermore, it is not clear how an explanation that refers to God is related to a sense of control, unless the rhetoric expects God's support or that, while "man proposes, God disposes." These attitudes could be close to the Buddhists' *karma,* and the prayerful resignation of saints, martyrs, or mystics, who may have sacrificed their own feelings of control in becoming aligned with a "higher purpose." These examples involve theories, beliefs, and doctrines about the way God (or nature) operate, and the belief that virtue will be rewarded and wickedness punished.

We might therefore distinguish the traditional forms of religious belief from what they can support, recognizing that an appeal to God's involvement is not necessarily to be taken at face-value, but could indicate an underlying confidence or resignation. Furthermore, to invoke God does not necessarily depend on any beliefs about whether (or how) God operates in the natural world. The ambiguities of religious belief and action (cf Godin, 1967) must be accepted, and a negative outcome does not have to reduce self-esteem should one believe that God produced it as a punishment, a warning, or as a test from which we might emerge strengthened and closer to God.

But no attributional model of religion overrides the silence of God in answer to prayer, or material successes as a sign of being among the 'elect' (Furnham, 1983). Material failures might even make some people work harder. Although attributions that appeal to God presuppose a God analogous to someone making contingent decisions, other views hold God to be an abstract power, a principle of order or justice, or a judge over final outcomes who is not concerned with day-by-day, event-by-event control. The arguments we accept, and those we reject shape what it is possible to believe about God's intervention, and when it can be appealed to.

Instead of looking for explanations that defer to God, we could look at the ways *appeals* for God's help in prayer or ritual explain or change the course of events. But religious explanations are not always coherent (cf Dittes, 1969), and beliefs about specific contexts or events can be invoked to accomplish other goals, or as a social display, which Lalljee, Brown, and Ginsberg (1984) argued is a major function of social attitudes. Psychologists of religion cannot disregard the contextual and other effects that tailor particular explanations. An account that might be appropriate at church is unlikely to fit with that for a psychological experiment, and explanations are also tuned for those to whom they are offered, whether they are a priest, scientist or lay person, and depend on whether the explainer hopes to be seen as 'religious' or not. Instead of expecting formal attributional models to apply to all appeals to 'God,' it would be better to establish how it is that a belief in God conveys an impression of religious piety or moral uprightness, and whether appeals to God are formulaic and declamatory, accepted implicitly, convey a lack of confidence in other explanations, involve an appeal of last resort, or ask for some other plan, as in "God knows" or in the koan "Show me God." Like *karma,* they might refer to "a theory of causation that supplies reasons for human fortune, good or bad, and that at least in theory can provide convincing explanations for human misfortune" (Keyes and Daniel, 1983, p. 3).

Keith Thomas argues in *Religion and the Decline of Magic* (1971) that we have a powerful 'need' to explain misfortune, if only to mitigate its rigors. Religion does that through its claim on supernatural power and support, and not because of our attributional skills, insight, or magical and superstitious perspectives. Thomas stresses that the emergence of Western Protestantism coincided with a changed understanding of the natural world and its boundaries, that reduced the intellectual power of religious beliefs, if not the motivational processes that supported those beliefs. That these boundaries have kept changing is shown by the Church of England's recent separation of its orthodox doctrines from whatever church-members find they can accept or use (in its Reports on *Christian Believing*, 1976 and *We Believe in God*, 1987).

The apparently noncontingent events that presented a problem to the Ancient Greeks (and still do for those with traditional rather than modern perspectives) were solved with reference to spirits, neglected duties, or a failure to recognize obligations. Our neglect of statistical rules (cf Nisbett and Ross, 1980) could be a modern manifestation of a similar process. Anecdotes, didactic teaching, and stories about exemplary events that are cast in a narrative mode (Zukier, 1987) draw more strongly on broadly moral codes and the search for causes, than on arguments about the penance or fasting that ensures control over ourselves (cf Thomas, 1971, p. 135), or the use of folk remedies and other cures that, like the placebos, work because of our faith in them or in those who prescribed them.

Attributions to God can therefore be understood as evaluative and communicative responses that display one's role or position, and make claims on one's beliefs. That such attributions *are* available validates their use, at least among those who accept them. The motives and the characteristics that are attributed to those who appeal to God's intervention can either refer to their personality and other needs, or to external events and the influence of powerful others, or to God's control. Although Heider and Kelley developed information processing models of attribution, religions do not expect such systematic tests of 'faith,' but a ready closure on the search for confirmatory evidence. In this sense they offer sanctioned theories that can be applied in retrospect and are never independently tested, because the religious language itself carries whatever intentions will be detected.

Criticism

Although there may be sound grounds for criticizing the superficiality of some psychological and social studies of religion (including their sampling procedures and the apparent irrelevance of the items that are used), Van Gogh suggested that art (like religion) contributes something greater than one's self to the power (and we might add the mystery) of creation and of life itself. This view contrasts against the sense of dryness, idleness, or lack of purpose that religious beliefs, doctrines, and practice have been expected to resolve. To accept that makes religious solutions societal rather than individual phenomena that, like counseling depend on relationships, if we are to identify the constructive role of religion. Although the stock of theological, scientific, and commonsense explanations is *not* available to all equally, as an additional cause, God could be part of a deep structure in which the meaning of both wanted and unwanted outcomes is reinforced.

A pervasive problem with prayer is its expected privacy, at least for prayers that are set against the public displays of religion that are a foil to bad behavior. We may recognize this problem, but it is hard to penetrate, except through the confessional literature and spiritual autobiographies, which can be ambiguous and more polemical than disclosive. When Bowker (1987) writes of the "unacceptable face of religion" (p. 1) in its involvement with genocidal and other instances of violent behavior, which led him to conclude that "religions are extremely dangerous animals" (p. 2), he stressed that the word 'religiously' has acquired a 'bad sense' that educated men and women have grown out of, "since religion belongs to the infancy of the human race" (p. 3). The other side of this ambiguity depends on the prayers that sustain many people through what they 'think about' or 'say' in their solitary rumination and meditation. This is no longer securely private now that investigative journalism and pornographic films and videos feed our fantasies about what others might be like, or in "what they do with their solitude," which was how Whitehead (1926, p. 16) described religion. William James might have agreed with that, although he had restricted himself to the experiences of "religious geniuses."

The individualism of religious experience must be accepted, as we learn from the accounts of the experiences of saints and mystics, reformers, innovators and others. That some have been prepared to be disclosive and unselfconscious about their prayer life gives examples of what prayer can do, although systematizing that information is difficult.

But Bowker (1987, p. 10) stressed that religions are organized "in immensely different ways" to facilitate (and constrain) the transmission of information. As he says, "Information, particularly in the religious case, is very far from being simply words, whether written, spoken, or sung. Much more is involved than the transfer of verbal items. What is being transmitted are such things as style, method, wisdom, insight, technique, behavior; and a great deal of all that is transmitted in the religious case by entirely non-verbal means, by action, liturgy, silence, ritual, dance, decoration, and so on." So prayers involve what we may "become in the transformation of life and its judgments, and might ultimately become in terms of salvation, nirvana, *moksha*, union with God, or whatever else may be held out as an ultimate goal or concern. It may be the case that the religions are entirely wrong, or even just partly wrong, about what they believe to be the ultimate case; but that does not affect the point" (p. 11).

In that sense religions involve "this-worldly discoveries," as do counseling, science, and many other activities that recognize pluralism and co-existence as the core of a realistic view that might also be found in poetry and other work (or 'fruits') of the imagination couched in language, and expressed directly or indirectly. Continuing disputes center, however, on the extent to which laws of nature, logic and mathematics, and our knowledge of ghosts or religion are human inventions (Pirsig, 1976, p. 34) or true discoveries (cf Penrose, 1990). The balance between public and private beliefs there, and in what religions are 'about' center on doubt and the objectivity or reality of the meaning of 'chaos,' being 'saved' or "washed in the blood of the Lamb." Others worry, or wonder, their way through a "spiritual journey" in which 'rest' is hard to find.

Everyday life has many contrasts between public facts and personal plans, pictures or programs that instantiate more than can be disclosed: if this were not the case, it would have been impossible for psychoanalysis (or perhaps a marriage) to go on for years. "That is why all accounts of God, in all religions, end up sooner or later by saying, much as Samuel Johnson said of Milton's religion, 'We know rather what he was not, than what he was.' So religions inevitably end up in the *via negativa* of Christianity, the *En Soph* of Judaism, the *bila kaif* of Islam, the *neti neti* of Hinduism (as not this not this), the *ik onkar* of Sikhism. In that limited sense there is a resemblance between our response to the universe and our response to God" (Bowker, 1987, p. 77). It is hard to establish how many have (or claim to have had) a direct contact with God in worship, meditation, prayer, or contemplation. As Tom Stoppard put it in his play, *Jumpers,* "How does one know what it is one believes when it's so difficult to know what it is one knows?"

The psychological necessities driving this process are as private (and obscure) as those that drive other actions—although we can produce accounts of what they might be. We are expected to explain ourselves, unless we can claim immunity from that demand because we are too busy, have another appointment or have perhaps gone mad. To say we have forgotten or don't know is less acceptable. These explanations themselves must be socially accepted and are likely to follow the conventions of a society (or religion) and its promises or constraints. If it is hard to face the futility of the world, we are expected to be able to compensate, or to blame something or someone else, as in the processes that Marx and Freud bequeathed to us, which lead to the conclusion that we believe because we must believe *in* something. That this is imagined is of less relevance, and it is less easily criticized now than it once was, because so many theories and explanations of deep scientific and sociopolitical processes appear transcendental. After all, few understand quantum effects or the money market.

The criteria by which mental health and maturity are evaluated are more social than biological. Youth and age follow prescribed roles, while judgments about adaptation, feelings, autonomy, hope, a sense of identity, and interpersonal skills are social. If we look at those problems in religious terms, they are vexed, because they involve obedience, lifestyles, and ethical actions. So Sabom (1985) as a religious psychologist, proposed that those with anorexia nervosa reject the principle that "the mind, body, and spirit are unified in a world-affirming biblical religion (1 Corinthians 6:19-20)," when they become involved with 'sinful' starvation or an unreal asceticism. But clinical interpretations of anorexia hold that those patients react to socio-cultural pressures that force vulnerable women (in particular) to starve themselves because of familial eating patterns, that they want to be thin because of low self-esteem, or in an attempt to cope in a way that might let them avoid the demands of adulthood. Sabom's religious interpretation is committed to a theory about a phenomenology that is neither testable or morally neutral. Scientific analyses can be tested, even if they involve an unfortunate scientism, and no explanation is independent of values and a trade-off between open and closed mindedness (Rokeach, 1960).

To ask who we might be talking to in prayer, or whether we 'talk' at all, either expects an answer or makes a claim on impossible questions, because those events are themselves unclear. We breathe and hardly question that, but require a leap of faith to understand what lies beyond religious experience. To explore relationships with God, as opposed to the concepts or ideas about who or what God might be like, does not expect God to be beyond words, although language could be a jailer to our thoughts. Prayers might simply recognize that life has a meaning that may itself be mysterious. Alternatively, prayer could be an irreducible response to God (whose presence we desire) that transforms our perspective on the world through the religious 'infrastructures' that constrain and control it.

God's silence and the politics of prayer

While God's silence is regarded as another weakness of prayer, because it pushes claims on it back to the one who prays, such silence is both a strength and a threat in its implicit challenges, especially when 'prayer vigils' are used as a political weapon against the actions (or inaction) of others. The apparent inaction of a psychoanalyst might even have been modeled on prayer, a view that is accentuated by using a 'third' or disembodied ear as an emblem of psychoanalysis, and accepting the silence of confessors. Another political (or ironic) use of prayer is found in Joyce's *Ulysses* when Mr Bloom, approaching a group of nuns, makes the sign of the cross and moves across the street. That sense of resignation needs neither explanation or over-interpretation, although both prayer and gambling can add spice and uncertainty to a life of routine, when they challenge fate or nature. Other explanations have face-validity and invoke a power that we can use to control ourselves, rather than the needs or demands of others.

Whether 'prayers' in times of distress draw from an urge to pray that is latent in everyone, or are an impetuous outburst in crisis, they can be trivialized once they are displayed. Phillips' criterion of prayer that contrasts religious prayers against an imprecation can only be satisfied when the context is known, or the crisis is over. A similar criterion could be applied to church-going, or when using Christian "instruments of worship" for "black magic." This again emphasizes an ambiguity of religious signs and practice that can only be resolved with reference to attitudes and actions in the rest of one's life.

Can we ever know, therefore, whether or how prayer might make a difference? Can we say that it changes God, others, or only the self? Is it necessarily explained (away) by those who do not believe? William James resolved those problems by noting that if prayer is not something "transacting, any feeling about it is illusory and rooted in delusion" (1902, p. 465). But even if our control is illusory, it still involves attributions about what might be involved (Langer, 1983).

While Marrett (1903) (and others later) identified the cultural development of prayer from "spell to prayer," that primal essence involved the need for control expressed in words or incantations. But if "God knows," is it necessary to be heard, especially if God is the one "from whom no secrets are hid"? We have noted that the psychological interpretations of magic, spells, and incantations are little used now, because the power of words is emphasized, especially when their meaning is subordinate to any effects they might have.

As D.W. Harding (1963) put this, a writer (and most researchers) "can offer only the verbal component of a pattern of experience the totality of which includes much else besides words and articulate thoughts. The reader reconstructs from the verbal component as much as he can of the rest of the pattern" (p. 175). Prayer might be similar to that, granted the attempt to identify or deconstruct the processes embedded in it, or to extract the meanings that others have found there or in the reactions to it. "Even in ordinary conversation the phrasing of an attitude is keyed to the context in which we are speaking and is apart altogether from polite concealments and hypocrisies in the phrasing we adopt as part of the attitude we find we have taken up" (Harding, 1963, p. 172). Harding's concern there, as with the language of prayer, was to put "experience into words."

The privacy of prayer
Prayer is not independent of those who pray, especially if the act of praying is its only reality and the meanings of prayer are taught, modeled, or learned by trial and error. Since it involves a spiritual expression of what is 'beyond,' the *privacy* of prayer is probably less important than its subjectivity and the confidence that can be placed in it. If we take it that prayer is only directly accessible through the 'collective mind' of a group or crowd, it could be similar to a poetic or aesthetic stance. Following 'Thouless's Law' (1935) which refers to the finding that uncertainty about matters of fact can be tolerated, while matters of belief tend to be resolved (pro or con) with confident certainty, another feature of prayer lies between those who can, and those who cannot accept it. Comparatively few are uncertain about their stance.

Those who reject the validity of personal prayer might accept its liturgical role and doctrines about the effects that are to be expected there. Beliefs surrounding the meaning of orthodox doctrines are similarly variable (Brown, 1988) (although sociobiology allows phenotypic variations around some genotypic core). Culturally, the concept of God involves symbolic control that ensures adaptation as it compels obedience: "Because he died for my sins; because when I was still far off he met me in his son and brought me home; because he revealed his will for me in the straight path which leads to heaven; because he guided our fathers through countless generations and laid his command upon us to be holy as he is holy" (Bowker, 1987, p. 217). Other formulations range across the creeds and the simple, direct cry, "Because I have been saved." This awareness of God does not depend on a rational calculus of propositions, although it might be explicated in that way. Believing 'religiously' involves an immediately self-validating experience for some, and it is a result of tortured intellectual debate for others.

While analyses of religious orientations emphasize the consequences of a religious stance (Batson and Ventis, 1982), the styles and meanings that are constructed around our beliefs have been neglected, perhaps because of their inherent variability and the difficulties in systematically documenting them, despite ready interpretations of a fit between religious meaning and personality that disregard the integrative role of religion itself. Whether these problems are religious or psychological, the validity and evidential force of the experiences that support them remains a problem (Davis, 1989) because any account can be reductionistic, and the doubts that might contradict what is expected could be understood as a test of faith. Spontaneous accounts of religious experiences, whether they are written or given orally are not usually offered within therapeutic or confessional encounters, but they can be expressed symbolically or with reference to some precipitants. Like the language of love, these experiences can be hard to talk about, not least because the language of feelings is tentative and approximate (Solomon, 1976).

We are not the last generation to accept theism as a 'live option' (to quote James again) on some balance of probabilities. When there are insufficient grounds for deciding rationally, it is accepted that we follow feelings or emotions. But having made that move about prayer or the existence of God, how much more of a religious 'package' are we prepared to accept? That might reflect our training or preferences when answering the question, "Why do you believe?" or a hope that the network of causes can be cut through by a socially appropriate reply, whether that moment is psychological, social or religious, or includes a vision for the future, in wish-fulfillment or as a working hypothesis. We must also face the problems of the content we accept, whether it derives from a set of doctrines or points to immanent truths. While the Buddha hesitated to teach, we confront the tension between our independence and the demands of a 'system' that can be creative, but may be misused (by either side).

While prayer can be discussed in psychological terms, and some studies of it have been experimentally controlled (cf Deconchy, 1985), a basic question asks how the religions from which the meaning of prayer is derived are held together by their members. Reference to personal narratives and accounts of religious practice and experience and the evidence that supports them gives more information about the contexts within which individuals operate than about the psychological processes that could be involved, since they are not accessible to introspection. Even our own personal histories are carefully tailored and elaborated.

At another level, the personality factors relating to a sense of subjective well-being include high self-esteem, internality, extraversion, sensation-seeking and sociability, and that social contact is itself related to a sense of well-being beyond extraversion because people are in general more sociable when they are happier. Findings about religion and subjective well-being are similarly confounded because of the different ways religion can be expressed although religious faith, the importance of religion and religious traditionalism generally relate positively to subjective well-being. Yet others have found that religiosity correlates inversely with positive moods, and that while most studies on church attendance and participation in religious groups show positive relations to subjective well-being, others have found no relationship. Other questions must ask about the factors that interact with subjective well-being, how various types of faith and participation relate to it, what happens when other effects are controlled and whether those who seek religion in a crisis find that it has a positive impact (cf Brown, 1993).

Religion and myth

The relationships between science and religion seldom distinguish between the old and new sciences, or between scientific and quasi-scientific beliefs, and the institutional structures that carry those traditions. Modernity is aligned with Western science since the Eastern or traditional perspectives represented by Buddhism or Hinduism entail less tangible solutions to the problems of life and its meaning that do not fit well into contrasts between instrumental and expressive attitudes, or between 'textuality' and a deep understanding of 'reincarnation,' for example. Those themes recur because the problems to which they relate concern control, position, and power, or accept the validity of myths without wanting to test them by scientific procedures. But what is 'natural' in these processes? Does our concept of 'man' (or person) imply a beast of prey, when we argue from historical evidence for continuing warfare? Or does it imply weakness if we take a simple-minded view of prayer?

A constructed view of the world accepts the psychological necessity of the archetypes that are supported socially (following Swanson, 1960). But the first step is to make sense of life within society, groups or families, and only then with reference to the self. At a later stage we might have to make sense of religious control over our needs and drives, and over the myths that support doctrines, or that interpret symbols and metaphors. The basic question is still, "What can one believe?" Whether the answers to that question are taken as fact, myth, dream, or they are driven by open- or closed-mindedness, and liberal or authoritarian attitudes, how should religious behavior or a religious perspective on life be explained? Does that perspective also involve attitudes to death, sex, 'after life,' or to social involvement and religious experience? Religions have shaped attitudes to illness or death. But is it reasonable to have rescued prayer from the assumption that it is irrational, if religious theories offer a coherent 'picture' through common sense alone? Whether those theories plausibly reduce the subjective validity of religion, or only interpret it, is another moot point.

Chapter Thirteen

Conclusion

Psychology began within theology and philosophy, as much as in physiology, to advance practical points of view that might interpret, modify, or control aspects of experience first, and then of 'behavior.' Its theories depended initially on "pure reason" with statements about experiences that lacked external validation by the empirical tests we now expect, although Augustine, Luther, and many others enunciated psychological principles that have become an essential part of our stock of common knowledge.

An important sub-set of those principles refers to the origins and nature of religion, whether in projection, fear, fantasy, example, social pressure, the control of others (including its leaders and followers), conviction, or by bluff and threats of damnation. Since prayer is central to religion, and theories about the consequences of religion are easier to test than most theories about its origins, we might find the consequences of prayer among those who have been explicitly taught to pray. Those experiences are, however, likely to follow the example of others. They are seldom 'invented,' although some forms of prayer are "cries or wishes from the heart." Prayer has therefore been described as a primitive or child-like plea for help. It might also be like a game that follows well-defined rules, as part of a great drama, or simply as a traditional activity.

Those who actively pray are likely to share different perspectives on the efficacy of their prayer, and on how they might explain its operation to those who can only watch that activity as outsiders. Specific questions about prayer are, however, differently understood, whether they concern the ways prayers are mediated and come to be accepted, what its evocative or arousal value might be, and to whom or through whom it is directed, with what effects. The answers to those questions *can* themselves convey positive or negative attitudes to prayer and to the beliefs about it. This alone guarantees its ambiguity, despite the fact that prayer is a widespread activity. In that sense prayer *is* different from the symptoms of any frank psychiatric illness or psychopathology, although it may not be easily distinguished from the fantasies that devel-

240

op around religion, which might entail *socially* accepted elaborations, perhaps of an '*as if*' kind that only become troublesome when directly translated into action. Spiritual direction about the 'excesses' of prayer depends on the attitudes (and knowledge) of the director or therapist. This is classically included under the heading of 'discernment,' which has political overtones, especially in its categorical use by Pentecostals. Any explanation of, or approach to prayer and other religious phenomena therefore depends on the order that is detected, or that can be assumed to lie behind (and beyond) the flux of immediate experiences. While skeptics and materialists may discard prayer, others regard it as an imaginative construction that helps to control their emotional life.

Specific thought-processes are unlikely to be involved or required for prayer. Reductionistic explanations, whether in terms of a brain dysfunction, misattribution, or social influence should, however, be shown to be generally supported before they can be applied to particular cases. A similar precision is needed about meditation, which does not easily align with either public or private petitionary prayer. Disputes in Australia, for example, have nevertheless centered on whether there should be *any* prayer (and if so, who might lead it) on public occasions like opening the War Memorial or the new Parliament Building in Canberra. For any context we need a systematic analysis of the available repertoires of prayer for both individuals and groups, a knowledge of the beliefs about its efficacy, and whether prayer expresses an inherent sense of trust or mistrust (following Erikson), or refers to our dependence and insecurity, or guarantees independence.

Prejudices which assume that modern religions have developed from primitive or 'earlier' forms, especially with reference to the Mass (if one is a Protestant) or Pentecost (for those stressing the Holy Spirit), or in magic and alchemy, contrast historicism against presentism as a basis for those explanations. Psychologists should, however, aim for psychological accounts of prayer that depend on some data and not on mere principle. Despite that, it is obvious that many people take over (or reject in various ways) a religious stance from their family or community thereby producing some prejudices against other religious traditions that integrate or sanction their appeals to a religious base. We all have *some* knowledge of prayer, and reject the aspects that we believe are too concrete (or abstract), wrongly directed, committed, not spontaneous enough, or too sacrificial, mindless, priestly, and so on. Those reactions have both social and personal perspectives and involve implicit assumptions about the nature of the world and our experience of it, and of religion, and how such information is made available. Furthermore, while we might recognize a range of emotions, including frustration, humility, confidence and so on, we seldom agree how they *ought* to be handled, or we fail to recognize that our emotional reactions to it are socially determined, as in Schachter and Singer's (1962) study of arousal, which showed that the meaning of bodily states of arousal are identified with reference to social cues. The emotions in religion are likely to be social and not dissimilar from those that are found in other social relationships that are organized in terms of subjection and kinship. Decisions about whether a particular action will help us to predict the reactions of others who pray about it, unless we ask whether their reactions to religion are concrete and specific (and if, for example, happiness can be compared with divine favor), or abstract and spiritual. They could simply involve surrendering to the hands of fate (like Stoicism) or praying in solemn contemplation or in adoration and praise. Perhaps scientific experiments *were* designed to cope with our over-confidence about the coherence of the environments that we have constructed for ourselves.

Reasons for retaining prayer have included the custom itself, coping with our ignorance of how the world works, taking a wager on God's existence (following Pascal), or challenging failure, self-deception, and the other pre-formed explanations of faithfulness that are available. Prayer might turn our contemplation toward God without petitionary components but within a context set by the imagination. Whatever analysis is accepted, there will be an inherent dialectic between the demands of rational thought and presuppositions about the results that might be produced by prayer. That contrast itself is psychologically interesting, demanding an answer to questions about its validity, and whether prayer can ever be a 'real' experience, or is only a 'shadow.' This allows it to be challenged or to be an affirmation of faith.

Our problems are therefore predominantly

a) theoretical, in which case we might follow fashion or tradition, using attributional analyses as a robust meta-theory to help understand prayer.

b) empirical, as we move between looking for any objective effects of prayer, or for what the effects are believed to be, while continuing to argue about the best methods to test for them.

c) practical, as we hope to improve our own prayer life or encourage others to pray.

d) leaving continuing questions about whether to concentrate on what is external and natural, cultural or traditional, immediately social and interactive, personal and psychological, or directly religious in prayer.

Psychologists will usually stress their findings, over the 'why' or 'what' questions that might have stimulated them. If we avoid the solutions and repeated findings or prejudices which suggest that 'prayer' has uniform meanings, its interpretation should nevertheless recognize denominational, sex and age differences, and the ambiguity of a 'no religion' category, since people may refuse to join a church and still accept religious beliefs. We should also identify the Christian fear or prejudices against Islam, the gods in Buddhism or Hinduism, or the influence of Jahweh.

While the symbolism in prayer might seem clear, its interpretation is not, since religions involve authority and dogma and they are celebrated by rituals that are not necessarily weakened by arguments about their truth (or infalli-bility). For Christians, that derives from the Fathers and their Councils, so that when one asks, "Why do you believe that?" the answer might refer to the tra-dition *or* to one's experience. Our task is, however, to find a way, without being reductionist or dismissive, to uncover the levels at which explanations of prayer are given.

Nonreligious perspectives on prayer are likely to center on political, eco-nomic, philosophical or psychological, rather than religious processes. Neither science or religion transmits innocent truths, since their findings can become like possessions (Abelson, 1988). But how are they used? What does psychology add to that? Are prayerful styles of thought and depths of feeling plumbed by single case studies? Does every religion have some tech-niques that allow even those who are closely involved to keep a discreet dis-tance from it? Are theater, poetry, and art, like religions, without the dogma? To what extent are the intellectual influences on prayer distinguished from the impact of other social movements on its practice?

These questions could go on, and we need a lexicon to capture all the views about prayer. One place to look for them is in various dictionaries. Alternatively we could be like the sufis and accept that miracles *have* hap-pened and spend our time looking for *them*. Even for many psychologists, life *is* mysterious.

Tourists who visit shrines and cathedrals go there for many reasons that include admiring them for their artistic, cultural, historical, or religious value, which the staff are expected to emphasize while giving "complete priority to the sense of worship" (English Tourist Board, 1979), despite the conflicts of interest between conducting services and satisfying the demands of a tourist trade. Other conflicts in formal religious contexts cut against the authenticity of an experience and what has been prescribed or hoped for by it. Pearce (1982, p. 116) notes that "the failure to fit the motives and expec-tations of the (touring) visitors to the experiences offered in that (or any) environment are not proving too severe in the cathedral settings," although the constraints there can compromise the authenticity of the experiences and whatever other interests might be served. Despite the varied interpreta-tions of how individuals' attitudes are formed (cf Fishbein and Ajzen, 1980), the processes by which imagination develops and religions change remain obscure, especially since many institutions force us to accommodate our-selves to their demands, regardless of our preference for open or closed cog-nitive systems (Rokeach, 1960, for example).

Existential questions about whether we should passively accept a received religious tradition or actively search for a more congenial form of prayer are easily answered with reference to processes of trial and error in an ide-alistic search for what it is that produced particular religious perspectives in the first place.

Another aim of any psychological analysis of prayer might be to broad-en the ways prayer might 'speak' in a dialogue between the past of a tradi-tion and one's present life. But whose voice will be heard, if the prayers of a "humble man availeth much"? Whether religion and psychology are both more closely associated with received solutions than with finding new solutions, and whether prayer is necessarily immature, are no longer at issue if the accepted definitions of what prayer involves are inherently social. But the early psychology of religion was dogged by the dilemma of documenting and interpreting what was available, and attempting to criticize or evaluate that. This is no longer a problem, except for those who, on principled grounds, reject the validity of the nonevaluative analyses that characterize 'religious studies.' Those for whom the truth of religion lies in a revelation beyond history seem to feel anxious about what psychologists 'think,' believe, or claim about their belief and practice. While religious responses are located initially within their own contexts, their meaning, like that of music, extends beyond specific performances to a cumulative tradition of practice and interpretation that continues to be elaborated, if only because the contexts and horizons of our predecessors were different from ours.

We may hear about witches and read about superstitions, yet only by examining the present can we find or 'hear' about the reality of the processes that justified them. When we find a meaning, it is likely to be interpreted through assumptions produced by the proto-histories of prayer that could be similar to the search for an 'authentic' performance of a piece of 'early' music (cf Kenyon, 1988). The validity of such performances are only evaluated against the uses to which they are put and must be first interpreted socially, then subjectively.

To maintain any religious tradition requires support from the cultural context from which it derives its meaning. To interpret that psychologically, we must first appeal to an historical analysis of the tradition, and then to behavioral data, reading the nonverbal signs in the gestures and postures for prayer or examining the language used in praying, when talking about or interpreting it, and in forming impressions of those who pray. While it might seem rather exaggerated, we should note the different information that actors and observers use to understand each other's stance (Ross and Nisbett, 1991). Both are caught in a trap that brings our own subjective impressions from a stream of consciousness, yet tends to reject others' perspectives as a source of valid data.

The focus of those analyses can be on public or private prayers for the self, others or the world. These styles may defer to matters of 'taste' or preference, attitude or tradition, and their theoretical explanations depend on frameworks of inclination and situated dispositions that involve radical or conservative attitudes. One goal of prayer is probably to preserve a tradition and its ideology, not through individual mechanisms of projection or wish-fulfillment, optimism, or self-fulfilling prophecies and placebo effects (Frank and Frank, 1991), but from a social or religious perspective. When used as a greeting or farewell, if someone is asked to "say a prayer when I get to Washington," that prayer loses its religious value.

Regardless of any specific conclusions, to understand what 'prayer' means could be to reconstruct some set of attitudes to it, and perhaps to religion itself, in resolving dilemmas about its appropriateness and efficacy for particular individuals, and to accept that 'unanswered' prayers are religiously defined. Conjectures about the role of personality factors or suggestibility are not well supported, although they are part of the ideology surrounding prayer, and the points of reference for its meaning that should be reconstructed.

Adopting a different perspective, to speak of 'God's agency' makes a distinction between our responsibilities and those of God, the effects of which are unlikely to be the same for Christians as for Moslems or Jews, who might attribute more, or perhaps a different responsibility to God. Across those groups, however, explanations that directly involve God are probably less important for severe events, but more relevant for the less severe events that could have been caused by individuals. This locates God and nature in different domains, at least among those who are not 'very religious' (Furnham and Brown, 1992).

We must accept the effects of prayer as matters of belief that depend on the context and the events being prayed about. On those grounds alone, 'experiments' on prayer presuppose a material rather than a spiritual or psychological reality for it, unless it is cast within a framework of self-efficacy and its objective or quantifiable effects there. While beliefs about the natural world are well-defined (as Keith Thomas has shown) they have changed over time, as have the explanations of what they involve that are grafted on to them. Despite the objectivity of prayer texts, a personal, mirrored-view of the world can be consoling: as Lacan said, "I pronounce the truth, but there is no truth." So psychological explanations need not over-simplify prayer, whether as mistaken, 'instinctual,' emotional (and wished for), or cognitive and intellectual, if it is accepted as self-referenced but not ego-centric. More eloquent models offered by dramaturgy or liturgy have yet to be explored psychologically, although their value might be more integrative than procedural, if prayer involves an affirmation of self. The issues surrounding psychosomatic illnesses raise similar problems, with dual diagnoses and doubt about the 'real' illness while avoiding the stigma attached to 'over-servicing' and factitious conditions. To identify God as "Husband, Lover, or Friend" involves a form of address that implies a metaphorical rather than a functional relationship through which our desires may give another 'reality' to the 'relationship.' If, as the popular phrase has it, "prayer changes things" it need not matter how that happens or what is changed, unless we have an academic rather than a religious interest in that question.

That the answers will be irrelevant to those who have no difficulty with unself-conscious prayers, or who are looking for spiritual guidance brings us back to a central problem in the psychology of religion concerning the priming and consolidation of religious claims.

In *Little Gidding*, Eliot makes the point that

> You are not here to verify,
> Instruct yourself, or inform curiosity

Or carry report. You are here to kneel
Where prayer has been valid. And prayer is more
Than an order of words, the conscious occupation
Of the praying mind, or the sound of the voice praying.

This analysis invalidates the psychologies of prayer that have looked for its specific efficacy, or that step over prayer itself to quantify and interpret the claims or experiences of those who pray. These interpretations range widely and have changed over the years, while avoiding "issues of determinism, free will, causality, explanation, evidence, and inference" (Gigerenzer et al, 1989, p. xv) that depend on fundamental propositions about chance, design and the existence of a divine plan. As in Pascal's wager "no matter how small we made the odds of God's existence, the pay-off is infinite; infinite bliss for the saved and infinite misery for the damned. Under such conditions, Pascal argued that rational self-interest dictates that we sacrifice our certain but merely finite worldly pleasures to the uncertain but infinite prospect of salvation" (ibid., p. 1). That perspective raises intangible questions about the reasonableness of our expectations, and about the evidence that turns doubt into confidence or certainty and then into faith, the regularity of the events which support that, and the extent to which those events are objective or only "in the mind." These problems contrast objective against subjective probabilities, or chance and luck against divine purpose or superstition. Whether prayer is within or outside some directly causal order has been a pervasive problem, resolved by Eliot (and others) with a move sideways that redefines prayer as what we *do*. This escapes questions about its reasonableness because of the social sanctions on prayer. Yet that issue remains alive, whether its solution depends on evidence or on what we believe. Prayer might also be like a game of chance that depends, not on the prayers' actual world but on their beliefs or expectations, which may themselves be reflexive or self-fulfilling. But any calculus of probable outcomes that surround prayer is likely to have moved from looking for external effects to emphasizing the value of prayer within a religious perspective, and at its uses or consequential effects on those who pray. That depends more on coping than on any definite (or probable) outcomes, if prayer is recognized as what we ought, or need to do.

This analysis is, however, compounded by the fact that 'chance' and 'fortune' are accepted parts of a philosophical vocabulary that could mean coincidence, absence of purpose or an "ample endowment of the 'external' goals of good health, wealth, beauty, and children" (Gigerenzer et al, 1989, p. 12), and a social acceptance of their importance. Prayer could also involve recognizing a divine purpose within or beyond the causal order, which has been aligned with magic by its critics. To ask if it is reasonable to pray could be like asking if a game of chance depends more on the wealth of the players or on their beliefs and expectations. Psychologists have tried to 'calculate' that, while hoping to demonstrate the outcomes rather than the uses of prayer. That still seems to be a preferred form of argument, even in religious contexts: and advertisements for lotteries argue that they have worked for others, so why not for you.

The seventeenth- and eighteenth-century mathematicians and philosophers who hoped to articulate the rules of probability or the laws of chance were criticized for "belaboring the obvious" (ibid., p. 16) with their descriptive or prescriptive theories. Bernoulli resolved that dispute in favor of a prescriptive model that made probability theory a tool rather than a model of enlightenment (ibid., p. 18). Perhaps we confront a similar dilemma with the psychological analyses of prayer, although prayer might be more like a mixed game of chance and skill than of chance alone. Some who pray still "put the improbability of winning against the still greater improbability that they could alter their situation in any other way" (ibid., p. 20). The outcome is then more like identifying the regularity in a mortality curve as a result of, rather than a reason for finding the hand of God in a predicted solution (ibid., p. 23). But there is still confusion about whether the independent variables involved in prayer are within those who pray, their prayers, or with God. If the answer is that "it depends," we must still decide what the mediating or moderator variables might be. Relying on immediate judgments, predictions or expectations there might involve blind faith or irrational beliefs, unless a better theory can be found within which to contextualize an explanation.

While the moral implications of prayer could make claims on its targets, just as a language speaks through us, so prayer prays in us, unlocking visions of a reality that interacts with symbols of the self, and of others who might be living or dead. That dynamic theory, within which we have been taught to pray as the Father was prayed to by the Son, is sustained by the social, cultural, and religious traditions of Christianity. We do not know how that theory should be modified for other traditions, especially if their interpretations were literal rather than metaphorical. Even 'childish' needs can be expressed symbolically and do not need to be taken at face value, although the Old Testament offered hope through dreams, visions, and history itself.

That the Church and other religious institutions are 'there' means that their processes are not simply 'psychological.' Ogres, witches, vampires, and mysterious fantasies are to be found in the language that contains them, as do religious explanations, art, and literature. Reality is seldom accepted without strain, and it can be relieved by a religion that allows, but does not challenge expressive coping. The rationality of millenarian questions and the typological nature of many 'psychological' answers are, however, questioned by the 'general explanations' that can be derogatory and even condemnatory when cast in psychiatric terms. Wilson (1973) noted, however, that "modern men expect their blessings mainly from the welfare state, scientific medicine, the development of technology, the availability of education, the operation of impersonal legal institutions, and disinterested agencies for the maintenance of social order" (p. 502). The prayers of any religion have little place there, although we have become increasingly cynical about those institutions and pray for "reassurance, solace, confirmation of worth . . . to be known as a person and not merely as a role-performer" (ibid.).

Despite the power of science and of the state, we yearn for *personal* solutions to questions about the meaning of life and death. Prayer is available to assist this, and it need not be understood as a self-defeating or irrational defense. As an illusion, religion is no more powerful than the illusions of art, literature or music that are all part of our own traditions, and that should be understood in those terms. We know that they depend on but are different from reality. Even those professionally involved with art and religion do not live the whole of their lives within that 'artificial' context, unless Searle's (1992) paradox is correct and "the appearance is the reality."

The argument developed here holds that prayer is psychologically complex and ambiguous. Ready-made or cliched explanations are of little help in explaining it with an external reference, whether that is to be called God, the Ultimate, the world, or even the self. That prayer is primarily within language, gesture, or posture and in attitudes of faith itself seems to have been disregarded by those who expect that it aims to change the 'real' world rather than those who are praying. Religion might be less easily accepted on another's authority, or as a technology that can achieve outcomes beyond itself than was previously the case. It is therefore parsimonious to look for the character of prayer within those who pray, by questioning those who do (or do not pray) about their understanding of what it involves. These questions, as well as their answers, may be biased by what people believe they ought to say, since the authenticity of prayer is guaranteed by indoctrination into a tradition which finds its meaning in the signs of God's action or failure to act, and in the expectations of what prayer can achieve in the quietness and privacy of thought, in a life of contemplative prayer, or in the passionate prayers of those in need. We should also remember that formal and ceremonial prayers accompany state occasions in some countries.

A casual use of 'prayer' is exemplified in an Australia Post advertisement for self-adhesive stamps that began, "Australia Post provides an answer to your prayers" (in May 1990). At another extreme is a definition of 'prayer' in the Concise Oxford Dictionary as a "solemn request or thanksgiving to God or [some other] object of worship." This definition accepts that a prayerful frame of mind is not necessarily linked to belief in God, or to any necessary effects, despite an implicit agreement about the events and other features of life for which prayer is appropriate, that contrast against whatever prayer is not expected to influence in physical, natural, or spiritual domains. Although the directly empirical tests of prayer have been taken seriously, their concreteness itself cuts against an expectation that prayers are always answered. As Szasz noted (1974), if one wishes to research the powers attributable to holy water, it does not help to analyze it chemically.

The apparent failures of prayer might carry some sense of shame about what was hoped for, with reports constrained by a sense of privacy. Rather than expecting some prayers to be effective, and having to explain why others seem to fail, or arguing that God always answers prayer and that on occasions the answer will be 'no,' we should look more closely at the talk or disclosures about how prayer has done.

Wittgenstein's cynicism contrasted the prayer that "two and two should make five" against a more common prayer that, "If I was sure I would die tonight I would repent at once." Such an urgent uncertainty gives prayer a peculiar status that is matched by Pascal's wager: "Let us weigh the gain and the loss involved by wagering that God exists. Let us estimate these two possibilities: if you win, you win all; if you lose, you lose nothing. Wager then, without hesitation, that He does exist" (Pensées, number 343). Pascal, who was much concerned with reason, also stressed the role of faith, in that "our religion is both wise and foolish" (at number 469) with "the two foundations, one inward, the other outward: grace and miracles—both supernatural" (number 470).

Our understanding of prayer seems to rely on anecdote, analogy, and experience, rather than on any abstract evidence about it, and although psychoses or other mental illnesses are likely to have disintegrative effects, religions play an integrative role. So Szasz noted that "when you speak to God, it is prayer. When God speaks to you it is schizophrenia," while Wagnick (1980, p. 336) observed that "the mystic provides the example of the method whereby the inner and outer may be joined; the schizophrenic, the tragic result when they are separated." This had not, however, stopped some psychiatrists and others from over-generalizing their diagnostic criteria, detecting psychotic signs in *any* religious thinking, without regard to the social contexts that support and interpret what will seem psychotic when it is detached from them, until the social sanctions for belief and behavior were appreciated.

Talk about God's activity and answers to prayer is therefore not to be understood directly, but as a 'way' or 'manner' of speaking about how the purposes of God might have been apprehended, expressed, or put into effect in a profound way (cf Wiles, 1974, p. 38). In that sense, claims on religious language must be understood with reference to the historical and scientific beliefs of a particular time, and the speaker's knowledge of that. As Davis (1989, p. 227) put it, "The word 'supernatural,' with its overtones of crude interventionism and magic, is therefore largely inappropriate; divine activity does not *violate* the natural order, but rather works with it not through it." But even that construction depends on the mental and linguistic models that represent the world and our actions through their own traditions. So Davis deferred to the evidence from psychological theories that implicate cognitive need, social learning, social deprivation, and projection, to explain religious and other objectifications or reactions to the external realities that we internalize.

No attempt has been made here to develop arguments for or against theism, since the goal was to explore the meanings of prayer and how it is possible to make sense of them, or understand them. The religious implications of that must be identified by others, whatever attitudes to prayer might be held. Belief in the efficacy of prayer is, however, more likely to be a result of teaching than of spontaneous beliefs about life after death, a loving God, recognition of the "divine spark," or from some other "cumulative argument" (Davis, 1989, p. 249). Except for those claiming a sudden conversion, growth and change in beliefs about the practice of prayer is to be expected, as our knowledge and prejudices about it are revised by the credibility of our own experiences. The accounts of that are unlikely to capture the classical descriptions of an Other working through us, or of the ways we might talk to ourselves (or others) when we need to be delivered from danger. We could find a parallel process in clinical or other professional consultations, when we share information about ourselves, guided by the relationship with those other people. There are, therefore, crucial differences psychologically between prayers modeled on reflection or self-discovery, and those in a more conversational or interactive mode. This immediately helps to understand the different forms of address in prayer, the politeness that pervades it, and the communications that become prayers, whether in church or not.

The current emphasis in health psychology on coping derived from the fact that the predominant causes of death have changed from infectious to chronic conditions like coronary artery disease and cancer, which are thought to implicate lifestyle as a risk factor and psychosocial events or threatening environmental processes. The interest in, and evidence for, the importance of coping skills has recently cumulated, and religious coping is now well-established in this literature (Pargament et al, 1990), bypassing the earlier reliance on testimonies to, or claims on the direct efficacy of prayer, and conflicts between the promises of scripture and miraculous claims on singular events. Our reliance on the statistical trends in numerous social surveys is well-established, and they carry great indicative weight. But religions themselves give more emphasis to commitment, claims by an institution, and personal insight, than to what an "average individual" might expect to experience or be able to do with prayer.

Conflicts over the place or usefulness of prayer could be similar to those in medicine that surround the specificity of a disease, which is independent of the patients' own judgments. While that has recently changed with the development of knowledge about the immune system, beliefs about prayer (and the questions individuals are asked about it) have assumed generic properties, especially in the 'stages' in its development from what is immature and concrete to abstract formulations of what prayer involves. Those issues are involved in the politics of prayer and take us back to Pascal's wager, and whether we could ever find enough evidence to reject the null hypothesis as it applies to prayer. Our problems with prayer are therefore psychological or philosophical. They only become practical when they involve a search for the meaning or significance of life. But we know too little about how judgments about prayer are made, or the evidence that resolves disputes about them, except in the most schematic way (cf Brown, 1994).

Attempts to resolve those questions will keep the psychology of prayer alive, if only through a search for its uses and socially constructed meanings (Bruner, 1990). If we want controlled data about that we should know how to predict whether a person will pray, and we must look for events in the real world that will elicit it. This requires an ecological perspective on the religious constraints on the data, and the conclusions they support. In that sense prayer, like perception, might be for 'doing,' just as a hole is for digging (Gibson, 1979, p. 226).

The meaning of prayer is limited if it is thought to be instrumental rather than attuned to a sense of otherness, or to a meditative solitude (Neitz and Spickard, 1990). Places, contexts, and the environments that frame or trigger experiences that give prayer its meaning are, like religious traditions themselves, carrying acts of prayer. Mere repetition could help to constitute those experiences, just as healing processes that are grounded in religion can generate a sense of harmony between self, society, and the world (Spickard, 1991).

To reduce any prayer to superstition, magic, suggestion, emotion, or primary needs neglects the social and religious traditions that define their meaning and their performative character. The impact of prayer must be more experiential than behavioral, with its complementarity between external and internal events, constraints and needs. Clements (1985, p. 13) asked what should be the most important or central goal of prayer. He answered, "That it is praise to God." As a discovery process, praise is matched by petition as a form of *self* discovery, and intercession as a deepening awareness of the place that other people have in our lives and in the world.

Chapter Fourteen

Postscript

The material presented here has been constrained by its psychological focus, which limits the issues that have been examined. The most important of these concern what a new senior high school syllabus in New South Wales identifies as the "Ways of Holiness." That syllabus prescribes the following content

*different ways of prayer and expressions of spirituality,
*concepts of the purpose and meaning of holy living,
*the relationships of the pursuit of holiness to everyday living,
*the ordinary way of holiness,
*a knowledge of the different forms of prayer and their place in everyday lives of believers,
*the cultural and religious influences on the ways of holiness practiced in two religious traditions.

While those paths are found, and justified in sacred writings, they must be realized in practice (and in its neglect), to which each person brings something of themselves and perhaps their needs, as they find that praying itself isn't always enough (cf Horton and Williamson, 1971). We all live in multiple worlds, with separate demands and prescriptions to which we respond.

It is unlikely that the range of prayers can be reduced to a single psychological explanation, or that psychological concepts will satisfy those who accept an objective God, rather than God's subjective reality. Yet both groups might expect that the functions, uses, or experience of prayer are more important than its mode of operation. While Taylor et al (1991) found that a belief in one's personal control is generally adaptive, reducing anxiety and depression, control by others yielded mixed results that depended, in their study of coping with illness, on the prognosis. That those with a good prognosis benefited from a sense of vicarious (if concurrent) control shows the crucial role of outcomes there. They might also be an important feature of prayer, if

252

it is used, not so much against present threats but future set-backs.

It is unlikely that one psychological theory will ever hold sway over prayer: if one were to be accepted it would of necessity be more ideological than strictly psychological, unless it related to social or contextual factors rather than to sets of 'mental' processes by themselves. We must recognize that prayer *is* an accepted practice that carries varied meanings, 'doing' different things at its surface and deeper levels, that have religious, psychological and commonsense implications. In these analyses we should disregard explanations in terms of illusions or fantasies, since they are not specific to religion. Yet a major problem with prayer is the apparent ease with which it can be criticized on one hand, and practiced on the other. In this sense prayer may not be a 'thing' or even a phenomenon, but something that is to be 'done.' The reality of prayer rests on the fact that people pray, and do so with varied intentions. What they actually pray for could be irrelevant, although a mature petition might be, "Lord have mercy."

Common psychological issues have focused on how people come to pray, what supports or sustains their prayer, and how it develops. While answers to those questions might be found by looking at the role of prayer in everyday life, that is highly variable and we must find data, if at least some psychological conclusions are to be supported. That Pargament, Steele, and Tyler (1979) found that satisfaction of Church members with their congregation have both negative and positive consequences, with those indicating greater satisfaction having a greater sense of control by God, and lower levels of efficacy and coping skills. This could be one 'price' that might have to be paid for aligning oneself with a religious orthodoxy (cf Deconchy, 1991).

Following Foucault (1988), prayer might therefore be understood as more like a technology of self than a way to access God, granted the confessional nature of religious institutions, and uncertainty about what God might be like. Foucault's analysis of sex, with its "strict rules of secrecy, decency, and modesty so that sexuality is related in a strange and complex way both to verbal prohibition and to the obligation to tell the truth, of hiding what one does, and of deciphering who one is" (Foucault, p. 16), could also apply to prayer. But what must we renounce if we are to pray, or to prepare for prayer? Foucault might answer that by asking, "What must one know about oneself in order to be willing to renounce anything?" and he stressed our ignorance of the history of the 'real practices' of self, within Christianity, for example. He noted that "the hermeneutics of the self has been confused with theologies of the soul—concupiscence, sin, and the fall from grace. A hermeneutics of the self has been so strongly diffused across Western culture that it is hard to isolate or separate it from our spontaneous experiences."

The other social technologies that Foucault examined cover material production, systems of signs and signification, and the power of others who dominate our conduct, so that we are objectivized. One implication of that analysis is the extent to which the practice of prayer can generate a form of consciousness that obscures our awareness of self, despite the claims that it brings us closer to an awareness of 'reality.' But it is hard to know the 'truth' about that (or any) reality, since the technologies of self have their 'effects' on body, mind, thought, actions, and ways of being, as accepted goals of prayer, especially when our relation with God is personal rather than social or 'causal.' The technologies of power control the conduct of individuals through semiotic and linguistic meanings, in which Christian morality "makes self-renunciation the condition for salvation" (Foucault, 1988, p. 22). That goal has been pursued in and out of monasteries, with a spiritual director, guide, or a guru who detects and shapes what we should do, since "the self must constitute self through obedience" (p. 45). If the goal is "permanent contemplation of God," Foucault stresses three possible types of self examination that are available "through thoughts in correspondence to reality (Cartesian)," by following rules (Seneca), or "with respect to the relation between the hidden thought and an inner impurity" found in Christian doctrine, because "there is something hidden in ourselves and we are always in a self-illusion which hides the secret" (p. 48). In that statement of how 'unconscious' attitudes might be construed, Foucault stresses a continuity in the negative psychological readings of Christian practice. Other readings yet to be verified offer other alternatives to 'suggestion' as an earlier interpretation that identified but also controlled prayer, as if petitionary or intercessory prayer were its only form.

Foucault dichotomizes the self-disclosures of early Christianity into the penitence of a sinner and their penance, and in renunciation and obedience to Another. This analysis neglects the other forms of self-control that align with prayer, while holding that verbalization is crucial, being used "without renunciation of the self but to constitute, positively, a new self" (p. 49). Foucault takes the recognition of that as a "decisive break" in the development of the human sciences. I wonder which other features of modern psychological practice and theory will be found to have such profound effects, although the importance of our coping repertoires, and the process-oriented theories of counseling are increasingly recognized. So Tice (1992) found that our attitudes are more likely to change "by internalizing public behavior than by internalizing behavior that is identical but lacks the interpersonal context" that can be given by religion.

A crucial feature of religions is their shared and interpersonal character or alignments, not only in their doctrines. These social features can, however, be obscured by the individualistic or personal orientations like those to be found in some forms of Protestantism. Tice also noted that when we have a "choice about making the self-portrayal, drawing on episodes from one's own past rather than relying on a yoked (provided) script and expecting future interaction with the audience all increased the internalization of a public behavior." The importances of our own coping or 'self-help' skills readily aligns with prayer. It could be this perspective, rather than that involving the control by others that was stressed by Foucault, that should be used to understand and teach about prayer. Teaching that, whether explicitly or implicitly, involves modeling and example. The effects are more reasonably understood in those terms, than as a 'natural' response, or as a reaction to externally imposed demands.

Prayer must be seen as one of the ways in which we can take care of ourselves. This is facilitated by casting it within a social or religious tradition that directs (and might constrain) the content of whatever self-directed thoughts are expressed in prayer.

Acknowledgements

After initially accepting the opinion that prayer had been neglected by psychologists of religion, conversations with Robert Thouless when he visited Australia from England following his retirement from Cambridge in 1962 sharpened my awareness of the problems that it presents. A few papers on the nature of religious thought, and the development of beliefs about the appropriateness and efficacy of prayer resulted from these discussions. The arguments in those papers were greatly helped by Andre Godin's editorial advice and support. He later became a friend. As my academic duties became more pressing, I put the psychology of religion aside for several years. On returning to it I focused primarily on religious belief, until a letter 'out-of-the-blue' from James Michael Lee asked if I would write this book for his Religious Education Press. I willingly accepted that task, which took my attention back to the early work on prayer.

It has taken a long time to prepare this manuscript because I was not confident that I was familiar enough with the practice of prayer to deal with it quickly. I have had many discussions with people inside and outside the Church and an extensive correspondence with Emma Shackle in London. We even considered joint authorship. But our differences of opinion meant that we made little progress. Emma and I have, however, continued to talk about prayer, and we have prepared the annotated bibliography in Appendix I and a joint paper contrasting the attitudes to prayer among schoolgirls and a group of middle-aged women who were meeting regularly for prayer. Emma is now involved with a study of those who follow the Spiritual Exercises of St Ignatius. I am grateful for her support, but I am uncertain how much of my argument she will agree with.

My debates with others may have validated their prejudice that psychology is the queen of the voyeuristic sciences. "Where do you come from in writing on prayer?" was one of the challenges I encountered. Another letter said that, "We will think of you—indeed 'pray' for you. You will no doubt write about it and we will 'do' it." But the only way to understand what prayer means, why it is practiced, and what it might achieve is in conversation with those who accept its validity. Any psychologist working sympathetically with religious material for a "psychology of religion" rather than a "religious psychology" must be prepared for criticism from all sides.

I could not list all who have helped me, whether positively or negatively, although I have relied heavily on Dorothy Brown's knowledge of Anglican traditions and her ability to remember and reconstruct fragments from it and other traditions. My reliance on David Wulff's (1991) book will be obvious, although some disagreements might be found by those who would compare our attitudes. James Michael Lee has tolerated a late typescript that was prepared most ably, and I hope with some interest, by Maxine Mackellar, my secretary in the School of Psychology at the University of New South Wales. I am grateful for that University's continued support of my research. My research assistant, Paul Adamson, analyzed some of the data and pursued many references. Gail Huon in the School of Psychology helped with her knowledge of counseling and gave advice about the analogues of prayer and the relevance of psychology to understanding what those who pray might be doing. I am also indebted to Anna Wierzbicka, David Turner, and Charles Creegan for the essays that they prepared so willingly.

An event that precipitated the completion of this book has been my appointment as Director of the Religious Experience Research Centre at Westminster College in Oxford, England. Readers who would like to debate any points I have made could write to me there.

Annotated Bibliography on the Psychology of Prayer

EMMA SHACKLE AND L.B. BROWN

This list does not claim to be exhaustive, and it is almost exclusively concerned with prayer in Christian traditions and in the English language. In preparing it, we tried to put the entries into separate categories, but found it hard to draw consistent boundaries, so the list is arranged alphabetically, with a few introductory notes. Other useful bibliographies are in Capps, Rambo & Ransohoff (1976), who cover "Prayer and Worship" on pages 129-134, Finney & Malony (1985a), and embedded in Wulff (1991). Van de Kemp's (1984) bibliography notes especially books on prayer by Strong (1909), Stolz (1913, 1923), Heiler (1918), Felix (1924) on the Sacraments, O'Brien (1927) on the Mass, Hodge (1931), Carter (1934) also on the Sacraments, Lee (1956), and Moore (1956). Suggestions about our omissions will be welcomed.

1. G.A. Coe (1916) in the *The psychology of religion* presented a "Topical bibliography" for the psychology of prayer in the following terms: "A brief classified bibliography of history and forms of prayer will be found in Marett's (1903) article 'Prayer,' in the *Encyclopaedia Britannica*. 'On the origins of prayer,' see Farnell (1905), Lecture IV, 'The Evolution of Prayer from Lower to Higher Forms'; Marrett (1909, chap. ii: 'From Spell to Prayer'), Ames (1910, chap. 5, viii); Wundt (1910-1915) (Vol. 3, last volume, pp. 449-459). On prayer as a present-day problem of Christians, see Coe (1916, chap. xi); Fosdick (1915); Ames (1915, 9). On the psychological structure and functions of prayer, see Strong (1906, 1909); Pratt (1910, 5); Calkins (1911, 6); Ranson (1904); Beck (1906); Hartshorne (1913)."

2. Books of direct relevance to the psychology of prayer include Godin

(1985), Heiler (1932), Hodge (1931), Pratt (1921), Stolz (1913, 1923), and Watts & Williams (1988).

3. Psychologically relevant philosophies of prayer are by Brummer (1984), and Phillips (1965).

4. Except for Mallory (1977), Pahnke & Richards (1966), Tart (1988), Underhill (1911), Van der Lans (1987), Von Hugel (1908), and West (1987), references to meditation and mysticism have not been included, largely because of the fuzzy boundaries between those practices and prayer, and no recent analyses of 'spirituality' are referred to.

5. Religious psychologies of prayer have not been included, except for Saliers (1980) and Ulanov & Ulanov (1985), papers from the *Review for Religious* by Clarke (1983), Helminiak (1983), and O'Connor (1975), and references to the current fashion for religious psychologists to rely on personality types, for example in Bunker (1991), Keating (1987), Metz & Burchill (1987), Michael & Morrisey (1984) and Thesing (1990). Modern approaches to spiritual direction are to be found in Culligan (1982), Leech (1977), May (1982), and Thornton (1984). Pennebaker (1990) is about the psychology of confession.

6a. The 15 empirical studies of prayer reviewed at length by Finney & Malony (1985a) cover: Brown (1966), Brown (1968), Carson & Huss (1979), Elkind, Anchor & Sandler (1979), Galton (1873), Godin & Van Rooey (1959), Goldman (1964), Long, Elkind & Spilka (1967), Mallory (1977), Parker & St Johns (1957), Sacks (1979), Sajwaj & Hedges (1973), Surwillo & Hobson (1978), Thouless & Brown (1964), and Welford (1947a).

6b. Other empirical studies in our list, which are typically based on survey data, include Beck (1906/7), Byrd (1988), Dubois-Dumee (1983), Carlson, Bacaseta & Simonton (1988), Duke & Johnson (1984), Finney & Malony (1985c), Francis & Brown (1990, 1991), Gronbaek (1969), Hood, Morris & Watson (1989), Imoda (1991), Jannsen, Hart & Draak (1989, 1990), Joyce & Welldon (1965), Krieger (1976), Loehr (1959), Lovekin & Malony (1977), Moore (1956), Morse & Allan (1912/13), Poloma & Gallup (1991a), Poloma & Pendleton (1991b), Poloma & Pendleton (1991c), Pratt (1910/11), Richards (1991), Samarin (1959), Shackle & Brown (1992), Trier (1983), Van der Lans (1987), Ware, Knapp & Schwarzin (1989), Welford (1947b). Some of these studies entail systematic experimental designs (e.g. Byrd, 1988 and Joyce & Welldon, 1965) although Lenington (1979) could exemplify the *reductio* of such studies.

7. Developmental accounts include Brown (1966, 1968), Francis & Brown (1990, 1991), Godin & Van Rooey (1959), Goldman (1964), Long, Elkind & Spilka (1967), Scarlett and Perriello (1991), and Thouless & Brown (1964).

8. The medical literature has several papers by F.J. Keefe and colleagues (Rosenstiel & Keefe, 1983, Keefe & Dolan, 1986, Crisson & Keefe, 1988). Brown & Nicassio (1987), Parker & Brown (1983), and Parker, Brown & Blignault (1986) identified prayer as a coping strategy, while J.C. Parker et al (1989) refer to prayer as a form of self control in the treatment of pain asso-

ciated with medical and psychiatric conditions. Galanter et al (1991) surveys its explicit uses in psychiatric practice.

9. Since swearing and taking oaths are sacrilegious and the opposite of prayer, for the sake of completeness the work by Brody (1975), Graves (1927), Chastaing (1976) could have been cited. Gilles de la Tourette's syndrome (or coprolalia) brings swearing into the psychiatric clinic (Fernando, 1976), and with some literary (or religious) license we include glossolalia or "speaking in tongues" here, which some accept as religiously valid and others as regressive. These dualities are commonplace in the phenomenology of religion, as Malony & Lovekin (1985) and Samarin (1972) note.

10. Marsh (n.d.) lists "all the prayers" in the Bible, while Clements (1985) examined 25 of them in detail. A useful collection is by Appleton (1982), and prayers of the Syriac fathers have been translated by Brock (1987) and the *Philokalia* by Kadlovbovsky & Palmer (1951/1992). The best account of Muslim devotions is in Padwick (1961), and some prayers written by children are in Durran (1987) and Marshall & Hample (1977). None of the almost innumerable religious manuals on how to pray has been referred to.

11. Unpublished studies and those, like Johnson & Spilka (1991) or Pargament et al (1990) in which prayer is identified primarily as a part of religion, or when it is used as an index of religiousness or as a resource (Neighbours et al, 1983), or that refer to it in passing (Lash, 1988) or from another social science perspective (Gill, 1987) have not been covered systematically.

****

Ames E.S. (1909) *The Psychology of Religious Experience*. London: Constable. (A reprint of this book in 1973 is available.)

An early classic.

Anonymous (1991) *Meditations on the Tarot: A Journey Into Christian Hermetism*. Rockport, Massachussetts: Dorset Element Books. (First published in a German translation from the French, 1972.)

A modern presentation of the ancient tradition of hermetic prayer.

Appleton, G. (Ed.) (1985) *The Oxford Book of Prayer*. Oxford University Press.

A collection of prayers from many sources.

Bearon, L.B., & Koenig, H.G. (1990) "Religious cognitions and use of prayer in health and illness." *The Gerontologist, 30*(2), 249-253.

A study of the use of prayer by 40 adults aged 65-74, which found that the least educated respondents and the Baptists were most likely to pray, that prayer is used for symptoms that are serious and that prayer and medical help-seeking are not mutually exclusive.

Beck, F.O. (1906) "Prayer: A study in its history and psychology." *American Journal of Religious Psychology and Education*, 2(1), 107-21.

A principled analysis of the history of prayer with a report of the data in answer to seventeen main questions. Beck's study was replicated by Shackle and Brown (1992).

Belshaw, G.P.M. (1972) "Prayer and personality." *Saint Luke's Journal of Theology, 16,* 57-67.

Cited in Capps et al (1976).

Bill-Harvey, D. et al (1989) "Methods used by urban, low-income minorities to care for their arthritis." *Arthritis Care and Research, 2*(2), 60-64.

Found that "Prayer (92%), equipment (70%) and heat (33%) were reported as 'most helpful' for the blacks. Hispanics reported prayer (50%) heat (40%) and topical ointments as 'most helpful.'"

Bowman, G.W. (1969) *The Dynamics of Confession.* Richmond VA: John Knox Press.

Cited in Capps et al (1976).

Brock, S. (1987) *The Syriac Fathers on Prayer and the Spiritual Life.* Kalamazoo, Michigan: Cistercian Publications, Inc.

The prayer of the "Syriac Orient," as distinguished from that of the "Latin West" and the "Greek East."

Brody, M. (1975) "Kol Nidre and the role of denial in depression." *Mental Health and Society, 2* (3-6), 151-160.

A Judaic perspective.

Brown, G.K., & Nicassio, P.M. (1987) "Development of a questionnaire for the assessment of active and passive coping strategies in chronic pain patients." *Pain, 31,* 53-64.

Identifies praying for relief as a form of passive coping with chronic pain.

Brown, L.B. (1966) "Egocentric thought in petitionary prayer: A cross-cultural study." *Journal of Social Psychology, 68,* 197-210.

When the responses of children aged 12-17 in the USA. Australia and New Zealand about the appropriateness and efficacy of prayer for seven separate situations were compared, consistant age-related trends away from causal efficacy but not for appropriateness were found within each culture.

Brown, L.B. (1968) "Some attitudes underlying petitionary prayer." In Godin, A. (Ed.) *From Cry to Word* (pp. 65-84). Brussels: Lumen Vitae Press.

A confirmatory replication and extension of Brown (1966) to cover the reasons offered for success or failure of prayer.

Brummer, V. (1984) *What Are We Doing When We Pray?: A Philosophical Enquiry.* London: SCM Press.

Argues that "in praying, the believer aims at really establishing, restoring and acknowledging his fellowship with God." (p. 113).

Bunker, D.E. (1986) "Ignatian Spirituality in the work of Morton Kelsey." *Journal of Psychology and Theology, 14*(3), 203-212.

Shows that Kelsey treats the Ignatian Spiritual Exercises as a traditional kataphatic spirituality incorporating a variety of prayer practices.

Bunker, D.E. (1991) "Spirituality and the four Jungian functions." *Journal of Psychology and Theology, 19*(1), 26-34.

Relates Jung's types to the devotional life, concluding that "we must bring to prayer the totallity of our personality" and that Jung's theory provides a way to help individuals identify their most suitable prayer forms.

Byrd, R.C. (1988) "Positive therapeutic effects of intercessory prayer in a Coronary Care Unit population." *Southern Medical Journal, 81* (7 July), 826-829.

Discussed by Poloma and Gallup (1991) on p. 12. This study was accepted by Wulff, but Spilka criticizes it on medical grounds.

Calkins, M.W. (1911) "The nature of prayer." *Theological Review, 6,* 489-500.

One of the first women psychologists writing on prayer.

Capps, D. (1982) "The psychology of petitionary prayer." *Theology Today, 39,* 130-141.

A principled interpretation of petitionary prayer as a communicative act or transaction with God, based on a 'co-orientation' that is analogous to non-verbal processes within family life, giving us freedom to express our desires.

Capps, D., Rambo, L., & Ransohoff, P. (1976) *Psychology of Religion: A Guide to Information Sources.* Detroit, Michigan: Gale Research Company.

An extensive bibliography in which are embedded several references to prayer.

Carlson, C.R., Bacaseta, P.E., & Simonton, D.A. (1988) "A controlled evaluation of devotional meditation and progressive relaxation." *Journal of Psychology and Theology, 16* (4), 362-368.

A study discussed by Poloma and Gallup (1991) on p. 12. Thirty-six participants were divided equally and by sex into three groups to study the effect of "devotional meditation" and progressive relaxation compared with a waiting list control. The hypothesis that devotional meditation could generate positive effects similar to progressive relaxation was partially confirmed.

Carroll, M.P. (1987) "Praying the rosary: The anal-erotic origins of a popular Catholic devotion." *Journal for the Scientific Study of Religion, 26*(4), 486-498.

Suggests that "praying the rosary is appealing because it represents the disguised gratification of repressed anal-erotic desires." See also Carroll & Capps (1988).

Carroll, M.P., & Capps. D. (1988) "Praying the rosary." *Journal for the Scientific Study of Religion, 27*(3), 429-441.

Capps interviews Carroll about readers' reaction to his psychoanalytic interpretation of "praying the rosary."

Carson, V., & Huss, K. (1979) "Prayer, an effective therapeutic and teaching tool." *Journal of Psychiatric Nursing, 17*, 34-37.

Carter, F.C. (1934) *Psychology and Sacraments.* London: Williams & Norgate.

"God is the great 'Hetero-Suggestor' and the Sacraments are means by which he sends the stream of his grace into the human soul" (van de Kemp, 1984).

Cary-Elwes, C. (1986) *Experiences With God: A Dictionary of Spirituality and Prayer.* London: Sheed & Ward.

Unpretentious dictionary of concepts, people and practices in the major traditions.

Chansou, J. (1927) *Etude de psychologie religieuse: Sur les sources et l'efficacite de la priere dans l'experience Chretienne.* Paris: M. Riviere.

In Capps et al (1976).

Ciccone, D.S., & Grzesiak, R.C. (1984) "Cognitive dimensions of chronic pain." *Social Science and Medicine, 19*, 1339-1345.

A broad analysis of cognitive-behavioral interventions in the treatment of pain from which a specific role for prayer is developed.

Clarke, T.E. (1983) "Jungian types and forms of prayer." *Review for Religious*, 42(5), 661-676.

A classical Jungian analysis of types.

Clements, R.E. (1985) *The Prayers of the Bible*. London: SCM Press.

An insightful exegesis of 25 prayers, from Abraham to St John the Divine.

Coats, R.H. (1920) *The Reality of Prayer*. London.

A commentary.

Culligan, K. (1982) "Toward a contemporary model of spiritual direction: A comparative study of St John of the Cross and Carl Rogers." In Sullivan, J. (Ed.) *Carmelite Studies: Contemporary Psychology and Carmel* (pp. 95-167). Washington DC: ICS Studies.

Formulates a "theoretical model for guiding practice and research in spiritual direction" (p. 155).

David, J.P., Ladd, K., & Spilka, B. (1992) "The multidimensionality of prayer and its role as a source of secondary control." Paper at the Centennial Convention of the APA, Washington, DC, August.

Identifies scales to measure prayers of confession, petition, thanksgiving, ritual, meditation, self-improvement, intercession, and habit.

Davis, T.N. (1986) "Can prayer facilitate healing and growth?" *Southern Medical Journal*, 79(6), 733-735.

A personal testimony that a prayer of confession had greater benefit than 'nine years of psychoanalytically oriented therapy.'

Donaghue, Q. & Shapiro, C. (1984) *Bless me, Father, for I Have Sinned: Catholics Speak Out About Confession*. Toronto: McClelland and Stewart.

A compilation of autobiographical narratives.

Dubois-Dumee, J.P. (1983) "A Renewal of Prayer." Brussels, *Lumen Vitae*, 38 (3), 259-274.

The editor of the journal 'Prier' reports a survey of 3000 respondents which supports the view that "the feeling for prayer has not died, but that its form has changed appreciably."

Duke, J.T., & Johnson, B.L. (1984) "Spiritual well-being and the consequential dimension of religiosity." *Review of Religious Research*, 26 (1), 59-72.

This study found a weak relationship between prayer and the consequential dimensions of religion.

Durran, M. (1987) *Dear God if I Ruled the World: Children's Prayers and Letters to God*. Basingstoke: Marshall and Pickering.

More children's prayers.

Edwards, J.C. (1982) *Ways of Praying*. London: CTS.

Defines prayer as "loving attention to God" and identifies 11 'prayer-styles' appropriate to different 'presences' of God.

Elkind, D., Anchor, K.N., & Sandler, H.M. (1979) "Relaxation training and prayer behavior as tension reduction techniques." *Behavioral Engineering*, 5, 81-87.

Referred to by Finney & Malony (1985a).

Ellens, J.H. (1977) "Communication theory and petitionary prayer." *Journal of Psychology and Theology*, 5, 48-54.

Referred to by Finney & Malony (1985a).

Farnell, F.R. (1905) *Evolution of religion*. New York.

Refers to prayer.

Felix, Richard W. (1924) *Some Principles of Psychology as Illustrated in the Sacramental System of the Church*. Washington, D.C.: Catholic University of America.

"Felix, a Benedictine, wrote this dissertation under the direction of Edward Aloysius Pace, and focuses his psychological analysis on the visible signs of the Sacraments" (Van de Kemp, 1984, p. 131).

Finney, J.R., & Malony, H.N. (1985a) "Empirical Studies of Christian prayer: A review of the literature." *Journal of Psychology and Theology, 13*(2), 104-115.

Discusses 15 studies of prayer, all of which are listed here.

Finney, J.R., & Malony, H.N. (1985b) "Contemplative prayer and its use in psychotherapy: A theoretical model." *Journal of Psychology and Theology, 13*(3), 172-181.

Describes contemplative prayer as "an imaginative mental interaction between one's idea of oneself and one's idea of God," suggesting its use as an adjunct to psychotherapy.

Finney, J.R., & Malony, H.N. (1985c) "An empirical study of contemplative prayer as an adjunct to psychotherapy." *Journal of Psychology and Theology, 13*(4), 284-290.

A controlled study of nine people, each as their own control, practicing contemplative prayer within the context of psychotherapy, which gave "only moderate support" for the hypothesis that contemplative prayer has a psychotherapeutic value.

Fosdick, H.E. (1915) *The Meaning of Prayer.* New York.

Referred to in Coe's (1916, p. 355) bibliography.

Francis, L.J., & Brown, L.B. (1990) "The predisposition to pray: A study of the social influence on the predisposition to pray among eleven year old children in England." *Journal of Empirical Theology, 3*(2), 23-34.

Studied 4,948 eleven-year-olds in England. A path analysis showed the direct influence of the child's church attendance, parental church attendance, and denominational identity in predicting their disposition to pray.

Francis, L.J., & Brown, L.B. (1991) "The influence of home, church and school on prayer among sixteen-year-old adolescents in England." *Review of Religious Research, 33*(2), 112-122.

Found that the influence of the Church is stronger and that of the parents weaker in influencing the predisposition to pray of sixteen-year-olds than for eleven-year-olds.

Galanter, M., Larson, D., & Rubenstone, E. (1991) "Christian psychiatry: The impact of evangelical belief on clinical practice." *American Journal of Psychiatry, 148*, 90-95.

Reports judgments of the therapeutic value of prayer among psychiatrists belonging to the Christian Medical and Dental Society in the USA. They rated the "Bible and prayer" as more effective for treating grief reaction and alcoholism among "Christian believers" than either psychotropic medication or insight psychotherapy.

Galton, F. (1873) "Statistical inquiries into the efficacy of prayer." *Fortnightly Review, 18* (vol XII, no. LXVIII New Series), 125-135.

Found that despite the prayers for the Royal Family prescribed by the Church of England they did not live longer than others.

Gill, S.D. (1977) "Prayer as person: the performative force in Navaho prayer acts." *History of Religions, 17*(2), 143-157.

Identifies the constituents of a prayer text within its context, as a "religious act of curing" with pragmatic effects.

Gill, S.D. (1987) *Native American Religious Action: A Performative Approach to Religion*. Columbia SC: University of South Carolina Press.

An anthropological focus on Navaho prayer, as 'performance' and as 'person,' from pp. 89-128.

Godin, A. (1958) "Psychological growth and Christian prayer." *Lumen Vitae, 13*, 517-530.

A developmental theory.

Godin, A., & Van Rooey, B. (1959) "Immanent justice and divine protection." *Lumen Vitae, 14*, 129-148.

A classic study showing that children believe in the causal efficacy of prayer in the sense that the objects of petition are thought to be observably obtained.

Godin, A. (Ed.) (1968) *From Cry to Word: Contributions toward a Psychology of Prayer*. Brussels: Lumen Vitae Press.

Thirteen papers with an editorial introduction.

Godin, A. (1985) *The Psychological Dynamics of Religious Experience*. Birmingham, Alabama: Religious Education Press.

Argues that prayer is crucial for functional religious experiences, affective experiences of God, and transforming experiences in the Christian faith within the group and socio-political contexts that make them possible.

Goldman, R. (1964) *Religious Thinking From Childhood to Adolescence*. London: Routledge and Kegan Paul.

A pivotal analysis that changed the understanding and practice of children's readiness for religious teaching.

Griffith, E.E.H., & Mahy, G.E. (1984) Psychological benefits of Spiritual Baptist 'mourning.' *American Journal of Psychiatry, 141*(6), 769-773.

Interviewed twenty-three people in the West Indies who had taken part in a ceremony that involves prayer, fasting, and experiencing dreams and visions while in isolation. They claimed relief of depressed mood, ability to foresee and avoid danger, improved decision making, ability to communicate with God and meditate, and some physical cures.

Gronbaek, V. (1969) "Visuelle Vorstellungen im Gebetsleden alter Menschen." In C. Horgl, et al. *Wesen und Weisen der Religion* (pp. 115-131).

A paper within the Dorpat tradition that refers to "spontaneous visual representations experienced by the aging during prayer" (Wulff, 1991, p. 562).

Heiler, F. (1932) *Prayer*. (Translated by S. McComb (Ed.) and J. Edgar Park) London and New York: Oxford University Press (first published under the title *"Das Gebet: Eine Religionsgeschichliche und Religionspyschologische Untersuchung,"* Munich, 1918).

This "widely admired book on prayer, which is considerably abridged in the English translation, is chiefly a study in typology, . . . it is also a work of analysis, in Koepp's sense of teleological illumination" (Wulff, 1991, p. 532).

Helminiak, D.A. (1982) "How is meditation prayer?" *Review for Religious*, *11*(5), 774-782.

Stresses centering prayer and aligns it with Transcendental Meditation.

Hodge, A.J. (1931) *Prayer and its Psychology*. London: SPCK.

A PhD thesis that examines the nature and evolution of prayer, and its psychological interpretation in terms of instincts, suggestion and the 'new psychology' (meaning Freud and Jung).

Hood, R.W. Jr., Morris, R.J., & Watson, P.J. (1989) "Prayer experience and religious orientation." *Review of Religious Research, 31*(1), 39-45.

In a sample of 198 people who prayed or meditated, they found that "actual prayer experiences and not simply the interpretation of these experiences may differ between extrinsics and intrinsics."

Imoda, F. (1991) "Ejercicios y cambio de la personalidad. Significado de un limite." In *Alemany*, Carlos & Carcia-Monge, Jose A. (Eds.) *Psicologia y Ejercios Ignacianos* (pp. 271-286). Coleccion "Manresa" Mensajero-Sal-Terrae Bilbao & Santander.

A longitudinal study of a group of 100 novices which showed that the measured effects of the Exercises on both the 'mature' and 'immature' had disappeared within four years.

Janssen, J., de Hart, J., & den Draak, C. (1989) "Praying practices." *Journal of Empirical Theology, 2*(2), 28-39.

An account of the praying practices of Dutch youth. See also Stachel (1989) who reflects on the educational implications of these findings.

Janssen, J., de Hart, J., & den Draak, C. (1990) "A content analysis of the praying practices of Dutch youth." *Journal for the Scientific Study of Religion, 29*(1), 99-107.

A content-analysis of the prayers of some Dutch youth.

Johnson, P.E. (1953) "A psychological understanding of prayer." *Pastoral Psychology, 4*(36), 33-39.

Cited by Wulff (1991).

Johnson, S.C., & Spilka, B. (1991) "Coping with breast cancer: the role of clergy and faith. *Journal of Religion and Health. 30*(1), 21-33.

Directs attention to "prayer, Bible or other religious reading, counseling, talking about the church, family, the future, irrelevancies and the feeling that the pastor or chaplain understood the patient."

Jones, C., Wainwright, G., & Yarnold, E. (Eds.) (1986) *The Study of Spirituality*. London: SPCK.

A reference book.

Joyce, C.R.B., & Welldon, R.M.C. (1965) "The objective efficacy of prayer: A double blind clinical trial." *Journal of Chronic Diseases, 18*, 367-377.

A controlled experiment among hospital patients criticized on methodological grounds by Wulff, 1991, pp. 169-171.

Jung, C.G. (1940) "Lectures on the *Exercitia Spiritualia of Ignatius Loyola.*" *Modern Psychology* (Zurich), 4, 146-264.

A set of twenty lectures which come to "a new chapter in the history of the development and application of the great problem of the active imagination" taking "the '*Exercitia Spiritualia*' of Ignatius of Loyola as a parallel to the Eastern texts which we have been studying."

Kadlovbovsky, E., & Palmer, G.E.H. (translators) (1992) *Writings from the Philokalia on Prayer of the Heart*. London: Faber and Faber (first published 1951).

Writings on prayer by Fathers of the Eastern Church from the fourth to fourteenth century.

Keating, C.J. (1987) *Who We Are Is How We Pray: Matching Personality and Spirituality*. Mystic, Connecticut: Twenty-Third Publications.

Relates Myers-Briggs personality types to various kinds of prayer practice.

Kelsey, M.T. (1977) *The Christian and the Supernatural*. London: Search Press.

Deals with the borders between parapsychology and prayer.

Krause, N., & Van Tran, T. (1989) "Stress and religious involvement among older blacks." *Journal of Gerontology. 44*, 1, S4-13.

A nation-wide sample of older black Americans evaluated moderator, suppressor and buffering models of the relationships between religions and stress. Only the stress-buffering model was supported; and it was found that those with higher levels of subjective religiosity because of their religious convictions and frequent prayer reported greater feelings of personal control.

Krieger, D. (1976) "Healing by the 'laying on of hands' as a facilitator of bioenergetic changes." *Psychoenergetic Systems, 1*, 121-129

Kristeva, J. (1983) *Histoires D'Amour*. Paris: Denoel.

Includes feminist psychoanalytic reflections on the Stabat Mater.

Lash, N. (1988) *Easter In Ordinary: Reflections on Human Experience and the Knowledge of God*. London: SCM Press.

Discusses the theology of James and Von Hugel, among others, and argues "that the occurrence of redemptive community is a necessary condition of the possibility of prayer" (p. 252).

Leach, K. (1977) *Soul Friend: A Study in Spirituality*. London: Sheldon Press.

Discusses the place of spiritual direction in Christian prayer, relying on psychoanalytic principles.

Lee, R.S. (1956) *Psychology and Worship*. New York: Philosophical Library.

A psychoanalytic perspective.

Lefevre, P. (1981) *Understandings of Prayer*. Philadelphia, Pennsylvania: The Westminster Press.

Theological accounts, including the views of Barth, Tillich, Bonhoeffer, C.S. Lewis, and Thomas Merton, which tend to rely on psychology.

Lenington, S. (1979) "Effect of holy water on the growth of radish plants." *Psychological Reports, 45*, 381-2.

"Mean growth of 12 radish seeds in peat pots watered with holy water were not significantly different from that of 12 watered with tap water. Limitations on data were listed" (which included storing the water in an aluminium container)—Journal Abstract.

Lilliston, L., and Brown, P.M. (1981) "Perceived effectiveness of religious solutions to personal problems." *Journal of Clinical Psychology, 37*(1), 118-122.

Lilliston, L., Brown, P.M., & Schliebe, H.P. (1982) "Perceptions of religious solutions to personal problems of women." *Journal of Clinical Psychology, 38*(3), 546-549.

Two controlled vignette studies that manipulated the type of problem and types of solution, including prayer, finding that "religious solutions were less highly valued than the information solution," no difference in the utility of "church attendance, prayer and a group emphasizing intense emotion religious experiences" for a man, although for a target woman church or prayer were valued more than an emotional religious experience.

Loehr, F. (1959) *The Power of Prayer on Plants.* Garden City, NY: Doubleday.

Reports that plants given holy water thrived.

Long, D., Elkind, D., & Spilka, B. (1967) "The child's conception of prayer." *Journal for the Scientific Study of Religion, 6,* 101-109.

Found among 160 elementary school children that the concept of prayer develops in three stages, from a global concept (ages 5-7), to a concrete (ages 7-9) and then to an abstract concept (ages 9-12). Replicated by Worten and Dollinger (1986).

Lovekin, A.A., & Malony, H.N. (1977) "Religious glossolalia: A scientific longitudinal study of personality changes." *Journal for the Scientific Study of Religion, 16,* 383-393.

Found that experiences of glossolalia were not related to prior psychopathology, with each group in the study changing towards personality integration after three months, which may not have been due to speaking in tongues itself.

Malony, H.N., & Lovekin, A.A. (1985) *Glossolalia: Behavioral Science Perspectives on Speaking in Tongues.* New York: Oxford University Press.

An authoritative text.

Mallory, M.M. (1977) *Christian Mysticism: Transcending Techniques.* Amsterdam: VanGorcum Assen.

An intensive study of the prayer life of 54 Carmelites (44 were female) which found that "concentration in prayer depends on the degree of libidinal involvement rather than on the degree of intellectual alertness" (p. 64).

Marrett, R.R. (1903) "Prayer." In the *Encyclopedia Britannica* (11th Edition).

An early anthropological account.

Marrett, R.R. (1909) *The Threshold of Religion.*

Chap. 2 is on prayer, and there was a second edition in 1914.

Marsh, John B. (n.d.) *The book of Bible prayers: containing all the prayers recorded to have been offered in the Bible, with a short introduction to each.* (Published early in the 19th century). London: Simpkin and Marshall (57 pages).

Marshall, E., & Hample, S. (1975) *Childrens' Letters to God.* Glasgow: Collins/Fontana.

A set of prayers written by children.

May, G. (1982) *Care of Mind/Care of Spirit: The Psychiatric Dimensions of Spiritual Direction.* San Francisco: Harper & Row.

Discusses problems that lie between psychiatry and spirituality.

Meadow, M.J., & Kahoe, R.D. (1984) *Psychology of Religion: Religion in Individual Lives.* New York: Harper & Row.

This textbook defines prayer as "communication with a (presumed) Divine Other" (p. 113).

Menashe, A. (1983) *The Face of Prayer: Photographs.* New York: Alfred A. Knopf.

"A striking exploration of the facial expressions and other gestures of prayer" (Wulff, p. 534).

Metz, B., & Burchill, J. (1987) *The Enneagram and Prayer: Discovering Our True Selves Before God.* Denville, New Jersey: Dimension Books.

Relates the Enneagram (introduced from the East by Gurdjieff to identify personality traits) to various types of prayer practices.

Michael, C.P., & Morrisey, M.C. (1984) *Prayer and Temperament: Different Prayer Forms for Different Personality Types.* Charlottesville, Virginia: Open Door.

Discusses relationships between the Myers-Briggs and Keirsey-Bates temperament types and prayer form preferences through sensing-judging or perceiving and intuition-thinking or feeling.

Mitchell, C.E. (1989) "Internal locus of control for expectation, perception and management of answered prayer." *Journal of Psychology and Theology, 17* (1), 21-26.

A principled study of the extent to which locus of control interacts with different types of prayer.

Moore, T.V. (1956) *The Life of Man With God*. New York: Harcourt, Brace & Co.

Reports the results of a questionnaire study of contemplative prayer before Vatican II among 200 Roman Catholics, which we found could not be replicated in 1987 because attitudes among religious appear to have changed so much, making the earlier questions irrelevant.

Morse, J., & Allan, J. Jr. (1912/13) "The religion of one hundred and twenty six college students." *Journal of Religious Psychology, 6,* 175-194.

A careful analysis of the responses of 126 college students to 14 primary questions, the results of which "speak more eloquently than anything that can be said for or about them."

Muelder, W.G. (1957) "The efficacy of prayer." In Doniger, S. (Ed.) *Healing: Human and Divine* (pp. 131-143). New York: Association Press.

Cited by Wulff (1991).

Neighbours, H.W., et al (1983) "Stress, coping and Black mental health: preliminary findings from a national study." *Prevention in the Human Services 2*(3), 5-29.

Found that "prayer was an extremely important coping response used by blacks especially among those making less than $10,000, above the age of 55, and women."

O'Brien, J.A. (1927) *Modern Psychology and the Mass: A Study in the Psychology of Religion*. New York: Paulist Press, 32 pp.

Referred to by Van de Kemp (1984).

O'Connor, J.E. (1975) "Motives and expectations in prayer." *Review for Religious, 34*(3), 403-408.

Oser, R., & Gmünder, P. (1991) *Religious Judgement [sic]: A Developmental Approach*. Birmingham, Alabama: Religious Education Press.

A contemporary European perspective deeply grounded in a North American intellectual heritage.

Padwick, C. (1961) *Muslim Devotions*. London: SPCK.

An account of Islamic prayer based on the numerous manuals of Sufi devotion that are used in the Arabic-speaking world.

Pahnke, W.N., & Richards, W.A. (1966) "Implications of LSD and experimental mysticism." *Journal of Religion and Health, 5,* 175-208.

A notorious, controlled study also known as the "Good Friday Experiment."

Pargament, K.I., et al (1990) "God help me: (I): Religious coping efforts as predictors of the outcomes to significant negative life events." *American Journal of Community Psychology, 18*(6), 793-823.

Accepts that "prayer as a coping strategy may be functionally equivalent to passive avoidant coping strategies such as day dreaming, accepting fate, or wishful thinking."

Parker, G.B., & Brown, L.B. (1982) "Coping behaviors that mediate between life events and depression." *Archives of General Psychiatry, 39,* 1386-1391.

Identifies the repertoires of coping that mediate life events and depression and shows that prayer fits into self-directed problem solving.

Parker, G.B., Brown, L.B. and Blignault, I. (1986) "Coping behaviors as predictors of the course of clinical depression." *Archives of General Psychiatry, 43,* 561-565.

This predictive study confirmed the relevance of self-directed coping in a clinically depressed group.

Parker, W.R., & St. Johns, E. (1957) *Prayer Can Change Your Life.* Carmel, NY: Guideposts.

Referred to at length by Finney and Malony (1985a).

Patterson, D.T. (1927) *Great Prayers of the Bible.* London: Williams and Norgate.

Offers yet another classification of prayer. Those attributed to "Jesus and his friends" are set out in our Appendix II.

Pennebaker, J.W. (1990) *Opening Up: The Healing Power of Confiding in Others.* New York: Morrow.

Reviewed by M.R. Leary in *Contemporary Psychology* 1992, *37*(4), 290-29, who says that it "summarizes a 10-year research program on the consequences of confiding one's secrets and offers advice regarding how to use confession to enhance psychological and physical health."

Phillips, D.Z. (1965) *The Concept of Prayer.* London: Routledge & Kegan Paul.

A philosophical analysis of what it might mean for a person to talk to and depend on God, and how, in a community, prayer differs from superstition.

Poloma, M.M., & Gallup, G.H. Jr. (1991) *Varieties of Prayer: A Survey Report*. Philadelphia: Trinity Press International.

This Gallup survey across the USA explores the practice of prayer, and the socio-economic factors that influence it and its effects on behavior and attitudes, and on the larger society.

Poloma, M.M., & Pendleton, B.F. (1989) "Exploring types of prayer and the quality of life." *Review of Religious Research, 31,* 46-53.

Identifies meditative and verbal types of prayer, noting that measures of the frequency of prayer gloss over important questions about what we do when we pray.

Poloma, M.M., & Pendleton, B.F. (1991a) "The effects of prayer and prayer experiences on measures of well-being." *Journal of Psychology and Theology, 19*(1), 71-83.

Reports a Gallup survey in Akron, Ohio, which distinguished colloquial, petitional, ritual, and meditative prayer, each of which relates differently to well-being.

Poloma, M.M., & Pendleton, B.F. (1991b) *Religiosity and Well-Being: Exploring Neglected Dimensions of Quality of Life Research*. Lewiston, NY: Edwin Mellen Press.

Continues the important work of this group in Akron.

Pratt, J.B. (1910-11) "An empirical study of prayer." *American Journal of Religious Psychology and Education, 4,* 48-67.

Reports the answers to a questionnaire study of 170 people.

Pratt, J.B. (1921) *The Religious Consciousness: A Psychological Study*. New York: Macmillan.

Another classical account of prayer in its religious context.

Rahner, K. (1967) *Theology of the Spiritual Life. Theological Investigations, Volume Three*. London: Darton, Longman & Todd.

Contains a "spiritual dialogue at evening: on sleep, prayer and other subjects" between a priest and a doctor.

Ranson, S.W. (1904/5) "Studies in the Psychology of Prayer." *Journal of Religious Psychology, 2,* 129-142.

Identifies questions that a psychology of prayer and of religious experience might address.

Reichard, G. (1944) *Prayer: The Compulsive Word*. New York: J.J. Augustin.

Referred to by Gill (1987) as crucial in the move from an evolutionist to a symbolic and structural perspective on Navaho prayer.

Reik, T. (1955) "From spell to prayer." *Psychoanalysis, 3,* 3-26.

A classical analysis.

Relton, H.M. (1925) "The psychology of prayer and religious experience." In O. Hardman (Ed.) *Psychology and the Church* (pp. 55-102). London: Macmillan.

Referred to in Finney & Malony (1985a).

Richards, D.G. (1991) "The phenomenology and psychological correlates of verbal prayer." *Journal of Psychology and Theology, 19*(4), 354-363.

Churched and unchurched people completed a questionnaire which asked what they typically include in their prayers, finding that "the intensity of prayer experience was correlated positively with purpose in life, negatively with external locus of control, and positively with absorption."

Rohr, R. (1990) *Discovering the Enneagram: An Ancient Tool for a New Spiritual Journey*. New York: Crossroad.

A sufi method for prescribing individual's preferred forms of prayer or meditation.

Rosenberg, R. (1990) "The development of the concept of prayer in Jewish-Israeli children and adolescents." *Studies in Jewish Education, 5,* 91-129.

Referred to by Oser and Gmünder (1991, p. 39).

Rosentiel, A.K., & Keefe, F.J. (1983) "The use of coping strategies in chronic low back pain patients: Relationship to patient characteristics and current adjustment." *Pain, 17,* 33-44.

Aligns "directing attention or praying" with cognitive coping and suppression, and helplessness as major coping strategies that predict behavioral and emotional adjustment.

Sacks, H.I.. (1979) "The effect of spiritual exercises on the integration of the self-system." *Journal for the Scientific Study of Religion, 18,* 46-50.

A longitudinal study of 46 Jesuit novices before and after a 30 day retreat which found marginal changes toward a "'conscientious' level of development" after the exercises (cf Imoda, 1991).

Sajwaj, T., & Hedges, D. (1973) "A note on the effects of saying grace on the behaviour of an oppositional retarded boy." *Journal of Applied Behaviour Analysis, 6*, 711-712.

A single case study within an operant context, discussed in terms of the "multiple behavioral effects of prayer."

Saliers, D.E. (1980) *The Soul in Paraphrase: Prayer and the Religious Affections*. New York: Seabury.

A religious psychology of prayer that relies on the emotions of gratitude, holy fear, joy and suffering, and love.

Samarin, W.J. (1959) "Glossolalia as learned behaviour." *Canadian Journal of Theology, 15* (1), 60-64.

A linguist's analysis of glossolalic prayer.

Samarin, W.J. (1972) *Tongues of Men and Angels*. New York: Macmillan.

Well-informed and fascinating accounts of glossolalia, covering both actor and observer perspectives.

Saudia, T.L., et al (1991) "Health locus of control and helpfulness of prayer." *Heart and Lung, 20*, 1, 60-65.

A questionnaire completed the day before cardiac surgery showed that 96% used prayer as a helpful direct action coping mechanism to deal with the stress.

Scarlett, W.G., & Perriello, L. (1991) "The development of prayer in adolescence." in Oser, F.K., & Scarlett, W.G. *Religious Development in Childhood and Adolescence* (pp. 63-76). (Number 52 in *New directions for child development*.) San Francisco: Jossey-Bass.

Reports a developmental study of 89 Catholics in 7th, 9th and undergraduate stages, who wrote prayers appropriate to each of six vignettes, and answered four questions about prayer. The results show changes from direct through conditional requests to intimate expression of search, struggle and doubt, and are supported by the spontaneous prayers and answers to the closed questions.

Segond, J. (1911) *La Prière. Etude de Psychologie Religieuse*. Paris: Alcan. (Referred to by Pratt, 1921, p. 314).

An almost forgotten reference.

Sevensky, R.L. (1981) "Religion and illness: an outline of their relationship." *Southern Medical Journal*, 74(6), 745-750.

A religious psychologist's plea for empirical studies of prayer, and for its acceptance by clinicians.

Shackle, E., & Brown, L.B. (1994) "Steps towards a psychology of prayer." In Brown, L.B. (Ed.) *Religion, Personality and Mental Health*. New York: Springer Verlag.

A replication of Beck (1906) and comparisons between the attitudes of girls at a Catholic school near London and women in an ecumenical prayer group.

Shapiro, D.H., Jr. (1982) "Overview: Clinical and physiological comparison of meditation with other self-control strategies." *American Journal of Psychiatry, 139,* 267-274.

A review of the literature bearing on clinical and physiological comparisons of meditation with other self-control strategies.

Stachel, G. (1989) "Praying and religious education." *Journal of Empirical Theology, 2*(2), 40-45.

Reflects on the educational implications of the findings of Janssen, Hart & Draak (1989).

Stolz, K.R. (1913) *Autosuggestion in Private Prayer: A Study in the Psychology of Prayer*. Grand Forks, ND.

An early analysis of answered and unanswered prayers which accepts that prayer constructs a personality at one with God. Originally a thesis for the University of Iowa.

Stolz, K.R. (1923) *The Psychology of Prayer*. New York: Abingdon Press.

A second edition of Stolz (1913).

Strong, A.L. (1906/7) "The relation of the subconscious to prayer." *American Journal of Religious Psychology and Education*, pp.160-167.

With reference to Beck's data and manuals of prayer, Strong presents a classification of prayer in terms of those results.

Strong, A.L. (1909) *The Psychology of Prayer*. Chicago: University of Chicago Press.

Originally a PhD thesis on "Prayer from the standpoint of social psychology."

Super, C.W. (1908-9) "The psychology of Christian hymns." *American Journal of Religious Psychology and Education, 3,* 1-15.

An early analysis.

Surwillo, W.W., & Hobson, D.P. (1978) "Brain electrical activity during prayer." *Psychological Reports, 43,* 135-143.

Discussed by Finney and Malony (1985a).

Sutton, T.D., & Murphy, S.P. (1989) "Stressors and patterns of coping in renal transplant patients." *Nursing Research, 38*(1), 46-49.

Found that "Prayer and looking at the problem objectively were used most in coping with stress."

Swatos, W.H., Jr. (1982) "The power of prayer: A prolegomenon to the ascetical sociology." *Review of Religious Research, 24*(2), 153-163.

Examines the way in which religions are made available through the power of prayer.

Tamminen, K. (1991) *Religious Development in Childhood and Youth: An Empirical Study.* Helsinki: Suomalainen Tiedeakatemia.

Chapter 8 (p. 209-245) of this longitudinal (from 1974 to 1986) and very systematic Finnish study covers the definitions and experience of changes in prayer, its appropriateness, efficacy, and the ways in which it might work.

Tart, C.T. (1988) *Waking-Up: Overcoming the Obstacles to Human Potential.* Shaftesbury: Dorset Element Books.

A fashionable but well-informed psychological perspective.

Thesing, R.J. (1990) "The Myers-Briggs, Enneagram and Spirituality." In *Spirituality and Psychology, The Way* Supplement 69 (Autumn) (pp. 50-60). Heythrop College London.

Argues that these systems, considered "as aids to spiritual growth," are best seen as "tools for self-understanding, rather than for understanding others."

Thornton, M. (1984) *Spiritual Direction: A Practical Introduction.* London: SPCK.

Regards "spiritual direction" as "the application of theology to the life of prayer" (p. 1).

Thouless, R.H., & Brown, L.B. (1964) "Petitionary prayer: Belief in its appropriateness and causal efficacy among adolescent girls." In Godin, A. (Ed.) *From Religious Experience to Religious Attitude* (pp. 123-136). Brussels: Lumen Vitae Press.

This vignette study comparing superstitious beliefs and practices with prayer among girls aged 12-17, found that the circumstances of prayer rather than its object is believed to be important in determining its causal efficacy.

Tillyard, A. (1927) *Spiritual Exercises and Their Results: An Essay in Psychology and Comparative Religion*. London: SPCK.

After examining Hindu, Buddhist, Muslim and Christian meditations and spiritual exercises, she concludes that "recognizable states of mind" occur that "cannot be accurately classified" since these states of consciousness are similar in the devotees of all religions, while they differ in the interpretations given to them.

Trier, K.K., & Shupe, A. (1991) "Prayer, religiosity & healing in the heartland USA: A research note." *Review of Religious Research, 32*(4), 351-357.

One third of a random sample of Midwesterners regarded prayer as "an efficacious tactic for maintaining and restoring health, but not at the expense of conventional biomedical care."

Turner, J.A., & Clancy, S. (1986) "Strategies for coping with chronic low back pain: Relationship to pain and disability." *Pain, 24*, 355-364.

Showed that "increased use of praying and hoping strategies was significantly related to decreases in pain intensity."

Ulanov, A., & Ulanov, B. (1985) *Primary Speech: Psychology of Prayer.* London: SCM Press.

A "religious psychology" which claims that in prayer we assert "our own being."

Underhill, E. (1911) *Mysticism: A Study of the Nature and Development of Man's Spiritual Consciousness*. London: Methuen. (Revised 1930.)

A seminal book divided into "The Mystic Fact" and "The Mystic Way," with a developmental model of adult mystical prayer.

Van de Kemp, H. (1984) *Psychology and Theology in Western Thought 1672-1965: A Historical and Annotated Bibliography*. New York: Kraus International Publications.

Another good bibliography.

Van der Lans, J. (1987) "The value of Sundén's role-theory demonstrated and tested with respect to religious experiences in meditation." *Journal for the Scientific Study of Religion, 16*, 383-393.

Examines hypnosis, psychoanalysis, psychophysiology, cognitive processes, and role theory as explanations of meditation as a source of religious experience and presents the results of a study in which thirty-five people gave daily reports of their experiences over four weeks of practicing a Zen meditation exercise. The results were interpreted within the context of

Sundēn's role theory which considers religious experience to be "a specific kind of perception."

Von Balthaser, H.U. (1961) *Prayer*. London: Geoffrey Chapman (first published under the title, *"Das Betrachtende Gebet"* by Johannes Verlag in 1957).

Argues that "prayer . . . is communication in which God's word has the initiative and we, at first, are simply listeners" (p. 12).

Von Hugel, F. (1908) *The Mystical Element of Religion as Studied in Saint Catherine of Genoa and Her Friends*. London: J.M. Dent & Sons (Fourth impression 1961, James Clarke & Co)

A two-volume work about Catherine of Genoa (1447-1510) commencing with an introduction that discusses the elements of religion, as "Fact and Thing," as "Thought, System and Philosophy," and as "the Experimental and Mystical" (pp. 51/54).

Wakefield, G.S. (Ed.) (1983) *A Dictionary of Christian Spirituality*. London: SCM Press.

A work of reference.

Ware, R., Knapp, C.R., Schwarzin, H. (1989) "Prayer form preferences of Keirsey temperaments and psychological types." *Journal of Psychological Type, 17,* 39-42.

Keirsey's temperament and Jungian personality types were related to a Prayer Form questionnaire answered by 170 people with rather inconclusive results, although sensation-judging types preferred "structured prayer."

Watts, F., & Williams, M. (1988) *The Psychology of Religious Knowing*. Cambridge University Press.

Approaches the psychology of religion from the standpoint of cognitive psychology and discusses "the interpretation of experience" in prayer.

Welford, A.T. (1947a) "Is religious behaviour dependent on affect or frustration?" *Journal of Abnormal and Social Psychology, 42,* 310-319.

Another important study using a vignette procedure.

Welford, A.T. (1947b) "A psychological footnote to prayer." *Theology Today, 3*(4), 498-501.

Reports a study which found a "small but reliable tendency for emotional stability to increase with the number of situations in which the subjects said they would pray."

West, M. (Ed.) (1987) *The Psychology of Meditation*. Oxford: Oxford University Science Publications.

A set of essays that examines the effects, practices and efficacy of meditation in relation to their theoretical bases in Eastern and Western psychology.

Worton, S.A., & Dollinger, S.J. (1986) "Mothers' intrinsic religious maturation, disciplinary preferences and children's conceptions of prayer." *Psychological Reports, 58*(1), 218.

A minor replication of Long, Elkind, and Spilka (1967).

Wulff, D. (1991) *Psychology of Religion: Classic and Contemporary Views*. New York: John Wiley & Sons.

A "comprehensive introduction to the psychology of religion" which recognizes the centrality of prayer, the importance of its experimental study, and of phenomenological analyses.

Wundt, W. (1910-1915) Last volume. *Vokerpsycholgie, 2 Band: Mythus und Religion*. Leipzig. Revised edition in 3 volumes.

Another classic that has not yet been translated.

Great Prayers of the Bible

COLLECTED BY DAVID T. PATTERSON (1927)

A baseline for Christian prayers beyond the Lord's Prayer is found in "Some directions of our Lord Jesus and his friends concerning prayer" from David Tait Patterson's (1927) *Great Prayers of the Bible*, London: William and Norgate. This collection suggests that to think about or try to understand prayer as if it were concerned with material goals, is a distortion of the kerygma.

"After this manner therefore pray ye:
Our Father which art in heaven,
Hallowed be Thy name. Thy kingdom come.
Thy will be done on earth, as it is in heaven.
Give us this day our daily bread:
And forgive us our trespasses, as we forgive them that trespass against us.
And lead us not into temptation, but deliver us from evil:
For Thine is the kingdom, and the power, and the glory, for ever. Amen."

(Matthew 6:9)

"When Thou prayest, enter into Thy closet, and when thou hast shut Thy door, pray to Thy Father, which is in secret; and Thy Father, which seeth in secret, shall reward thee openly."

(Matthew 6:6)

"What things soever ye desire when ye pray, believe that ye receive them, and ye shall have them. And when ye stand praying, forgive, if ye have ought against any: that your Father also which is in heaven may forgive you your trespasses."

(Mark 11:24-25)

"If ye abide in me, and my words abide in you, ye shall ask what ye will, and it shall be done unto you."

(John 15:7)

"If two of you shall agree on earth as touching anything that they shall ask, it shall be done for them of my Father which is in heaven. For where two or three are gathered together in my name, there am I in the midst of them."

(Matthew 18:19-20)

"Continue in prayer (. . . with thanksgiving)."

(Colossians 4:2)

"Pray for one another."

(James 5:16)

"And this is the confidence that we have in Him that, if we ask anything according to His will, He heareth us."

(1 John 5:14)

"The Spirit also helpeth our infirmities: for we know not what we should pray for as we ought: but the Spirit itself maketh intercession for us with groanings which cannot be uttered . . . He maketh intercession for the saints according to the will of God."

(Romans 8:26-27)

"Be careful for nothing; but in everything by prayer and supplication, with thanksgiving, let your requests be made known unto God."

(Philippians 4:6)

(It is ironic that one of the prayers that Patterson included in this section, "God forbid that I should sin against the Lord in ceasing to pray for you", he failed to identify, but it is from 1 Samuel 12:23.)

References

Abelson, R.P. (1986) "Beliefs are like possessions." *Journal for the Theory of Social Behavior, 16*(3), 223-250.

Abrams, M., et al (1985) *Values and Social Change in Britain*. Basingstoke: Macmillan, Houndmills.

Abramson, L.Y., Seligman, M.E.P., & Teasdale, J. (1978) "Learned helplessness in humans: Critique and reformulation." *Journal of Abnormal Psychology, 87*, 49-74.

Adams Smith, D.E. (1989) "Linguistic and semantic changmes in the revised Anglican liturgy." *Applied Linguistics, 10*(3), 268-280.

Adorno, T.W. (1973) *Philosophy of Modern Music*. (A.G. Mitchell & W.V. Blomster, Trans.). New York: Seabury.

Alcock J.E. (1987) "Parapsychology: Science of the anomalous or search for the soul." *Behavioral and Brain Sciences, 10*, 553-565.

Alexander, H.B. (1918) "Prayer (American)." In James Hastings (Ed.), *Encyclopaedia of Religion and Ethics* (Vol 10:158-159). Edinburgh: T. & T. Clark.

Allport, F.H. (1934) "The J-curve hypothesis of conforming behavior." *Journal of Social Psychology, 5*, 141-183.

Allport, G.W. (1950) *The Individual and His Religion: A Psychological Interpretation*. New York: Macmillan.

Allport, G.W., Gillespie, J.M., & Young, J. (1948) "The religion of the post-war college student." *The Journal of Psychology, 25*, 3-33.

Alston, W. (1985) "Divine-human dialogue and the nature of God." *In Faith and Philosophy*, 2, 5-20.

Ames, E.S. (1910) *The Psychology of Religious Experience*. Boston: Houghton Mifflin.

Anesaki, M. (1918) "Prayer (Buddhist)." In James Hastings (Ed.), *Encyclopaedia of Religion and Ethics* (Vol. 10: 166-170). Edinburgh: T. & T. Clark.

Antaki, C. (1986) "Ordinary explanations in conversation: causal structures and their defence." *European Journal of Social Psychology, 15*, 213-230.

Appleton, G. (Ed.) (1985) *The Oxford Book of Prayer*. Oxford University Press.

Apresjan, J. (1974) *Leksiceskaja Semantika*. Moscow: Nauka.

Aquinas, St Thomas (1965) *Summa Theologiae*. London: Blackfriars.

Arbesmann, R. (1967) Prayer. *New Catholic Encyclopaedia* (Vol. 11: 667-669). New York: McGraw Hill.

Arbib, M.A. & Hesse, M.B. (1986) *The Construction of Reality*. Cambridge University Press.

Archbishop's Commission on Christian Doctrine (1971) *Prayer and the Departed*. London: SPCK.

Argyle, M.A. (1958) *Religious Behaviour*. London: Routledge and Kegan Paul.

Argyle, M.A., & Beit-Hallahmi, B. (1975) *The Social Psychology of Religion*. London: Routledge and Kegan Paul.

Astington, J.W., Harris, P.C., & Olson, D.R. (1988) *Developing Theories of Mind*. Cambridge University Press.

Augustine, Saint (1991) *Confessions: Translated With An Introduction and Notes by Henry Chadwick*. Oxford University Press.

Austin, J.L (1962, 1975) *How To Do Things With Words*. Cambridge, MA: Harvard University Press. Second Edition edited by J.O. Urmson and M. Sbisa.

Ayeroff, F., & Abelson, R.P. (1976) "ESP and ESB: belief in personal success at mental telepathy." *Journal of Personality and Social Psychology*, *34*, 240-247.

Back, C.W., & Bourque, L.B. (1970) "Can feelings be enumerated?" *Behavioral Science*, 15, 487-496.

Baelz, P.R. (1968) *Prayer and Providence*. London: SCM Press; New York: Seabury.

Baelz, P.R. (1982) *Does God Answer Prayer?* London: Darton, Longman and Todd.

Bains, G. (1983) "Explanations and the need for control." In M. Hewstone, *Attribution Theory*. Oxford: Blackwell.

Bakan, D. (1958) *S. Freud and the Jewish mystical tradition*. Princeton University Press.

Bandura, A. (1972) "Self-efficacy: Toward a unifying theory of behavioral change." *Psychological Review*, *84*, 191-215.

Barabat, R. (1975) "On the ambiguity of Cistercian sign language." *Sign Language Studies*, *8*, 275-289.

Barker, E. (1986) "Religious movements: cult and anti-cult since Jonestown." *Annual Review of Sociology*, *12*, 329-346.

Barker, E. (1989) *New Religious Movements: A Practical Introduction*. London: Her Majesty's Stationery Office.

Barry, W.A. (1987) *God and You: Prayer as a Personal Relationship*. New York: Paulist Press.

Bartlett, F.C. (1973) *Political propaganda*. New York: Octagon Books.

Batson, C.D., & Schoenrade, P. (1991) "Measuring religion as quest: 1) Validity concerns, 2) Reliability concerns." *Journal for the Scientific Study of Religion*, 30(4), 416-447.

Batson, C.D., & Ventis, W.L. (1982) *The Religious Experience: A Social-Psychological Perspective*. New York: Oxford University Press.

Bauml, B., & Bauml, F. (1975) *A Dictionary of Gestures*. Metuchan, NJ: Scarecrow.

Beck, A.T. (1990) *Cognitive Therapy of Personality Disorders*. New York: Guilford Press.

Beck, F.O. (1906) "Prayer: A study in its history and psychology." *American Journal of Religious Psychology and Education, 2*(1), 107-121.

Beit-Hallahmi, B. (1989) *Prolegomena to the Psychological Study of Religion.* Lewisburg: Bucknell University Press.

Bell, R.M. (1985) *Holy Anorexia.* Chicago: University of Chicago Press.

Benoit, Pierre (1981) "La priere dans les religions greco-romaines et dans le Christianisme primitif." In *Prayer in Late Antiquity and Early Christianity.* Yearbook 1978-1979. Tantur/Jerusalem: Ecumenical Institute for Advanced Theological Studies, pp. 19-43.

Berger, P.L. & Luckmann, T. (1966) *The Social Construction of Reality: A Treatise in the Sociology of Knowledge.* Garden City, NY: Doubleday. (1972) Harmondsworth: Penguin Books.

Bergin, A.E. (1980) "Negative effects revisited: A reply." *Professional Psychology,* 11, 93-100.

Bettelheim, B. (1962) *The Uses of Enchantment: The Meaning and Importance of Fairy Tales.* New York: Random House.

Bharati, A. (1980) *The Ochre Robe.* Santa Barbara: Ross-Erikson.

Blackburn, R. (1988) "On moral judgements and personality disorders: the myth of psychopathic personality revisited." *British Journal of Psychiatry, 153,* 505-512.

Blackmore, S. (1990) "The lure of the paranormal." *New Scientist,* 46-49.

Bonhoeffer, D. (1959) *Letters and Papers from Prison.* London: Fontana Books.

Bootzin, R.R. (1985) "The role of expectancy in behavior change." In L. White, B. Tursky, & G.E. Schwartz, *Placebo: Theory, Research, and Mechanism* (pp. 196-210). New York: Guilford Press.

Bordin, E.S. (1979) "The generalizability of the psychoanalytic concept of the working alliance." *Psychotherapy: Theory, Research and Practice,* 16, 252-260.

Boring, E.G. (1950) *A History of Experimental Psychology* (2nd ed.). New York: Appleton-Century Crafts.

Bourguignon, E. (1973) *Religion, Altered States of Consciousness and Social Change.* Columbus, Ohio: Ohio State University Press.

Bovet, P. (1925) *Le sentiment religieuse et la psychologie de l'enfant.* Paris: Delachaux.

Bowker, J. (1973) *The Sense of God: Sociological, Anthropological and Psychological Approaches to the Origin of the Sense of God.* Oxford: Clarendon Press.

Bowker, J. (1987) *Licensed Insanities: Religions and Belief in God in the Contemporary World.* London: Darton, Longman and Todd.

Brandon, S.G.F. (Ed.) (1970) "Prayer." In *A Dictionary of Comparative Religion* (pp. 507-509). London: Weidenfeld & Nicolson.

Brewer, C. (1986) In D.C. Rubin (Ed.), *Autobiographical Memory.* Cambridge University Press.

Broad, W., & Wade, N. (1986) *Betrayers of the Truth: Fraud and Deceit in Science.* Oxford University Press.

Brown, G.K., & Nicassio, P.M. (1987) "Development of a questionnaire for the assessment of active and passive coping strategies in chronic pain patients." *Pain, 31,* 53-64.

Brown, L.B. (1966) "Ego-centric thought in petitionary prayer: a cross-cultural study." *Journal of Social Psychology*, *48*(2), 197-210.

Brown, L.B. (1987) *The Psychology of Religious Belief.* London: Academic Press.

Brown, L.B. (1988) *Introduction to the Psychology of Religion.* London: Academic Press.

Brown, L.B. (1989) *Dr. Thouless and Psychical Research.* In G.K. Zollschan et al, (1989) *Exploring the Paranormal: Perspectives on Belief and Experience.* (pp. 250-269). Dorset: Prism Press.

Brown, L.B. (1994) *Religion, Personality and Mental Health.* New York: Springer-Verlag.

Brown, L.B. (1993) *A Schematic View of Religion.* (in preparation)

Brown, L.B., & Moore, A.C. (1990) "Art and the structure of religion." *Journal of Empirical Theology, 3*(2), 23-34.

Brown, L.B., & Thouless, R.H. (1964) "Petitionary prayer: belief in its appropriateness and causal efficacy among adolescent girls." *Studies in Religious Psychology.* Lumen Vitae, 3, 123-136.

Brown, L.B., & Thouless, R.H. (1965) "Animistic thought in civilized adults." *Journal of Genetic Psychology, 107* (1), 33-42.

Brummer, V. (1984) *What Are We Doing When We Pray?: A Philosophical Enquiry.* London: SCM Press.

Bruner, J. (1965) *On Knowing: Essays for the Left-Hand.* Cambridge, MA: Harvard University Press.

Bruner, J. (1990) *Acts of Meaning.* Cambridge, MA: Harvard University Press.

Brush, S.J. (1974) "The prayer test." *American Scientist, 62*, 561-563.

Buber, M. (1958) *I and Thou* (Trans. by Ronald Gregor, 1878-1965) (2nd. rev. ed.) Edinburgh: T and T Clark.

Bulman, R.J., & Wortman, C.B. (1977) "Attribution of blame and agency in the 'real world': Severe accident victims' attitudes to their lot." *Journal of Personality and Social Psychology, 35*(5), 351-363.

Buono, A.M. (1990) *Praying with the Church.* New York: Alba House.

Burnam, T. (1975) *Dictionary of Misinformation.* New York: Crowell.

Burnett, D. (1988) *Unearthly Powers.* MARC

Byrd, R.C. (1988) "Positive therapeutic effects of intercessary prayer in a coronary care unit population." *Southern Medical Journal, 81*(7), 826-829.

Calkins, M.W. (1911) "The nature of prayer." *Theological Review, 6, 489-500.*

Cambry, J. (1838) *Voyage dans le Finistere.* Paris.

Campbell, J. (1972) *Myths to Live By.* New York: Viking.

Capps, D. & Dittes, J.E. (1990) *The Hunger of the Heart: Reflections on the Confessions of Augustine.* SSSR Monograph Series, Number 8.

Capps, D., Rambo, L., & Ransohoff, P. (1976) *Psychology of Religion: A Guide to Information Sources.* Detroit: Gale Research Company.

Carlson, J.G. (1989) "Affirmative: In support of researching the Myers-Briggs Type indicator." *Journal of Counselling and Development, 67*(8), 494-486.

Carothers, J.C. (1959) "Culture, psychiatry and the written word." *Psychiatry, 22*, 307-320.

Carroll, M.P. (1987) "Praying the rosary: The anal-erotic origins of a popular Catholic devotion." *Journal of the Scientific Study of Religion, 26*(4), 486-498.

Carse, J.P. (1985) *The Silence of God: Meditations on Prayer.* New York: Macmillan.

Carver, C.S., Scheier, M.F., & Weintraub, J.K. (1989) "Assessing coping strategies: A theoretically based approach." *Journal of Personality and Social Psychology,* 56(2), 267-283.

Cassirer, E. (1946) *Language and Myth.* (Susanne Langer, Trans.) New York: Harper & Row.

Castles, I. (1990) *Year Book Australia, Number 73.* Canberra: Australian Bureau of Statistics.

Chastaing, M. (1976) "The psychology of swearing." *Journal de Psychologie-Normale-et Pathologique, 73*(3-4), pp. 443-468.

Chertok, L. (1986) "Suggestion revisted." *Psychotherapy, 23*(4), 563-569.

Chi, M.T.H. (1978) "Knowledge, structure and memory development." In R. Siegler (Ed.), *Children's Thinking: What Develops* (pp. 73-96). Hillsdale, NJ: Lawrence Erlbaum.

The Complete Works of Chuang Tzu (1968) (Burton Watson, Trans.). New York: Columbia University Press.

Clanchy, M.T. (1979) *From Memory to Written Record: England 1066-1307.* Cambridge, MA: Harvard University Press.

Clark, W.H. (1958) *The Psychology of Religion: An Introduction to Religous Experience and Behavior.* New York: Macmillan.

Clarke, T.E. (1983) "Jungian types and forms of prayer." *Review for Religious, 42*(5), 661-676.

Claxton, G. (1987) "Meditation in Buddhist psychology." In M.A. West (Ed.), *The Psychology of Meditation* (pp. 23-38). Oxford: Clarendon Press.

Clayton, R.R., & Gladden, J.W. (1969) "The five dimensions of religiosity: Toward demythologizing a sacred artifact." *Journal for the Scientific Study of Religion, 13*, 135-143.

Clements, R.E. (1985) *The Prayers of the Bible.* London: SCM Press.

Coe, G.A. (1916) *The Psychology of Religion.* Chicago: University of Chicago Press.

Coles, R. (1990) *The Spiritual Life of Children.* Boston: Houghton Mifflin.

Collins Cobild English Language Dictionary (1987) London: Collins.

Collipp, P.J. (1969) "The efficacy of prayer: a triple blind study." *Medical Times, 97,* 201-204.

Comstock, G.W., & Partridge, K.B. (1972) "Church attendance and health." *Journal of Chronic Diseases, 22*, 665-672.

Conn, J.W. (1989) *Spiritual and Personal Maturity.* New York: Paulist Press: Interpretive Books.

Constitution of the Sacred Liturgy (C. Howell, Trans., p. 7) (quoted by Crystal, 1965, p. 151).

Corlu, A. (1966) *Recherches sur les mots relatifs a l'idee de priere, d'Homer aux tragiques.* Paris: Librarie C. Klincksieck.

Crisson, J.E., & Keefe, F.J. (1988) "The relationship of locus of control to pain coping strategies and psychological distress in chronic pain patients." *Pain, 35*, 147-154.

Crook, J.H. (1988) *The Evolution of Human Consciousness.* Oxford: Clarendon Press.

Crystal, D. (1965) *Linguistics, Language and Religion.* London: Burns and Oates.

Crystal, D. (1987) *The Cambridge Encyclopedia of Language.* Cambridge University Press.

Csikzentmihalyi, M., & Csikzentmihalyi, I.S. (Eds.) (1988) *Optimal Experience: Psychology Studies of Flow in Consciousness.* Cambridge University Press.

Cupitt, D. (1982) *The World to Come.* London: SCM Press.

Cupitt, D. (1988) *The New Christian Ethics.* London: SCM Press.

Currie, R., Gilbert, A., & Horsley, L. (1977) *Churches and Church-goers: Patterns of Church Growth in the British Isles Since 1700.* Oxford: Clarendon Press.

Curtis, R.C., Rietdorff, P., & Donell, D. (1980) "Appeasing the gods? Suffering to reduce probable future suffering." *Personality and Social Psychology Bulletin, 6,* 234-241.

D'Arcy, C.F. (1918) "Prayer (Christian, Theological)." In James Hastings (Ed.), *Encyclopaedia of Religion and Ethics* (Vol. 10: 171-177). Edinburgh: T. & T. Clark.

Darley, J. & Batson, C.D. (1973) "From Jerusalem to Jericho: A study of situational and dispositional variables in helping behavior." *Journal of Personality and Social Psychology, 27*(2), 100-108.

Daston, L. (1989) *Classical Probability in the Enlightenment.* Princeton University Press.

David, J.P., Ladd, K., & Spilka, B. (1992) "The multidimensionality of prayer and its role as a source of secondary control." Paper at the Centennial Convention of the APA, Washington, DC.

Davis, C. Franks (1989) *The Evidential Force of Religious Experience.* Oxford: Clarendon Press.

Dawkins, R. (1976) *The Selfish Gene.* Oxford University Press.

De Charms, R., & Muir, M.S. (1978) "Motivation: social approaches." *Annual Review of Psychology, 29,* 91-113.

Deconchy, J-P. (1985) "Non-experimental and experimental methods in the psychology of religion." In L.B. Brown (Ed.), *Advances in the Psychology of Religion* (pp. 76-112). Oxford: Pergamon.

Deconchy, J-P. (1991) "Religious belief systems: Their ideological representations and practical constraints." *International Journal for the Psychology of Religion, 1*(1), 5-21.

Delmonte, M.M. (1987) "Personality and meditation." In M.A. West, *The Psychology of Meditation* (pp. 118-134). Oxford: Clarendon Press.

Dennett, D.C. (1991) *Consciousness Explained.* Boston: Little, Brown.

Devlin, J. (1987) *The Superstitious Mind: French Peasants and the Supernatural in the Nineteenth Century.* New Haven: Yale University Press.

Dittes, J.E. (1969) "Psychology of religion." In G. Lindzey & E. Aronson (Eds.), *The Handbook of Social Psychology* (2nd. ed., pp. 602-659). Reading, Mass. Addison-Wesley.

Doctrine Commission of the Church of England (1976) *Christian Believing.* London: SPCK.

Doctrine Commission fo the Church of England (1981) *Believing in the Church: The Corporate Nature of Faith.* London: SPCK.

Doctrine Commission of the Church of England (1987) *We Believe in God.* London: Church House Publishing.

Dodds, E.R. (1951) *The Greeks and the Irrational.* Berkeley: University of California Press.

Douglas, M. (1966) *Purity and Danger.* Harmondsworth: Penguin Books.

Dubois-Dumee, Jean-Pierre (1989) *Becoming Prayer.* (Anne White, Trans.) Middlegreen, England: St Paul Publications.

Dudley, M. (1992) "Melancholy or depression: sacred or secular?" *International Journal for the Psychology of Religion, 2*(2), 87-100.

Dumont, L. (1971) *Religion, Politics and History in India.* The Hague: Mouton.

Durran, M. (1987) *Dear God if I Ruled the World: Children's Prayers and Letters to God.* Bassingstoke: Marshall and Pickering.

Dyer Ball, J. (1918) "Prayer (Chinese)." In James Hastings (Ed.), *Encyclopaedia of Religion and Ethics* (Vol. 10: 170-171). Edinburgh: T. & T. Clark.

Easting, R., & Sharpe, R. (1988) "Peter of Cornwall: The visions of Ailsi and his son." *Mediaevistik, 1*, 207-262.

Edelstein, E.J.L. (1945) *Asclepius: A Collection and Interpretation of the Testimonies.* 2 volumes. Baltimore: Johns Hopkins Press.

Eiser, J.R. (1980) *Cognitive Social Psychology: A Guide Book to Theory and Research.* London: McGraw-Hill.

El Azayem, G.A. (1993) "Psychological aspects of Islam." *Journal for the Psychology of Religion.* (in press)

Eliade, Mircea (1973) *Australian Religions: An Introduction.* Ithaca: Cornell University Press.

Elias, N. (1978) *The Civilizing Process.* New York: Urizen Press.

Elkind, D. (1964) "Piaget's semi-clinical interview and the study of spontaneous religion." *Journal for the Scientific Study of Religion, 4*(1), 40-47.

English, H.B., & English, A.C. (1958) *A Comprehensive Dictionary of Psychological and Psychoanalytical Terms.* New York: Longmans Green.

English Tourist Board (1979) *English Cathedrals and Tourism.* London: English Tourist Board.

Ericsson, K.A., & Simon, H.A. (1980) "Verbal reports as data." *Psychological Review, 87*, 215-251.

Erikson, E. (1958) *Young Man Luther: A Study in Psychoanalysis and History.* New York: Norton.

Eysenck, H.J. (Ed.) (1981) *A Model for Personality.* New York: Springer-Verlag.

Fallaize, E.N. (1918) Prayer (Introductory and Primitive). In James Hastings (Ed.), *Encyclopaedia of Religion and Ethics* (Vol. 10: 154-158). Edinburgh: T. & T. Clark.

Farberow, N.L. (1963) *Taboo Topics.* New York: Atherton.

Farnell, L.R. (1905) *The Evolution of Religion: An Anthropological Study.* London: Williams & Norgate, and New York: G.P. Putnam's Sons.

Farr, R.M., & Moscovici, S. (1984) *Social Representations.* Cambridge University Press.

Feagin, J. (1972) "Poverty: We still believe that God helps those who help themselves." *Psychology Today, 6*, 101-129.

Felix, R.W. (1924) *Some Principles of Psychology as Illustrated in the Sacramental*

System of the Church. Washington DC: Catholic University of America.

Fenwick, P. (1987) "Meditation and the EEG." In M.A. West (Ed.), *The Psychology of Meditation* (pp. 104-117). Oxford: Clarendon Press.

Ferré, F. (1962) *Language, Logic and God.* London: Eyre and Spottiswoode.

Festinger, L. (1957) *A Theory of Cognitive Dissonance.* Evanston: Row, Peterson.

Festinger, L., & Carlsmith, J.M. (1959) "Cognitive consequences of forced compliance." *Journal of Abnormal and Social Psychology, 58,* 203-210.

Fichter, J.H. (1954) *Social Relations in the Urban Parish.* Chicago: University of Chicago Press.

Finney, J.R., & Malony, H.N. (1985) "Empirical studies of Christian prayer: A review of the literature. *Journal of Psychology and Theology, 13*(2), 104-115.

Fisch, R., & Daniel, H.D. (1982) "Research and publication trends in experimental social psychology: 1971-1980." *European Journal of Social Psychology, 12,* 335-412.

Fishbein, M., & Ajzen, F. (1975) *Belief, Attitude, Intention and Behavior: An Introduction to Theory and Research.* Reading, MA: Addison-Wesley.

Fogarty, M., Ryan, L., & Lee, J. (1984) *Irish Values and Attitudes: The Irish Report of the European Values Systems Study.* Dublin: Dominican Publications.

Fong, G.T., Krantz, D.H., & Nisbett, R.E. (1986) "The effects of statistical training on thinking about everyday problems." *Cognitive Psychology, 18*(3), 253-292.

Foucault, M. (1988) *Technologies of the Self.* (Eds. L.H. Martin, H. Gutman, & P.H. Hutton). Amherst: University of Massachusetts Press.

Francis, L.J., & Brown, L.B. (1990) "The predisposition to pray." *Journal of Empirical Theology, 3*(2), 23-34.

Francis, L.J., & Brown, L.B. (1991) "The influence of home, Church and school on prayer among sixteen year old adolescents in England." *Review of Religious Research, 33*(2), 112-122.

Frank, J.D., & Frank, J.B. (1991) *Persuasion and Healing: A Comparative Study of Psychotherapy* (3rd. ed.). Baltimore: The John Hopkins University Press.

Frayn, M. (1968) *A Very Private Life.* London: Collins.

Frazer, J.G. (1923) *The Golden Bough: A Study in Magic and Religion.* London: Macmillan.

Freud, S. (1933) *New Introductory Lectures on Psychoanalysis.* Standard Edition, Vol 22 (1964) London: Hogarth Press.

Freud, S. (1974) *The Freud/Jung Letters.* Princeton University Press.

Frye, N. (1964) *The Educated Imagination.* Bloomington: Indiana University Press.

Frye, N. (1982) *The Great Code: The Bible and Literature.* London: Routledge and Kegan Paul.

Furnham, A. (1983) "Attribution for affluence." *Personality and Individual Differences, 4,* 31-40

Furnham, A., & Brown, L.B. (1992) "Theodicy: a neglected aspect of the psychology of religion." *International Journal for the Psychology of Religion, 2*(1), 37-45.

Gallistel, C.R. (1990) *The Organization of Learning.* Boston: M.I.T. Press.

Gallup, G., & Castelli, J. (1989) *The People's Religion: American Faith in the 90's.* New York: Macmillan.

Galton, F. (1873) "Statistical enquiries into the efficacy of prayer." *Fortnightly Review, 12*, 125-135.

Galton, F. (1883) "Objective efficacy of prayer." (Reprint of Galton, 1873) in *Inquiries into Human Faculty and Its Development*. London: Macmillan.

Gardener, M. (1957) *Fads and Fallacies in the Name of Science*. New York: Daver.

Gardner, H. (1987) *The Mind's New Science: A History of the Cognitive Revolution*. New York: Basic Books.

Gaston, J.E., & Brown, L.B. (1992) "Religion and gender prototypes." *International Journal for the Psychology of Religion, 1*(2), 101-106.

Gergen, M. (1987) "The case of the undetermined theory." *Behavioral and Brain Sciences, 10*, 588.

Gibb, H.A.R. (1969) *Mohammedanism*. London: Oxford University Press.

Gibson, J.J. (1979) *The Ecological Approach to Useful Perception*. Boston: Houghton Mifflin.

Gigerenzer, G., et al (1989) *The Empire of Chance: How Probability Changed Science and Everyday Life*. Cambridge University Press.

Gill, S.D. (1977) "Prayer as person: the performative force in Navaho prayer acts." *History of Religions, 17*, 143-157.

Gill, S.D. (1986) "Prayer." In M. Eliade (Ed.), *The Encyclopedia of Religion* (Volume II: 489-494). New York: Macmillan.

Gill, S.D. (1987) *Native American Religious Action: A Performance Approach to Religion*. University of South Carolina Press.

Girgensohn, K. (1923) *Religion psychologie, Religions wissenschaft und Theologie*. Leipzig: A. Deichert.

Glik, D.C. (1986) "Psychosocial wellness among spiritual healing participants." *Social Science and Medicine, 22*, 579-586.

Glock, C.Y., & Stark, R. (1965) *Religion and Society in Tension*. Chicago: Rand McNally.

Godin, A. (1964) *From Religious Experience to Religious Attitude*. Brussels: Lumen Vitae Press.

Godin, A. (1967) "The psychology of religion." *Quarterly Review of Religion and Mental Health, 5*(4), 1-6.

Godin, A. (1971) "Some developmental tasks in Christian education." In M.P. Strommen (Ed.), *Research on Religious Development and Comprehensive Handbook*. New York: Hawthorn Books.

Godin, A. (1985) *The Psychological Dynamics of Religious Experience*. Birmingham, AL: Religious Education Press.

Godin, A., & Sister Marthe (1960) "Magical mentality and sacramental life." *Lumen Vitae, 15*(2), 277-296.

Godin, A., & Van Roey (1959) "Immanent justice and divine protection." *Lumen Vitae, 14*, 129-148.

Godin, A. (Ed.), (1968) *From Cry to Word: Contributions Toward a Psychology of Religion*. Brussels: Lumen Vitae Press.

Goldman, R. (1964) *Religious Thinking From Childhood to Adolescence*. London: Routledge and Kegan Paul.

Goleman, D.J. (1988) *The Meditative Mind: The Varieties of Meditative Experience*.

Wellingborough: The Aquarian Press.

Goll, R. (1988) *Beyond Decline: A Challenge for the Churches.* London: SCM.

Gorsuch, R. (1984) "Measurement: The boon and the bane of investigating religions." *American Psychologist, 39*(3), 228-236.

Gorsuch, R.L., & Smith, C.S. (1983) "Attribution and responsibi'.y to God: An interaction of religious beliefs and outcomes." *Journal for the Scientific Study of Religion, 22*, 340-352.

Graves, R. (1927) *Lars Porsena or the Future of Swearing and Improper Language.* London: Kegan Paul Trench and Trubner.

Greeley, A. (1991) "The practice of prayer." *The Tablet,* 24 August, pp. 1021-1022.

Greimas, A.J. (1983) *Structural Semantics: An Attempt At a Method.* Lincoln: University of Nebraska Press.

Grice, H.P. (1975) "Logic and conversion." In P. Cole, & J.C. Morgan (Eds.), *Syntax and semantics,* vol 3. *Speech Acts.* New York: Academic Press.

Grice, H.P. (1978) "Further notes on logic and conversation." In Cole (Ed.), *Syntax and semantics,* vol 9. *Pragmatics.* New York: Academic Press.

Grimmet, M. (1987) "Religious education and value assumptions." *British Journal of Religious Education, 9*(3), 160-170.

Halliday, M.A.K. (1973) *Exploration in the Functions of Language.* London: Arnold.

Halliday, M.A.K. (1975) *Learning How to Mean: Exploration in the Development of Language.* London: Arnold.

Halliday, M.A.K. (1978) *Language as Social Semiotic: The Social Interpretation of Language and Meaning.* London: Arnold.

Halliday, M.A.K. (1985) *Spoken and written language.* Victoria: Deakin University Press.

Hameedullah, M. (1991) *Islam.* Lahore: Kazi.

Harakas, S.S. (1990) *Health and Medicine in the Eastern Orthodox Tradition: Faith, Liturgy and Wholeness.* New York: Crossroad.

Harding, D.W. (1963) *Experience Into Words.* Harmondsworth: Penguin.

Harding, D.W. (1976) *Words in Rhythm: English Speech Rhythm in Verse and Prose.* Cambridge University Press.

Harding, S., Phillips, D., & Fogarty, M. (1986) *Contrasting Values in Western Europe: Unity, Diversity and Change.* London: Macmillan.

Hardy, A. (1979) *The Spiritual Nature of Man: A Study of Contemporary Religious Experience.* Oxford University Press.

Harré, R., & Finlay-Jones, R. (1986) "Emotion, talk across times." In R. Harré (Ed.), *The Social Construction of Emotions* (pp. 220-233). Oxford: Blackwell.

Harries, R. (1984) *Turning to Prayer.* London: Mowbray.

Harris, P.L. (1989) *Children and Emotion: The Development of Psychological Understanding.* Oxford: Basil Blackwell.

Hay, D. (1982) *Exploring Inner Space: Scientists and Religious Experience.* Harmondsworth: Penguin Books.

Healy, C.C. (1989) "Negative: The MBTI." *Journal of Counselling and Development, 67*(8), 487-488.

Heffer, D. (1986) *The Children's God.* University of Chicago Press.

Heider, F. (1946) "Attitudes and cognitive organization." *Journal of Psychology, 21,* 107-112.

Heider, F. (1958) *The Psychology of Interpersonal Relations.* New York: John Wiley and Sons.

Heiler, F. (1918) *Das Gebet: Eine religionsgeschichtliche und religionspsychologische Untersuchung.* Munich: Ernst Reinhardt, 1969.

Heiler, F. (1932) *Prayer: A Study in the History and Psychology of Religion.* New York: Oxford University Press.

Helminiak, D.A. (1982) "How is meditation prayer?" *Review for Religious, 41*(5), 774-782.

Hendlen, S.J. (1979) "Initial Zen intensive (Sesshin: A subjective account)." *Journal of Pastoral Counselling, 14,* 27-43. (Cited by Pekola).

Heppner, P.P. & Claiborn, C.D. (1989) "Social influence research in counselling: A review and critique." *Journal of Counselling Psychology Monograph, 36*(3), 365-387.

Hewstone, M. (1989) *Causal Attribution: From Cognitive Processes to Collective Beliefs.* Oxford: Basil Backwell.

Hilgard, E.R. (1987) *Psychology in America: A Historical Survey.* San Diego: Harcourt, Brace, Jovanovich.

Hill, J.M.M. (1965) *The Holiday.* London: Tavistock Institute.

Hocking, P. (1912) *The Meaning of God in Human Experience.* New Haven: Yale University Press.

Hodge, A.J. (1931) *Prayer and Its Psychology.* London: SPCK.

Holahan, C.J. & Moose, R.H. (1987) "Personal and contextual determinants of coping strategies." *Journal of Personality and Social Psychology, 52*(5), 946-955.

Holland, J.C., Magoon, T.M., & Spokane, A.R. (1981) "Counseling psychology: Career interventions, research and theory." *Annual Review of Psychology, 32,* 279-305.

Holmes, T.H., & Rahe, R.H. (1967) "The social readjustment rating scale." *Journal of Psychosomatic Research, 11,* 213-218.

Horton, A.L., & Williamson, J.A. (Eds.) (1971) *Abuse and Religion: When Praying Isn't Enough.* Lexington: MA: Lexington.

Horton, P.C. & Sharp, S.L. (1986) "Language, solace and transitional relatedness." *Psychoanalytic Study of the Child,* pp. 167-194.

Howard, P. (1988) *Winged Words.* New York: Oxford University Press.

Hunsberger, B.E., & Brown, L.B. (1984) "Religious socialization, apostasy and the impact of family background." *Journal for the Scientific Study of Religion, 23*(3), 239-251.

Hunt, R.A., & King, M.B. (1971) "The intrinsic-extrinsic concept: a review and evaluation." *Journal for the Scientific Study of Religion, 10,* 339-356.

Huon, G.F., & Brown, L.B. (1988) *Fighting with Food: Overcoming Bulimia Nervosa.* Sydney: University of New South Wales Press.

Hynes, Kiernan (1989) *Pray As You Can.* Homebush, NSW: St Paul Publications.

Ichheiser, G. (1943) "Misinterpretation of personality in everyday life and the psychologist's frame of reference." *Character and Personality, 12,* 145-160.

Inglis, Brian (1989) *Trance: A Natural History of Altered States of Mind.* Grafton: Collins.

Jacks, L.P. (1911) *The Alchemy of Thought.* London: Williams and Norgate.

Jackson, F. (1982) "Epiphenomenal qualia." *Philosophical Quarterly, 32,* 127-136.

Jacobs, A., & Sachs, L.B. (1971) *The Psychology of Private Events: Perspectives on Covert Response Systems.* New York: Academic Press.

Jahoda, G. (1969) *The Psychology of Superstition.* London: Allen Lane.

Jaksa, James A., & E.L. Stech (Eds.) (1980) *Voices From Silence: The Trappists Speak.* Toronto: Griffin House.

James, Henry (1898) *The Turn of the Screw.* Oxford: Everyman.

James, W. (1902) *The Varieties of Religious Experience: A Study in Human Nature.* Cambridge, MA: Harvard University Press (1985).

James, W. (1907) *Pragmatism.* Cambridge, MA: Harvard University Press (1976).

Janis, I.L. (Ed.) (1982) *Counselling on Personal Decisions: Theory and Research on Short-term Helping Relationships.* New Haven: Yale University Press.

Janis, I.L. (Ed.) (1983) *Short-term Counselling: Guidelines Based on Recent Research.* New Haven: Yale University Press.

Jaynes, J. (1976) *The Origin of Consciousness in the Breakdown of the Bicameral Mind.* London: Allen Lane.

Jenkins, W.O., & Stanley, J.C. (1950) "Partial reinforcement: A review and critique." *Psychological Bulletin, 47,* 193-234.

Jennings, M., & Niemi, R. (1968) "The transmission of political values from parent to child." *American Political Science Review, 62,* 169-184.

Johnson, P.E. (1953) "A psychological understanding of prayer." *Pastoral Psychology, 4*(36), 33-39.

Johnson, S.C., & Spilka, B. (1991) "Coping with breast cancer: The roles of clergy and faith." *Journal of Religion and Health, 30*(1), 21-33.

Joyce, C.R.B., & Welldon, R.M.C. (1965) "The objective efficacy of prayer: A double-blind clinical trial." *Journal of Chronic Diseases, 18,* 367-377.

Jung, C.G. (1958) "Answer to Job" In *Psychology and Religion: West and East* (pp. 355-470). London: Routledge and Kegan Paul.

Kahneman, D., Slovic, P., & Tversky, A. (Eds.) (1982) *Judgment Under Uncertainty: Heuristics and Biases.* Cambridge University Press.

Keefe, F.J., & Dolan, E. (1986) "Pain behavior and pain coping strategies in low back pain and myofascial pain dysfunction syndrome patients." *Pain, 74,* 49-56.

Keller, E.F. (1987) *Reflections on Gender and Science.* New Haven: Yale University Press.

Kelley, H.H., & Michela, J.L. (1980) "Attribution theory and research." *Annual Review of Psychology, 31,* 457-501.

Kelley, H.H. (1971) "Moral evaluation." *American Psychologist, 26,* 293-300.

Kelley, H.H. (1973) "The process of causal attribution." *American Psychologist, 28,* 107-128.

Kelley, H.H. (1992) "Common sense psychology and scientific psychology." *Annual Review of Psychology, 43,* 1-20.

Kendon, A. (1980) "The sign language of the women of Yuendumu." *Sign Language Studies, 27,* 101-112.

Kenny, A. (1985) *The Path from Rome.* London: Sidgwick & Jackson.

Kenyon, C.H. (1988) *Authenticity and Early Music.* Oxford University Press.

Keyes, C.F., & Daniel, E.V. (1983) *Karma: An Anthropological Enquiry*. Berkeley: University of California Press.

Kieckhefer, R. (1990) *Magic in the Middle Ages*. Cambridge University Press.

Kierkegaard, S. (1956) *Purity of Heart Is to Will One Thing: Spiritual Preparation for the Office of Confession*. New York: Harper & Row.

Kierkegaard, S. (1941) *Concluding Unscientific Postscript*. (D.F. Swenson and W. Lowrie, Trans.). Princeton: Princeton University Press.

Kierkegaard, S. (1962) *Works of Love*. (H.V. Hong and E.H. Hong, Trans.). New York: Harper Torchbooks.

Kierkegaard, S. (1967-73) *Søren Kierkegaard's Journals and Papers,* 7 vols. (H.V. Hong and E.H. Hong, Eds. and Trans., with G. Malantschuk). Bloomington: Indiana University Press.

Kierkegaard, S. (1980) *The Sickness Unto Death*. (H.V. Hong and E.H. Hong, Eds. and Trans.). Princeton: Princeton University Press.

Kierkegaard, S. (1983) *Fear and Trembling*. (H.V. Hong and E.H. Hong, Eds. and Trans.) Princeton: Princeton University Press.

King, M. (1967) "Measuring the religious variable: Nine proposed dimensions." *Journal for the Scientific Study of Religion, 6,* 173-190.

King, N. (1986) *African Cosmos: An Introduction to Religion in Africa*. Belmont, CA: Wadsworth.

Kirkpatrick, L.A., & Hood, R.W. (1990) "Intrinsic-extrinsic religious orientation: The 'boon or 'bane' of contemporary psychology of religion." *Journal for the Scientific Study of Religion, 29,* 442-462.

Kirkpatrick, L.A. (1992) "An attachment theory approach to the psychology of religion." *International Journal for the Psychology of Religion, 2*(1), 3-28.

Klausner, William J. (1985) *Reflections on Thai Culture: Collected Writings of William J. Klausner*. Bangkok: Siam Society.

Knox, R. (1950) *Enthusiasm*. New York: Oxford University Press.

Koep, W. (1920) *Einführung in das Studium der Religionpsychologie*. Tubingen: J.C.B. Mohr (Paul Siebeck).

Koestler, A. (1972) *The Roots of Coincidence*. London: Hutchinson.

Krause, N., & Van Tran, T. (1989) "Stress and religious involvement among older Blacks." *Journal of Gerontology, 44*(1), S4-13

Laing, R.D. (1967) *The Politics of Experience and the Bird of Paradise*. Harmondsworth: Penguin.

Lalljee, M., & Abelson, R.P. (1983) "The organization of explanations." In M. Hewstone (Ed.), *Attribution Theory and Research: Conceptual, Developmental and Social Dimensions*. London: Academic Press.

Lalljee, M., Brown, L.B. & Ginsberg, G.P. (1984) "Attitudes: disposition in behavior or evaluation." *British Journal of Social Psychology, 23,* 233-244.

Lalljee, M., Brown, L.B., & Hilton, D. (1990) "The relationship between images of God, explanations for failure to do one's duty to God, and invoking God's agency." *Journal of Psychology and Theology, 18*(2), 166-173.

Lambert, M.J., Shapiro, D.A., & Bergin, A.E. (1986) "The effectiveness of synchotherapy." In S.C. Garfield, & A.E. Bergin, *Handbook of Psychotherapy and Behavior Change* (pp. 157-211). New York: Wiley.

Langdon, S. (1981) "Prayer (Babylonian)." In James Hastings (Ed.), *Encyclopaedia of Religion and Ethics* (Vol. 10: 159-166). Edinburgh: T. & T. Clark.

Langer, E.J. (1983) *The Psychology of Control*. Beverly Hills: Sage.

Langer, S. (1951) *Philosophy in a New Key*. Cambridge, MA: Harvard University Press.

Lansing, J. S. (1983) *The Three Worlds of Bali*. New York: Praeger.

Lazarus, A. (1976) *Multi-model Behavior Therapy*. New York: Springer.

Le Bon, G. (1895) *Psychologie des foules*. (Translated as *The Crowd*. London: Kegan Paul, 1903).

Leary, D.E. (1987) "Telling likely stories: The rhetoric of the new psychology, 1880-1920." *Journal of the History of the Behavioral Sciences, 23,* 315-331.

Leary, D.E. (1990) *Metaphors in the History of Psychology*. Cambridge University Press.

Legge, J.W. (1914) *English Church Life from the Restoration to the Tractarian Movement*.

Lenington, S. (1979) "Effect of holy water on the growth of radish plants." *Psychological Reports, 45,* 381-382.

Lerner, M.J. (1980) *The Belief in a Just World: A Fundamental Delusion*. New York: Plenum Press.

Lester, D. (1990) *Understanding and Preventing Suicide: New Perspectives*. New York: C.C. Thomas.

Leuba, J.H. (1925) *The Psychology of Religious Mysticism*. London: Routledge and Kegan Paul.

Levy-Bruhl, L. (1926) *How Natives Think*. London: Allen and Unwin.

Lienhardt, G. (1961) *Divinity and Experience. The Religion of the Dinka*. Oxford: Clarendon Press.

Lilliston, L., & Brown, P.M. (1981) "Perceived effectiveness of relegous solutions to personal problems." *Journal of Clinical Psychology, 37*(1), 118-122.

Lilliston, L., Brown, P.M. & Schliebe, H.P. (1982) "Perception of religious solutions to personal problems of women." *Journal of Clinical Psychology, 38*(3), 546-549.

Lilliston, L., & Klein, D.G. (1991) "A self-discrepancy reduction model of religious coping." *Journal of Clinical Psychology, 47*(6), 854-860.

Lindbeck, George A. (1981) Hesychastic prayer and the Christianizing of Platonism: Some Protestant reflections. In *Prayer in Late Antiquity and in Early Christianity*. Yearbook 1978-1979 (pp. 71-88). Tantur/Jerusalem: Ecumenical Institute for Advanced Theological Studies.

Lindzey, G. & Aronson, E. (1985) (Eds.) *Handbook of Social Psychology* (3rd. ed.). New York: Random House/Erlbaum.

Loehr, F. (1959). *The Power of Prayer on Plants*. New York: Doubleday.

Long, D., Elkind, D., & Spilka, B. (1967) "The child's conception of prayer." *Journal for the Scientific Study of Religion, 6,* 101-109.

Long, E.L. Jr. (1952) *Religious Beliefs of American Scientists*. Philadelphia: Westminster Press.

Loveland, G.G. (1968) "The effects of bereavement on certain religious attitudes." *Sociological Symposium, 1,* 17-27.

MacDonald, M. (1981) *Mystical Bedlam*. Cambridge University Press.

Macquarrie, John (1972) *Paths in Spirituality.* London: SCM Press.

Maddock, Kenneth (1984) "The world-creative powers." In Max Charlesworth et al (Eds.). *Religion in Aboriginal Australia: An Anthology* (pp. 85-104). St Lucia, Qld: University of Queensland Press.

Malinowski, B. (1925) *Magic, Science and Religion and Other Essays.* New York: Doubleday (1954).

Malony, H.N., & Lovekin, A.A. (1985) *Glossolalia: Behavioral Science Perspectives on Speaking in Tongues.* New York: Oxford University Press.

Marmor, J. (1956) *American Journal of Orthopsychiatry, 26,* 119-130.

Marrett, R.R. (1903) "Prayer" in the *Encyclopedia Brittanica,* 11th Edition.

Martin, A. (1985) *The Knowledge of Ignorance: From Genesis to Jules Verne.* Cambridge University Press.

Marty, M., Rosenberg, S.E., & Greeley, A.M. (1968) *What Do We Believe? The Stance of Religion in America.* New York: Meredith Press.

Masih, Y. (1983) *The Hindu Religious Thought.* Delhi: Motilal Banarsidass.

Mavrodes, G.I. (1966) "Bliks, Proofs, and Prayers." *Philosophy Forum, 5,* 49-62.

McCallum, J. (1987) "Secularisation in Australia between 1966 and 1985: A research note." *Australia and New Zealand Journal of Sociology, 23*(3), 407-422.

McCann, R.V. (1962) "The Churches and mental health." *Joint Commission on Mental Illness and Health. Monograph Series 8.* New York: Basic Books.

McDannell, C., & Lang, B. (1990) *Heaven: A History.* New Haven: Yale University Press.

McDougall, W. (1908) *Introduction to Social Psychology.* London: Methuen.

McFague, S. (1987) *Models of God.* London: SCM.

McFarland, S.G.. (1989) "Religious orientations and the targets of discrimination." *Journal for the Scientific Study of Religion, 28,* 324-336.

McFarland, T. (1990) "The transformation of historical material: the case of Dorothea von Mantau." In P. Brady, T. McFarland, & J. White (Eds.), *Gunter Grass's Der Butt: Sexual Politics and the Male Myths of History.* (pp. 69-96). Oxford University Press.

McKenzie, P. (1988) *The Christians: Their Practices and Beliefs* (An adaptation of Friedrich Heiler's *Phenomenology of Religion.*). London: SPCK.

McNamara, (1981) *Christian Mysticism and Psychotheology.* Chicago: Franciscan Herald Press.

Mead, G.H. (1934) *Mind, Self and Society.* Chicago: University of Chicago Press.

Meehl, P.E. (1978) "Theoretical risks and tabular asterisks: Sir Karl, Sir Ronald and the slow progress of soft psychology." *Journal of Consulting and Clinical Psychology, 48,* 806-834.

Mehrabian, A., & Russell, J.A. (1974) *An Approach to Environmental Psychology.* Cambridge, MA: M.I.T. Press.

Meissner, W.W. (1984) *Psychoanalysis and Religious Experience* (pp. 160-184). New Haven: Yale University Press.

Merton, T. (1956) *Silence in Heaven: A Book of the Monastic Life.* London: Thames and Hudson.

Merton, R.K. (1948) *The Self-fulfilling Prophecy in Social Theory and Social Structure.* New York: Free Press.

Metropolitan Anthony of Sourozh (1987) *Creative Prayer: Dailing Readings With Metropolitan Anthony of Sourozh.* London: Darton, Longman & Todd.

Michotte, A. (1950) *La perception de la Causalite.* Louvain: Institut Superieur de Philosphie.

Miller, G.A., & McNeil, D. (1969) "Psycholinguistics." In G. Lindzey & E. Aronson (Eds.), *Handbook of Social Psychology* (Volume III.) (pp. 666-794). Reading, MA: Addison-Wesley.

Miller, H. (1961) *The Tropic of Capricorn* (p. 176). New York: Grove.

Minsky, M. (1985) *The Society of Mind.* New York: Simon and Schuster.

Misiak, H. & Stoudt, V.M. (1954) *Catholicism in Psychology: A Historical Survey.* New York: McGraw-Hill.

Moberg, D. (1971) "Religious practices." In M.P. Strommen (Ed.), *Research on Religious Development: A Comprehensive Handbook* (pp. 551-598). New York: Hawthorn.

Monden, L. (1966) *Signs and Wonders: A Study of the Miraculous Element in Religion.* New York: Desclee.

Moore, H.T. (1921) "The comparative influence of majority and minority opinion." *American Journal of Psychology, 32,* 16-20.

Moore, T.V. (1956) *The Life of Man With God.* New York: Harcourt, Brace & Co.

Morphy, H. (1984) "Introduction: Forms of religious experience." In Max Charlesworth et al (Eds). *Religion in Aboriginal Australia: An Anthology* (pp. 215-217). St Lucia, Qld: University of Queensland Press.

Morse, J. & Allan, J.R. (1912/13) "The religion of 126 college students." *Journal of Religious Psychology, 6,* 175-194.

Muelder, W.G. (1957) "The efficacy of prayer." In S. Doniger (Ed.), *Healing: Human and Divine* (pp. 131-143). New York: Association Press.

Myers, D.G., & Jeeves, M.A. (1987) *Psychology Through the Eyes of Faith.* New York: Harper & Row.

Naranjo, C., & Ornstein, R.E. (1973) *On the Psychology of Meditation.* London: Allen and Unwin.

Nedoncelle, M. (1964) *The Nature and Use of Prayer.* London: Burns and Oates.

Neighbours, H.W., et al (1983) "Stress, coping, and Black mental health: Preliminary findings from a national study." *Prevention in the Human Services, 2*(3), 5-29.

Neitz, M.J., & Spickard, J.V. (1990) "Steps toward a sociology of religious experience: The theories of Mihalyi Csikszentmihalyi and Alfred Schutz." *Sociological Analysis, 51*(1), 15-33.

Nisard, C. (1964) *Histoire de livres populaires ou de la Litterature de Colportage, depuis l'origine de l'Imprimerie jusqu'a l'Establissement de la Commission d'Examen de livres de Colpartage.* (2nd ed. 2 vol.) Paris.

Nisbett, R.E. & Ross, L. (1980) *Human Inference. Strategies and Shortcomings of Social Judgment.* Englewood Cliffs, NJ: Prentice-Hall.

Nishitani, Keiji (1983) *Religion and Nothingness.* Berkeley: University of California Press.

O'Connor, J.E. (1975) "Motives and expectations in prayer." *Review for Religious, 34*(3), 403-408.

O'Donnell, D. (Ed.) (1977) *Praying is like this ... : Ten Australian Oblates Share Their Own Experience of Prayer.* Homebush, NSW: Alba House.

Oden, T.C. (1969) *Structures of Awareness.* Nashville: Abingdon Press.

Ogden, C.K. & Richards, I.A. (1923/1949) *The Meaning of Meaning.* London: Routledge.

Ong, W.J. (1982) *Orality and Literacy: The Technologizing of the Word.* London: Methuen.

Orne, M.T. (1969) "Demand characteristics and the concept of quasi controls." In B. Rosenthal and R.L. Rosnow (Eds.), *Artifact in Behavioral Research.* New York: Academic Press.

Oser, F., & Gmünder, P. (1991) *Religious Judgement: A Developmental Approach.* Birmingham, AL: Religious Education Press.

Oser, F., & Reich, K.H. (1990) "Moral judgment, religious judgment, world views and logical thought: A review of their relationship." *British Journal of Religious Education, 12*(2), 94-101, and (3), 172-181.

Oser, F.K., & Reich, K.H. (1987) "The challenge of competing explanations: The development of thinking in terms of complementarity of 'theories'." *Human Development, 30,* 178-186.

Oser, F.K., & Scarlett, W.G. (1991) *Religious Development in Childhood and Adolescence.* San Francisco: Jossey-Bass.

Osgood, C.E. (1952) "The nature and measurement of meaning." *Psychological Bulletin, 49,* 197-237.

Oskamps (1965) "A study of clinical judgment." (Conference paper ms.)

Otto, R. (1917) *The idea of the holy: An inquiry into the non-rational factor in the idea of the divine and its relation to the rational.* Oxford University Press. (1923).

Oxford Dictionary of Quotations. (1979) Third Edition: Oxford University Press.

Pahnke, W.N. (1966) "Drugs and mysticism." *International Journal of Parapsychology, 52*(2), 295-324.

Pahnke, W.N., & Richards, W.A. (1966) "Implications of LSD and experimental mysticism." *Journal of Religion and Health, 5,* 175-208.

Pailin, D.A. (1990) *The Cultic Character of Theology.* Cambridge University Press.

Pargament, K. (1992) "Of means and ends: Religion and the search for significance." *International Journal for the Psychology of Religion, 2*(4), 201-229.

Pargament, K.I., & Hahn, J. (1986) "God and the just world: Causal and coping attributions to God in health situations." *Journal for the Scientific Study of Religion, 25,* 193-207.

Pargament, K.I., et al (1990) "God help me (I): Religious coping efforts as predictors of the outcomes to significant negative life events." *American Journal of Community Psychology, 18*(6), 793-823.

Pargament, K.I., Steele, R., & Tyler, F.B. (1979) "Religious participation, religious maturation, and individual psychological competence." *Journal for the Scientific Study of Religion, 18,* 412-419.

Parker, G.B. (1983) *Parental Overprotection a Risk Factor in Psychosocial Development.* New York: Grune and Stratton.

Parker, G.B., & Brown, L.B. (1982) "Coping behaviors that mediate between life events and depression." *Archives of General Psychiatry, 39,* 1386-1391.

Parker, G.B., & Brown, L.B. (1984) "Coping behaviors as predictors of the course of clinical depression." *Archives of General Psychiatry, 43,* 561-565.

Parker, J.C., et al (1989) "Pain control and rational thinking: Implications for rheumatoid arthritis." *Arthritis and Rheumatism, 32,* 984-990.

Parker, W.R., & St. Johns, E. (1957) *Prayer Can Change Your Life: Experiments and Techniques in Prayer Therapy.* Carmel, NY: Guideposts Associates.

Parkins, D. (1985) *The Anthropology of Evil.* New York: Blackwell.

Parsifal-Charles, N. (1986) *The Dream: 4000 Years of Theory and Practice* 2 vols.

Parsons, M.J. (1987) *How We Understand Art.* Cambridge University Press.

Pascal, B. (1670) *Pensées: Notes on Religion and Other Subjects.* London: Dent (1960).

Patterson, D.T. (1927) *Great Prayers in the Bible.* London: Williams and Norgate.

Pattison, E.M., Lapins, N.A., & Doerr, H.A. (1973) "Faith healing: a study of personality and function." *Journal of Nervous and Mental Diseases, 157,* 397-409.

Pearce, P.L. (1982) *The Social Psychology of Tourist Behaviour.* Oxford: Pergamon.

Pekola, R.J. (1987) "The phenomenology of meditation." In M. West (Ed.), *The Psychology of Meditation* (pp. 59-80). Oxford: Oxford University Science Publications.

Penrose, R. (1990) *The Emperor's New Mind: Concerning Computers, Minds and the Laws of Physics.* Oxford University Press.

Persinger, M.A. (1987) *Neuropsychological Bases of God Beliefs.* New York: Praeger.

Pervin, L.A. (1963) "The need to predict and control under conditions of threat." *Journal of Personality, 31,* 570-587.

Petty, R.E., & Cacioppo, J.T. (1985) "The elaboration likelihood model of persuasion." In L. Berkowitz (Ed.), *Advances in Experimental Social Psychology,* vol. 19. New York: Academic Press.

Phillips, D.Z. (1965) *The Concept of Prayer.* London: Routledge and Kegan Paul.

Phillips, D.Z. (1981) "Religion in Wittgenstein's mirror." In A.P. Griffiths (Ed.), *Wittgenstein Centenary Essays* (pp. 135-150). Cambridge: Cambridge University Press.

Piaget, J. (1931) "Children's philosophies." In C.A. Murchison (Ed.), *A Handbook of Child Psychology.* Oxford University Press.

Piaget, J. (1954) *The Construction of Reality in the Child.* New York: Basic Books.

Pickering, J., & Skinner, M. (1990) *From Sentence to Symbols.* Brighton: Harvester.

Pirsig, R.M. (1974) *Zen and the Art of Motorcycle Maintenance.* New York: Morrow.

Plato, *The Republic.* Translated with an Introduction by D. Lee (1987) Harmondsworth: Penguin.

Poloma, M.M., & Gallup, G.H. (1991) *Varieties of Prayer: A Survey Report.* Philadelphia: Trinity Press International.

Poloma, M.M., & Pendleton, B.F. (1991) *Religiosity and Well-being: Exploring Neglected Dimensions of Quality of Life Research.* Lewiston, NY: Edwin Mellen Press.

Pratt, J.B. (1907) *The Psychology of Religious Belief.* New York: Macmillan.

Pratt, J.B. (1910) "An empirical study of prayer." *American Journal of Religious Psychology and Education, 4,* 48-67.

Pratt, J.B. (1921) *The Religious Consciousness: A Psychological Study.* New York: Macmillan.

Proudfoot, W. (1985) *Religious Experience.* Berkeley: University of California Press.

Proudfoot, W., & Shaver, P. (1975) "Attribution theory and the psychology of religion." *Journal for the Scientific Study of Religion, 141,* 317-330.

Pullum, G.K. (1991) *The Great Eskimo Vocabulary Hoax and Other Irrevent Essays on the Study of Language.* Chicago: University of Chicago Press.

Rabinowitz, J.., Kim, I., & Lazerwitz, B. (1992) "Metropolitan size and participation in religio-ethnic communities." *Journal for the Scientific Study of Religion, 31*(3), 339-345.

Rambo, L.R. (1982) "Current research on religious conversion." *Religious Studies Review, 8,* 146-159.

Radhakrishna, S. (1953) *The Principal Upanishads.* London: George Allen and Unwin.

Rao, K.R., & Palmer, J. (1987) "The anomaly called psi: Recent research and criticism." *Behavioral and Brain Sciences, 10,* 539-551.

Ravenhill, P.L. (1976) "Religious utterances and the theory of speech acts." In W.J. Samarin (Ed.), *Language in Religious Practice.* Rowley, MA: Newberry House.

Rehder, H. (1955) "Wunderheilungen, ein Experiment." *Hippokrates, 26,* 577-580.

Reichard, G.A. (1944) *Prayer: The Compulsive Word.* New York: Augustin.

Reik, T. (1955) "From spell to prayer." *Psychoanalysis, 3*(4), 3-26.

Reynolds, V., & Tanner, R.E. (1983) *The Biology of Religion.* London: Longmans.

Richardson, A. (1984) *The Experiential Dimension of Psychology.* Brisbane: University of Queensland Press.

Rivers, W.H.R. (1906) *The Todas.* London.

Robinson, J.P., Shaver, P.R., & Wrightsman, L.S. (1991) *Measures of Personality and Social Psychological Attitudes.* San Diego: Academic Press.

Rogers, C. (1951) *Client-centered Therapy.* Boston: Houghton Mifflin.

Rohr, R. (1990) *Discovering the Enneagram: An Ancient Tool for a New Spiritual Journey.* New York: Crossroad.

Rokeach, M. (1960) *Open and Closed Mind: Investigations into the Nature of Belief Systems and Personality Systems.* New York: Basic Books.

Rokeach, M. (1918-) *The Nature of Human Values.* New York: Free Press.

Rokeach, M. (1964) *The Three Christs of Ypsilanti: A Psychological Study.* New York: Knopf.

Rosenberg, B.A. (1970) "The formulaic quality of spontaneous sermons." *Journal of American Folk-lore, 83,* 3-20.

Rosenberg, M.J., & Abelson, R.P. (1960) "An analysis of cognitive balancing." In M.J. Rosenberg et al (Eds.), *Attitude Organization and Change: An Analysis of Consistencies Among Attitude Components.* New Haven: Yale University Press.

Rosensteil, A.K., & Keefe, F.J. (1983) "The use of coping strategies in chronic low back pain patients: Relationship to patient characteristics and current adjustment." *Pain, 17,* 33-44.

Rosenthal, R. (1964) "The effects of the experimenter in the results of psychological research." In B.A. Maher (Ed.), *Progress in Experimental Personality Research, 1,* pp. 79-114.

Rosenthal, R., & Jacobson, L. (1968) *Pygmalian in the Classroom.* New York: Holt, Rinehart and Winston.

Ross, L., & Nisbett, R.E. (1991) *The Person and the Situation: Perspectives of Social Psychology.* New York: McGraw-Hill.

Ross, M.G. (1950) *Religious Beliefs of Youth.* New York: Association Press.

Rothbaum, F., Weisz, J.R., & Snyder, S.S. (1982) "Changing the world and changing the self. A two-process model of perceived control." *Journal of Personality and Social Psychology, 42,* 5-37.

Ruf, F.J. (1991) *The Creation of Chaos: William James and the Stylistic Making of a Disorderly World.* State University of New York Press.

Ryan, J. (1991) *The Vanishing Subject: Early Psychology and Literary Modernism.* Chicago: The University of Chicago Press.

Sabatier, A. (n.d.) *An Outline of the Philosophy of Religion* (referred to by Pratt, 1907).

Sabom, M.B. (1982) *Recollections of Death: A Medical Investigation.* New York: Harper & Row.

Sacks, O. (1986a) *A Leg to Stand On.* London: Picador.

Sacks, O. (1986b) *The Man Who Mistook His Wife For a Hat.* London: Pan Books.

Salter, D.L. (1986) *Spirit and Intellect: Thomas Upham's Holiness Theory.* Metuchan: Scarecrow Press.

Samarin, W.J. (1976) *Language in Religious Practice.* Rowley, MA: Newbury House.

Sangharakshita (1987) *A Survey of Buddhism: Its Doctrines and Methods Through the Ages.* London: Tharpa.

Saudia, T.L., et al (1991) "Health locus of control and helpfulness of prayer." *Heart and Lung, 20*(1), 60-65.

Scarlett, W.G. & Perriello, L. (1991) "The development of prayer in adolescence." In F.K. Oser & W.G. Scarlett, *Religious Development in Childhood and Adolescence.* San Francisco: Jossey-Bass.

Schachter, S., & Singer, J.E. (1962) "Cognitive, social and physiological determinants of emotional state." *Psychological Review, 69,* 379-399.

Scheler, M. (1921) *On the Eternal in Man.* (B. Noble, Trans., 1960) New York: Harper & Brothers.

Schmeidler, G.R., & McConnell, R.A. (1973) *ESP and Personality Patterns.* Westport, CT: Greenwood Press.

Schneiders, S. (1986) *New Wine-skins: Reimagining Religious Life Today.* New York: Paulist Press.

Schultz (in Jaspars, J. 1983) *Attribution Theory and Research: Conceptual Developmental and Social Dimensions.* London: Academic Press.

Schweitzer, A. (1913) *The Quest of the Historical Jesus: A Critical Study of its Progress from Reimarus to Wrede.* New York: Macmillan (1948).

Searle, J.R. (1992) *The Rediscovery of Mind.* Boston: MIT Press (review by T. Roszack, *New Scientist,* 3 Oct 1992, p. 41).

Segond, J. (1911) *La Prière: Etude de Psychologie Religiouse.* Paris: Alcan.

Shackle, E. (1988) "Pioneer questionnaires on prayer revisted." Paper presented to XXIV International Congress of Psychology, Sydney, N.S.W.

Shackle, E., & Brown, L.B. (1994) "Steps towards a psychology of prayer." In L.B. Brown (Ed.), *Religion, Personality and Mental Health*. New York: Springer Verlag.

Shallice, T. (1988) *From Neuropsychology to Mental Structure*. Cambridge University Press.

Shephard, R.N. (1971) "Mental rotation of 3-D objects." *Science, 171*, 701-703.

Sherif, M., Taub, D., & Houland, G.T. (1958) "Assimilation and contrast effects of anchoring stimuli on judgment." *Journal of Experimental Psychology, 55*, 150-155.

Sills, D.L., & Merton, R.K. (1991) "Social science quotations." *International Encyclopedia of the Social Sciences,* Volume 19. New York: Macmillan.

Skinner, B.F. (1989) *Recent Issues in the Analysis of Behavior*. Columbus, Ohio: Merrill.

Smart, N. (1969) *The Religious Experience of Mankind*. New York: Scribners.

Snider, J.G., & Osgood, C.E. (1969) *Semantic Differential Technique*. Chicago: Aldine.

Snow, A. (1974) "Folk medical beliefs." *Annals of Internal Medicine, 81*, 82-96.

Snyder, C.R. (1989) "Reality negotiation: From excuse to hope and beyond." *Journal of Social and Clinical Psychology, 8*(2), 130-157.

Solomon, R.C. (1976) *The Passions*. New York: Doubleday.

Speiber, D., & Wilson, D. (1986) *Relevance: A Theory of Communication*. Cambridge, MA: Harvard University Press.

Spencer, B., & F.J. Gillen (1904) *The Northern Tribes of Central Australia*. London: Macmillan.

Spero, M. (1980) *Judaism and Psychology*. New York: Kitav.

Spickard, J.V. (1991) "Experiencing religous rituals: A Schutzian analysis of Navajo cermonies." *Sociological Analysis, 52*(2), 191-204.

Spilka, B., & Schmidt, G. (1983) "General attribution theory for the psychology of religion: The influence of event character on attributions to God." *Journal for the Scientific Study of Religion, 22*, 326-339.

Spilka, B., Hood, R.W., & Gorsuch, R.L. (1985) *The Psychology of Religion: An Empirical Approach*. Englewood Cliffs, NJ: Prentice-Hall.

Spitzer, M. (1990) "On defining delusions." *Comprehensive Psychiatry, 31*(5), 377-397.

Staal, F. (1991) "Vedic Mantras." In Harvey Alper (Ed.), *Understanding Mantras*. Delhi: Motilal Banarsidass.

Staat, F. (1975) *Exploring Mysticism*. Harmondsworth: Penguin.

Stace, W.T. (1960a) *Mysticism and Philosophy*. Philadelphia: Lippincott.

Stace, W.T. (1960b) *The Teachings of the Mystics: Being Selections from the Great Mystics and Metaphysical Writings of the World*. New York: American Library.

Stanner, W.E.H. (1963) On Aboriginal religion, VI. *Oceania* 33, 239-73.

Stanner, W.E.H. (1976) Some aspects of Australian religion. *Colloquium* 9(1): 19-35.

Stanner, W.E.H. (1984) *Religion, Totemism and Symbolism*. In Max Charlesworth et al (Eds.), *Religion in Aboriginal Australia: An Anthology* (pp. 137-172). St Lucia, Qld: University of Queensland Press..

Starbuck, E.D. (1897) "Psychology of religion." *American Journal of Psychology,* *9,* 70-124.

Stark, R., & Glock, C.Y. (1968) *American Piety: The Nature of Religious Commitment.* Berkeley: University of California Press.

Stevens, W. (1953) *Selected poems.* London: Faber & Faber.

Stolz, K.R. (1913) *Autosuggestion in Private Prayer: A Study in the Psychology of Prayer.* Grand Forks, ND

Stolz, K.R. (1923) *The Psychology of Prayer.* New York: Abingdon Press.

Stouffer, S.A., et al (1949) *The American Soldier: Volume 2: Combat and its Aftermath.* Princeton University Press.

Streeter, B.H. (1921) *Concerning Prayer: Its Nature, Its Difficulties and Its Value.* London: Macmillan.

Strong, A.L. (1909) *The Psychology of Prayer.* Chicago: University of Chicago Press.

Swanson, G.E. (1960) *The Birth of the Gods: The Origin of Primitive Beliefs.* Ann Arbor: University of Michigan Press.

Swatos, W.H. Jr (1987) *Religious Sociology: Interfaces and Boundaries.* Westport, CT: Greenwood Press.

Szasz, T. (1974) *Ceremonial Chemistry.* New York: Doubleday.

Tamminen, K. (1991) *Religious Development in Childhood and Youth: An Empirical Study.* Helsinki: Suomalainen Tiedeakatemia.

Tarde, G. (1898) "Le public et la Foule." *Revue de Paris, 5,* 615-635.

Tart, C. (1988) *Waking Up: Overcoming the Obstacles to Human Potential.* Shaftesbury: Dorset Element Books.

Taylor, S.E. (1989) *Positive Illusions: Creative Self-deception and the Healthy Mind.* New York: Basic Books.

Taylor, S.E., & Brown, J.D. (1988) "Illusion and well-being: A social psychological perspective on mental health." *Psychological Bulletin, 103,* 193-210.

Taylor, S.E., et al (1991) "Self-generated feelings of control and adjustment to physical illness." *Journal of Social Issues,* 47 (4), 91-110.

Thiel-Horstmann, M. (1989) "Bhakti and monasticism." In G.D. Southeimer & H. Kulke (Eds.), *Hinduism Reconsidered.* New Delhi: Manohar Publications.

Thomas, K. (1971) *Religion and the Decline of Magic: Studies in Popular Beliefs in Sixteenth and Seventeenth England.* London: Weidenfeld and Nicolson.

Thouless, R.H. (1935) "The tendency to certainty in religious belief." *British Journal of Psychology, 26,* 16-31.

Thouless, R.H. (1954) *Authority and Freedom: Some Psychological Problems of Religious Belief.* Greenwich, CT: Seabury Press.

Thouless, R.H. (1971) *An Introduction to the Psychology of Religion* (3rd. ed.). Cambridge University Press.

Threadgold, D. (1987) "Changing the subject." In *Language Topics.* Amsterdam: John Benjamin Publishing.

Tice, D.M. (1992) "Self-concept change and self-presentation: The looking glass self is also a magnifying glass." *Journal of Personality and Social Psychology, 63*(3), 435-451.

Tolman, E.C. (1925) "Purpose and cognition: The determiners of animal learning."

Psychological Review, 32, 285-197.

Tolstoy, L. (1982) *Anna Karenina.* Harmondsworth: Penguin.

Treisman, A. (1988) "Features and objects: The fourteenth Bartlett Memorial Lecture." *Quarterly Journal of Experimental Psychology, 40A,* 201-237.

Tucci, Giuseppe (1988) *The Religions of Tibet.* Berkeley: University of California Press.

Turner, David H. (1985) "The Incarnation of Nambirrirra." In T. Swain & D. Rose (Eds.), *Aborigines and Christian Missions.* Adelaide: Australian Association for the Study of Religion.

Turner, David H. (1989) *Return to Eden: A Journey Through the Promised Landscape of Amagalyuagbe.* New York: Peter Lang.

Turner, J.A., & Clancy, S. (1986) "Strategies for coping with chronic low back pain: Relationship to pain and disability." *Pain, 24,* 355-364.

Turner, V., & Turner, E. (1978) *Image and Pilgrimage in Christian Culture: Anthropological Perspectives.* New York: Columbia University Press.

Tversky, A., & Kahneman, D. (1974) "Judgment under uncertainty: Heuristics and biases." *Science, 185,* 1124-1131.

Twain, Mark (1869) *The Innocents Abroad.* New York: Airmend (1936 reprint).

Tylor, E.B. (1873) *Primitive Culture: Researches Into the Development of Mythology, Philosophy, Religion, Language, Art and Custom.* London: John Murray.

Tyrrel, G.N.M. (1953) *Apparitions.* London: Duckworth.

Uberman, H.P. (1990) *Luther: Man Between God and the Devil.* New Haven: Yale University Press.

Ulanov, A., & Ulanov, B. (1985) *Primary Speech: A Psychology of Prayer.* London: SCM Press.

Underhill, E. (1911) *Mysticism: A Study in the Nature and Development of Man's Spiritual Consciousness.* London: Methuen (revised, 1930).

Van de Kemp, H. (1984) *Psychology and Theology in Western Thought 1672-1965: A Historical and Annotated Bibliography.* White Plains: Kraus International.

Vergote, A. (1988) *Guilt and Desire: Religious Attitudes and Their Pathological Derivatives.* New Haven: Yale University Press.

Vergote, A., & Tamayo, A. (1980) *The Parental Figures and the Representation of God.* The Hague: Mouton.

Wach, J. (1944) *Sociology of Religion.* Chicago: University of Chicago Press.

Wagnick, K. (1980) "Mysticism and schizophrenia." In R. Woods (Ed.), *Understanding Mysticism* (pp. 321-337). New York: Doubleday.

Wakefield, G.S. (Ed.) (1983) *A Dictionary of Christian Spirituality.* London: SCM Press.

Walster, E., Aronson, E., & Brown, Z. (1966) "Choosing to suffer as a consequence of expecting to suffer." *Journal of Experimental Social Psychology. 22,* 400-406.

Watson, P., Morris, R., & Hood, R. (1990) "Attributional complexity, religious orientation and indiscriminate pro-religion." *Review of Religious Research, 32,* 110-121.

Welford, A.T. (1946) "An attempt at an experimental approach to the psychology of religion." *British Journal of Psychology, 36,* 55-73.

Welford, A.T. (1947a) "Is religion behavior dependent on affect or frustration?" *Journal of Abnormal and Social Psychology, 42,* 310-319.

Welford, A.T. (1947b) "A psychological footnote to prayer." *Theology Today, 3*(4), 498-501.

Welford, A.T. (1948) "The use of archaic language in religious expression: An example of a canalised response." *British Journal of Psychology, 38,* 209-218.

Wellman, H.M., & Gelman, S.A. (1992) "Cognitive development: foundational theories of core domains. *Annual Review of Psychology, 43,* 337-375.

Wells, H.G. (1934) *Experiment in Autobiography: Discoveries and Conclusions of a Very Ordinary Brain.* New York: Macmillan.

West, M.A. (Ed.) (1987) *The Psychology of Meditation.* Oxford: Clarendon Press.

Wheaton, B. (1985) "Models of the stress-buffering functions of coping resources." *Journal of Health and Social Behavior, 26,* 352-364.

Whitehead, A.N. (1926) *Religion in the Making.* Cambridge University Press.

Wicker, A.W. (1971) "An examination of the 'other variables' explanations of attitude-behavior inconsistency." *Journal of Abnormal and Social Psychology, 38,* 209-218.

Wierzbicka, A. (1985) *Lexicography and Conceptual Analysis.* Ann Arbor: Karoma.

Wierzbicka, A. (1987) *English Speech Act Verbs: A Semantic Dictionary.* Sydney: Academic.

Wierzbicka, A. (1988) *The Semantics of Grammar.* Amsterdam: John Benjamins.

Wierzbicka, A. (1991) *Cross-cultural Pragmatics: The Semantics of Human Interaction.* Berlin: Mouton de Gruyter.

Wierzbicka, A. (1992). *Semantics, Culture and Cognition: Universal Human Concepts in Culture-specific Configurations.* New York: Oxford University Press.

Wierzbicka, A. (1994) "Back to Definitions." *Lexicographica, 8,* 146-174.

Wierzbicka, A. (Forthcoming). The semantics of non-verbal communication.

Wierzbicka, A. (In press). Semantic primitives and semantic fields. In A. Lehrer & E. Kittay (Eds.), *Frames, Fields, and Contrasts.*

Wiles, M. (1974) *The Remaking of Christian Doctrine.* London: SCM Press.

Wiles, M. (1976) *What Is Theology?* Oxford: Oxford University Press.

Williams, H.A. (1972) *Some Day I'll Find You: An Autobiography.* London: Mitchell Beazley.

Wilson, B. (1973) *Magic and the Millenium.* Frogmore: Palladin.

Winnicott, D.W. (1971) *Playing and Reality.* London: Tavistock.

Wittgenstein, L. (1921) *Tractatus Logico-Philosophicus.* London: Routledge and Kegan Paul (1981).

Wittgenstein, Ludwig (1953) *Philosophical Investigations.* (G.E.M. Anscombe, Trans.). Oxford: Basil Blackwell.

Wittgenstein, Ludwig (1970) *Zettel,* ed. G.E.M. Anscombe and G.H. von Wright, trans. G.E.M. Anscombe. Berkeley: University of California Press.

Woodworth, R.S., & Sells, S.B. (1935) "An atmosphere effect in formal sylogistic reasoning." *Journal of Experimental Psychology, 18,* 451-460.

Woods, R. (Ed.) (1986) *Understanding Mysticism.* New York: Doubleday.

Wright, D. (1976) *Moral Development: A Cognitive Approach.* Milton Keynes: Open University Press.

Wulff, D.M. (1991) *Psychology of Religion: Classic and Contemporary Views*. New York: Wiley.

Wundt, W. (1900-1920) *Volker-psychologie,* Leipzig 10 volumes.

Wuthnow, R. (1988) *The Restructuring of American Religion: Society and Faith Since World War II*. Princeton: Princeton University Press.

Yates, F.A. (1966) *The Art of Memory*. London: Routledge and Kegan Paul.

Zajonc, R.B. (1965) "Social facilitation." *Science, 149*, 269-274.

Zajonc, R.B. (1980) "Feeling and thinking: Preferences need no inferences." *American Psychologist, 35*, 151-175.

Zaleski, C. (1987) *Otherworld Journeys: Accounts of Near-death Experience in Medieval and Modern Times*. New York: Oxford University Press.

Zollschan, G.K. et al (1989) *Exploring the Paranormal: Perspectives on Belief and Experiences*. Dorset: Prism Press.

Zukier, H. (1986) "The paradigmatic and narrative modes in goal-guided inference." In R.M. Sorrentino & E.T. Higgins (Eds.), *Handbook of Motivation and Cognition: Foundations of Social Behavior* (pp. 465-502). New York: Wiley.

Zusne, L., & Jones, W.H. (1989) *Anomalistic Psychology: A Study of Magical Thinking*. Hillsdale, NJ: Lawrence Erlbaum.

Index of Names

Abelson, R.P. 142, 228, 230, 243, 284f, 296, 302
Abraham 108, 263
Abrams, M. 284
Abramson, L.Y. 177, 284
Achilles 9
Adamson, P. 256
Adams Smith, D.E. 284
Adorno, T.W. 224, 284
Agamemnon 9
Ajzen, F. 243, 291
Alcock, J.E. 113, 284
Alemany, C. 267
Alexander, H.B. 39f, 284
Allah 80
Allan, J.R. 54, 60, 258, 272, 299
Allport, F.H. 145, 284
Allport, G.W. 88, 112, 133, 158, 284
Alper, H. 304
Alston, W. 101, 284
Ames, E.S. 48, 53, 257, 259, 284
Anchor, K.N. 258, 264
Anesaki, M. 40f, 284
Anscombe, G.E.M. 307
Antaki, C. 227, 284
Anthony of Sourozh 27, 299
Anthony, St. 112, 136
Apollo 33, 138
Appleton, G. 17, 83, 149, 259, 284
Apresjan, J. 30, 285

Aquinas, T. 27, 162, 285
Arbesmann, R. 28, 285
Arbib, M.A. 285
Argyle, M.A. 158, 161, 170f, 193, 285
Aristotle 10, 33
Aronson, E. 180, 227, 289, 297, 299, 306
Asclepius 10
Astington, J.W. 50, 285
Athene 33
Augustine 18, 27, 33, 61, 100, 139, 148, 162, 212, 240, 285, 287
Aurangzeb 79
Austin, J.L. 127ff, 139, 191, 285
Ayeroff, F. 285

Bacaseta, P.E. 258, 262
Back, C.W. 60, 285
Bacon, R. 119
Baelz, P.R. 285
Baiame 42
Bains, G. 229, 285
Bakan, D. 285
Ball, D. 33
Bandura, A. 122, 285
Barabat, R. 285
Barker, E. 175, 285
Baroffio, B. 26
Barry, W.A. 27, 285
Barth, K. 269
Bartlett, F.C. 285

Bates, M. 271
Bateson, C.D. 112, 164, 237, 285, 289
Bauml, B. 145, 285
Bauml, F. 145, 285
Bearon, L.B. 259
Beck, A.T. 202, 222, 285
Beck, F.O. 50, 54f, 60, 150, 168, 170, 257f, 260, 277, 286
Beit-Hallahmi, B. 161, 170f, 285, 286
Bell, R.M. 121, 286
Belshaw, G.P.M. 260
Benedict, St. 69
Benoit, P. 33, 286
Berger, P.L. 111, 286
Bergin, A.E. 178, 220ff, 286, 295f
Berkowitz, L. 301
Bernadette Soubirous, St. 37
Bernoulli, D. 247
Bertram, St. 58
Bettelheim, B. 286
Bharati, A. 286
Bill-Harvey, D. 260
Blackburn, R. 286
Blackmore, S. 114, 286
Blignault, I. 258, 273
Blomster, W.V. 284
Bloom, L. 235
Bonhoeffer, D. 103, 134, 269, 286
Bootzin, R.R. 221, 286
Bordin, E.S. 221, 286
Boring, E.G. 223, 286
Borst, J. 27
Boulding, M. 27
Bourguignon, E. 286
Bourque, L.B. 60, 285
Bovet, P. 197, 286
Bowker, J. 8, 54, 96, 181, 204, 214, 233f, 237, 286
Bowman, G.W. 260
Brady, P. 298
Brahman 71f, 76f
Brandon, S.G.F. 25, 39, 286
Brentano, F. 223
Brewer, C. 286
Broad, W. 286
Brock, S. 259, 260

Brody, M. 259, 260
Brown, D.F. 255
Brown, G.K. 258, 260, 286
Brown, J.D. 305
Brown, L.B. 2, 4,18f, 49f, 55f, 85f, 90, 92, 125, 128, 132, 140, 145, 151, 153ff, 157f, 169, 180, 189, 192, 195, 208, 213, 215, 218, 220, 231, 237fr, 245, 250, 257f, 260f, 265, 273f, 277f, 286f, 289, 291, 292, 294, 296, 300, 304
Brown, P.M. 186ff, 269, 297
Brown, Z. 180, 306
Brummer, V. 88, 200, 258, 261, 287
Bruner, J. 131, 250, 287
Brush, S.J. 88, 287
Bryant, C. 22, 23
Buber, M. 1, 21, 92, 287
Buddha, Gautama 40, 41, 44, 52, 77f, 237
Bulman, R.J. 287
Bunker, D.E. 258, 261
Bunyan, J. 55
Buono, A.M. 26, 28, 287
Burchill, J. 258, 271
Burnam, T. 125, 287
Burnett, D. 287
Butler, S. 137
Byrd, R.C. 49, 158, 165ff, 193, 258, 261, 287

Cacioppo, J.T. 218, 301
Calkins, M.W. 161, 257, 261, 287
Calvin, J. 88
Cambry, J. 115, 287
Campbell, J. 287
Capps, D. 18, 119, 212, 217, 257, 260, 261, 262, 287
Carcia-Monge, J.A. 267
Carlsmith, J.M. 180, 291
Carlson, C.R. 258, 262
Carlson, J.G. 287
Carothers, J.C. 287
Carroll, M.P. 121, 197, 262, 287
Carse, J.P. 84, 288
Carson, V. 258, 262

Carter, F.C. 257, 262
Carver, C.S. 288
Cary-Elwes, C. 262
Cassirer, E. 143, 288
Castelli, J. 160, 291
Castles, I. 5, 288
Catherine of Genoa 280
Chadwick, H. 285
Chansou, J. 262
Charcot, J.M. 221
Charlesworth, M. 298, 299, 304
Chastaing, M. 138, 259, 288
Chertok, L. 51, 288
Chi, M.T.H. 131, 288
Christopher, St. 134
Chuang Tzu 67, 288
Ciccone, D.S. 262
Claiborn, C.D. 218, 294
Clanchy, M.T. 288
Clancy, S. 185, 279, 306
Clark, W.H. 8, 143, 198f, 225, 288
Clarke, T.E. 258, 263, 288
Claxton, G. 179, 288
Clayton, R.R. 21, 288
Clements, R.E. 251, 259, 263, 288
Coats, R.H. 263
Coe, G.A. 47, 49, 50, 51, 52, 53, 56, 62,
    63, 152, 257, 265, 288
Cole, P. 293
Coles, R. 95, 288
Collipp, P.J. 166, 288
Comstock, G.W. 4, 288
Conn, J.W. 288
Copernicus, N. 142
Corlu, A. 44, 288
Coué, E. 221
Creegan, C. 97, 256
Crispin, St. 136
Crisson, J.E. 185, 258, 288
Crook, J.H. 175, 288
Cruden, A. 62
Crystal, D. 126, 134f, 138, 206, 288f
Csikszentmihalyi, I.S. 8, 201, 289
Csikszentmihalyi, M. 8, 201, 289, 299
Culligan, K. 258, 263
Cupitt, D. 93f, 97f, 100ff, 109, 289

Curnow, T. 26
Currie, R. 4, 289
Curtis, R.C. 180, 289

Damascene, J. 26
Daniel, E.V. 232, 296
Daniel, H.D. 291
D'Arcy, C.F. 25, 28, 289
Darley, J. 164, 289
Daston, L. 289
David, J.P. 161, 263, 289
Davis, C.F. 213ff, 237, 249, 289
Davis, T.N. 263
Dawkins, R. 201, 289
De Charms, R. 289
Deconchy, J.P. 119, 164, 167, 180, 182,
    202, 237, 289
de Hart, J. 258, 267, 277
de la Tourette, G. 138, 259
Delmonte, M.M. 178, 289
Demeter 33
Dennett, D.C. 51f, 201f, 289
Devil, The 137f
Devlin, J. 112, 114ff, 139, 289
Diller, A. 26, 44
Dittes, J.E. 4, 8, 18, 182, 200, 212, 231,
    287, 289
Dodds, E.R. 8ff, 52, 290
Doerr, H.A. 209, 301
Dolan, E. 258, 295
Dollinger, S.J. 270, 281
Donaghue, Q. 143, 263
Donell, D. 180, 289
Doniger, S. 272, 299
Douglas, M. 290
Draak, C. den 258, 267, 277
Dubois-Dumee, J.P. 25ff, 31f, 258, 263,
    290
Dudley, M. 150, 290
Duke, I.T. 258, 263
Dumont, L. 173, 290
Durkheim, E., 15, 201, 211, 214f
Durran, M. 153, 259, 264, 290
Dyer Ball, J. 290

Easting, R 290

Eckhardt, Meister 179
Edelstein, E.J.L. 290
Edwards, J.C. 264
Einstein, A. 125
Eiser, J.R. 142, 290
El Azayem, G.A. 53, 290
Eliade, M. 42f, 190, 290, 292
Elias, N. 196, 290
Eliot, T.S. 245f
Elizabeth of the Trinity 27
Elkin, A.P. 42
Elkind, D. 190f, 193f, 202, 258, 264, 270, 281, 290, 297
Ellens, J.H. 264
Emerson, R.W. 55, 142
English, A.C. 221, 290
English, H.B. 221, 290
Ericsson, K.A. 122, 290
Erikson, E. 18, 196, 212, 241, 290
Ernulphus, Bishop 138
Escott, H. 306
Evans, C.S. 109
Evely, L. 27
Eysenck, H.J. 290

Fallaize, E.N. 28, 39, 290
Farberow, N.L. 4, 290
Farnell, F.R. 35f, 257, 264, 290
Farr, R.M. 151, 201, 290
Farrar, Dean 137
Feagin, J. 229, 290
Fechner, G.T. 162
Felix, R.W. 257, 264, 290
Fenwick, P. 176, 291
Fernando, S.J. 259
Ferré, F. 125, 291
Festinger, L. 142, 169, 180, 291
Feuerbach, L.-A. 18, 101, 210, 212
Fichter, J.H. 198, 291
Finlay-Jones, R. 150, 293
Finney, J.R. 47, 83, 257f, 264f, 273, 275, 278, 291
Fisch, R. 291
Fishbein, M. 243, 291
Flaubert, G. 125
Fogarty, M. 4, 291, 293

Fong, G.T. 291
Fosdick, H.E. 257, 265
Foucault, M. 63, 253f, 291
Fowler, J. 194
Fox, G. 139
Francis of Assisi, St. 4, 17f
Francis, L.J. 58, 90, 140, 153f, 189f, 258, 265, 291
Frank, J.B. 122, 208ff, 216, 220ff, 244, 291
Frank, J.D. 122, 208ff, 216, 220ff, 244, 291
Frayn, M. 291
Frazer, J.G. 20, 291
Freud, S. 9, 18, 51, 95, 120, 134, 149, 196, 201, 210, 212, 222, 234, 267, 291
Fromm, E. 196
Frye, N. 291
Furnham, A. 50, 56, 85, 169, 231, 245, 291

Gabriel 80
Galanter, M. 259, 265
Galileo, G. 142, 143
Gallistel, C.R. 291
Gallup, G.H. 94, 151, 159f, 168, 258, 261f, 274, 291, 301
Galton, F. 52, 123, 157, 165, 258, 265, 292
Gardener, M. 292
Gardner, H. 122, 292
Garfield, S.C. 296
Gaston, J.E. 19, 86, 292
Gelman, S.A. 49, 119, 131, 191, 307
George, St. 136
Gergen, M. 114, 292
Gibb, H.A.R. 292
Gibson, J.J. 251, 292
Gigerenzer, G. 178, 246, 292
Gilbert, A. 4, 289
Gill, S.D. 25, 28, 30, 39, 41, 45, 189f, 191, 259, 265, 266, 275, 292
Gillen, F.J. 42, 48, 304
Gillespie, J.M. 284
Ginsberg, G.P. 231, 296
Girgensohn, K. 15, 211, 292

Gladden, J.W. 21, 288
Glik, D.C. 209, 292
Glock, C.Y. 21, 292, 305
Gmünder, P. 131, 151, 194f, 272, 300
Goddard, C. 45, 292
Godin, A. 18, 47, 49, 53, 61, 65, 84, 93, 128, 150f, 169, 189, 192f, 196f, 231, 255, 257f, 261, 266, 278, 292
Goldman, R. 192f, 258, 266, 292
Goleman, D.J. 176, 218, 220, 292
Goll, R. 293
Gorer, G. 170
Gorsuch, R. 4, 56, 83, 85, 119, 162, 172, 255, 293, 304
Grass, G. 16, 298
Graves, R. 135, 138, 259, 293
Greeley, A.M. 171, 293, 298
Gregor, R. 287
Gregory of Nyssa 26
Greimas, A.J. 293
Grice, H.P. 200, 293
Griffith, E.E.H. 266
Griffiths, A.P. 301
Grimmet, M. 293
Gronbaek, V. 258, 266
Grzesiak, R.C. 262
Gurdjieff, G.I. 271
Gutman, H. 291

Hahn, J. 230, 300
Hall, G.S. 50, 150
Halliday, M.A.K. 92, 130, 293
Hameedullah, M. 293
Hamlet 147f
Hample, S. 259, 271
Harakas, S.S. 293
Harding, D.W. 162, 236, 293
Harding, S. 293
Hardman, O. 275
Hardy, A. 162, 293
Harkins, J. 26
Harré, R. 150, 293
Harries, R. 23, 293
Harris, P.C. 285
Harris, P.L. 293
Hartshorne, H. 257

Hastings, J. 284, 289f, 297
Havel, V. 90
Hay, D. 16, 168, 293
Healy, C.C. 293
Heber, R. 91
Hedges, D. 258, 276
Heffer, D. 293
Heider, F. 84, 142, 232, 294
Heiler, F. 6, 15, 18f, 28f, 47, 94, 145, 150, 183ff, 191, 210, 212f, 257f, 267, 294
Helminiak, D.A. 258, 267, 294
Hemingway, E. 135
Hendlen, S.J. 172, 294
Heppner, P.P. 218, 294
Herbert, G. 85f
Herodotus 10
Hesiod 10, 33
Hesse, M.B. 285
Hewstone, M. 226, 229, 285, 294, 296
Higgins, E.T. 308
Hilgard, E.R. 223, 294
Hill, J.M.M. 294
Hilton, D. 296
Hippocrates, 222, 302
Hippolytus 128
Hobson, D.P. 258, 278
Hocking, P. 56, 294
Hodge, A.J. 47, 257f, 267, 294
Holahan, C.J. 294
Holland, J.C. 217, 294
Holmes, T.H. 112, 294
Homer 8, 33
Hong, E.H. 296
Hong, H.V. 296
Hood, R.W. 4, 83, 85, 119, 167, 172, 258, 267, 296, 304, 306
Hopkins, G.M. 135
Horgl, C. 266
Horsley, L. 4, 289
Horton, A.L. 252, 294
Horton, P.C. 205f, 294
Houland, G.T. 304
Howard, P. 144, 294
Howell, C. 126, 288
Hunsberger, B. 19, 213, 294

Hunt, R.A. 204, 294
Huon, G.F. 145, 220, 256, 294
Huss, K. 258, 262
Hutton, P.H. 291
Hynes, K. 27, 28, 294

Ichheiser, G. 229, 294
Ignatius of Loyola, St. 26, 129, 140, 268
Imoda, F. 258, 267, 275
Inglis, B. 294
Isaac the Syrian 27
Ishtar 34

Jacks, L.P. 61, 295
Jackson, F. 206, 295
Jacobs, A. 122, 295
Jacobson, L. 303
Jahoda, G. 159, 295
Jaksa, J.A. 295
Jam, J. 70
James, H. 224, 295
James, W. 17, 45f, 56, 62f, 65, 96, 120ff,
    139, 141f, 148, 151, 173, 175, 182,
    198, 211, 221, 223f, 233, 236f, 269,
    295, 303
Janis, I.L. 216f, 219, 295
Janssen, J. 258, 267, 277
Jaspars, J. 303
Jaynes, J. 202, 295
Jeeves, M.A. 85, 88, 299
Jehla, J.K.M. 75
Jendon 116
Jenkins, W.O. 60, 295
Jennings, M. 295
Jensen, J.P. 221, 295
Jesus Christ 14, 24, 27, 32, 65, 69, 78,
    80, 84f, 89, 91, 101f, 116, 118, 120,
    124, 137, 139, 141, 171, 273
Job 7, 22
John Chrysostom, St. 28, 37
John of the Cross, St. 107f, 206, 263
John the Divine, St. 263
John, St. 111, 120, 124, 148, 283
Johnson, B.L. 258, 263
Johnson, P.E. 171, 268, 295
Johnson, S. 114, 234

Johnson, S.C. 185f, 259, 268, 295
Jones, C. 122, 268
Jones, W.H. 308
Joyce, C.R.B. 165f, 258, 268, 295
Joyce, J. 130, 235
Jung, C.G. 7, 9f, 22f, 181, 261, 267f,
    291, 295

Kadlovbovsky, E. 259, 268
Kahneman, D. 85f, 178, 295, 306
Kahoe, R.D. 271
Karenina, A. 33
Keating, C.J. 258, 268
Keefe, F.J. 185f, 258, 275, 288, 295, 302
Keirsey, D. 271, 280
Keller, E.F. 62, 295
Kelley, H.H. 6, 13, 51, 84, 132, 141,
    226ff, 230, 232, 295
Kelsey, M.T. 261, 268
Kendon, A. 295
Kenny, A. 295
Kenyon, C.H. 244, 295
Keyes, C.F. 232, 296
Khan, Abdul Hamid 79, 81, 120
Kieckhefer, R. 50, 117ff, 296
Kierkegaard, S. 14, 61, 66, 102, 106ff,
    296
Kim, I. 302
King, M.B. 21, 204, 294, 296
King, N. 296
Kinsey, A.C. 168
Kirkpatrick, L.A. 121, 181, 218, 296
Kittay, E. 307
Klausner, W.J. 40, 296
Klein, D.G. 297
Klein, M. 196
Knapp, C.R. 258, 280
Knox, R. 56, 296
Koenig, H.G. 259
Koepp, W. 182, 267, 296
Kohlberg, L. 194
Koestler, A. 206, 296
Krantz, D.H. 291
Krause, N. 63ff, 268, 296
Krieger, D. 258, 269
Kristeva, J. 269

Kulke, H. 305
Kumbu, Madi, 73
Kunmanggur 42

Lacan, J. 245
Ladd, K. 161, 263, 289
Laing, R.D. 220, 296
Lakshana Devi 75
Lalljee, M. 85, 228, 230, 231, 296
Lambert, M.J. 178f, 220, 296
Lang, B. 111, 298
Langdon, S. 34, 297
Lange, C. 148
Langer, E.J. 175, 177, 224, 236, 297
Langer, S. 131, 288, 297
Lansing, J.S. 71f, 297
Lapins, N.A. 209, 301
Laplace, P.S. de 84
Larson, D. 265
Lash, N. 259, 269
Lazarus, A. 297
Lazerwitz, B. 302
Leach, K. 258, 269
Leary, D.E. 297
Leary, M.R. 113, 273
Le Bon, G. 51, 297
Le Bouthillier de Rance, D.A.J. 69
Lecky, A. 112, 297
Le Corbusier 125
Lee, D. 301
Lee, J. 4, 291
Lee, J.M. 255ff
Lee, R.S. 269
Lefevre, P. 269
Legge, J.W. 92, 297
Lehrer, A. 307
Lenington, S. 258, 265, 269, 297
Lerner, M.J. 159, 180, 225, 230, 297
Lessing, G.E. 102
Lester, D. 297
Leuba, J.H. 1, 47, 297
Lewis, C.S. 85, 269
Levy-Bruhl, L. 130, 297
Lienhardt, G. 297
Likert, R. 151
Lindbeck, G.A. 32, 297

Lilliston, L. 186f, 190, 269, 297
Lindzey, G. 277, 289, 297, 299
Locke, J. 204
Loehr, F. 49, 165, 258, 270, 297
Lokko, J. 69
Long, D. 151, 190f, 193f, 258, 270, 281, 297
Long, E.L. 181, 297
Lovekin, A.A. 138, 258f, 270, 298
Loveland, G.G. 167, 297
Lowrie, W. 296
Lucifer 38
Luckmann, T. 111, 286
Luke, St. 120, 260
Luther, M. 15, 18, 142, 212, 240, 290

MacDonald, M. 297
Mackellar, M. 256
Macquarrie, J. 28, 298
Maddock, K. 42, 298
Magoon, T.M. 217, 294
Maharaj Jee 75
Mahy, G.E. 266
Malaachi 210
Malantschuk, G. 296
Malinowski, B. 126f, 135, 265, 298
Mallory, M.M. 258, 270
Malony, H.N. 47, 83, 138, 257ff, 264, 270, 273, 275, 278, 291, 298
Mann, L. 219
Marcel, G. 21
Marduk 34
Mark, St. 282
Marmor, J. 298
Marrett, R.R. 5, 20, 48, 53, 114, 257, 270, 298
Marsh, J.B. 259, 271
Marshall, E. 259, 271
Marthe, Sr. 193, 292
Martin, A. 298
Martin, L.H. 11f, 117, 291
Marty, M. 171, 298
Marx, K. 18, 210, 212, 234
Mary Magdalene 118
Mary (the mother) of James 118
Masih, Y. 298

Maslow, A. 162
Matthew, St. 124, 148, 282, 283
Mavrodes, G.I. 101, 298
May, G. 258, 271
McCallum, J. 16, 298
McCann, R.V. 167, 298
McComb, S. 267
McConnell, R.A. 114, 303
McDannell, C. 111, 298
McDougall, W. 53, 298
McFague, S. 298
McFarland, S.G. 16, 298
McFarland, T. 298
McKenzie, P. 148, 298
McLuhan, M. 207
McNamara, W. 208, 298
McNeil, D. 299
Mead, G.H. 51, 298
Meadow, M.J. 271
Meehl, P.E. 144, 298
Mehrabian, A. 298
Meissner, W.W. 298
Menashe, A. 271
Mephisto 38
Mercury 138
Meredith, G. 11
Merton, R.K. 298, 304
Merton, T. 84, 86, 139, 269, 298
Mesmer, F.A. 221F
Metz, B. 258, 271
Michael, C.P. 258, 271
Michela, J.L. 226, 295
Michotte, A. 84, 299
Miller, G.A. 299
Miller, H. 116, 299
Milne, A.A. 205
Milton, J. 234
Minsky, M. 299
Misiak, H. 299
Mitchell, A.G. 284
Mitchell, C.E. 271
Moberg, D. 170, 299
Mohr, J.C.B. 296
Monden, L. 299
Monty Python 3
Moore, A.C. 18, 145, 208, 187

Moore, H.T. 299
Moore, T.V. 150, 169f, 257f, 272, 299
Moose, R.H. 294
Morgan, J.C. 293
Morgan, S.P. 281
Morphy, H. 42, 299
Morris, R.J. 258, 267, 306
Morrisey, M.C. 258, 271
Morse, J. 54, 60, 258, 272, 299
Moscovici, S. 151, 201, 214, 290
Mosel, U. 26
Muelder, W.G. 171, 272, 299
Muhammad 80
Muir, M.S. 289
Murchison, C.A. 301
Murphy, S.P., 278
Musil, R. 164
Myers, C.S. 56, 85, 88
Myers, D.G. 299
Myers-Briggs, I. 132, 199, 268, 271, 278, 287

Nagabada 75
Nambirrirrma 76
Napoleon Bonaparte 84
Naranjo, C. 299
Narsingh 75
Nebo 34
Nedoncelle, M. 195, 299
Needham, J. 120
Neighbours, H.W. 185, 259, 272, 299
Neitz, M.J. 251, 299
Newton, I. 142
Nicanor 33
Nicassio, P.M. 258, 260, 286
Niemi, R. 295
Nietzsche, F.W. 210
Nisard, C. 115, 299
Nisbett, R.E. 122,. 127, 178, 229, 232, 244, 291, 299, 303
Nishitani, K. 299
Noble, B. 303
Nogamain 43
Novalis 24

O'Brien, J.A. 257, 272

O'Connor, J.E. 258, 299
Oden, T.C. 300
O'Donnell, d. 27, 300
Ogden, C.K. 124, 300
Olson, D.R. 285
Ong, W.J. 11, 197, 300
Orlan 176
Orne, M.T. 178, 300
Ornstein, R.E. 176, 299, 300
Oser, F.K. 131, 151, 176, 194f, 197, 276, 300, 303
Oser, R. 272, 275
Osgood, C.E. 66, 126, 145, 300, 304
Oskamp, S. 86, 300
Otto, R. 10, 21, 148, 183, 210, 300

Pace, E.A. 264
Padwick, C. 259, 272
Pahnke, W.N. 173, 179, 225, 258, 272, 300
Pailin, D.A. 20, 300
Palmer, G.E.H. 113, 259, 268
Palmer, J. 302
Pargament, K.I. 61, 151, 186, 193, 230, 250, 253, 259, 273, 300
Park, J.E. 267
Parker, G.B. 151, 157f, 258, 273, 300
Parker, J.C. 185, 258, 301
Parker, W.R. 165, 258, 273, 301
Parkins, D. 301
Parsifal-Charles, N. 301
Parsons, M.J. 301
Partridge, K.B. 4, 288
Pascal, B. 87, 95, 242, 246, 249f, 301
Patterson, D.T. 273, 282, 301
Pattison, E.M. 209, 301
Paul, St. 170
Pavlov, I.P. 222
Pearce, P.L. 243, 301
Pekola, R.J. 172f, 294, 301
Pendleton, B.F. 190, 258, 274, 301
Pennebaker, J.W. 258, 273
Penrose, R. 20, 234, 301
Perriello, L. 194, 258, 276, 303
Persinger, M.A. 181, 301
Pervin, L.A. 301

Petty, R.E. 218, 301
Phillips, D.Z. 13f, 28f, 61f, 65f, 98ff, 107, 110, 134, 140, 143, 191, 200, 236, 258, 273, 293, 301
Piaget, J. 51, 119, 130f, 191, 194, 197, 290, 301
Pickering, J. 301
Pirsig, R.M. 234, 301
Plato, 183, 301
Polma, M.M. 94, 151, 159f, 168, 190, 258, 261f, 274, 301
Pope, The 136, 143
Powles, G. 2
Praimahil Mahara 75
Pratt, J.B. 53ff, 60f, 114, 149, 151ff, 207, 257f, 274, 276 301ff
Procrustes 224
Proudfoot, W. 50, 89, 214, 224, 302
Pullum, G.K. 125, 302
Punch 134
Pusey, E.B. 92
Pythagoras 142

Rabinowitz, J. 302
Radhakrishna, S. 302
Rahe, R.H. 112, 294
Rahner, K. 274
Rambo, L.R. 119, 257, 261, 287, 302
Ransohoff, P. 119, 257, 261, 287
Ranson, S.W. 257, 274
Ravenhill, P.L. 191, 302
Rao, K.R. 113, 302
Rehder, H. 209, 302
Reich, K.H. 176, 197, 300
Reichard, G.A. 191, 275, 302
Reik, T. 190, 275, 302
Relton, H.M. 275
Reynolds, V. 162, 302
Richards, D.G. 258, 275
Richards, I.A. 124, 300
Richards, W.A. 173, 258, 272, 300
Richardson, A. 122, 302
Rietdorff, P. 180, 289
Rilke, R.M. 62
Rivers, W.H.R. 39, 302
Robinson, J.P. 3, 302

Rocal 116
Roger of Taize 32
Rogers, C. 217, 263, 302
Rohr, R. 132, 197, 275, 302
Rokeach, M. 201, 235, 243, 302
Ronell, D. 289
Rorschach, H. 220
Rose, D. 306
Rosenberg, B.A. 302
Rosenberg, M.J. 302
Rosenberg, R. 275
Rosenberg, S.E. 142, 171, 298
Rosenstiel, A.K. 185f, 258, 275, 302
Rosenthal, B. 300
Rosenthal, R. 178, 302f
Rosnow, R.L. 300
Ross, L. 122, 127, 178, 299, 232, 244, 299, 303
Ross, M.G. 193, 303
Roszack, T. 303
Rothbaum, F. 161, 303
Rousseau, J.J. 19, 213
Rubenstone, E. 265
Rubin, D.C. 286
Ruf, F.J. 142, 303
Rushdie, S. 130
Russell, J.A. 298
Ryan, J. 62, 122, 141, 223f, 303
Ryan, L. 4, 291

St. Johns, E. 165, 258, 273, 301
Sabatier, A. 20, 153, 303
Sabom, M.B. 235, 303
Sachs, L.B. 122, 295
Sacks, H.L. 17, 52, 258, 275
Sacks, O. 303
Sajwaj, T. 258, 276
Sakhi 81
Saliers, D.E. 258, 276
Salome 118
Salter, D.L. 303
Samarin, W.J. 258f, 276, 302f
Sandler, H.M. 258, 264
Sangharakshita 303
Satan 108, 137
Saudia, T.L. 185, 276, 303

Sbisa, M. 285
Scarlett, W.G. 194f, 258, 276, 300, 303
Schachter, S. 241, 303
Scheier, M.F. 288
Scheler, M. 180, 303
Schleiermacher, F.D.E. 21, 89
Schliebe, H.P. 186F, 269, 297
Schmeidler, G.R. 114, 303
Schmidt, G. 225, 304
Schneiders, S. 169, 303
Schoenrade, P. 199, 285
Schopenhauer, A. 18, 212
Schultz, A. 299, 303
Schwartz, G.E. 286
Schwarzin, H. 258, 280
Schweitzer, A. 141, 303
Searle, J.R. 248, 303
Segond, J. 53, 276, 303
Seligman, M.E.P. 176, 284
Sells, S.B. 126, 307
Seneca 254
Sevensky, R.L. 276
Shackle, E. 50, 55, 150, 169, 218, 255, 257, 258, 260, 274, 277, 304
Shallice, T., 176, 304
Shandy, Tristram 137
Shang Ti 33
Shapiro, C. 263
Shapiro, D.A. 178, 220, 296
Shapiro, D.H. 176, 277
Sharpe, R. 290
Sharpe, S.L. 205f, 294
Shaver, P.R. 3, 50, 225, 302
Shephard, R.N. 122, 304
Sherif, M. 180, 304
Shiva, 71f, 74f
Shupe, A. 279
Siegler, R. 288
Sills, D.L. 84, 304
Simes, E. 2
Simon, H.A. 122, 290
Simonton, D.A. 258, 262
Singer, J.E. 241, 303
Singh, Harjit 74
Skinner, B.F. 60, 141, 206, 222, 304
Skinner, M. 301

Slovic, P. 178, 295
Smart, N. 21, 304
Smith, A. 126
Smith, C.S. 225, 293
Smith, D. 27
Smith, S. 114
Snider, J.G. 126, 304
Snow, A. 304
Snyder, C.R. 304
Snyder, S.S. 303
Socrates 19, 142
Solomon, R.C. 237, 304
Sorrentino, R.M 308
Southeimer, G.D. 21, 305
Speiber, D. 304
Spencer, B. 42, 48, 304
Spero, M. 304
Spickard, J.V. 251, 299, 304
Spilka, B. 4, 83, 85, 119, 161, 167, 170,
    172, 185f, 190f, 193f, 225f, 228, 230f,
    258f, 261, 263, 268, 270, 281, 289,
    295, 297, 304
Spitzer, M. 304
Spokane, A.R. 217, 294
Staal, F. 79, 82, 304
Stace, W.T. 173, 304
Stachel, G. 267, 277
Stanley, J.C. 60, 295
Stanner, W.E.H. 25, 41ff, 304
Starbuck, E.D. 3, 50, 305
Stark, R. 21, 292, 305
Stech, E.L. 295
Steele, R. 253, 300
Stevens, W. 111, 305
Stolz, K.R. 47, 150, 257f, 277, 305
Stoppard, T. 234
Stoudt, V.M. 299
Stouffer, S.A. 158, 167, 305
Stravinsky, I. 96, 257
Streeter, B.H. 305
Strommen, M.P. 292, 299
Strong, A.L. 47, 52, 60, 150, 257, 277,
    305
Sullivan, J. 263
Sunden, H. 279, 280
Super, C.W. 277

Surwillo, W.W. 258, 278
Sutton, T.D. 278
Swain, T. 306
Swanson, G.E. 19, 111, 238, 305
Swatos, W.H. 278, 305
Swenson, D.F. 296
Szasz, T. 222, 248f, 305

Tamminen, K. 195, 278, 305
Tamayo, A. 56, 205, 225, 306
Tanner, R. E. 162, 302
Tarde, G. 51, 305
Tart, C.T. 175, 258, 278, 305
Taub, D. 304
Taylor, S.E. 64, 111, 252, 305
Teasdale, J. 176, 284
Teresa of Avila, St. 17f, 27, 37, 170,
    211f
Thesing, R.J. 258, 278
Thiel-Horstmann, M. 173f, 305
Thomas, K. 232, 245, 305
Thornton, M. 258, 278
Thouless, R.H. 2, 49, 92, 128, 132, 165,
    180, 192, 195, 198, 231, 236, 255,
    258, 278, 287, 305
Threadgold, D. 305
Tice, D.M. 254, 305
Tillich, P. 269
Tillyard, A. 279
Tolman, E.C. 159, 305
Tolstoy, L. 33, 306
Topping, F. 27
Treisman, A. 203, 306
Trier, K.K. 258, 279
Tucci, G. 306
Turing, A. 203
Turner, D.H. 67, 256, 306
Turner, E. 306
Turner, J.A. 185, 279, 306
Turner, V. 306
Tursky, B. 286
Tversky, A. 85f, 178, 295, 306
Twain, M. 133, 306
Tyler, F.B. 253, 300
Tylor, E.B. 9, 39, 191, 306
Tyrrell, G.N.M. 214, 306

Uberman, H.P. 306
Ulanov, A. 12, 47, 49, 258, 279, 306
Ulanov, B. 12, 47, 49, 258, 279, 306
Underhill, E. 148, 258, 279, 306
Upham, T. 303
Urmson, J.O. 285

van de Kemp, H. 150, 257f, 262, 264,
   272, 279, 306
van der Lans, J. 258, 279
van Gogh, V. 233
van Rooey, B. 49, 192, 258, 266, 292
Van Tran, T. 63ff, 268, 296
Ventis, W.L. 112, 237, 285
Vergote, A. 18, 56, 59, 95, 204, 225, 306
Vishnu 71f
Voltaire, F.M.A. de 20, 213
von Balthaser, H.U. 280
von Hugel, F. 96, 258, 269, 280
von Montau, D. 16, 298
von Wright, G.H. 307

Wach, J. 198, 306
Wade, N. 286
Wagnick, K. 249, 306
Wainwright, G. 268
Wakefield, G.S. 22f, 280, 306
Walker, A. 157
Wallace, R.K. 281
Walster, E. 180, 306
Ware, R. 258, 280
Watson, B. 288
Watson, P.J. 258, 267, 306
Watts, F. 258, 280
Watts, I. 205, 306
Weil, S. 14, 27, 66
Weintraub, J.K. 288
Weisz, J.R. 303
Welford, A.T. 18, 93, 126, 167, 170, 175,
   258, 280, 306, 307
Welldon, R.M.C. 165f, 258, 268, 295
Wellman, H.M. 49, 119, 131, 191, 307
Wells, H.G. 161, 307
West, M.A. 172, 175f, 178, 258, 281,
   288f, 291, 300, 307

Wheaton, B. 64, 307
White, A. 290
White, J. 298
White, L. 286
Whitehead, A.N. 20, 233, 307
Whorf, B.L. 125
Wicker, A.W. 307
Wierzbicka, A. 6, 25ff, 30, 31, 38, 45f,
   256, 307
Wiles, M. 214, 249, 307
Wilkins, J. 281
William, King 136
Williams, H.A. 307
Williams, M. 258, 280
Williamson, J.A. 252, 294
Wilson, D. 304
Wilson, B. 247, 307
Winch, P. 206
Winnicott, D.W. 204f, 307
Wittgenstein, L. 26, 29, 62, 65, 89, 99ff,
   114, 149, 207, 248, 301, 307
Woods, R. 306, 308
Woodworth, R.S. 126, 307
Wordsworth, W. 223
Worten, S.A. 270, 281
Wortman, C.B. 287
Wright, D. 215, 308
Wrightsman, L.S. 3, 302
Wulff, D.M., 4, 22, 47, 83, 119, 162,
   164f, 171, 175, 180f, 182f, 255, 257,
   261, 267f, 271f, 281, 308
Wundt, W. 162, 257, 281, 308
Wuthnow, R. 308
Wynn, F.W. 91

Yarnold, E. 268
Yates, F.A. 308
Young, J. 284

Zajonc, R.B. 125, 308
Zaleski, C. 11, 308
Zeus 9, 33
Zollschan, G.K. 159, 287, 308
Zukier, H. 229, 232, 308
Zusne, L. 122, 308

Index of Subjects

(Prepared by L.B. Brown)

Aboriginal religion 25f, 41, 48, 67ff
accounts 231
alchemy 113, 210
altruism 164
ambiguity 11, 117, 120
Ancient Greece 8f
animism 48f, 56, 84, 119, 191ff
anthropology 67ff
apparitions 37
archetypes 7f, 11, 22
atmosphere 126
attitudes 121, 128, 243
attribution 50, 84f, 127, 169, 225ff
awe 148

Bali 72ff
behavior 13
belief 163, 180, 231
bhakti 173f
bibliographies 150f, 257ff
blasphemy 135f, 143
Buddhism 76ff, 96, 117, 145, 162

cases 17
causality 84, 104
censorship 130, 167
chakra 172
chance 178, 246
children 95f

collects 62
common-sense 13, 15, 23f, 30, 51, 140
communication 28ff
complaints 2
computing 203
conformity 180
consciousness 52, 172, 224
conspiracy 229
contexts 224
contrasts 122
control 161, 224f, 236
converts 180
coping 112, 134, 157, 216, 250
cosmology 111
counselling 216f, 220

decentration 52
defining 30f
development 131
developmental tasks 196
dharma 210
dissociation 8
dissonance 142, 169, 180
divine 225
dream-time 68

efficacy 65f
emotion 237
ethics 106

exercises 129, 140
experience 16f, 94, 236
experiments 140, 164
expertise 131
explanations 234

faith 180
false 128
flow 8
folklore 115f
fools 12
functions of religion 95

gambling 12
games 14
God 9, 14, 19, 22f, 28, 32, 34, 47, 56, 61,
  68, 84f, 93, 95, 110, 140, 167, 170,
  203f, 218, 223, 225, 228ff, 233
grammar 110, 143

healing 64, 209, 216ff
health 171
heaven 111
helplessness 177
heresy 143
heroes 33
heuristics 86
Hinduism 21, 71f

icons 147
illusion 22, 24
imagination 224
individual differences 197ff
Islam 80f

jokes 128

karma 73, 231f

lexical universals 31
language 124f, 134ff, 236
Lourdes 10, 209
luck 178

magic 49, 117f, 122, 193, 217, 232
mana 53

manuals 118f
materialism 211
meaning 226
measurement 3f, 162
mechanisms 164
mental acts 223
metaphor 28, 61
mindfulness 175, 220
mindlessness 178
miracles 141
misfortune 230
modernism
music 96, 182
mystery 15, 141
mysticism 47, 50
myth 238f

neuropsychology 176, 181
new movements 182
new psychologies 223
numinous 10f

optimism 111
orientations 133, 182
orthodoxy 119, 146f
over-belief 142

partial reinforcement 60
personality 19, 198f, 238
perspectives 112
persuasion 208ff
physiology 171, 176, 181
pietism 23
pilgrimage 209
politeness 14
positivism 223
power 18
practice 181
prayer
  Aboriginal 41ff, 48, 50
  across cultures 33ff
  act 144
  advice 86
  agnosticism 91
  ambiguity 139
  American 160

American Indian 39
answered 60, 153, 175
archetype 181
attacks 199
attitude(s) 36, 85, 93, 113, 133, 148,
    156f, 200, 207
authentic 143
Babylonian 34
barriers 91
beliefs 231f
bibliographies 150, 257ff
Buddhist 40f, 139
children 49, 189ff
claims 10f
collects 62, 133
common-sense 152
communication 101, 200
conclusions 240ff
confession 23
consequences 144, 181f, 240
consolation 95
context 3, 24, 153
control 12, 164ff, 177
coping 112, 160, 185
correlates 171
cries 134, 211f
death 90f, 98
decentration 200
deficiency 210
defined 3, 13f, 22, 26ff, 175, 183
delusion 121
denial 105
dependency 184
designs 165
development 149f, 189ff, 199, 250
devotion 121
disclosures 18
diversity 183f
divine power 36
doctrine 88ff
early work 47ff, 168ff
efficacy 7, 12, 14, 19, 49, 52, 65f, 85,
    94, 104, 114, 121, 123, 134, 142,
    162, 165, 171, 186, 192, 199
ego-centric 12, 200
emotion 148

European 160
evidence 211ff
expectation 121, 162, 177
experience 89, 94, 98f, 149
experiments 145ff, 164ff
expertise 170
explanations 114, 163, 173ff, 194,
    214, 243
factor analysis 155f
failure 139f, 231
faith 87
faith-healing 51f
fruits 17, 21, 23, 109
frustration 167
futile 12
gestures 145, 184
goals 218
grace 160
grammar 100, 102
healing 64, 120, 122, 208ff
in private 110
intangible 1
intention 170
intercession 91, 166, 171
interpretation 122
Islam 198
issues 163
language 15, 18, 25ff, 92ff, 98, 101,
    120, 124f, 176, 205f
logic 200
Lord's 83
magic 113, 117ff, 122, 150, 191, 209,
    236
mantra 79, 82
Mass 139
maturity 61, 143, 196, 199f
meanings, 24, 25ff, 194
measures 4, 161f
meditation 164ff, 172f
miracle 102, 120
modeling 207
Muslim 53, 81
mystery 113
mysticism 150
non-Christians 6
numinous 183

(prayer cont.)
  oaths 135
  objects 153
  observations of 2
  observed 144
  offering 148
  offices 69
  opportunities 185
  origins 5, 8f, 17, 20
  outcomes 186
  parallels 201
  performance 2, 127
  performative 127f
  pervasive 155
  petitionary 7, 46, 55, 128
  petitions 58ff, 115f, 167, 192
  phenomenology 6, 10, 12, 19, 172, 190
  philosophy 13
  placebo 158, 179, 221
  plants 165
  politics 235
  posture 53f, 145f, 148, 184
  power 233
  practice 127, 155, 159, 175
  praying 62
  prier 30
  privacy 94, 97ff, 112, 142, 233, 236
  private 103f, 208
  propers 139
  Protestant 150
  psychology 5, 13, 47, 84f
  psychotherapy 178f, 216f
  public 17f
  questionnaire 151f
  rain 123
  reasons 20
  rituals 215
  rosary 121, 197
  sacramental 128
  self-fulfilling 168
  selfhood 93
  semantics 44
  sex 171
  silence 90, 149
  sociality 201
  sounds 125
  spiritual 168
  spiritual direction 18
  spoken 31
  stages 193f
  stereotypes 170
  studies 164
  success 56, 186
  surveys 4, 16, 54f, 150f, 159, 170
  talk 15, 97
  technology 63f
  testimony 157, 212
  tests 88, 186
  thanks 59, 65
  therapy 165, 167, 202
  tradition 61
  types 161, 173f, 181ff, 190, 198, 204, 206, 213
  unanswered 169
  understood 127
  universal 45
  validity 61, 167, 175
  variety 3
  war 158
  why? 153
  'windows' for 185
  wish 148
  words 123f, 133, 143
prediction 162
probability 85f
process 218
projection 8, 10, 18
psi 113f
psychical research 113f
psycho-logic 132
psychology 19, 119f, 162f, 182
psychotherapy 208

quest 199

rationalization 142
realism 99f
reductionism 214, 251
relationship 67
religion 162f
religionism 163

religious components 21f
religious problems 11, 15
religious psychology 7, 84f, 132, 149, 179, 212, 235
religiousness 4, 7
revelation 244
Royals 158, 165

sacrament 193
sanctions 162
science 15, 17 20, 87, 143, 182, 211, 238
self 61, 93, 97ff, 111, 113, 117f
semantic differential 145
shamans 11
silence 69
skill 178
sorcery 116, 118
spells 20, 53, 149, 236
states 203
strategies 178
structuralism 100ff
subjectivity 60f, 141f, 122, 182, 210
suggestion 51, 122
summary 162f
supernature 10, 115, 209

superstition 85
surveys 16, 50, 53
swearing 134ff, 143
symbols 120

thanksgiving 65
theory 221ff
time 61
TM 175
tourism 243
Trappists 69f
Trinity 22
Turing test 203
types 183f, 196f, 223

unconscious 10

valves 221
variables 164, 217ff
via negativa 149
virtuality 173, 200, 202

wagers 87
witchcraft 229
worship 68